Emerson's Liberalism

Emerson's Liberalism

Neal Dolan

THE UNIVERSITY OF WISCONSIN PRESS

Publication of this volume has been made possible,
in part, through support from
THE ANONYMOUS FUND OF THE COLLEGE OF LETTERS AND SCIENCE
at the University of Wisconsin–Madison.

The University of Wisconsin Press
1930 Monroe Street, 3rd Floor
Madison, Wisconsin 53711-2059

www.wisc.edu/wisconsinpress/

3 Henrietta Street
London WC2E 8LU, England

1   3   5   4   2

Printed in the United States of America

Library of Congress Cataloging-in-Publication Data
Dolan, Neal.
Emerson's liberalism / Neal Dolan.
p.   cm.—(Studies in American thought and culture)
Includes bibliographical references and index.
ISBN 978-0-299-22804-0 (pbk.: alk. paper)
ISBN 978-0-299-22803-3 (e-book)
1. Emerson, Ralph Waldo, 1803–1882—Political and social views.
2. Emerson, Ralph Waldo, 1803–1882—Criticism and interpretation.
3. Liberalism in literature.
I. Title.   II. Series.
PS1642.S58D65   2009
814'.3—dc22   2008038489

To
my mother and my brothers,

in memory of
Dad and Brian.

And to
Laura Jane and Rory,
with unending love.

We must try to understand that which we have suddenly discovered we possess and value. . . . [W]e need to know just what it is we love.

Ernest Gellner, *Conditions of Liberty*

Contents

Acknowledgments

Whatever merits this book may have I owe largely to the intellectual inspiration, example, and guidance given over many years by an extraordinary sequence of teachers. At St. Anthony's High School almost thirty years ago Brother Owen Justinian Sadlier, Brother Cletus Burke, and Mr. Kevin Ahearne recognized and encouraged my curiosity about philosophy, American history, and literature. I will never forget their generosity, humor, unpretentious learning, love of teaching, and genuine Christian kindness. At Yale Leslie Brisman showed an Irish Italian Catholic boy how to bring Talmudic scrutiny to bear on the secularized Protestant literature of English Romanticism, and found time also for occasional and much-needed paternal admonitions. Without his help and his confidence in me I never would have found my way in the strange world of academia. And at Harvard the late Alan Heimert put his vast historical learning at my disposal while allowing me to think things through, however slowly, for myself. Alan embodied and extended the legacy of his great teacher Perry Miller, and I hope this book does honor to that tradition. Lawrence Buell stepped in after Heimert's death to advise this project at its dissertation stage and has given me the utmost professional support and good counsel every step of the way since then. And I owe special words of thanks to Helen Vendler, who took an interest in me, who never insisted I write about poetry, who read and commented on every word of the first draft of this book despite not being on my dissertation committee, and who remains, to me and many others, a model of dedicated teaching, inspired scholarship, and candid, undogmatic intelligence.

I would also like to thank Peter Berkowitz, Stephen Macedo, and Rob Devigne for letting a literature scholar join their evening seminars on liberal political thought at Harvard back in the mid- and late 1990s. This book is in many ways a continuation of those discussions, which were taken up further in those years with John Moser, Terence Moore, Richard Boyd, and others under the good auspices of Marty Zuppan at the Institute of Humane Studies.

I am grateful also to the late Wilson Carey McWilliams for supporting this project at a crucial juncture and for thus allowing me the time necessary to, in his words, "make it good." John Stauffer read and made characteristically thorough and thoughtful comments on the manuscript at an intermediate stage. And I thank Paul Boyer for finding merit in the final product and seeing it through to publication.

On a more personal level, I wish to thank my mother, Frances, for her example of hard work and perseverance. I'm grateful also to Claudia Nelson and her parents, Janet and Merlin, for their unstinting encouragement and support during much of the time I was working on this project.

Thanks also to my friend Seth Moglen, who taught me the love of intellectual conversation and with whom I have been conversing about literature, history, politics, and life for more than twenty-five years. Even when we disagree, my thinking and writing owe much to him.

My deepest gratitude goes to my wife, Laura Jane. Every aspect of this book benefited from her patient attention, fine mind, and ear for language. And every aspect of my life benefits from being shared with her.

Abbreviations

AW   *Emerson's Antislavery Writings.* Edited by Len Gougeon and Joel
         Myerson. New Haven, CT: Yale University Press, 1995.

EL   *The Early Lectures of Ralph Waldo Emerson.* 3 volumes. Edited by
         Stephen E. Whicher and Robert E. Spiller. Cambridge, MA:
         Harvard University Press, 1959–1972.

E&L   *Essays and Lectures.* Edited by Joel Porte. New York: Library of
         America, 1983.

JMN   *The Journals and Miscellaneous Notebooks of Ralph Waldo Emerson.*
         16 volumes. Edited by William H. Gilman et al. Cambridge,
         MA: Harvard University Press, 1960–1982.

LL   *The Later Lectures of Ralph Waldo Emerson, 1843–1871.* 2 volumes.
         Edited by Ronald A. Bosco. Athens: University of Georgia
         Press, 2001.

Emerson's Liberalism

Introduction

The Political Reception of Emerson

This book presents Ralph Waldo Emerson as a <u>preacher of liberal</u>
<u>culture.</u> The challenges of Emerson's task are implicit in the par-
adox of the term "liberal culture." From an anthropological perspective, the word "culture" usually implies a traditional "cult"—an established set of symbols, narratives, and rituals that ensure the transmission
of a given society's values from one generation to the next. And yet the
idea of liberty contained in the word "liberal" connotes, in part, emancipation from tradition and its cults. In the modern West, specifically,
the emergence of liberal civilization has entailed the uprooting of the
traditional ideas and institutions of feudal-aristocratic Europe as they
were underwritten by the cult(s) of Roman Catholicism—the political-
cultural complex Tocqueville called "the old regime." Reason displaced
authority. Science undermined faith. Liberal democracy ousted monarchy. Capitalism dissolved feudalism. Rights replaced privileges. Self-
assertion dispensed with deference. Equality subverted hierarchy. Self-
interest took the place of virtue. "Organic solidarity," to use Durkheim's
terms, replaced "mechanical solidarity." Criticism and the expectation
of progress overtook reverence for the past. But these new values
needed to be symbolized and transmitted no less than the old ones. In
the early stages of the full emergence of liberal civilization in the
West—in the late eighteenth and early nineteenth centuries—it was by

3

no means clear how this might be done. The papier-mâché figures of "Reason" and "Liberty" with which the French revolutionaries replaced the statues of the Virgin and the saints in Notre Dame cathedral were neither aesthetically nor ceremonially compelling and hardly built to last. How does a society go about enshrining, symbolizing, and transmitting countertraditional liberal values without creating another potentially rigid and repressive tradition? It was Ralph Waldo Emerson's distinctive achievement, I argue in the pages that follow, to have answered this question by a certain kind of example.

Two classic essays help to flesh out what I am suggesting by situating Emerson's achievement in its specifically American context. In "From Edwards to Emerson" (1940) Perry Miller asserted a deep continuity between the Puritans and Emerson insofar as both possessed and attempted to inspire an intense mystical awareness of the presence of God in the universe.[1] In "From Franklin to Emerson" (1976) William L. Hedges offered a counterpart to Miller's essay by pointing out a strong continuity between Emerson and Benjamin Franklin insofar as both were eminently practical, empirical, tough-minded, disciplined, and market oriented—devotees of "the Protestant ethic in highly exalted form."[2] The following study synthesizes these two perspectives and transposes them into political-cultural and psychological terms. I argue that Emerson was a descendant of the Puritan ministry not only in his mysticism, a pantheistic version of which Miller was right to see everywhere in his writing, but also in his conception of his relationship as an intellectual to his society. Emerson was trained as a Protestant minister, like his father and his father's fathers for several generations, and while as a young man he may have left both pulpit and Unitarian orthodoxy for the lyceum and transcendentalism, he never ceased to perform a quasi-ministerial role of cultural-symbolic exposition and exhortation. But the values he thus communicated were on the whole secular and liberal, Franklinesque, if you will, rather than Christian, and the symbolic language and style were freshly self-invented rather than biblical. For two hundred years New England ministers had drawn upon the enormous symbolic resources of the Bible to inspire the members of their congregations with such Christian values as awe before God, charity to their neighbors, and faith in the next life. Emerson drew on what he saw as the no less potent symbolism of nature, history, and the marketplace to inspire the citizens of his young nation with liberal values such as rational wonder at the cosmos, disciplined work in pursuit of property, a critical attitude toward tradition, suspicion of government, and respect for natural rights, especially the core right to liberty. Emerson thus found a distinctive way to carry out what he himself described as the paradoxical "two fold office" of a "true culture": "to rid itself of superstition and to deepen the piety" (*EL* 2:335).

No one will be surprised to hear that Emerson was a liberal. Most scholars acknowledge it in passing, if only in order to lament the fact. George Kateb has given the matter the most serious attention. Kateb has written intensive, original, and insightful studies of Emerson's political significance, which I will discuss later in this introduction, but he surprisingly declines, as we will see, to call Emerson a liberal. Sacvan Bercovitch also gives the topic unusually searching analysis in construing Emerson as developing "a form of utopian consciousness . . . within the premises of liberal culture" but regrets what he sees as Emerson's lapsing back into the more conservative national liberal mythos during the latter half of his career.[3] (I will discuss Bercovitch's reading at some length in chapter 1.) Robert Richardson opens the issue most generously, saying, "It is the ambition . . . of transcendentalism to provide a soul for modern liberalism and thereby to enlarge the possibilities of modern life."[4] But the all-inclusive scope of Richardson's remarkable book does not leave time for an in-depth discussion of this aspect of Emerson's thinking. No scholar, to my knowledge, has offered a thorough and sympathetic study of the role of liberal ideas and values in Emerson's work. Given the centrality of such ideas and values to American life and the centrality of Emerson to American literature, this is in itself an intriguing fact, worthy of a study of its own that might reveal much about what Lionel Trilling called the "adversary culture" of American intellectuals.[5] Perhaps because my own attitude toward mainstream American liberalism is on the whole grateful rather than adversarial, I have undertaken in the following study to fill in this significant gap in the historical understanding of one of its great voices.

Len Gougeon has demonstrated how a tendency to downplay aspects of Emerson's liberalism took root in the earliest stages of the reception history of his work.[6] Focusing on the question of Emerson's degree of commitment to the antislavery cause prior to the Civil War, Gougeon surveys the long history of Emerson biographies from the early efforts of George Willis Cooke (1881), Moncure Daniel Conway (1882), Alexander Ireland (1882), Oliver Wendell Holmes (1884), and

James Eliot Cabot (1887) to the relatively recent works of Gay Wilson Allen (1981) and John McAleer (1984).[7] He shows how the treatment of Emerson's antislavery activity generally reflects the political orientation of the biographer. Conservative biographers such as Holmes, Cabot, Stephen E. Whicher, and McAleer downplayed Emerson's activism, while more "progressive" chroniclers such as Conway, Ireland, and Ralph Rusk gave it more importance.[8] Gougeon himself performs a great deal of painstaking original research in an effort to resolve the question. He concludes that on the whole the "progressive" interpreters were correct about Emerson's position after 1850, while the conservatives added necessary shading in emphasizing Emerson's initial reluctance to get involved.[9]

Both Gougeon's findings and his method are relevant to this study. I find his empiricism exemplary in many respects and will rely on his and other empirical studies throughout. But my initial point here has less to do with Gougeon's claims about what may actually have been true for Emerson than with his demonstration of how malleable that truth has been in the hands of different interpreters. If it is the case that Emerson's biographers, working in an empirically oriented genre, have tended to reshape Emerson's political image according to their own biases, it should not surprise us to find that literary scholars and essayists working with fewer empirical constraints have tended toward similarly strong misreadings. I have found several pervasive patterns of misprision in the long record of political commentaries on Emerson written since his death in 1882. They may be roughly grouped under three headings: (1) the "pragmatist" or "antifoundationalist," (2) the "antihistorical," and (3) the "democratic." It is worth critically reviewing these types of reading at some length, selecting representative examples for closer inspection, because the general emphases of my own interpretation may be most precisely introduced by contrast to this large body of previous work.

I will start with the most recently popular way of reading Emerson— the pragmatist and/or antifoundationalist approach. The revival of pragmatism, to borrow the title of an important collection published in 1998, has been an enormously stimulating and multifaceted development in American humanistic scholarship over the past twenty years or so.[10] In William James especially, many American scholars influenced by poststructuralism have seemed to find a generous, eminently humane philosopher who had worked his way out of the illusions of Western metaphysics without succumbing to nihilism. As propounded in different ways by Richard Rorty, Cornel West, Richard Poirier, Hilary and Ana Putnam, James Kloppenberg, Richard Bernstein, Ross Posnock, and Louis Menand, among others, pragmatism has seemed to promise nothing less than a pluralistic, grittily empiricist, affirmative, and somehow uniquely open reinvigoration of American philosophy and high culture, and many have sought to anoint Emerson high literary priest. Writing from what he presents as a Jamesian perspective, for example, Cornel West sees Emerson as the originating source of American pragmatism. He argues that Emerson "evades modern philosophy" by "ingeniously and skillfully refusing (1) its quest for certainty and its hope for professional, i.e., scientific sensibility, and (2) its search for foundations." Instead of a quest for objective truths, West suggests that Emerson "pursued a mode of cultural criticism which indulges in a quest for power, a perennial experimental search sustained by provocation and a hope for the enhancement and expansion of the self."[11] Like Harold Bloom, West also sees Emerson as a proto-Nietzschean immoralist: "The major events of Emerson's life," he writes, "fanned and fueled his deep belief in moral transgression against any limits or constraints."[12]

Richard Poirier also names Emerson as "the father of American pragmatism." He presents Emerson as coming to pragmatist conclusions by way of a proto-postmodern linguistic skepticism. Initially seduced in *Nature* by the notion of direct correspondence between word and thing, Poirier's Emerson soon comes around to the more sophisticated postmodern view that "the human situation in language . . . is barely negotiable; it is precarious, limiting, tense, belabored." Duly chastened, Emerson gives up on naive efforts to ground the self, or morality, or politics, on accurate representations of objective reality. He turns instead to complex rhetorical strategies of punning, troping, and playing one type of discourse against another in the hopes of occasionally finding seams in the entangling net of language, knowing all the while that the most such breakthroughs can provide is a momentary and unstable self-enhancement. "For Emerson, the reading of life or art is not a search for morally stabilizing moments or summary, but for infusions and diffusions of energy, for that constant redistribution of forces called troping, including the troping of the self." In anticipation of Nietzsche and Foucault, Poirier argues, Emerson grasped that "there is nothing sacred on the far side of language except the desire that the words should exist," that "he might have to use the words 'God' or 'soul,' but would go on to suppose, as I do, that there was in fact really nothing outside to depend on, and nothing inside either, nothing except the desire that there should be more than nothing."[13]

Such a deeply skeptical epistemological stance does not provide much of a basis for any coherent set of religious, ethical, or political commitments. For Poirier, this is precisely what makes Emerson worthy of our attention. To his mind, it is Emerson's capacity to face up to and even to celebrate our fundamental moral and epistemological groundlessness that makes him continually interesting and attractive. Indeed, in focusing narrowly on Emerson's proto-postmodern "obsession with language," Poirier claims to be rescuing Emerson from all efforts to put him to extra-literary political-cultural uses. Unlike Matthew Arnold and other such heroes of cultural conservatives, Poirier argues, Emerson is the founding member of a literary tradition that is profoundly skeptical about any effort to settle on fundamental values, including the value of literature. "Troubled within itself . . . discernibly on edge about its own rhetorical status, especially when the rhetoric is conspicuously indebted to any of the great, historically rooted institutions," the Emersonian tradition "shows the futility of this search for truth, values, and exaltations."[14]

"Pragmatist" readings of Emerson such as West's and Poirier's have been immensely influential, and they have tended to push the interpretation of Emerson in the direction of Nietzsche. As David Robinson puts it in the first sentences of his 1993 study of pragmatism in Emerson's later work, "a generation of scholars has come to read Emerson as a philosopher of power. The discovery that power was 'Emerson's True Grail,' as Barbara Packer put it, has secured on quite new grounds his place as a founder of American culture."[15] No less a critic than Harold Bloom, for example, speaks of Emerson's "cheerfully amoral dialectics of power." He claims that it was Emerson who "gave our politics its particular view of power as freed from all moral limitations." "Emerson remains," Bloom writes, "the American theoretician of power—be it political, literary, spiritual, economic—because he took the risk of exalting transition from one activity or state of mind or kind of spiritual being to another for its own sake."[16]

My own reading of Emerson's complete works and journals, the major biographies written about him, and much of the older critical commentary, however, has led me to the conclusion that this Nietzschean-pragmatist characterization of Emerson's moral and epistemological stance is starkly anachronistic. If we approach Emerson's writings with appropriate openness to his historical distinctness and with appropriate wariness of imposing our own ideas and assumptions, what emerges is far from the amoral, agnostic, and "transgressive" Nietzschean-pragmatist skeptic these critics have constructed. Indeed, far from conveying a sense of futility, Emerson's work tries everywhere to inspire precisely the sort of exaltation in shared (liberal) values that Poirier dismisses. I intend no disparagement of pragmatism when, from an empirical-historical point of view, I strongly second Stanley Cavell's cautions about assigning the term to Emerson.[17] Indeed, it seems to me precisely false to the best aspects of pragmatism—its empiricism and pluralism and pleasure in heterogeneity—to so aggressively assimilate Emerson to its outlook. Such colonization manifests in its approach to history the same "blindness in human beings" that James diagnosed and attempted to overcome in his own work—the inability to recognize and register the "feelings of creatures and people different from ourselves."[18] And in ignoring the large body of both primary and secondary literature that directly contradicts their pragmatist readings, these scholars also fail to heed what Louis Menand has presented as one of pragmatism's most important epistemological insights—that knowledge is cumulative, cross-generational, collective, social.[19]

It is useful to establish a few of the most important points of difference. Biographers, literary historians, and intellectual historians, for example, generally agree that in both his manner of life and his thinking Emerson held strictly, persistently, and often jubilantly to what he saw as a universal moral law. The dictates of this law were the same as the Kantian categorical imperative. All human beings were capable of discovering it by following the intuitive promptings of innate moral sentiments. It could also be discovered in a variety of forms throughout the world's great moral and religious literature—especially in the writings of the Stoics and their modern descendants such as Montaigne, in the epigrams of the great Indian epics, and in the axioms and proverbs of other Eastern sages such as Hafiz and Confucius. This universal law, it is generally agreed, formed the backbone of Emerson's moral thought and the structuring principle of many of his essays. Earlier scholars also concur that Emerson believed persistently in the validity of both natural science and Platonic philosophy, a combination of beliefs he saw reflected in such intellectual heroes as Goethe and Francis Bacon and that was instrumental in his departure from the Unitarian Church.[20] There is still further agreement that Emerson generally followed the pattern of the Unitarianism in which he grew up in attempting to reconcile an idiosyncratic form of radical Protestant spirituality with Enlightenment rationalism.[21] This was an unlikely marriage, resulting in a strange hybrid neither recognizably Christian nor strictly rationalist in the Enlightenment sense of the word, but nevertheless distinctively marked by both legacies.

To recognize such foreign beliefs (and others) in Emerson is not to say that we today should share them. On the contrary, it seems to me that Emerson may be interesting and valuable to us precisely to the extent that he does not exactly share our contemporary views. His excitement about new insights into nature provided by science; his comfort in the legitimacy of moral sentiment; his ecstatic intuitions of imminent divinity; his conviction in the political principle of natural right, or his general confidence in our capacity to remake our reality and ourselves through work—the fact that our contemporary literary-intellectual culture does not generally share these feelings should only make their presence in Emerson more interesting. A monolithic tradition, even if it is a sophisticated Nietzschean-pragmatist monolith, seems to me no better than the old kinds of tradition. A tradition tolerant of the otherness of its own voices, by contrast, seems worthy of the name "liberal."

Christopher Newfield shows little such tolerance in his ambitious postmodernist political commentary on Emerson entitled *The Emerson Effect*.[22] Rather than attempting a sympathetic appreciation of Emerson's distinctive political outlook, Newfield aggressively takes him to task for failing to share a certain kind of postmodernist political radicalism. Emerson's respect for law, Newfield argues, makes him insufficiently anarchistic. His nineteenth-century preference for liberty over equality makes him insufficiently egalitarian. He is insufficiently skeptical or "antifoundationalist" in his attitude toward knowledge and the authority claimed in its name. And he is insufficiently liberated in his attitudes toward sexuality. In all of these respects, Newfield argues, Emerson is typical of the moderate liberal tradition that has dominated American politics throughout its history. As a "principal architect" of this tradition, Emerson is charged with initiating its tendency toward fatal compromise. Because Emerson always checks himself rather than taking his individualist or antinomian or democratic impulses to their extremes, Newfield argues, Emerson ultimately vitiates the values for which he claims to stand. By attempting to accommodate the demands of society within his individualism, for example, Emerson weakens the claims of both community and self. Most ominously, Newfield argues, by attempting to accommodate a regard for natural law within his conception of freedom, Emerson gives himself and his readers over to an incipient "authoritarianism."

As his principal evidence for this claim, Newfield offers an interesting analysis of a three-step pattern in Emerson's thought and writing. He cites a passage from "Self-Reliance" wherein Emerson "performs a series of moves which . . . typify his thought as a whole":

> Trust thyself: every heart vibrates to that iron string. Accept the place the divine providence has found for you, the society of your contemporaries, the connection of events. Great men have always done so. . . . And now we are men, and must accept in the highest mind the same transcendent destiny . . . obeying the Almighty effort. (*E&L* 260)

The first sentence, Newfield argues, pronounces the liberating, nonconformist message we have come to associate with Emerson. "This," as Newfield puts it, "is Emerson the individualist radical, Emerson the anarchist, Emerson the creative artist, who insists that the truth requires that we first sever our ties to established knowledge and society. This is, in short, Emerson the radical liberal, putting self-possession first, but for the sake of any social change the soul decrees." But in the next sentence, Newfield complains, Emerson seems completely to forgo this radicalism in favor of its opposite. "He defines self-trust as a form of accepting one's place in precisely the 'society of one's contemporaries,' and in 'the connection of events' that we might think self-trust was designed to evade. Self-reliance is not simple possessive individualism—self-ownership, freedom of control, autonomy, but a complex relationship to actually existing society." Then, in his third step, Emerson moves beyond accommodation with society to what Newfield sees as a posture of craven submissiveness to a larger order. "This familiar injunction," Newfield writes, "to move beyond conventional understanding into harmony with Being means that we must 'accept,' 'obey.' The transcendentalizing of the law does not appear as a specifiable rule or quality, but as the rule of superiority, that which compels obedience. Superiority forms the content of transcendent law; accepting an external superiority is 'what makes men great.'"[23]

To Newfield's dismay, Emerson thus moves, in the space of one brief passage, from a celebration of "the revolutionary genius of your own

unique being" to a condition of "rapturous servitude." Newfield argues
that this basic trajectory is repeated throughout Emerson's work. It is
symptomatic, he believes, of a fatal contradiction at the core of the cen-
trist liberal tradition of which Emerson is a founding voice. Most important, it reveals an ominous tendency toward "authoritarianism" in this
tradition.

One cannot dispute that Newfield has put his finger on a central
problem in Emerson. Lou Ann Lange has worried at length about precisely the same puzzling conjunction of liberation and submission—she
calls it a "paradox"—in her iconoclastic 1986 study entitled *The Riddle of
Liberty: Emerson on Alienation, Freedom, and Obedience.*[24] One could similarly
summarize the thesis of Stephen Whicher's landmark 1953 study *Freedom and Fate* as a claim that, over the course of his career, Emerson
moved from an early emphasis on the first of the positions Newfield describes ("freedom") to a late emphasis on the third ("fate"). And in 1991
Christopher Lasch bucked the general critical emphasis on the "emancipatory" Emerson by arguing that an insistence on submission to necessary limits was always at the heart of his message.[25] Newfield is thus
in good company when he puzzles over this apparent contradiction in
Emerson's writing. But in puzzling through this crux, as in reading Emerson in general, it is crucial to keep in mind that one of the most important differences between Emerson's historical moment and our own was
his relatively close connection to the Enlightenment intellectual revolution. Newfield's commentary, like that of Bloom, West, and Poirier, col-
lapses the difference between Emerson's Enlightenment-based concept
of self-reliant freedom as a means to truth and a more skeptical late-
twentieth-century stance that sees radical autonomy as a valuable end in
itself.

Newfield betrays a failure to grasp this difference in his paraphrase of
what he takes to be the character of Emerson's basic nonconformity. An
"individualist radical," an "anarchist," and a "creative artist" who "puts
the self first for any social change the soul decrees" describes a certain
popular image of the Emersonian nonconformist reflective of American
radical culture of the 1960s and 1970s. But it says little about the historical Emerson of the 1820s, 1830s, and 1840s. The crucial difference, as I
have suggested, is that the early decades of the nineteenth century were
a great deal closer to the Enlightenment, and they were thus still dominated, especially in Unitarian and late Federalist New England, by the
preeminent value of reason.[26] It is true, of course, that Emerson rejected

Enlightenment epistemology—particularly its skeptical empiricism and materialism—in favor of a Romantic confidence in imagination and intuition. But this in no way implied a rejection of reason, or rationality, or the Enlightenment per se. On the contrary, it meant only an expanded conception of the means of enlightenment. The word Emerson chose to designate what he saw as the highest faculty of the mind—the intuitive and imaginative capacity to synthesize a whole from its parts—was "Reason." He did not see imagination and intuition in opposition to rationality; he saw them as higher forms of it. He appropriated Kant, Coleridge, and German Romanticism not as alternatives to the Enlightenment but as the necessary next stage in its fulfillment.

It is important to remember this here because it reminds us of *why* Emerson believed that self-reliance was better than other kinds of reliance. Emerson did not advocate self-trust, as Newfield and other postmodernist commentators would argue, because he believed that unchecked, "radical," "anarchistic" autonomy, self-expression, and the pursuit of power were good for their own sake without reference to any external laws or standards. Emerson preached self-reliance because the self was the locus of reason as he understood it. It was only through the independent exercise of reason that one could free oneself from the falsehoods promulgated by tradition and come to grasp real truths about nature, the self, and the cosmos. Following Plato, Stoicism, and the general Enlightenment critique of custom and received opinion, Emerson believed that in the ordinary course of things most people were prey to false images and illusions perpetrated by society in its need to sustain order. Like Plato, he understood the value of such stability, and in his own manner of living he was generally respectful of convention as long as this did not cause him to compromise his deeper beliefs. But, like Plato, he also believed that genuine insight into the higher realities required one to liberate oneself from conventional views in favor of an independent, critical, philosophical perspective. Contra Cornel West, Emerson did not "evade" philosophy; he put it at the center of his life. He preached solitude, self-communion, and criticism of society not for their own rebellious sake but because they were difficult but necessary stages on the way out of the cave of illusion.

The most important of these truths took the form not of anarchy but of law. Directly following Plato and the Stoics, Emerson believed that an immutable moral law bound nature, God, and the soul into one great, harmonious, and intelligible cosmos. Newfield, like Lange and

Lasch, is right to observe that verbal expressions of submission usually follow not long after Emerson's calls for self-liberation. But Newfield is wrong to identify an "authoritarian" impulse in Emerson as the projected source of this pattern. It is not the ominous vagary Newfield calls "the principle of superiority" that compels Emerson's submission. It is, rather, as both Lange and Lasch point out, the "highest-minded" knowledge of the fundamental cosmic law—here spoken of as the "divine providence." To conform to this law was for Emerson, as for Jonathan Edwards and much of the Western and Eastern speculative tradition, to partake directly of the divine energy that shaped and governed the universe.

Servitude at this exalted level often demanded resistance on lower levels—as the whole history of Puritanism, in which Emerson was also steeped, illustrated. It was in service to the higher law and in explicit resistance to "the principle of superiority per se" that Emerson protested the removal of the Cherokee Indians from Georgia by the forces of the U.S. government in 1838. His resistance in the 1850s to the enslavement of Africans by legally, financially, and socially "superior" Southern American white men was similarly motivated, as was his rage at the members of the New England establishment who benefited from this practice. His support for the enfranchisement of women was similarly dictated by his allegiance to a principle of right that he believed was built into nature itself. If submission to such an exacting and generous higher law implies creeping "authoritarianism," then Jefferson, Kant, Thoreau, Gandhi, and Martin Luther King, Jr., were also incipiently "authoritarian."

By losing sight of the foundational role of Enlightenment reason in Emerson and thus of the moral law that reason discovered, not only do Newfield and the postmodernist critics in general make Emerson's particular political stances unintelligible, they make it far more difficult to appreciate Emerson's writing. His prose is laced with proclamations of the moral law, with celebrations of the moral sentiment that helps us to know it, and with countless protean refigurations of its basic teaching. I am not suggesting that Emerson never doubted the moral law. One only need read "Experience" to know that he at times found it slippery, evanescent, and obscure. But it is important to remember that "Experience," however great, is only one of Emerson's many essays and lectures. Postmodernist scholars often write as if "Experience" and "Self-Reliance" were the only important essays Emerson wrote. But for every expression of skeptical despair in "Experience," one finds a score of ringing affirmations of moral clarity elsewhere—in his later no less than in his earlier work. And even in "Experience," as throughout Emerson's writing, spiritual crisis is allayed by a recovery of faith in the moral law. This is precisely the "axis," as he says toward the end of the essay, that we must "possess more firmly" (*E&L* 490).

Emerson's use of the word "axis" in "Experience" is reminiscent of his use of the word "iron" in "Self-Reliance"—"Trust thyself: every heart vibrates to that iron string." These terms are meant to suggest reassuring strength and firmness. Emerson chooses such terms precisely to ward off the inevitable charge that he is propounding a soft, subjective doctrine where anything goes if it expresses one's "true" feelings. He thus emphasizes that self-reliance does not mean, as Newfield suggests, "put[ting] the self first for any social change the soul decrees." Nor does it, as Bloom suggests, invite us to join a "cheerfully amoral dialectics of power." Nor is it, as West suggests, an incitement to "moral transgression." Nor is it a call to stare into Poirier's abyss of linguistic self-referentiality. If any of these claims were true, how would one explain Emerson's disgust when he heard that members of Congress laughed at William Henry Seward's invocation of a higher law in a speech against the Fugitive Slave Act?[27] How, furthermore, would one explain Emerson's volcanic outpouring of vituperation for Daniel Webster when he "cheerfully" acquiesced to the "amoral dialectics of power" and supported the Compromise of 1850?[28] For Emerson, self-reliance implied not liberation from moral standards but rather allegiance to a higher standard than society generally heeded. It implied disciplined obedience to the stern dictates of a truly rational conscience. "If anyone imagines that this law is lax," Emerson warned, "let him keep its commandment one day" (*E&L* 274). The universality of reason's voice is implicit in the suggestion that "every heart" hears it, but this does not mean it is easily discernable. It makes its commands clear not in the familiar customs and conventions that dominate public life but in the private resonances of philosophical intuitions.

Against the antifoundationalist misreading, then, I argue that Emerson's work, both as a whole and in its details, is structured by an Enlightenment-Platonic hierarchy of values in which experience, observation, and independent critical reason are given preference over authority and tradition as guides to basic truths about the world. The most important of these truths is an objectively intelligible moral law. Virtue is achieved by bringing one's actions into conformity with the dictates of this law. Calling human beings toward such virtue, not toward transgression, was the central aim of Emerson's work.

Emerson's morality is not the only aspect of his thought that is misunderstood if we underestimate the importance to him of reason and natural law. Emerson was a Romantic heir of the Enlightenment not only in his conception of virtue but in his conception of history. Like a great many nineteenth-century thinkers and statesmen, Hegel not least among them, Emerson tended to view history as the progressive realization of universal metaphysical principles of freedom and natural right. According to this view, a benign providential hand guides humankind through history toward the gradual attainment of universal freedom, equality, dignity, and general well-being. The decay of feudalism, the growth of commerce, the discovery of America, the Protestant reformation of moral life and religious institutions, the Renaissance flowering of the arts, technological improvements in agriculture and transportation, Enlightenment advances in science, the decline of monarchy and aristocracy, and the national emancipation movements of the nineteenth century were all seen as decisive stages in this inexorable process. Based in Enlightenment confidence about the capacity of reason to liberate humankind from age-old blinders of provincial custom and priestly tradition, this general sense of history became pervasive among progressive intellectuals and politicians of many varieties during the late eighteenth century and throughout the nineteenth century. It provides the necessary context, I will argue, for an understanding of several of Emerson's most prominent and variously interpreted political preoccupations. His distinctive version of American nationalism; his high regard for the history and culture of England; and his positive view of capitalism, commercialism, and industrial technology are all rooted in a "liberal" or "Whig" sense of history.

Such horrors as World War I, Nazism, World War II, and Stalinism have since significantly chastened the Western historical imagination. But our current wariness of such optimistic historical teleologies should not render us incapable of appreciating their role in shaping the historical imagination of previous eras. Nor should we jump too quickly to a charge of naiveté. Whiggish liberals indeed saw human history unfolding toward progressively higher levels of rationality, decency, well-being, and respect for rights. But they did not envision any sudden, decisive, or permanent transformation of human nature. And even if such a transformation were possible, liberals of this sort were loath to see politics as its appropriate agent. Their political outlook was based on a wariness of any significant consolidation of political power. Their careful attention to history taught them not only that humankind was progressing in the direction of greater freedom and equality but also that human beings have almost always abused power when given too much of it. They believed that human beings may well slowly learn to govern themselves more justly and provide for one another more fairly, but in politics above all human beings must remain always wary of their intrinsic selfishness and lust for domination. As Hamilton put it in *The Federalist* 51, "If men were angels, no government would be necessary. If angels were to govern men, neither external nor internal controls on government would be necessary." The liberal sense of history is rooted in the balanced, wary view of human nature expressed here and in *The Federalist* 55: "As there is a degree of depravity in mankind which requires a certain degree of circumspection and distrust: So there are other qualities in human nature which justify a certain portion of esteem and confidence."[29]

From the beginning to the end of his intellectual career Emerson's work was significantly shaped by this cautiously optimistic "Whig" or "liberal" sense of history. He derived it from several sources: extensive early reading of Enlightenment and early-nineteenth-century Whiggish thinkers such as Montesquieu, Adam Smith, David Hume, Benjamin Constant, and Madame de Staël; the American Federalist and Whig political cultures in which he was raised and came to maturity; and the Scottish Enlightenment outlook that was so pervasive in his Harvard training, both as an undergraduate and as a divinity student. The combination of these sources formed a deeply held and distinctively liberal sense of history that played a significant role in his early crisis of vocation, that simmered under the surface of his early works, and that burst into full and powerful expression in the political lectures and addresses of the early 1840s and the antislavery writings of the 1840s and 1850s. And there are countless passages throughout his work that only become fully intelligible if one assumes the tacit acceptance of this historical metanarrative in the background.

By attributing such a historical sensibility to Emerson, I contend against the second of the three strains of misprision I referred to above—what I called the "antihistorical" school. Long before the "antifoundationalist" assimilation of Emerson, an essentially hostile reading arose that emphasized the absence in his work of any realistic appreciation of the impact of history and society on human character. Writers in this mode took Emerson at his word when, in his early works, he said things like "build, therefore, your own world," or "strictly speaking, there is no history, only biography," or "insist on yourself, never imitate." Behind such exhortations these scholars discerned a misguided effort to deny the limits imposed by history and society on the individual human will. In advocating such denial Emerson was charged with fostering what these writers saw as the shallowest tendencies of American culture—its naiveté with respect to other cultures; its lack of reverence for the past; its valorization of self-aggrandizing egotism; its want of a reasonable sense of limits; its uprooting and alienating of individuals from the healthy constraints imposed by tradition, family, and community.

In the broadest sense, this line of criticism started with the famous complaints of Herman Melville and Nathaniel Hawthorne about Emerson's failure to heed the darker side of human life. It found what was perhaps its most influential voice in George Santayana's inclusion of Emerson in the group of spiritually effete late Puritan writers he famously labeled and attacked as the "genteel tradition" in 1913. To Santayana, the outlook of these writers was bloodless—"a little thin," "abstract," "becalmed," escapist. They had retained the ascetic wariness of the Puritans without their magnificent moral intensity. The intellectualism of these writers was a retreat from actualities rather than an effort to grasp them. The transcendental "egotism" and "subjectivism" of Emerson's essays were typical of this sensibility at its worst. In his poems Emerson occasionally showed signs of breaking free of this sterile mindset, but even there he tended to fall back on a soft "aestheticization of the landscape." A writer with such a deficient sense of reality could not possibly have any meaningful grasp of history, so, for Santayana, it was not surprising to find Emerson trying to deny its importance.[30]

Santayana was not himself a politically minded writer, but his critique of the escapist Emerson struck a chord with young leftists of the next generation, including Van Wyck Brooks. Brooks found Emerson's highbrow gentility more than a little thin. Unable as yet to assimilate Emerson to a radical agenda in the manner of F. O. Matthiessen, Brooks went on the offensive. *America's Coming of Age* (1915), in addition to introducing the phrases "highbrow" and "lowbrow" into our critical vocabulary, raised Santayana's criticisms of Emersonian "unreality" to a scathing pitch: "The truth is that Emerson was not interested in human life; he cared nothing for experience or emotion, possessing so little himself."[31]

To a large extent, the Santayana-Brooks characterization of a vapid, disconnected, "unreal" Emerson became the mainstream view in American literary and cultural criticism through the modernist–new critical era. Matthiessen went against the grain in the early 1940s by offering a sophisticated appreciation of Emerson's formal achievement, especially his use of proverbs.[32] But T. S. Eliot's dismissal of Emerson's essays had long since set the tone. Edmund Wilson had little to say about Emerson. In 1953 Whicher's *Freedom and Fate* provided a beautifully written and exhaustively well informed interpretation of Emerson's life and work that still stands as the most sensitive and searching account available. But for all his fine appreciation of Emerson, Whicher ultimately lends credence to the Santayana-Brooks image of a detached, unworldly introvert, ultimately uninterested in the concrete workings of history.

Quentin Anderson's publication of *The Imperial Self* in 1971 extended the Santayana-Brooks critique nearly into our own moment. Anderson's angle of attack parallels more recent "communitarian" critiques of liberal political philosophy. For Anderson, Emerson's principal sin is his effort to deny the importance of society and community in shaping a person's identity. In emphasizing the radical freedom and infinite power of the private individual, Anderson argues, Emerson ignores the vital fact that individuals are "fatally" shaped by their relationships to their parents, siblings, neighbors, friends, lovers, and fellow citizens. Like Alasdair Macintyre or Michael Sandel, Anderson believes that our identities are largely determined by our social roles—the particular positions we occupy in our interactions with other members of our communities. Emerson goes dangerously wrong by trying to disencumber the self from these roles. He offers his readers a delusion of egotistical power purchased at the high price of social disconnection—what Anderson calls "imaginative desocialization." The desocialized imagination was inevitably also an ahistorical imagination: Emerson "was saying that time must have a stop, that society was unthinkable, that history was an insult to the being of our immediate perceptions—that we were our own fathers."[33] In making such a futile attempt to father ourselves, we disown our rightful patrimony:

> The qualities of expansiveness and abstraction which came to characterize our diction and locutions in the 1820s were new not in the sense that they were our first response to our newness as a people, or the vastness of our land and expectations, they were new in contrast to the vocabulary of the Founding Fathers, the tough-mindedness of the Tenth

Federalist paper, the subtle, aristocratic boldness of Jefferson. . . . How suddenly remote is the world of *The Federalist Papers*! Reading them, one enters a world in which the life of the community is the paramount fact about human beings, and the arrangements to govern it are assumed to have the decisive power to qualify that life. To read Emerson is to find that associated life has become almost unreal, that the middle ground is filled, insofar as it is filled, with projects out of the self.[34]

By arguing for the importance to Emerson of a "liberal sense of history," I place Emerson in the mainstream of precisely the moderate Enlightenment tradition from which Anderson here attempts to remove him. The "tough-mindedness of the Tenth *Federalist* paper"; the "subtle, aristocratic boldness of Jefferson"; the general spirit of caution and moderation; the instinct for the middle ground: many of the habits of mind for which the Founding Fathers have long been celebrated were rooted in a balanced and wary vision of history that was progressive without being utopian or eschatological. Emerson derived a similar sense of history from similar sources, and it had similarly salutary effects on his thought. Rather than being dismissed as a cloudy mystic with a deficient sense of reality, Emerson belongs in the company of Lincoln as one of the great extenders of the Founders' legacy of sanguine, temperate, historically alert political realism.

In order to come to such an appreciation, however, it is first necessary to sharpen a fundamental distinction that Anderson blurs. In *The Spirit of Modern Republicanism*, the Straussian political theorist Thomas Pangle argues that Locke and his followers made a decisive moral shift that permanently separated modern republican thought from its classical predecessors. Stated simply, Locke endorsed as virtuous a kind of life that classical political theorists viewed as morally and spiritually mediocre or even vicious—the private and self-interested pursuit of material comfort and personal autonomy.[35] The ethos promoted by classical-republican thought had been Spartan—harsh, rigorous, martial, exacting. It demanded heroic commitment to high and difficult standards of selfless patriotism. Its tone of feeling was ardent, intense, and devoted. And it had given highest place to the active public life of military, civic, and political participation. The ethos of modern republicanism, by contrast, was soft, inward looking, moderate, and urbane. A firm line was drawn to protect the sacrosanct private sphere from public interference, and moral precedence was given to domesticity and inner spirituality. The virtues in demand were the middling commercial ones of prudence, thrift, sobriety, orderliness, and moderation. Rather than heroic self-sacrifice for one's fellows, it encouraged an attitude of cool but peaceable tolerance. Shrewd calculation was preferred to reckless courage. In shaping their political systems to promote this commercial ethic, Pangle suggests, Locke, Montesquieu, and the Founders made a tough-minded trade-off. Aware of the immense damage done by ardent political sectarianism during the seventeenth-century wars of religion, they knowingly gave up the volatile emotional intensity and xenophobic social integrity of militant republicanism in exchange for the cosmopolitan flexibility, balance, and stability of commercial liberalism. *The Federalist* 10 is the classic defense of the political benefits of this trade-off. Benjamin Franklin's autobiography is the classic illustration of the good life made possible by it. And Emerson's work, I would add, is an effort to charge this ethos with inspired moral feeling.

Anderson misleadingly implies that the Founders were more classically republican than Emerson in giving more priority to "the life of the community" and "the arrangements to govern it." Pangle, Joyce Appleby, and Isaac Kramnick, among others, have made a convincing case that the Founders were more libertarian than republican.[36] Emerson was liberal in a very similar way. Having read Bacon, Locke, Montesquieu, Hume, and Adam Smith as carefully as did Adams, Hamilton, and Madison, Emerson's instinctive response to political power was a wary desire to limit it as far as possible. Sharing these authors' and Burke's devotion to English common-law liberties, he generally preferred the slow, spontaneous evolution of complex social orders to any efforts at utopian rational design from above. No one knew better than the author of "Compensation" that "nothing is got for nothing," and he was more than ready to follow *The Federalist* 10 and trade off the public glories and civic intensity of the small, homogeneous patria in favor of the moderate private pleasures of a diffuse and cosmopolitan commercial republic. Emerson belongs in the company of Hume, Adam Smith, and Franklin in his faith in the educative value of the marketplace. He surpasses these great liberals in his passionate conviction of the dignity and sanctity of the private sphere. And while many have criticized him for political passivity, his record of action is actually strong, consistent, and coherent when seen from a libertarian-liberal perspective. Emerson generally refused to participate in utopian schemes because, like the modern liberal tradition in general, he did not see politics as a means for reshaping human nature. He resisted most calls to piecemeal activism

out of a principled allegiance to his private projects. But when he believed that the fundamental liberal political principle of natural right
was being threatened—as in the case of the removal of the Cherokees
from their ancestral lands in Georgia in 1838 or the slavery issue in the
1850s—he swung aggressively into rhetorical action.

I have suggested that Emerson's liberal concept of nationalism con-
tended against the cruder, more imperialistic nationalism of the contemporary Democratic Party. In general, Emerson, like Lincoln, resisted
the jingoistic rhetoric of Jackson and his many subsequent imitators. But
their imperialist and proslavery positions were not the only things Emerson disliked about the Democrats. His visceral antipathy to the general
populist ethos of the Jacksonians is unmistakable to a careful reader of
his letters or voluminous journals.[37] This hostility must be given due
weight in any effort to assess Emerson's general political outlook. But
Emerson's pervasive contempt for the vibrant popular politics of his
own day has not prevented many of his most influential twentieth-
century interpreters from seeing his thought and writings as profoundly
democratic at a deeper level.

No less a figure than John Dewey eloquently initiated this tradition
at the beginning of the twentieth century. In 1903 Dewey wrote, "When
Democracy has articulated itself, it will have no difficulty in finding itself
already proposed in Emerson. . . . Against creed and system, convention
and institution, Emerson stands for restoring to the common man that
which in the name of religion, philosophy, of art, and of morality, has
been embezzled from the common store and appropriated to sectarian
and class use. For such reasons, the coming century may well make evident what is just now dawning, that Emerson is not only a philosopher,
but he is the philosopher of Democracy."[38] Vernon Parrington struck a
similar tone in the 1920s, placing Emerson in a long Jeffersonian democratic tradition.[39] Matthiessen approvingly cites Dewey's remarks at the
beginning of his important work of 1941, *American Renaissance*. He goes on
to argue that Emerson shared with Hawthorne, Melville, Thoreau, and
Whitman a "devotion to the possibilities of democracy." "His value,"
Matthiessen went further, assimilating Emerson to his own socialist view-
point, "can hardly be exaggerated for those who believe now in the dynamic extension of democracy on economic as well as political levels."[40]
Daniel Aaron follows suit in his 1951 chronicle of American literary progressives, finding "marked Jeffersonian and Jacksonian overtones" in

Emerson's political philosophy.[41] And Wilson Allen concludes his major 1981 biography with a ringing endorsement of the same Dewey passage quoted above.[42]

The most recent major statement of the "democratic" reading of Emerson must be considered at greater length. In a number of seminal essays and in his book *Emerson and Self-Reliance* (1994), George Kateb has developed what many see as the fullest, most ambitious, and most insightful interpretation of Emerson's politics yet written.[43] I agree on the whole with this assessment, but with one important caveat. In the bulk of *Emerson and Self-Reliance* and in most of his essays, Kateb has painted a richly textured, nuanced, and, I believe, accurate portrait of Emerson's political sensibility. The problem is that he has given his painting the wrong title. He has completed a compelling portrait of a great liberal but called it a portrait of a democrat.

Kateb concludes, for example, that for Emerson "democracy" was the only form of political life that gave ultimate precedence to the individual: "Emerson's guiding sense [was] that society is a means for the end of individuals, who are themselves ends. Democracy is the set of political arrangements that provide the protections and encouragements to become individuals, rather than servants of society."[44] This statement is an accurate summary of Emerson's priorities except in its choice of the term "democracy" over "liberalism" or even "liberal democracy." It was no more difficult for Emerson than it is for us to imagine a democratic form of society in which individuals would *not* be protected. He need only have recalled the works of Rousseau, with which he was familiar, or of the classical-republican tradition, which played such a large part in America's founding period. Emerson pointedly refrained from tapping into the available classical-republican concept of democracy precisely because it implied the sacrifice of individuals to the needs of the community or the state.[45] Instead, he richly endorsed the liberal concept of democracy because it contains a check on the potential excesses of democratic communitarianism. Thus, only if one strikes out "democracy" and writes in "liberalism" or "liberal democracy" does Kateb's statement stand as an accurate summary of Emerson's basic political outlook.

The difference might seem small, but it is crucial. Stated simply, it is the difference between giving priority to the value of freedom or to the value of equality. Both of these values are at the heart of liberal democracy. For the most part they are complementary, as when we say that "equality before the law" guarantees to all the same basic liberties. But they do sometimes come into conflict, as when the will of the majority threatens the basic liberties of a minority. And there is always at least some tension between these two values to the extent that one of liberal democracy's most sacred liberties—the right to acquire and hold property—implies the development of substantive economic inequalities within the overarching framework of legal equality.[46] When forced to confront these basic tensions, it is fair to say that nineteenth-century liberals tended to throw their weight behind liberty and against equality, while twentieth-century liberalism has tended in the other direction.[47]

The liberal tendency to pit freedom against equality became especially prominent toward the middle of the nineteenth century in Europe. As working-class suffrage movements and the specter of communism increasingly seemed to threaten the sacred middle-class right to property, liberal political thought and practice was increasingly pervaded by a profound anxiety about equality and a compensatory emphasis on freedom as a value that would provide a bulwark against the leveling tendencies of mass democracy. This pattern is timelessly expressed in such major political-cultural works of the midcentury as Alexis de Tocqueville's *Democracy in America* (1835, 1840), John Stuart Mill's *On Liberty* (1859), and Matthew Arnold's *Culture and Anarchy* (1869) and, I would add, in the journals, essays, and books of Emerson. Like the more overtly political works of these European contemporaries, Emerson's writings are well characterized in political terms as efforts to find supplements with which to bolster liberal democratic societies against the moral and spiritual deficiencies intrinsic to what Tocqueville warily called democratic "equality of condition."

By mistitling his Emerson a "democrat" rather than a "liberal," Kateb joins the members of the Deweyan tradition in overlooking the decisive importance of this anxiety about equality in Emerson's work. This oversight is especially surprising in the case of Kateb because, unlike Parrington or Matthiessen, he does not for the most part aim to present a democratically sanitized image of Emerson. For example, Kateb is alone among recent political interpreters in reminding us of the central importance of Plato to Emerson's outlook. "Emerson's premise is roughly Plato's," Kateb writes in expounding "Self-Reliance," "to see right is at once (and inter-connectedly) a source of intense pleasure, the highest manifestation of doing justice and the most intimate embrace of reality."[48] This is an important observation about the Platonic roots of

Emerson's emphasis on the interconnection between virtue, truth, and beauty. Until recently, most nonpolitical readers readily acknowledged the pervasive presence throughout Emerson's work of an essentially Platonic structure of values. But most democratically minded critics have shied away from this connection because they are wary of the aristocratic political preferences associated with Platonism. Kateb, by contrast, is quite candid. He points out that the root of the much-touted affinity between Nietzsche and Emerson is their shared debt to their great Greek predecessor: "Plato is their common bond and allegiance." And Kateb does not back away from the antidemocratic implications of this shared allegiance. "Emerson," he acknowledges, "exceeds Nietzsche in queasiness."[49]

By "queasiness" Kateb means precisely revulsion toward humans in the unwashed mass, toward "the herd," the demos. As Kateb eloquently suggests, Emerson, even more than Nietzsche, "is temperamentally given to shuddering at the thought of clustered humanity, lost together because each is lost to himself or herself."[50] This shudder is especially audible, Kateb points out, in Emerson's expressions of bewildered contempt for the shallow way in which most people spend their time.[51] The only activities finally worthy of respect for Kateb's Emerson are contemplative ones—reading, writing, thinking, and worship. But this emphatically omits ordinary perusal of the newspaper, writing letters, and going dutifully to services on the weekend. It only includes the kind of poetic, intense, unconventional, and high-minded personal reflection, devotion, and creative expression cultivated by rare free spirits.

Kateb acknowledges that on the surface these would not seem to be the raw materials of a "democratic" outlook. "It must be conceded," he writes, "that before the slavery crisis in the 1850s permanently changes Emerson's sensibility, he can speak with a certain lightness of his commitment to democracy." But Kateb insists nonetheless that in the final estimate "Emerson's work is soaked in democratic spirit."[52] Emerson is indeed like Nietzsche in his profound wariness of the crowd, Kateb argues, but he is unlike Nietzsche in his confidence that every person is capable of emancipating himself or herself from the crowd and achieving spiritual elevation. Similarly, Emerson is like Plato in insisting on a rank order for human activities in which philosophical contemplation takes the highest place, but he is unlike Plato in believing that "everyone's vocation is to philosophize." To quote one of his most succinct formulations of the issue, "[self-reliance] is thus not a doctrine of superiority to average humanity. Rather it is a doctrine urging the elevation of democracy to its full height, free of the aristocratic, but also free of the demotic."[53]

Here Kateb tries unsuccessfully to have it both ways. Is it really possible to have a democracy free of the demotic? And should we really call that thinker a "democrat" who attempts to cure democracy of the demotic? To answer these questions, it is instructive to contrast Emerson with a contemporary who conspicuously reveled in the colloquial speech of the people—Walt Whitman. Kateb, like Parrington, Matthiessen, and the Deweyan strain in general, tends to lump Emerson together with Whitman. In doing so he blurs the distinctive political character of both writers. The characteristic social gesture of Whitman's writing is relaxed, expansive, inclusive, and outward, as in "I lean and loaf at my ease observing a spear of summer grass" and "Flood-tide below me! I see you face to face! . . . Crowds of men and women attired in the usual costumes, how curious you are to me!"[54] The characteristic social gesture of Emerson's writing, by contrast, is tense, exclusive, reclusive, inward, and upward, as in "the air clears, and the clouds lift a little, there are the gods still sitting around him on their thrones,—they alone with him alone" (*E&L* 1124). At the most intimate levels of his sensibility, Emerson was profoundly discomfited by precisely that surging "Flood-tide" of humanity in the mass that elicited Whitman's great effusions of democratic sentiment. This is not to say that Emerson was hostile to democracy, only that he was often made very uneasy by it. This uneasiness takes him out of the company of such radically democratic contemporaries as Whitman and the early Bancroft and puts him firmly in the company of the European liberal contemporaries I have already mentioned—Tocqueville, Mill, and Arnold. These writers shared Emerson's essential friendliness toward democracy in the abstract as well as his "queasiness" in the face of democracy's actual plebeian grittiness. It is only by exploring the liberal anxieties he shared with these illustrious contemporaries rather than by projecting back our own democratic certainties that we may hope to come to an accurate understanding of Emerson's general political position.

Kateb has made a valuable contribution to this understanding by restoring Emerson to a Platonic context. Emerson's work, as I have already suggested, is drenched in Plato and Neoplatonism and thus everywhere preoccupied with ideas of what is "high," "noble," "refined," "excellent," and "virtuous." There is hardly a paragraph in all of his work, including his journals, that does not follow a steep upward trajectory. One feels everywhere a constant push for elevation, ascent, distinction. He is rivaled perhaps only by Franklin among American writers in his unflagging focus on the pursuit of excellence at every significant level of human endeavor—moral, philosophical, political, aesthetic, and material. But in so persistently aiming for the "high," Emerson operates almost always in considerable tension with democratic egalitarianism as he perceived it flowering around him in Jacksonian America.

1

Progress

Journals (1820–1824); "Self-Reliance" (1841)

D o not believe the past" (*E&L* 101). "The centuries are conspirators against the sanity and authority of the soul" (*E&L* 270). "When we have new perception, we shall gladly disburden the memory of its hoarded treasures as old rubbish" (*E&L* 271). Most readers will recognize Emerson's "antihistorical" strain. A perhaps all-too-American irreverence toward the past is one of the characteristics most commonly associated with Emerson's work. But readers who take Emerson too simply at his word in such statements (and many have done so) might be surprised by his earliest journals.[1] From 1821, when as a college student at Harvard he began regularly transcribing thoughts and passages from his reading into notebooks, to roughly 1826, when he completed his divinity studies and was approbated to preach, it is fair to say that history, broadly understood as the overarching pattern of human experience as a whole, was Emerson's most pervasive concern. Emerson read an enormous number and range of historical works during these years, and the sequence of his reading indicates that the young scholar had undertaken no less a task than orienting himself with respect to the course of human history in its entirety. It was as if he could not settle the problem of his own vocation until he understood what history as a whole required of him.[2] And the wonder is that he heard such a clear calling! Rather than a denial of history, the statements above and countless others like them throughout Emerson's opus derive directly from a comprehensive liberal conception of history at which Emerson arrived during these early studies and on which all of his subsequent work may be said to pivot. Influenced by a distinctive set of liberal sources as well as the many emancipatory tendencies and portents of his own historical moment, including especially in later years the antislavery movement and the Civil War, Emerson came to see history in no uncertain liberal terms as, to use Hegel's phrase, "the progress of the consciousness of freedom," and he conceived his own work as an agent of this progress.[3] Indeed, Emerson's unique new prose style would serve in part to embody, enact, and evoke this new consciousness. It was on the basis of a profound sense of history, in other words, that Emerson so distinctively declared freedom from it.[4]

So pervasive has been the perception of Emerson as antihistorical, however, that surprisingly little has been written in depth about the historical aspect of his work. The relevant material can be briefly surveyed. As far back as 1943 Rene Wellek confirmed that in the latter half of Emerson's career (after 1849) he was significantly, if indirectly, influenced by Hegel's *The Philosophy of Right* and *The Philosophy of History*.[5] The next significant statement was not until 1961. Philip Nicoloff's *Emerson on Race and History: An Examination of English Traits* remains valuable as one of only two book-length studies of the historical theme in Emerson's work and will be summarized below.[6] A full fifteen years later, in 1976, Gustaaf Van Cromphout expanded upon the Hegel connection to suggest that Emerson saw history as a "dialectical process involving hero and society," wherein great men serve as agents of progress by periodically shattering old conventions and ideas.[7] Robert Richardson also emphasized Hegel in making a strong case for the centrality of history to Emerson's thought in his important 1982 article, "Emerson and History," also summarized below.[8] In 1990 Len Gougeon ushered in the current historical turn in Emerson criticism with his detailed study of Emerson's involvement in the antislavery movement.[9] Gougeon notes repeatedly how Emerson's response to slavery was framed within a larger sense of the quasi-providential "ameliorative" course of human history. In the same year, but on a somewhat different track, Sacvan Bercovitch, in "Emerson, Individualism, and the Ambiguities of Dissent," offered a characteristically multilayered and complex analysis of Emerson's "journey into [American liberal] ideology," with its associated notions of progress.[10] Eduardo Cadava has recently stressed how Emerson's engagement with the major political issues of his day, especially slavery, drew him into serious moral and philosophical reflections on history per se.[11] And, most recently, Lawrence Buell has commented trenchantly on the persistence of an Anglo-Saxon liberal myth of history in Emerson's writing.[12] All of these are lasting contributions, relevant to our concerns in different ways. Most generally, they provide substantial corroboration that Emerson was indeed centrally concerned with history. And in the cases of Wellek, Richardson, Gougeon, Bercovitch, and Buell, they confirm that Emerson's general historical orientation was liberal, though it must be noted that both Bercovitch and Buell do so with differing degrees of distaste. In what might be seen as a new version of Whicher's retraction narrative, Bercovitch partially laments what he sees as Emerson's midcareer retreat into American liberal orthodoxy from an early radical moment of interest in European socialism. And Buell sees Emerson's long preoccupation with America's Anglo-Saxon liberal roots as nothing more than a "juvenile fixation" that refused to go away.[13] We will come back to both of these.

Nicoloff and Richardson provide the most helpful overviews of Emerson's sources and emphases. Nicoloff, to start with, breaks down Emerson's vast reading into a lucid and accessible schema, focusing on the oft-ignored *English Traits* (1856) as a mature and serious statement. As Nicoloff sees it, Emerson's thinking about history had two main stages. His early outlook derived principally from ancient Greek thought (pre-Socratic, Platonic, and Neoplatonic) and saw history as a cyclical pattern of growth and decay whose fluxions could be at best temporarily transcended in privileged moments of intuitive flight to the eternal. Emerson then supplemented this outlook, starting roughly in the midthirties, with a quasi-biological natural-scientific conception of slow, long-term, evolutionary ascent derived from Lyell, proto-Darwinians such as Robert Chambers, and an eclectic blend of early-nineteenth-century philosophers of history such as Coleridge, Herder, Cousin, Hegel (via Cousin), Carlyle, and Stallo. An additional—and regrettable—aspect of this later stage, Nicoloff emphasizes, was Emerson's partial absorption of some now notorious strains of racialist nineteenth-century ethnography, an issue we will address in chapter 7.[14] In any case, Nicoloff says that Emerson's mature view was a combination of his earlier and later perspectives. By the time he was writing *English Traits* and *The Conduct of Life* (1860), he had come to envision history as a vast, two-level pattern in which discrete local cycles of efflorescence, struggle (including racial struggle), dominance (including racial dominance), and decay feed into a larger, all-embracing, cosmic progression toward the physical, moral, and even spiritual development of the species as a whole.

Richardson opens up yet another dimension of Emerson's historical outlook by focusing on the essay "History." He suggests that Emerson ultimately rejected both positivist and prophetic claims about history's direction in favor of "subjective historicism," "a concept of history as meaningful only when validated by individual experience."[15] Not to be confused with relativism, which denies the possibility of arriving at any authoritative truth, this view gives each individual access to the laws of nature via self-reliant reflection on his or her own mind and experience. Its antipositivism notwithstanding, Richardson emphasizes the Enlightenment secularity of this outlook—its "sweeping repudiation" of the Christian-typological approach. Just as Herder reveled in the Copernican decentering and the subsequent Enlightenment doctrine of the plurality of worlds because it implied that any observer from any cosmic position had, in a sense, equally valid purchase on the objective laws of the universe, so Emerson's historical subjectivism, derived in part from Herder, gave all authentically reflective individuals equal access to the truths of history.

Together, Nicoloff and Richardson provide a lucid exposition of many of the important main features of Emerson's multifaceted, at times contradictory, and ever-evolving conception of history. But for all their combined thoroughness, I would suggest that they do not cast their nets quite widely enough. They are missing two crucial pieces, one from the beginning of Emerson's career and one from near the end, but both conceptually closely linked. On the early end, Nicoloff overlooks the important fact that the mature Emerson was predisposed to embrace an evolutionary-progressive sense of history by the distinctive brand of liberal progressivism he had long since absorbed from the Scottish Enlightenment authorities of his Harvard Unitarian schooling. And on the later end, Gougeon's book has now made it impossible to ignore the significance for Emerson of his involvement in the antislavery movement after 1844, an experience that initially pushed Emerson back on his Anglo-Scottish liberal intellectual roots and that, I will suggest, ultimately had the effect of deepening his liberal convictions in a way surprising even to himself.[16] We will discuss this important midcareer consolidation of Emerson's liberal outlook later in the book. To begin with now we must examine more closely the foundations of the liberal-historical orientation that would continue to fundamentally shape Emerson's thinking throughout his life.

Nicoloff and Richardson both acknowledge that the young Emerson read Hume's history and his historical essays as well as Gibbon and Voltaire. But Nicoloff especially downplays the importance of these Enlightenment historians in shaping Emerson's thought, and neither he nor Richardson makes any mention of Adam Smith, William Robertson, Adam Ferguson, or of the distinctive liberal-historical temper of the Scottish Enlightenment in general. The fact so amply demonstrated by Daniel Walker Howe, that all of Emerson's teachers at Harvard, William Ellery Channing not least among them, were steeped in the Scottish outlook, would not perhaps in itself be sufficient to assure its influence on Emerson.[17] But Emerson's notebooks from the early 1820s, as we will see, betray the Scottish influence at every turn. By looking closely at revealing passages from these years, I suggest that Emerson's earliest conception of history was not one of repeating cycles of decay but rather his own distinctively American and personally reflexive variant of the eighteenth-century Scottish liberal and Victorian Whig stories of the history of liberty—a decidedly linear narrative of gradual emancipatory ascent that in Emerson as in many of his English Victorian contemporaries would in time meld with the Darwinian account.[18] Happily, since I approach Emerson as a historical-contextual literary scholar rather than as a historian per se, I need not address the substance of Herbert Butterfield's and others' concerns about how Whig preconceptions inevitably slanted the historical record.[19] I will be concerned only to recognize the Whig categories as such, and to observe how a great literary mythmaker absorbed and then transmuted them into the rhetorically propulsive narrative axis of a larger liberal-cultural symbolic system.

The principal events and heroes of the Victorian "history of liberty" are perhaps familiar enough, but it is worth reviewing them briefly not only for the purposes of this chapter but because they are contextually relevant to every aspect of Emerson's work. In Lord Acton's classic account the Hebrew prophets are presented as the earliest founders: they "laid down the parallel lines on which all freedom has been won—the doctrine of national tradition and the doctrine of the higher law."[20] When Ezekiel or Isaiah castigated the rulers of ancient Israel by reference to God's law and the founding covenant, he invoked an authority higher than the established positive authority and thus opened up a space, in principle at least, for legitimate independent thought and conscience, and possible reform. Solon opened up similar space in classical Athens by giving all citizens some say in their governance and constructing a constitution open in principle to change: "Government by consent superseded government by compulsion, and the pyramid which had stood on its point was made to stand on its base." Socrates went further still by questioning the religious no less than the political authorities and setting up human reason — "the test of incessant inquiry" — as the final authority: "The epoch of doubt and transition during which the Greeks passed from the dim fancies of mythology to the fierce light of science was the age of Pericles, and the endeavor to substitute certain truth for the prescriptions of impaired authorities, which was then beginning to absorb the energies of the Greek intellect, is the grandest movement in the profane annals of mankind." The Stoics then carried these seeds of liberty from the classical Greek into the Roman and Christian eras. Their personal and inward ethical attunement to an overarching cosmic moral order "speaks almost the language of Christianity" and met the transcultural needs of a vast empire encompassing multiple legal and political cultures. According to Acton, the Stoics also initiated the liberal tradition's long theoretical opposition to slavery. For the Stoics, "the great question is to discover, not what governments prescribe, but what they ought to prescribe; for no prescription is valid against the conscience of mankind. Before God, there is neither Greek nor barbarian, neither rich nor poor, and the slave is as good as his master, for by birth all men are free; they are the citizens of that universal commonwealth which embraces all the world, brethren of one family, and children of God."[21]

Hebrews and Hellenes thus each helped to start liberty on its way by questioning traditional political authority, opening a space for higher morality in the former case and higher reason in the latter. But neither yet gave up on the utopian hope for an ultimately perfected political structure — the Messiah's restored Zion or the philosophers' ideal republic. According to Acton, it was only when Christ said, "My kingdom is not of this world," or "The kingdom of Heaven is within you," or "Render unto Caesar what is Caesar's and unto God what is God's" that the West was liberated in principle from utopian enclosure. Neither Hebraic prophecy nor Greek philosophy intended any denigration of politics; it sought rather to make politicians answerable to authorities higher than custom, tradition, or corrupt conventional practice. These words of Christ, on the other hand, especially as expounded by St. Augustine in *The City of God,* imposed a limit upon the value of politics per se by placing it second in importance to the inward and transcendent reality of the spirit. In protecting a space for faith, in other words, Christianity implicitly asserted a principle of limited government.[22] In the protracted power struggle that ensued between the Roman Catholic Church and the monarchs of Europe, both sides sought to curtail the authority of the other. The cunning of history is such that in thus attempting to aggrandize their respective powers, both sides appealed, in theory, to the will of the people, and thus a set of protoliberal ideas regarding popular will, limited government, and boundaries between church and state began to work their way into the institutional fabric of Western life. Consciousness of this boundary remained largely dormant at the popular level during the long agrarian sleep of the feudal era, the Whig narrative allows, but the early modern rise of towns, trade, humanism, print technology, and, most important, Protestantism brought to the many members of the newly emerging middle class an increasingly sharp sense that, along with their newly acquired properties, they might also be entitled to ownership of themselves.[23]

"All history must tend to become more whig in proportion as it becomes more abridged," Herbert Butterfield quipped in his famous critique of this general outlook, and the comment clearly holds true of the early Emerson.[24] By the time Emerson wrote *Nature* he had absorbed variants of this entire Whig narrative to such an extent that it had become axiomatic. It needed no demonstration or argumentation; he assumes that his readers understand and accept it. He sketches a redacted version of the whole trajectory in an extended passage from *Nature,* invoking a "noble" line of liberty's martyrs from Socrates and Jesus through the Swiss Arnold Winkelried, who cried out "For Liberty!" as he cast himself against a phalanx of Austrian spears, and concluding with seventeenth-century English republicans such as Harry Vane and Lord Russel, who chose to die rather than submit to what they saw as the tyranny of Charles II. Emerson had further occasion to rehearse the full account again later in response to the slavery crisis. But generally a sense of history as progress toward freedom remains implicit or tersely abbreviated, though fully active, in Emerson's published work. Indeed, Emerson's entire voluminous early body of writing from roughly 1820 to 1840, taken together, reveals an extended process of crystallization of these ideas about history. He moves from the journals' loose, youthful efforts to comprehend the pattern of history as a whole; toward the lectures' increasingly clear, semisystematic, and unmistakably Anglo Whiggish account of decisive forces, figures, and moments; and finally to the poetic liberal-historical abridgments of the early published essays and addresses. It forms a kind of pyramidal iceberg structure in which the wide base of unpublished historical reflections sits under the abrupt epigrammatic points of the published prose. Emerson is able to say "Do not believe the past" so confidently and concisely in "Literary Ethics" because he has already spent a great deal of time figuring out that the whole pattern of history leads to this moment of departure from history. And, as befits the "subjective historicism" that insisted that the truths of history must be, in Richardson's phrase, "validated by personal experience," the force of Emerson's ever-clarifying perception of history as progress toward freedom was reflexively redoubled in these early years by the parallel narrative of his own difficult personal liberation from his family's religious-cultural tradition.

Let us now look at some of the relevant texts.

Many scholars have been struck by the first sentence of Emerson's youthful journal of May 1822: "I dedicate my book to the spirit of America" (*JMN* 2:3). But few have noted how his immediately preceding and following set of notebooks, starting from his very first journal in June 1820, frame this declaration. In one of his very first entries Emerson casts a jaundiced Gibbonesque eye over the long, lamentable history of human religious self-abasement: "What odious vice, what sottish and debasing enormity the degenerate naughtiness of man has never crouch[ed] unto and adored?" he rhetorically asks. But he then apprehends "a joyful change" when, through reason, "human nature unshackl[es] herself and assert[s] her divine origin" (*JMN* 2:18). In much of what follows Emerson proceeds to chart across time and geography his version of the classical-Enlightenment opposition between "sottish" tradition and "joyful" reason. No cultural relativist, he imagines that even the remotest archaic idolater must have had "a stupid consciousness of going wrong": "While he kneels before the false altar, in obedience to a greater idol, Custom, the moral sense rebels within him" (*JMN* 1:78). Emerson speculates that the fall of Rome, which he "does not deplore," might nonetheless have been averted if the Romans had introduced into their political structure the balances of modern bicameralism—"the rational hope of our own institutions" (*JMN* 1:70). He marvels in horror at the Catholic "Dark ages" of the "six centuries 5, 6, 7, 8, 9, 10": "It is a fearful phenomenon that the mind should thus sleep for 6 hundred years and under the influence of such tremendous dreams" (*JMN* 1:66). He sees this era as "an emphatic night preceded and followed by Days of extraordinary glory"—classical Greece before and the Italian Renaissance after, in the latter of which we predictably find "the dawn of the restoration of human honour," as philosophy now "extend[s] her influence in a thousand branches," "reviv[ing] all that was worthy in Ancient Science" (*JMN* 1:66, 68). Early modern Italy is then doubly instructive "because it demonstrated better than any other the remarkable and vast effects upon national prosperity of free Commerce and agriculture, which exalted individual character, and filled the public treasury with a boundless wealth," but it failed to reap the full benefits of these advantages "by neglecting to lay deeply the civil order upon the sound principles of the interests and inclinations of men" (*JMN* 1:77–78).

Early modern Italy became rich, in other words, because it was economically liberal but eventually lost its wealth because it was not liberal enough. "Commerce had raised a counterpoise to the privileges of the nobles," but in Italy, as in the rest of Europe, "in that disastrous twilight . . . all were equalized by the common submission of the freedom of opinion to the ordinances of the councils and courts of Rome" (*JMN* 1:306). Trade brought prosperity, refinement of manners, and tolerance everywhere it was allowed, but only when thought, conscience, and speech could be as free would the full promise of modernity be realized. For this the "convulsion" of the Reformation was first required to "break the slumber of the dark ages" (*JMN* 1:151). "After the decline of the Roman Church the lower orders of Europe had no Indian Brahmin to tell them that in the eternal rounds of transmigration their soul could never rise above the jackal, and the license which the Press immediately brought tended directly to enlighten and emancipate them. . . . When at length moral discussions which before were strange and unintelligible to their ears began to be understood and they comprehended the nature of property and government, things were in train for amendment." Once the printing press was invented and the foundational liberal principle of private property fully established, freedom's momentum became inexorable. "To the diffusion of knowledge through the lower orders of Society must be attributed in the first place the rise of the commons in the monarchies of Europe which began the demolition of the feudal system" and "lastly the rebellion of the people against the throne which has everywhere manifested itself either in dangerous symptoms or in actual revolution. . . . [T]he Moralist regards this commotion as the inevitable effect of the progress of knowledge which might have been foretold almost from the time of the invention of Printing and which must proceed, with whatever disastrous evils the crisis may be attended, to the calm and secure possession of equal rights and laws which it was intended to obtain" (*JMN* 1:344). The narrative draws to a fitting conclusion with Emerson's self-consciously eccentric conception of an extended "Age of Reason."

> The curse which is landed on the Roman Church records that she substituted authority for reason, that she took the Bible from the hands of men and commanded them to believe. The bondage was so crafty and so strong that it was long before the mind was hardy enough to break it. But it was finally broken, and thenceforward the Age of Reason commenced. I use a term which has been perverted and abused, but I apply it with propriety to the era of Luther and Calvin, with still more propriety to the advanced reason of Clarke and Newton, and with still more perfect propriety to this latter day when our eyes read with all the added splendor of these great and various lights. (*JMN* 2:17)

This entire Whig narrative, derived principally from the Scottish Enlightenment via the Harvard teachers with whom Emerson studied from 1817 to 1821, and some of whose lectures he still attended, stands freshly in the background when Emerson dedicates his 1822 journal to the "spirit of America." Twice in the process of transposing this material from lectures and reading into his notebooks he was moved proudly to claim its legacy as his American "birthright." First in May 1822, after reflecting on the disruptive effects of the activities of "the church faction" throughout Europe in the Middle Ages, he writes: "I will not believe that it is ignorance to esteem my *birthright* in America as a preferable gift to the honors of any other nation that breathes upon Earth." And then following the above dedication in May 1822 he puts it this way: "If the nations of Europe can find anything to idolize in their ruinous and enslaved institutions, we are content. . . . But let them not ignorantly mock at the pride of an American . . . when that freeman is giving an imperfect expression to his sense of his condition. He rejoices in the *birthright* of a country where the freedom of opinion and action is so perfect that every man enjoys exactly that consideration to which he is entitled" (*JMN* 2:4, italics mine). The word "birthright" is telling here because at this tender psychological moment in the nineteen-year-old Emerson's formation, as he begins to sample the "wide world" of his notebooks' title, his cultural "birthright" would inevitably have been at issue. One of the most fundamental tasks of cultural symbolism, Geertz reminds us, is to provide the self with primordial temporal orientation— a sense of a past and future that he or she unconsciously inherits, precisely as a "birthright," from the previous generation, shares with his or her own generation, and then passes along to the next in the same gratuitous form.[25] Intellectuals tend to make this process critically self-conscious. In so consciously avowing his American "birthright" in this context of the Anglo Whig history of liberty, the young intellectual Emerson claims for himself and for his young country both deep and definite roots and a clearly directed future. The tone of hostile defensiveness with regard to Europe belies a degree of anxiety about his cultural identity not surprising in one of his or his country's youthful age and appropriate to the psychic importance of the matter. The psycho-cultural stakes are only poignantly raised by the premature assertion of cultural leadership implicit in the young man presumptuously dedicating to "the spirit of America" the pages of what was, after all, little more than a college notebook—a device usually devoted more to the passive reception of cultural wisdom than to its transmission. In any case, it is crucial for the understanding of Emerson's work as a whole to see that he first lays claim to the symbolic identity with which he is to be permanently associated in this particular Enlightenment-Whig historical context. I would suggest that "America" and "American" retain this particular Enlightenment-historical meaning, and continue to perform this particular role of temporal orientation, throughout Emerson's work.

But one cannot comment even in a preliminary way upon the cultural-symbolic meaning of "America" in a discussion of Emerson without acknowledging the readings of Sacvan Bercovitch. No one has done more to advance our understanding of the use and abuse of "America" as a cultural symbol, especially in the major works of the U.S. literary tradition. It is sufficient to say that to a large extent Bercovitch reads Emerson as extending a unique tradition of cultural exhortation that he has traced back to the New England Puritans and taught a generation of scholars to recognize as the "American jeremiad." As Bercovitch reads it, the jeremiad is an extraordinarily sophisticated and flexible cultural-symbolic practice that evolved over the course of the seventeenth, eighteenth, and nineteenth centuries to supply the distinctive psychosocial needs for temporal orientation and social cohesion of the United States' new kind of modern middle-class society, committed as it was in an unprecedented fashion to the values of process and progress. In the original Puritan jeremiads of the seventeenth century, Bercovitch argues contra Perry Miller that what appeared to be largely pessimistic catalogs of collective backsliding actually functioned optimistically both to reorient the community toward its sacred origin—the New Englanders' special original "covenant" with God—and to rally their spirits toward the transcendent millennial future promised therein. Over time the elusive, ambiguous, ever-retreating character of this future promise turned out to be perfectly suited to a society committed to an infinitely expansive conception of the self and to apparently unbounded economic and geopolitical growth. The jeremiad's channeling of dissenting energies into an ongoing process of social renewal and rededication thus provided extraordinary cohesion and continuity to a dynamic society that would have seemed especially vulnerable to the atomizing forces of modern capitalism. Indeed, Bercovitch suggests that the jeremiad's distinctive fusion of sacred and secular served not only to accommodate dissent but to elide the incipient problem of individualist ennui by investing the profane pursuit of middle-class self-interest with an aura of collective eschatological mission. "The latter day Jeremiahs forged a powerful vehicle of middle-class ideology: a ritual of progress through consensus, a system of sacred-secular symbols for a laissez-faire creed, a 'civil religion' for a people chosen to spring fully formed into the modern world." In the nineteenth century, Bercovitch asserts, the leading Jeremiah was Emerson: "His career exemplifies the possibilities and constrictions of the nineteenth-century Jeremiad."[26] "By 1860 he was the oracle of an ideology fully matured, a ritual of crisis and control that had virtually assumed a dynamic of its own."[27]

Bercovitch's reading thus supports my initial suggestion above that from early on Emerson found in "America" a cultural symbol oriented progressively toward the future. But for Bercovitch, Emerson's American hope is ultimately eschatological and nationalist. He places Emerson in a long line of millenarian exhorters stretching from Thomas Hooker through Edward Johnson, Increase Mather, Samuel Danforth, and Jonathan Edwards, and notes the persistence everywhere in Emerson of secularized Calvinist modes of conceiving self, society, and history.[28] Emerson, Bercovitch suggests, offers a "dream-vision" of social unity through laissez-faire, a "liberal millennium" based on a "Christic paradox[ical]" figuring of the individual as mystical social body and carrying forward a "typological" sense of history in which "America" is now nationalistically figured as the promised land of Canaan.[29] By pointing out the decisive early importance of what is ultimately an Enlightenment-historical orientation, I prepare to read the symbolism of Emerson's "America" somewhat differently. Bercovitch's powerful readings depend upon a conception of secularization against which Hans Blumenberg has mounted a telling critique, arguing that it tends to blur the difference between scientific-secular-skeptical modernity and its Christian-traditional antecedents. The modern scientific idea of progress, Blumenberg argues, may have taken the cultural "position" formerly occupied by Christian eschatology insofar as it provides a hopeful orientation toward the long-term future, but the nature of its hope, the form of its expectation, is radically different. For Blumenberg, the idea of progress is more humanly self-assertive than Christian eschatology insofar as it insists upon a human capacity for knowledge reserved by Christianity only to God. It is at the same time more modest insofar as it anticipates ultimate reward not by extrahistorical messianic intervention from on high but only by the gradual, secular, intrahistorical accumulation and transmission of knowledge across many generations of a universal human community. "The idea of (modern scientific) method is not a kind of planning, not a transformation of the divine salvation plan, but rather the establishment of a disposition: the disposition of the subject, in his place, to take part in a process that generates knowledge in a transsubjective manner."[30] Blumenberg's critique is especially pertinent to Emerson because he argues that the Western intellect was initially provoked toward this epochal modern "self-assertion" in much the same way that the young Emerson will be provoked toward his own "self-reliance"—by the severity of the Calvinist denial of the efficacy of human rational agency. "The escape into transcendence," Blumenberg writes regarding Calvinism, "as the possibility that is held out to man and has only to be grasped, has lost its human relevance precisely on account of the absolutism of the decisions of divine grace, that is, on account of the dependence of the individual's salvation on a faith that he can no longer choose to have. This changed set of presuppositions brings into the horizon of possible intentions the alternative of the immanent self-assertion of reason through the mastery and alteration of reality."[31] With Blumenberg in mind, I would argue that Emerson, rather than a mouthpiece of secularized Calvinism, is best understood as a participant, albeit in a peculiarly Romantic idiom, of this "self-assertion of reason" against the strictures of

Christianity, Calvinist no less than Roman Catholic. Bercovitch ultimately sees Emerson's "America" as a surrogate for the Old Testament Canaan, operating within a biblical-typological sense of history to unify, sanctify, and inspire a latter-day chosen people in preparation for their ever-imminent redemption. I would draw on Blumenberg to read Emerson's "America," its frequent quasi-religious tonalities notwithstanding, as a more ecumenical symbol, operating within an Enlightenment-Whig sense of history to join its particular citizens to the slow, secular, global movement of human beings per se toward higher levels of political and intellectual freedom, scientific knowledge, technological control of nature, and material prosperity.[32]

I cite for initial support Lawrence Buell's recent well-taken objections to the tendency to associate Emerson with American cultural nationalism.[33] Buell notes accurately that Emerson was often dismissive of nationalism; he is sharply critical of it at moments even in these early notebooks. Just one year and a half after dedicating his book to "the spirit of America," Emerson "confess[es]" in it that "I am a little cynical on some topics and when a whole nation is roaring Patriotism at the top of its voice I am fain to explore the cleanness of its hands and the purity of its heart" (*JMN* 2:302). My Enlightenment-historical contextualization helps us to see why for Emerson there was no contradiction here. From these earliest years of his thinking Emerson's attachment to America was not particularist or tribal in the usual manner of European (or biblical) nationalisms but rather liberal universalist—a matter of shared principles rather than shared blood. Emerson saw America as playing a special role in the ever-unfolding world-historical realization of the universal values of human freedom and rationality, and he loved and celebrated America to the extent that he saw it carrying out this role—but no further. Emerson's love for his country, unlike Lincoln's, was not unconditional. When Emerson saw America betraying its Enlightenment-historical heritage, as we will see that he did during the worst days of the slavery crisis in the 1850s, he withdrew his affections, approved tearing up the Constitution, and spoke out in favor of a preemptive dissolution of the Union. Emerson, young or old, might fairly be called an American exceptionalist but not, in the usual sense of the word, an American nationalist.

A sequence of entries from just six months after Emerson's initial dedication is further revealing in this context:

The past—in all its grand characters of horror and evil—lies open before us. The whole of it amounts to what? The bones of its children and
the monument of its bad example, its terrific wrongs, and its Gothic ignorance . . . God forbid that the mind should bow down before this huge
chaos to worship; or, that, the world's dark barbarism, or darker vice,
should be the best idol intellect can set up. . . . There is another prospect
before. We have gathered what we could that was precious from the
past; we are preparing to add the results of present science and civilization to these, and this shall form a legacy to the future. (*JMN* 2:75)

To the Genius of the Future, I dedicate my page. (*JMN* 2:76)

It is not the freak of a Youthful or Utopian imagination to anticipate
more from the future than the past has produced. . . . Casual & general /
recurrences/ appeal to the melancholy uniformity of human history
may plausibly support the declamations of those false prophets who denounce tribulation and wrath to all the years of man as they rise in the
long succession of futurity. But a cautious and profound philosophy
would be loath to believe the denunciation. For his survey of humankind suggests the opinion that there is no experience in its annals,
from which a fair judgment could be formed, with respect to its future
history—because there is no age in its whole history bearing any likeness, in its character, to the present. (*JMN* 2:76)

What is extraordinary in these passages is at once the grand scale of the
young Emerson's cultural ambition, the intuitive clarity of his perception of his options, and the care with which he chooses his path among
them. Emerson here acknowledges that he is taking his bearings, as I
suggested in my opening, from nothing less than a complete historical
"survey of humankind," reviewing its "annals," "the whole of it." And
he understands that it is precisely fundamental temporal orientation that
is at stake, the sort of cultural work traditionally performed by religion,
with its "monuments," "worship," "idols," "prophets," and "wrath." As
a budding cultural leader, Emerson at this early moment sees for himself
two alternatives. The first, the jeremiad, comes from his own religious
birthright. As the descendant of several generations of New England
Calvinist ministers, however mild they may have turned by his time,
Emerson was authentically linked to a long line of "those . . . prophets
who denounce tribulation and wrath to all the years of man." Indeed, he
seems to tap readily enough into their denunciatory eloquence when he
writes here of "the past—in all its grand character of horror and evil . . .
the bones of its children, and the monument of its bad example, its

terrific wrongs, and its Gothic ignorance." But just as he will in fact decide to do when he leaves the ministry roughly ten years after this passage
is written, Emerson here imaginatively rejects what he sees as an incur-
ably pessimistic religious outlook and its messianic-redemptive complement in favor of an as-yet-undefined "philosophy" at once more "cautious" and more "profound." To call his favored outlook a "philosophy"
in the midst of so much religious language already associates it with the
classical-Enlightenment-critical progression we have seen him tracing
in his notebooks up to this point, and his subsequent characterization sounds much like Blumenberg's modest, secular, cross-generational
gradualism: "We have gathered what we could that was precious from
the past; we are preparing to add the results of present science and civilization to these, and this shall form a legacy to the future." Emerson
justifies his hopeful choice on the grounds that while his survey of history has indeed revealed a long record of "chaos" and "barbarism," it
has also made him aware of the unprecedented uniqueness of his own
historical moment: "There is no age in its whole history bearing any
likeness, in its character, to the present." This was not just a nationalis-
tic projection of "new-world" difference; Eric Hobsbawm notes the
epochal uniqueness of this historical moment in an authoritative transatlantic study that could hardly be accused of American chauvinism: "A
sudden, qualitative, and fundamental transformation . . . happened in
the 1780s, . . ." Hobsbawm writes of the whole transatlantic region,
"[whose] essence was that henceforward revolutionary change became
the norm."[34] So when in a manner precisely analogous to the "dedication" of his "book" a few months earlier to "the spirit of America,"
Emerson here "dedicates" his "page" to "the genius of the future," it
takes no great leap to see that "America" and "future" are linked by more
than just syntax. In "America" the young Emerson has found a cultural
symbol whose optimistic, open-ended futurism, for lack of a better word,
aligns with and expresses his now crystallizing sense that all of history
leads to the unique present opportunity for departure from history. For
Emerson, to revise Joyce slightly, history was a nightmare from which,
with a splash from reason's bracing stream, we were about to awake.

And Emerson perhaps intuitively sensed that the symbol of America
would provide cultural ballast in these new historical waters. Unlike
most traditional conceptions of history in which long-standing patterns
of occurrence set the boundaries of what may be anticipated in the future, the idea of progress, Reinhart Koselleck has pointed out, presumes

a divorce between experience and expectation. For Koselleck as for Hobsbawm, this break is definitive of modernity and largely responsible for its pervasive anxiety: "The divide between previous experience and coming expectations opened up, and a difference between past and present increased so that lived time was experienced as a rupture, as a period of transition in which the new and unexpected continually happened."[35] Emerson's strongest writing enacts precisely this experience of rupture and continuing newness in moods of joy, alacrity, freedom, and release: "Power," he writes in "Self-Reliance," "resides in the moment of transition from a past to a new state, in the shooting of the gulf, in the darting to an aim" (*E&L* 271). And experience itself, in the great essay of that name, is defined as what occurs in the collapse of expectation: "Life is a series of surprises, and would not be worth taking or keeping, if it were not" (*E&L* 483). Here Emerson's characteristically rapid, even choppy sentence structure mimics the motion it celebrates as it "darts" across the commas from phrase to synonymous but refigured phrase—"in the shooting of the gulf, in the darting to an aim"—or from word to associated word—"taking or keeping." And this delight in abrupt transition is characteristic of Emerson's prose in general. Many, including Emerson himself, have commented on the absence in his essays of the conventional transitional niceties by which most writers step back from the flow of thought to guide their readers from one paragraph or sentence to the next. An Emerson paragraph, by contrast, is typically composed of many short, semiaphoristic, metaphorical, or imagistic sentences in no obvious logical order. These sentences are themselves then broken up by frequent commas into many short, sharp, emphatic, often syntactically parallel phrases. The result for the reader is a bracing experience of multiple small leaps across what sometimes seem vertiginous logical gulfs in ever-shifting metaphorical vehicles. Indeed, it is fair to say that Emerson's writing in general achieves its distinctive energy precisely by multiplying an effect of ever-uncertain but always surprisingly successful transition. It is no wonder that Nietzsche, who preached dancing and metamorphosis, loved this prose. When it works, as it often does, it turns the ruptures of modernity into the raptures of progress. It transfers a sense of ever-unfolding freedom from the distant realm of history to the intimate realm of the reader's exhilarated nervous system.

In the subsequent notebooks of the early 1820s Emerson continues to write frequently about "America" in relation to a universal sense of human history and human progress, but with a slightly different and very interesting new emphasis. Just a month or so after the passage above, he defends the "meagerness" of U.S. history since the Revolution as a function of its unprecedented religious, moral, political, and commercial vitality. He assumes that this is indicative of a global tendency: "History will continually grow less interesting as the world grows better" (*JMN* 2:90). And he has little doubt that it is getting better. In the following entry he suggests organizing the narrative of world history on a transnational basis according to the progressive moral achievements of what he calls "the communities of men" "such as the Reformation, the Revival of Letters, the progressive Abolition of the Slave-trade." And a month later we find a remarkable passage in which he fully anticipates, with his own characteristic moral slant, the twentieth-century historiographical innovations of the Annales school and social history:

> All our researches into antiquity look to this ultimate end—of ascertaining the private life of our fellow beings who have occupied the different parts of the globe before us. . . . If we had a series of faithful portraits of private life in Egypt, Assyria, Greece, & Rome we might relinquish without a sigh their national annals. . . . Our vague and pompous outlines of history serve but to define in geographical and chronological limits the faint vestiges we possess of former nations. . . . Give us the bare narrative of the *moral* beings engaged, the *moral* feelings concerned & the result—and you have answered all our purpose, all the ultimate design which leads the mind to explore the past. (*JMN* 2:94)

Any lingering doubt as to Emerson's interest in history or his sophistication regarding it should be dispelled by passages like this one. His historical curiosity here is sufficiently personal and intense as to leave him dissatisfied with all the currently available resources. He finds most of the standard historical representations crude ("vague," "pompous," "faint," "vestigial"), partly due to their tendency to proceed at a national level of generality. Preoccupied with wars and treaties and the vicissitudes of empire, they are not "delicate" enough to capture what to him is most interesting about the past—the vast, intimate variety of ordinary moral feeling. In recognizing the full depth and range of cultural difference—"the Englishman," "the Tartan," "the Roman," and "the Chinese" "fill up the hours of the day with very different thoughts & different actions" (*JMN* 2:94)—Emerson shows a profound grasp of the full import of the concept of cultural pluralism, which Herder had only recently formulated: human beings at different times and places not only *behave* differently, they actually *feel* and *think* differently. But Emerson is also sufficiently a child of the Enlightenment not to relinquish all universal categories: the "ultimate design" of this intricate process of "estimates & comparisons" would be to arrive at knowledge of "human nature" per se (*JMN* 2:94). The conventions of history writing did not change soon enough, of course, to meet Emerson's complex demands during his lifetime, although he later regarded Madame de Staël's *De l'Allemagne* (Of Germany) as one exemplar. Nor did he himself ultimately devote his own literary energies to the historical portraiture of private life. But the passage nonetheless reveals the intimate level of human consciousness and behavior that Emerson found historically most significant and that, as I have suggested, he eventually sought to influence in his own writing. For Emerson, the history of liberty was in part the history of a "moral feeling." For its past progress he mostly had to make do with remote sketches; for the future he would himself provide from his own experience and with his own inspirational words appropriately intimate and fine-grained instigations.

He did find one useful sketch about a year later in Hume's *History of England*. Just as Hume saw an advance in "liberality" over the course of the seventeenth century as political control in England passed from Puritan extremism to the moderation of the 1688 settlement, so Emerson saw an evolution in American attitudes toward liberty from the early-seventeenth-century Puritan migration to the Revolution of 1776. The later revolutionary generation "had dropped so much of the Puritanism of their sires, that they would hardly have been acknowledged by them as sound members of their rigorous society" (*JMN* 2:226). Emerson salutes the English Puritans for "fram[ing] the English constitution," and he honors the immigrant "adventurousness" that helped them to found a new society in the wilderness—"a spirit which confides in its own strength for the accomplishment of its ends & disdains to calculate the chance of failure." But he regrets their "intolerance," "bigotry," and "ecclesiastical tyranny," their "persecution" of Quakers and "hanging" of witches. "Liberality of religion & of politics," he observes ironically, "do not always go hand in hand." He then emphatically welcomes the comparative "*Good Sense*" of their descendants—the generation of Otis, Adams, Washington, and, especially, Franklin, who were able to "correct the faults of inexperience" (*JMN* 2:227). He seems shortly hereafter to have planned to write a historical study of some sort about Franklin

(*JMN* 2:242). He credits Franklin's generation with "A Revolution" that "bears the palm away from Greek & Roman achievement." Again, the accuracy of the history here is less important than its object of interest—the complex progressive-historical development of an originally Anglo-American, but incipiently global, Enlightenment-liberal mentalité.

This, like most positive historical developments, could only occur slowly. "Many," Emerson writes about five months later, "nay, most of the great blessings of humanity require cycles of a thousand years to bring them to their light." "The Compass, Press, Steam Engine; Astronomy, Mathematics, Politics; have scarce begun to exist till within a thousand years. Yet the principles of which they are results are surely in our Nature" (*JMN* 2:277). For this reason Emerson devotes several pages a month later to an extended repudiation and reversal of the then-fashionable Rousseauian Romantic association of advanced civilization with false consciousness and immorality. "Modern science," he writes, has now "circumnavigated the globe," but has discovered no "Elysian fields" nor "Fortunate isles" nor "golden age." On the contrary, Western encounters with "rudimentary" societies around the world have shown that "fraud," "violence," "depravity," and "very defective morality" were "not the consequence of refinement but [were] planted wherever the seed of man was sown" (*JMN* 2:287). Nor, upon historical reflection, does it seem to be true that material scarcity or natural adversity fosters compensatory noble traits of character. In western Europe the "Era of the Plague," for example, brought about extreme "licentiousness" as "Vices and Crimes ascended to a pitch, to a madness that had no parallel" (*JMN* 2:289). Indeed, the moral direction of history seems to be precisely the opposite of what Rousseau suggested: as the Scottish historians emphasized, basic material and technological progress tends to bring with it a discernibly higher level of general social morality: "On the whole the advancement from the first to the second stage of civilization is attended by a cotemporary moral advancement" (*JMN* 2:288). Emerson does not seek to diminish the achievement of those heroic few who managed to uphold high moral standards in the face of material deprivation or other obstacles, but he does want to mark and celebrate what he sees as a distinctive benefit of modern life:

It has ceased to require any heroism to avow one's self the disciple of Christ. *The stake is not dressed, the faggot is not kindled, the lean beasts of the*

amphitheatre are not unchained to compel the incompellable service of your soul. . . .
It has ceased to be a sacrifice to be virtuous. You chime in with the tune of the
time. You but follow a fashion to espouse this ancient cause. (*JMN* 2:
292, italics mine)

Two weeks later he fleshes out this insight further:

> It must have often occurred to a contemplative man that individual ad-
> vantage is inseparably linked to the general welfare so that wheresoever
> & whatsoever efforts are made for the most confined personal better-
> ment the same effort ameliorates the condition of mankind. . . .
>
> The further we follow this inquiry, the more exact consistence we
> shall discover . . . In all districts of all lands, in all the classes of commu-
> nities thousands of minds are intently occupied, the merchant in his
> compting house, the mechanist over his plans, the statesman at his map,
> his treaty & his tariff, the scholar in the skilful history, each stung to
> the quick with the desire of exalting himself to a hasty & yet unfound
> height above the level of his peers. Each is absorbed in the prospect of
> good accruing to himself but each is no less contributing to the utmost
> of his ability to set forward the march of the human race & adorn
> human civilization. (*JMN* 2:304)

Emerson uses the word "sacrifice" only once in these passages, but
the concept of sacrifice is important throughout. His primary reference
point for his initial comments on the greater "liberality" of the age of
the American Revolution versus the age of the Puritans had been the
relative absence in Franklin's era of the practice of what may be called
communal-sacrificial scapegoating—the "hanging of witches" and the
"persecution of Quakers." Here, Emerson frames the story of Christianity's imperceptibly gradual progress from persecuted heterodoxy to
benign contemporary hegemony as also a movement away from sacrifice. This is true on two distinct levels: (1) Christians are no longer themselves treated as communal-sacrificial scapegoats ("The stake is not
dressed, the faggot is not kindled") and (2) in his own Unitarian moment
Christian morality is no longer imposed on human beings as itself an essentially sacrificial ethic (Christians "insist at this day not so much on
the imperative *obligation* as on the *beauty* of virtue & have invited men to
receive her not so much in the capacity of accountable as intellectual
beings" [*JMN* 2:292]). On the level of moral feeling, then, these passages together indicate that the intimate history of liberty must be at
least in part a story of the growth of human societies away from the

emotional intensities of sacrificial solidarity. And, like many thinkers with roots in Christian-communalist traditions, Emerson marvels at the capacity of liberal moral economy to sustain collective harmony, cooperation, and even a kind of abstract solidarity without the sacrifice of individual self-interest: "Each is absorbed in the prospect of good accruing to himself but each is no less contributing to the utmost of his ability to set forward the march of the human race & adorn human civilization." These last sentences are significant as the first full instance of what becomes a (historical) topos in Emerson's writing—the elaboration of what he sees as the happy paradox of liberal moral economy. His frequent strictures against the narrowness of his society's materialism notwithstanding, the mature Emerson never ceased to marvel approvingly at how in free-market societies, to use Mandeville's famous phrase, "private vice makes public virtue."

Emerson thus distinguishes the "modern" age from its predecessors according to a criterion he shared with, among others, his French-liberal contemporary Benjamin Constant: whereas the essence of ancient politics and society was the subordination of the individual to the greater good of the collectivity, the essence of modern liberal society was the priority of the individual to the group. With the foregoing passages in mind, it is useful to recall that the former, "ancient" value system would have found public expression in myriad symbols, rituals, or commemorations of sacrifice meant to evoke socially bonding emotions of solidarity. The latter, modern revaluation of values was principally expressed in the legal formulae of "rights," which may be said to function in part as ultimate "trumps," to borrow Ronald Dworkin's term, of an incipient collective will toward sacrifice of individuals for its own ends.

But what were the symbolic forms appropriate to this defensive, legalistic, libertarian principle? What emotions should they evoke? In his youthful wonder in the early notebook passages quoted above Emerson was inchoately feeling his way toward what would become his self-appointed historical task as high-rhetorical literary priest-celebrant of the moral emotions appropriate to a postsacrificial, rights-based social order. In a sense, although he had not realized it yet, Emerson's lifelong project, the goal of virtually every one of his essays, becomes the historically unprecedented articulation and evocation of what we might call nonsacrificial moral feeling—the deep psychic sustenance of liberty at last historically come of age.

But Emerson's own coming of age had to be attended to first. History recedes somewhat as an overt topic in the journals of the later years of the 1820s as Emerson turned his attention to the internal debate between reason and tradition that culminated in the turning point of his life and career—his resignation of his ministry in September 1832 on the grounds that he could no longer in good conscience administer the sacrament of Communion as the body and blood of Christ. I will trace this debate in detail in the next chapter. But in the context of this chapter, it becomes possible to jump ahead and see the liberal-historical dimension in Emerson's life-altering decision. Recent scholarship has reminded us of the enormous difficulty of Emerson's choice: "Emerson's new life seemed to those around him only a new failure," Robert Richardson writes. "Leaving the Second Church in Boston was a repudiation of the world of his father. Emerson was also giving up institutional affiliation and support, a guaranteed social position, and a generous and assured salary. . . . In the late fall of 1832 [he] suffered a physical and emotional letdown after the great crisis. . . . 'Things,' his brother Charles wrote to his Aunt, 'seem flying to pieces.'"[36] What, one might ask, saw the young man through? Having now reviewed in some detail his principal intellectual interest of the foregoing five years, it is fair to suggest that history, as embodied in the emancipatory symbolism of America, must be part of the answer. "There is a relation between the hours of our life and the centuries of time," Emerson says in one of many lovely reflexive formulations in the essay "History." "We are always coming up with the emphatic facts of history in our private experience, and verifying them there" (*E&L* 240). In leaving the ministry, in repudiating the world of his father, Emerson was not only decisively giving precedence to reason over tradition, he was reenacting within his own life narrative the essential emancipating pattern as he understood it of the larger narrative of human history itself. He was emboldened to cut his moorings in part because he knew he would be taken up into liberty's inexorable current. Emerson often quoted in Latin a particular sentence from Horace's epistles, on one occasion adapting its exhortation regarding time's ceaseless progression to what he called "the stream of liberty which the Holy Alliance are striving to dam": "Labitur et labetur in omne volubilis aevum." "Yet on it glides, and on it will glide, rolling its flood forever" (*JMN* 2:250).

It is therefore not incidental that the ritual upon which Emerson focused his departing protest was a sacrificial one. Although Emerson does not address this aspect of Communion in the sermon entitled "The Lord's Supper" in which he details his objections, at this stage of his reading and thinking it could not have been lost on him that the performance of this ceremony not only demanded the subordination of his skepticism to the particular collective consciousness of the congregation of the Second Church but also that the symbolism of sacrifice per se always connotes the priority of the collectivity over the individual. Perhaps this is why this sermon is, as Lawrence Buell has pointed out, so surprisingly "confrontational," self-assertive, and, in its final turn, subjective.[37] "This mode of commemorating Christ is not suitable to me," Emerson says with a seeming shrug. "That is reason enough why I should abandon it" (*E&L* 1138). And several lines later he declares: "Freedom is the essence of this faith [Christianity]" (*E&L* 1139). It was to be the first of a great many moments in which Emerson would take a provocatively arbitrary tone in opposing the sacrificial authority of a traditional collectivity. "I shun father and mother and wife and brother, when my genius calls me," he writes notoriously in a crucial passage of "Self-Reliance." "I would write on the lintels of the door-post, *Whim*" (*E&L* 262). Read in the context of a liberal sense of history as progress toward freedom, the passage's complex allusion to Exodus takes on its full resonance. In a kind of ritual of countersacrifice, the biblical Jews spared themselves from God's anger and ensured their subsequent release from Egyptian bondage by marking the lintels of their doorposts with lamb's blood—a surrogate for their own. The New Testament Christ then extended this symbolism of countersacrifice by offering himself as the Lamb of God whose blood would obviate the need for all future blood sacrifice by Christians. Emerson takes this emancipatory progression a step further in this passage by a radical assertion of the priority of his own autonomous moral will to the incipiently sacrificial claims of the primordial collectivity—the family. But where the biblical Jews and Jesus retained forms of sacrifice even as they attempted to move beyond it, Emerson here attempts to jettison this long-standing structure of moral experience altogether. To insert a term as seemingly light and volatile as "whim" in the place formerly occupied by sacrificial blood is a profoundly individualist gesture that indicates the intimate psychohistorical depth of Emerson's liberalism. It at once places itself within a long Judeo-Christian history of liberty and effects a dramatic reversal of traditional Hebraic, especially Calvinist, emphasis on collective guilt and atonement. "I do not wish to expiate," Emerson writes a few sentences later in "Self-Reliance," "but to live." And he reasserts his independence even as he assures us that such living will not be lawless: "I hope it is not whim at last, but I cannot spend the day in explanation." Again, Emerson here does not so much preach a secularized Calvinism as he deliberately finds a secular-liberal-individualist-Enlightenment substitute—"whim" as negative liberty—to occupy the position formerly held by the Christian-Calvinist symbolism of collective sacrifice. Having traced the river of liberty back to its sources, he meant now to turn it into a fresh new channel.

2

Reason I, Science

Journals (1826–1832)

Emerson's Romantic epistemology and his Romantic style of writing would seem to put him at a considerable distance from his Enlightenment predecessors. But his substantial innovations of thought and manner occurred within a stable structure of recognizably Enlightenment-based values that emphasized above all the freedom of the individual to philosophize, or, in Kant's words, to "use his own understanding"—to reason without slavish or superstitious deference to established authorities or ancestral teachings. We could easily be reading the most famous of Emerson's essays, "Self-Reliance," when in "What Is Enlightenment?" Kant chides the reader: "If I have a book which understands for me, a pastor who has a conscience for me, a physician who decides my diet, and so forth, I need not trouble myself. I need not think, if only I can pay: others will readily undertake the irksome work for me."[1] The language of Emerson's essay is sharper, swifter, more charged and abrupt than that of Kant. It employs a dazzling array of vivid images to compel imaginative assent from a reader or listener. And, for reasons we will examine later in the chapter, Emerson explicitly preferred the term "reason" to "understanding." But the fundamental teaching of "Self-Reliance" and of most of Emerson's early writing is closely akin to Kant's in "What Is Enlightenment?" and to Plato's throughout his dialogues: it is better to learn to think for yourself than to allow others to do the thinking for you, not because this gives you power or allows you to express yourself, though these may be incidental benefits, but because it is a necessary step toward knowledge of truths about the nature of things.

Like all terms of historical periodization, the word "Enlightenment" must be used warily. It confers deceptive unity on a vast revolution of ideas, values, and methods of inquiry that evolved in complex ways over time and took on a wide variety of forms and colorings in different locales. The tone of Locke's and Newton's Enlightenment in late-seventeenth-century England was not the same as that of David Hume and Adam Smith in mid-eighteenth-century Scotland. None of these politically moderate British luminaries struck the radical and peculiarly French notes of Voltaire or Rousseau or Diderot, each of whom in turn distrusted the other. In mid-eighteenth-century Philadelphia, Benjamin Franklin fashioned both French and English influences into a uniquely American Enlightenment style, while a generation later in Virginia and Boston Thomas Jefferson and John Adams took opposite sides in a bitter political-cultural contest between a Francophilic American Enlightenment, on the one hand, and an Anglophilic American Enlightenment, on the other. Both Jefferson and Adams paid homage to Newton, Locke, and Franklin, and in their magnificent late-life correspondence they rediscovered abundant common ground, but their enmity had been substantial. To place Emerson in an "Enlightenment" context it is necessary to speak both generally and specifically, both internationally and locally, of the fundamental philosophical orientation he shared with the broad European intellectual movement known as the Enlightenment and of the particular form and flavor of Enlightenment he adapted from sources closer to home.

Starting in the 1970s, historical scholarship has greatly enriched our understanding of the vast influence of the Scottish Enlightenment on the literary and political culture of the young American republic.[2] In *Inventing America*, Garry Wills argued controversially that it was the communitarian Scots rather than the individualistic Locke who most fundamentally informed Thomas Jefferson's thought, even providing some of the specific language of the Declaration of Independence. In *The Unitarian Conscience*, Daniel Walker Howe painstakingly demonstrated the pervasive influence of Scottish Enlightenment thought on the Unitarian educators who dominated Harvard and Boston's intellectual life throughout the first half of the nineteenth century. And Howe was no less thorough in detailing the Scottish underpinnings of antebellum Whig "political culture" in general in *The Political Culture of the American Whigs:* "They poured the new wine of commerce and industrialization into the old bottles of deference, patriarchalism, Scottish moral philosophy, and classical rhetoric."[3] But it is the intellectual-historical investigations of Henry May and Charles Taylor that provide the most help in focusing our understanding of the distinctively "Scottish" aspect of Emerson's Enlightenment framework.

In his acclaimed study of 1976, Henry May divided the Enlightenment in America into four overlapping phases. He called the first the "moderate Enlightenment." Starting with "the rational and Protestant Revolution" of 1688 and ending with the writing and ratification of the American Constitution in 1787, thinkers of this cautiously Whiggish outlook sought middle ground wherever possible. In matters of religion they tried to blend Newtonian science and Christian revelation. The title of Locke's major theological work, *The Reasonableness of Christianity,* is itself exemplary of this compromising spirit, as were Newton's own efforts to find mathematical proof of the biblical account of human history. In America moderate Congregationalists such as Lemuel Briant, Charles Chauncy, and Jonathan Mayhew defended a decorous, emotionally restrained style of piety against what they saw as the hysterical excesses of the revivalists. These ministers were also principal American champions of moderate Enlightenment literary preferences—the cheerful bourgeois moralism of Addison, the cosmic harmonies of Pope, and the simple, natural virtues advocated by Tacitus, Plutarch, and the classics. In politics, May argues, the American Constitution was the culminating realization of the moderate Enlightenment outlook, balancing democratic fickleness with aristocratic restraint, executive prerogative with congressional accountability, national centralization with the local interests of the states, and the general will with judicial review. The careful young architect of this delicately balanced structure, James Madison, was second only to Benjamin Franklin as a representative American figure of the moderate Enlightenment spirit. It was an urbane, prudent mindset with an instinct for the center. It sought harmony, balance, and compromise in all things.

The next two phases of May's American Enlightenment veered away from this moderate center. The "skeptical Enlightenment," which May dates from 1750 to 1789, and the "radical Enlightenment," which he dates from 1776 to 1800, tended toward opposite extremes. Typified by Voltaire's satiric wit, Hume's urbane skepticism, and Gibbon's learned sadness, the thinkers of the skeptical Enlightenment, May observes, possessed a keen sense of irony and tragedy, a concomitant tendency toward stoic resignation, and little patience for Christianity in any form.[4] May suggests that the youthful, pious, and optimistic tone of American life did not foster many thinkers of this type, although John Adams possessed something of its acerbic pessimism, and Alexander Hamilton's dark view of history took much of its gloomy tinge from Hume and Gibbon.

"Radical Enlightenment" figures were far more common in America, and, for a time, more popular. Thomas Jefferson himself belonged to this category, as did several prominent intellectuals who benefited, however briefly, from the political patronage of the sage of Monticello. Men such as Thomas Paine, Joel Barlow, and Philip Freneau shared the skeptics' hostility toward traditional Christianity but not the skeptics' patrician approval of aristocratic social arrangements or their acquiescence to a host of repressive conventions. Where Gibbon, Hume, and Voltaire somberly tallied up the long historical record of human delusion and cruelty, Paine and his cohort looked bracingly ahead toward a utopian new dawn of equality, freedom, technological mastery of the environment, and harmonious relations between nations, races, and sexes. They believed fervently that the success of the American Revolution heralded a new age of universal human emancipation.

The brutal denouement of the French Revolution shattered these dreams for most radicals and left moderates and skeptics increasingly uneasy. As the eighteenth century gave way to the nineteenth, May suggests, American cultural leaders faced a problem. They were too deeply invested in some aspects of Enlightenment ideology to dismiss it altogether, but events in France had borne out their worst misgivings about its potential excesses. Some fundamental distinctions had to be made: "Locke, Newton, Montesquieu, science, progress, intellectual freedom, republicanism were good; Voltaire, Hume, Rousseau, religious skepticism, frantic innovation, undisciplined emotion, the French Revolution, were bad." It was not enough simply to assert these oppositions, however; they had to be supported by rational argument. This is where the Scots came in. Many of the Presbyterian and Unitarian leaders of "the semi-official culture of early nineteenth-century America" took their orientation from Scotland, May suggests, because thinkers such as Francis Hutcheson, Thomas Reid, Adam Ferguson, Dugald Stewart, and

Adam Smith provided a fresh and intellectually respectable defense of the familiar moderate Enlightenment program of balance, order, and centrism. Like old Ben Franklin or young James Madison at the time of the constitutional convention, educated Americans in the first quarter of the nineteenth century, as May puts it, "wanted to believe at once in social and even scientific progress and in unchanging moral principles." The solid Scots comfortably contained this tension and thus helped thoughtful Americans to define and occupy the middle ground: "[The Scots were] moderate progressives in provincial politics as well as religion. . . . Cautious by instinct, personally genial and not unworldly, they were always concerned to distinguish themselves from Jacobites and other extremists, from wild Highlanders, and from ignorant bigots. Within their many differences from each other, according to their closest student, they had a common purpose: to show that culture, science, and urbanity were compatible with morality, religion, and law."[5] From the turn of the century to the Civil War and beyond, this morally and socially conservative, religiously moderate, and cautiously progressive political outlook, which May labels "the didactic Enlightenment," was advanced in pulpits, university classrooms, newspapers, literary reviews, and Whig political platforms throughout the United States. Its enlightened, neomoderate consensus exercised what May calls a "massive" influence on American life and thought.

Not least among those influenced was the young Ralph Waldo Emerson. Howe leaves no doubt about the extensive Boston Unitarian debt to the Scottish Enlightenment, and we have already noted Emerson's extensive debt to the Unitarians.[6] Emerson's prize-winning undergraduate essay of 1821, "The Present State of Ethical Philosophy," showed detailed knowledge of the works of Thomas Reid and Dugald Stewart and concluded by predicting that future developments in this field would follow the Scots' lead.[7] He seems to have maintained this conviction after graduating; a student from a school he kept in 1822 later told Edward Emerson that the girls "found out that to praise Dugald Stewart's Philosophy, which he had lately read, and which was one of the few metaphysical works he liked, was a way to please him."[8] Emerson was surely attracted to the Scots for many of the same reasons as his teachers and so many other intellectual Americans of his moment. Reid, Stewart, and their colleagues managed to preserve the fundamental Enlightenment structure of values, to which we will return later in the chapter, without giving in to naturalist materialism, Humean

skepticism, or radical democracy. But Emerson took the Scots' premises in surprising new directions. Before the emergence of the current
"pragmatist" reading of Emerson, Merrell Davis and many others had
noted that the concepts of "reason" and the "sentiment of virtue," which
play such a crucial role in Emerson's major works, were derived directly
from Scottish Enlightenment thought.[9] To grasp the full significance of
this connection, and to thus come to fuller historical understanding of
Emerson's major works, it is first necessary to trace, as concisely as possible, an extended chain of intellectual influence that reaches to Emerson
from Plato, the Stoics, and Plotinus, through the Cambridge Platonists,
to the Earl of Shaftesbury, Francis Hutcheson, Thomas Reid, Dugald
Stewart, and, finally, the English and German Romantics.

Charles Taylor has established this genealogy most fruitfully. Taylor's general aim is to trace the deep cultural roots of what he calls the
"affirmation of ordinary life"—a distinctively modern Western ethic
that gives moral priority to the private sphere, individualism, subjective
feeling, marriage, childrearing, domesticity, work in a vocation, democracy, and bourgeois competence. The Protestant Reformation, he notes,
was the first and most potent agent of the general Western cultural shift
toward these values. Where Roman Catholicism had ranked ordinary
life lower than monastic devotion or priestly celibacy, Protestantism
implicitly placed all believers on an equal plane and gave all worldly activities equal dignity in the eyes of God, including, as Max Weber most
influentially noted, the formerly profane business of middle-class getting and spending. But Protestantism was never a unified phenomenon,
and it took on divergent forms as it moved into the eighteenth century
and struggled to assimilate Enlightenment ideas. "Lockean deism" and
"counter-Lockean deism" were two forms that proved especially influential for later developments in Western culture. Lockean deism provided moral and theological support for the early career of modern science as well as, needless to say, for modern liberalism. Counter-Lockean
deism, Taylor argues, was a direct source of the Scottish Enlightenment and an indirect source of the Romantic movement—parallel cultural currents that blended felicitously in the flow of Emerson's capacious eclecticism. In political terms it may be said that Emerson's
eclectic thought drew upon the Scottish counter-Lockean Enlightenment and Romantic epistemology to advance essentially Lockean political principles.

Lockean religious rationalism, Taylor points out, was at once Carte-sian and Calvinist. Following Descartes, Locke understood the activity of reason to be fundamentally analytical, procedural, calculative, repre-sentational, and abstract. The knowing mind was an immaterial and unstructured internal agency that assembled more or less accurate pic-tures of the outside world by combining sense impressions according to certain protocols. Its relationship both to the world and to its own physi-cal and passionate selfhood was detached, disengaged, and instrumen-tal. To know the world or oneself was to be able to analyze and control it. Benjamin Franklin exemplified this stance at many levels. His famous chart of virtues was the moral corollary of his scientific experiments. He attempted to gain control over his moral selfhood in the same way he at-tempted to gain control over a natural phenomenon such as lightning— by observing it carefully and dispassionately, breaking it down into its constituent parts, charting its tendencies, and finding the law or prin-ciple or pattern that governed it. The residual Calvinism of this Lockean procedure was also visible in Franklin's underlying assumption that his natural inclinations required vigilant monitoring. He took it for granted that innate tendencies toward sloth, pride, concupiscence, and so on would always militate against his aspirations to virtue. As in Calvinism, Taylor emphasizes, the moral theology of Lockean deism was "volun-taristic" or "extrinsic"; God's will was just because it was God's will, not because it somehow accorded with nature or answered to reason. On the contrary, obedience to the moral law instituted by God's will re-quired human beings to overcome a nature understood by Locke, as by Calvin and Hobbes, to be nasty, brutish, and selfish. In Lockean deism unaided reason was capable of understanding the dictates of God's will or the moral law, but an appreciation of the natural depravity of the un-regenerate human heart was an essential component of such rationality.

Where Lockean deism was thus Cartesian and Calvinist, counter-Lockean deism was Platonic and Erasmian. In other words, where Lock-ean deism saw reason as detached analysis, counter-Lockean deism saw reason as a kind of intuitive "attunement" of the whole self to God. And where Lockeans retained a tendency to see human beings as fundamen-tally depraved, counter-Lockeans tended to see human nature as basi-cally inclined toward the good. The "Cambridge Platonists"—Ralph Cudworth, John Smith, Henry More, and Benjamin Whichcote—had laid the groundwork for this outlook in their debate with Hobbes in the second half of the seventeenth century. Against Hobbes's voluntaristic view of a corrupt human will dependent on external coercion by an angry God or a tyrannical state, these thinkers had drawn on the Renaissance Neoplatonism of Ficino and Pico to argue that human beings had an innate, organic inclination toward harmonious integration into orderly wholes. Like the later Unitarians, they called for a "thawing" of the naturally joyous moral love of the divine whole that had been "frozen" by Calvin's dour legalism.

In the next generation the Earl of Shaftesbury incorporated the affirmative outlook of the Cambridge Platonists into an eloquent and moving version of Stoicism. Taylor paraphrases the Earl as follows:

> The highest good for humans is to love and take joy in the whole course of the world. Someone who achieves this love reaches a perfect tranquility and equanimity; he is proof against all the buffetings of adverse fortune; and above all, he can love those around him constantly and steadily, undiverted by his own pain and disappointments, or his own partial interests. He attains "a generous affection, an exercise of friendship uninterrupted, a constant kindness and benignity." Moreover, this love carries itself the greatest intrinsic satisfaction. Since by nature we love the ordered and beautiful, the highest and most complete order and beauty is an object of the greatest joy. "For it is impossible that such a divine order should be contemplated without ecstacy and rapture."[10]

Shaftesbury never pretended to originality in these views. He would have granted readily that this wisdom could just as easily have been found in the pages of Epictetus or Marcus Aurelius. But Taylor points out that there was a newly modern aspect to Shaftesbury's stoicism. Where Plato and the Stoics attained love of the whole by means of a strictly rational contemplation of the cosmic order of things, Shaftesbury attained it via a turn inward, an attentiveness to the inner voice of what he called our "natural affections."[11] For Plato and the Stoics, the properly educated soul was freed from erroneous opinion so that it could behold the true order of the cosmos; the soul was said to be virtuous when its order reflected that of the cosmos. For Shaftesbury, the process of moral education was slightly different. As in Augustine and the Augustinian tradition in general, more attention was paid to the subjective condition of the self than to the objective cosmic harmonies. One came to love the whole less because one was drawn toward its intrinsic grandeur and loveliness (although this is implicit) and more because one learned to give heed to the inner voice of one's higher longings, one's "agape" rather than one's "concupiscence." Of course, this turn inward was never so fraught with peril for Shaftesbury as it was for Augustine. Shaftesbury's view of human nature was comparatively sanguine. Where the bishop of Hippo's inward ear strained to distinguish the still, small voice of the good from the clamorings of a thousand lusts, the third earl was immediately attuned to the wholesome counsels of what he was the first to call "the moral sense."

Francis Hutcheson put the concept of a "moral sense" at the center of Scottish Enlightenment thought. Hutcheson followed his mentor, Shaftesbury, and the Cambridge Platonists in rejecting the "extrinsic" and pessimistic moral theory of Hobbes and his followers—particularly Mandeville. Where Hobbes and Mandeville placed their hopes in a political structure designed to check and channel human nature's innate selfish aggressiveness, Hutcheson argued that human beings possessed a natural tendency toward the good. This tendency expressed itself in instinctive emotional responses. Morally offensive words or acts, Hutcheson argued, inspired in all sane human beings a similar emotion of revulsion and condemnation, while morally admirable behavior elicited in all people similar feelings of pleasure, approval, and solidarity. In *An Inquiry into the Original of Our Ideas of Beauty and Virtue*, he phrased it this way: "Some Actions have to Men an immediate goodness," and this is perceived by "a superiour Sense, which I call a Moral one."[12] The defining characteristic of "good" actions was their "benevolence." For Hutcheson, there was cause for optimism not only in our own natural inclination to benevolence but in the abundant evidence that this inclination fits us harmoniously into a benevolent universe. By acting benevolently we not only contribute to the happiness of others but enhance our own well-being by participating affirmatively in the divine order. There was more than a little of Shaftesbury's Stoicism in this emphasis on integrating oneself harmoniously into an orderly whole. And like Shaftesbury, Taylor reminds us, Hutcheson gave Stoicism a modern twist by relying on sentiment for this cosmic orientation. Plato and the Stoics had depended upon "reason" to provide the necessary information about the universal order with which they sought to align themselves. And they conceived of "reason" explicitly by its opposition to passion and sentiment. Hutcheson sought a kind of cosmic integration reminiscent of Plato and the Stoics, but the sentimental means by which he attempted to achieve this was distinctively modern. Hutcheson's sentimentalism, like Shaftesbury's, had roots in post-Reformation Augustinian pietism, with its emphasis on the ordering of the psyche's "two loves."

The next generation of Scottish philosophers began where Hutcheson left off. Most influentially, Thomas Reid expanded Hutcheson's notion of "the moral sense" to a broader epistemological conception of what he called "common sense." Berkeley and Hume had demonstrated that Locke's epistemology led inevitably to radical skepticism. Reid responded to Hume by dropping Locke's passive schema in favor of a more tactile and active conception of the mind. Where Locke's metaphor of the "blank slate" suggested ghostly remoteness from phenomenological experience, Reid's term, "common sense," at once evoked immediate contact with ordinary things and a reassuringly familiar level of shared reference. He pictured the mind as a kind of amorphous, prehensile entity capable of moving out actively into the world and achieving a direct, unmediated, intuitive grasp of external reality. The most striking feature of this reality was the way in which its complex interlocking order meshed with and enhanced human purposes. Like Hutcheson's response to Mandeville, Reid's response to Hume's skeptical reading of Locke gave metaphysical legitimacy to ordinary intuitions. Where Hume denied any ultimate legitimacy, for example, to the commonsense notion of causation, Reid saw the very commonness of the idea as evidence of its validity.

Wills has helpfully characterized Reid's epistemology as "egalitarian."[13] He links it as such with what he calls Reid's "humble" empiricism and "communitarian" morality. Reid, Wills points out, taught that an untutored plowman's grasp of reality was every bit as valid as that of an esteemed scholar. Indeed, because the plowman would be less distracted by abstract notions, his apprehension of the world would tend to be clearer, surer, and less cluttered. Since all knowledge was built on the basis of ordinary perceptions and intuitions, the boy in the field had as good a chance at the truth as the scholar in the classroom. And since moral responses, for Reid as for Hutcheson, were governed by universal moral sentiments rather than abstract ratiocination, there was also no reason to expect the educated person to act more decently than the rustic. It is not hard to see the shortcomings of this outlook as a rigorous philosophical system, but it is also not hard to see why Reid's views found vast numbers of willing students among the new republic's active, practical, down-to-earth, egalitarian, and morally assured middle classes.

Nor is it hard to see the affinities between the "common sense" school and the contemporaneous early stirrings of European Romanticism. The moral tone of the Scottish thinkers was rather more buttoned-up and bourgeois than that of Rousseau, but in epochal early works of the Romantic movement such as *Émile* and *Discours sur l'origine et les fondements de l'inégalité parmi les hommes* (Discourse on the Origins and Foundations of Inequality between Men), Rousseau made similarly egalitarian claims for the wisdom of ordinary moral sentiment and untutored intuition. The Savoyard vicar of *Émile* is a veritable prophet of moral sentiment, and no one asserted the moral equality of the plowboy and the professor more passionately than Rousseau.

Rousseau differed significantly from the Scots, however, in his radical distrust of social convention. The moderate Scots tended to see conventions as expressions of shared communal intuitions—as part of what was "common" in common sense. The radical Rousseau famously saw the social, political, and ideological conventions then prevalent in European culture as invidious artificial constructs that corrupted and enervated individuals by alienating them from authentic selfhood. For Rousseau, in Taylor's apt summary, "the original impulse of nature is right, but the effect of a depraved culture is that we lose contact with it. We suffer this loss because we no longer depend on ourselves and this inner impulse, but rather on others and what they think of us, admire or despise in us, reward or punish in us. We are separated from nature by the dense web of opinion which is woven between us in society and can no longer recover contact with it."[14] One antidote to this alienated condition was solitary communion with nature. Rousseau applied the spark to a vast and still-resonating European cultural explosion by advocating retreat from crowded urban centers to lonely and untamed natural settings. He valued the poetic emotions and slow, unforced, meditative wisdom fostered by natural surroundings. He established the basic pattern of Romantic literature by arguing that only by attuning oneself in solitude to nature's timeless forms and rhythms could one hope to recover emotional wholeness and moral autonomy. And it was only on the basis of such autonomy, Rousseau argued in a notorious paradox, that meaningful social solidarity could be established.

Rousseau thus followed an increasingly pervasive modern pattern, Taylor argues, of achieving moral integration into a greater whole by means of a turn inward. Rousseau, of course, followed this inward route much further and with far greater abandon than any of his predecessors, thus preparing the way at once for the purely "expressivist" strain of European Romanticism as well as the more "holistic" or "integrationist" strain that leads to Emerson. Taylor associates the purely expressivist strain mainly with French Romantic writers such as Lamartine and Musset who principally "sought in their poetry to give authentic expression to their feelings." The German Romantics and their English and American followers tended, he suggests, to take the more holistic approach, reading the inner voice or impulse as the intimation of "the larger order in which we are set." Herder and Goethe were prominent German writers of this type who both exercised a profound and lasting influence on Emerson. One of Emerson's most basic teachings was concisely expressed in Herder's admonition to "see the whole of nature, behold the great analogy of creation. Everything feels itself and its like, life reverberates to life."[15] Goethe returned repeatedly to the same point, declaring that "all is in each . . . that every natural form to the smallest, a leaf, a sunbeam, a moment of time, a drop, is related to the whole, and partakes of the beauty of the whole." Robert Richardson has remarked that it would be impossible to exaggerate the influence of Goethe on Emerson and that what distinguished Goethe from the other Romantics for Emerson was precisely his "hard edge of realism, classicism, and clarity," his insistence on "facing outward," his Olympian objectivity. "So long as [the poet] only speaks out his few subjective feelings, he deserves not the name," Goethe wrote, "but as soon as he knows how to appropriate to himself and to express the world, he is a poet."[16]

I do not mean to suggest that Emerson took the idea of turning inward to find moral integration principally from Rousseau or even from Goethe. It was initially via English and American interpretations of Immanuel Kant that Emerson found his way into the broad cultural movement of which Rousseau and Goethe were representative figures. At the risk of oversimplifying, one can say that Kant followed Rousseau in placing freedom or autonomy at the core of authentic human being. For Kant, as for Rousseau, one was truly human to the extent that one was free to choose one's own ends. And Kant, like Rousseau, believed that throughout most of history and even in eighteenth-century Europe most people were prevented by custom, convention, tradition, and political tyranny from fulfilling their true humanity in this sense. But Kant departed dramatically from Rousseau in his understanding of how best to break these chains. Both thinkers turned inward, as Taylor points out, but Rousseau and his Romantic heirs turned inward toward the intimate, particular, and spontaneous voice of nature and/or primordial selfhood, while Kant turned inward to the rational command of a universalizing moral imperative. Thus, Taylor summarizes, "Kant gives a firm but quite new base to the subjectivization or internalization of moral sources which Rousseau inaugurates. The moral law is what comes from within; it can no longer be defined by any external order. But it is not defined by the impulse of nature in me either, but only by the nature of reasoning, by, one might say, the procedures of practical reasoning, which demand that one act by general principles."[17] Kant's thought, in other words, followed a pattern broadly similar to that of the Cambridge Platonists, Hutcheson's Scottish Enlightenment, and Rousseau's *Émile:* in an effort at once to liberate the self from dependence on alienating external norms and to protect the self from disorienting skepticism or subjectivism, he turned inward to the certainty of fundamental moral knowledge. But where Hutcheson, Reid, and Rousseau were content to call this knowledge an intuition—the product of a loosely defined "sense" or "sentiment," Kant saw it as the primary product of "reason" rightly understood, and he built a comprehensive and rigorous rational system upon this conception of reason. It is not necessary for our purposes to submit to Kant's subtler rigors. It is sufficient to note that something of Shaftesbury's serenity and joy in knowing his rightful place within a grand rational whole was present in Kant's invocation of "the starry skies above me and the moral law within me." Emerson was immensely attracted to an idea of order at once so cosmically vast and so psychologically intimate.

Moving from Cambridge Neoplatonism through Shaftesbury's neo-Stoicism to Hutcheson's moral sense, Reid's common sense, Rousseau's voice of nature, Goethe's holism, and Kant's categorical imperative, I have attempted to trace the sweeping trajectory of a broad strain of "counter-Lockean" Enlightenment thought. Notwithstanding considerable differences of tone, terminology, and emphasis, all of these thinkers made similar turns inward to moral sentiment, moral intuition, and moral knowledge in an effort to overcome what Blake called "spectral dualities"—the self-alienation, affective impoverishment, and self-mechanization they believed to be implicit in Cartesian epistemology and Hobbesian or Lockean moral psychology. Unlike Blake, however, none of these thinkers saw their rejection of Cartesian epistemology as a basis for the rejection of Enlightenment values altogether. On the whole, these thinkers retained a firm conviction in the preeminent value of autonomous rational inquiry, but they attempted to expand, enhance, or completely replace the prevailing Cartesian-Lockean conception of rationality. Where Descartes and Locke advanced an essentially analytical and instrumental conception of reason in which the knowing subject broke down and analyzed the object of knowledge from a position of neutral distance, Cudworth, Shaftesbury, and Hutcheson et al. developed a more affective, intuitive, holistic conception of reason based upon the integration of parts into orderly wholes. Similarly, where Locke and Hobbes conceived of morality in terms of the subordination of selfish and aggressive individuals to externally imposed authority, the counter-Lockean tradition conceived of morality in terms of the harmonious integration of essentially benevolent individuals into an analogously benevolent cosmos. This integration required not the suppression or channeling of depraved impulses but rather the uncovering and heeding of the true inner voice—the natural or authentic selfhood hitherto obscured, corrupted, or silenced outright by tradition, prejudice, or social convention.

Ironically, Emerson was first given access to the ethos of Enlightenment by his earliest intellectual guardians, starting with his father. William Emerson, Sr., was a literate, socially polished, and theologically liberal Congregationalist minister who held one of the most prestigious pulpits in Boston in the last decade of the eighteenth century and the first decade of the nineteenth. As a cofounder and editor, for a brief period, of the *Monthly Anthology,* one of the new nation's first sophisticated literary-political reviews, he promoted the conservative sociopolitical views, Augustan literary tastes, and enlightened Christianity of the New England Federalist elite. He also gave personal encouragement wherever possible to clubs, societies, and other institutions dedicated to the pursuit of natural science.[18] Although William Sr. died when Ralph was only eight, he had already established the cultural tone of the bookish household in which the boy and his four brothers grew up. It is no accident that the authors to whom the precocious eleven-year-old minister's son refers in his earliest surviving letters are Vergil, Cicero, Samuel Johnson, and Pope.[19] Before the bereaved family sold William Sr.'s library for needed cash, the young scholar and his no less scholarly brothers would have found among its volumes well-thumbed editions of any of these Augustan standbys. Ralph Waldo's lifelong devotion to Plutarchan virtue and the middle way must have taken some early impetus from the neoclassicism of the *Monthly Anthology*. And some of the most central preoccupations of Emerson's mature writing, such as the question of human progress, the importance of a national literature, the responsibilities of elite leadership, and what Lewis Simpson calls a "humanist attitude" toward "the integral relation of virtue and learning," were clearly prefigured in the pages of his father's magazine.[20]

In *New England Literary Culture: From Revolution through Renaissance*, Lawrence Buell has established a number of important continuities between the literary strategies of early national neoclassicism and antebellum Romanticism. He suggests a connection, for example, between the detached quality of closed-couplet neoclassical verses and the mutually repellent aphoristic atoms of Emerson's prose. He also points out a resemblance between the "self-appointed monitorship" of the Federalist aristocrats (such as William Emerson, Sr.) and that of the transcendentalist prophets (such as Ralph Waldo).[21] It seems equally plausible to suggest some consistency in the structure of values underlying these continuities of stance and style. Perhaps the most important continuity between the two generations was a bedrock conviction of the preeminent value of reason. Although Emerson came to understand the process of reasoning and the relationship of reason to religion in a way very different from that of his father or his father's Augustan models, he remained equally convinced of reason's excellence and importance.

The acute phase of the crisis that led to Emerson's departure from the Unitarian Church in the summer of 1832 is often said to be signaled by a telling passage from his journal of that winter. "It is the best part of the man, I think," Emerson recorded on 10 January 1832, "that revolts most against his being the minister." But almost a year earlier Emerson had already begun decisively to articulate the substantive conflict of values that lay beneath this "revolt." In March 1831 he wrote:

> The Religion that is afraid of science dishonors God & commits suicide. It acknowledges that it is not equal to the whole of truth, that it legislates, tyrannizes over a village of God's empire but is not the immutable, universal law. Every influx of atheism, of skepticism is thus made useful as a mercury pill assaulting and removing a diseased religion & making a way for truth, & itself is presently purged into the draught. The only way to stand is to cling to the Rock. Keep the soul always turned towards God. Nothing so vast but feel that he contains it. (*JMN* 3:239)

It is worth following the logic of this passage in some detail. First, it is not entirely clear that the "suicidal" religion to which Emerson here refers is Unitarianism, although it is very likely to be. This passage could be construed as praise of Unitarianism's relative openness toward science as opposed to the more fearful attitude of orthodox Calvinism. But even if we accept this cautious reading, we must also notice the priority given to science. Science is aligned with a dialectical process of cleansing and healing that brings the mind from partiality and doubt to an apprehension of "the whole of truth" and "the universal law." These phrases and others like them are pervasive throughout Emerson and in themselves go a long way toward suggesting the limits of the pragmatist reading of his work, since pragmatism explicitly eschews the possibility or the importance of apprehending "the whole" or "the universal." Emerson here and elsewhere clings unpragmatically to an objective absolute in the figure of "The Rock," which here represents stark truth, however recalcitrant and disillusioning. This truth is the stable foundation to which one must cling while shallow and limited dogmas are washed away. Skepticism and atheism are useful as tools that help one arrive at this foundation, but since they deny the possibility of resting on any such foundation, they too must finally be washed away. Clinging to the rock of truth and keeping the soul turned toward God are here figured as one and the same—which is to suggest that truthful science is more sacred than illusory religion—a stance to which Emerson subsequently becomes more decisively and explicitly attached. Indeed, in his closing line—"Nothing so vast but feel that [God] contains it"—Emerson implies that open-minded scientists have more faith than dogmatic religionists. They are willing to contemplate vast, new, and surprising truths against which the dogmatist timidly and "suicidally" protects himself.

Perhaps Emerson has not yet entirely given up on the Unitarian "confluence" of revelation and reason, but he has clearly begun to give reason higher priority. In the next year and a half the voice of reason becomes increasingly dominant. Copernicus, Galileo, Kepler, Leonardo da Vinci, Bacon, Goethe, and contemporary scientific authors increasingly take the place of liberal theologians in Emerson's reading. His sense of the burden of tradition becomes more acute and explicit. He more frequently allows himself critical remarks about sectarianism and organized religion. And in general his focus shifts from the harmony between scientific reason and Christian revelation to their ultimate incompatibility.

In the last few months prior to his official departure from the Second Church, this new clarity finds its most forceful expression in a series of journal entries and a sermon on the subject of astronomy. The names of Copernicus and Galileo, as I have suggested, had been appearing frequently in his journals for the past year or so. In the spring before his crisis summer he begins to tap the poetic power of these and other astronomers' discoveries:

> Indeed is truth stranger than fiction. For what has imagination created to compare with the science of Astronomy? What is there in Paradise Lost to elevate and astonish like Herschel & Somerville? . . . Not a (dot) white spot but is a lump of Suns, the roe, the milt of light & life. Who can be a Calvinist or who an Atheist? God has opened this knowledge to us to correct our theology & educate the mind. (*JMN* 3:24)

The comparison to *Paradise Lost* is significant. At this point in his career Emerson still harbored serious and as yet unchecked poetic ambitions. As the history of Victorian poetry in England makes clear, it was never an easy matter for poets to abandon the vast imaginative resources provided by Christian scripture and theology. What is extraordinary about this passage and many others like it in Emerson's early work is the apparent alacrity with which he makes this departure. Emerson confidently dismisses the grand poetic heritage of Calvinist theology in order to clear the slate for grander and more bracing inspiration. Unlike Matthew Arnold, or Tennyson, or Hardy, for whom the transition from a Christian to a scientific worldview was fraught with an anguished sense of imaginative impoverishment, Emerson declares his confidence that the universe according to science will exceed Calvin's universe in its power to "elevate and astonish." As if in evidence, he presents some fresh and startling poetic imagery: "a lump of Suns, the roe, the milt of light & life."

A few lines later Emerson shifts into a more understated but no less poetic register. "I hope the time will come when there will be a telescope in every street," he remarks whimsically.[22] For Emerson, astronomy and its instrument, the telescope, are symbols of philosophical wonder in its purest form. Stargazing is for him what "water-gazing" is for Melville's Ishmael. In a sermon entitled "Astronomy" delivered at about this time Emerson urges stargazing on all of his parishioners in terms that equate it with the highest aspirations to a rational understanding of the universe. "He who made the eye and the light and clothed the globe with its transparent atmosphere did thereby teach his creature to observe the stars and write their laws." And he draws upon the same image four years later in the opening passages of *Nature,* where he calls upon his readers to become more philosophical, to put some distance between themselves and their guardians: "If a man would be alone, let him look at the stars" (*E&L* 9).

For Emerson as for his poetic heir, Robert Frost, "looking at the stars" is never merely an idle pastime. Just as the man in Frost's "Star-Splitter" must burn down his house to get the insurance money to buy a telescope, Emerson warns us that to learn the law of the heavens we must be ready to sacrifice the comfort of customary beliefs. By introducing us directly to nature, a telescope has the power permanently to undermine our fealty to tradition:

> Calvinism suited Ptolemaism. The irresistible effect of Copernican astronomy has been to make the great scheme for the salvation of man absolutely incredible. Hence great geniuses who studied the mechanism of the heavens became unbelievers in the popular faith: Newton became a Unitarian. Laplace in a Catholic country became an infidel, substituting Necessity for God but a self intelligent necessity is God. (*JMN* 4:26)

Thus Emerson discards the Unitarian balance between science and scripture. Science here has the unrivalled authority to decide which parts of the Bible remain credible. Astronomy, not the New Testament, is rooted in "Eternity" (*JMN* 4:27). It "establish[es] the moral laws" (*JMN* 4:26), and its vast time frame exhausts "temporary" constructions, including that of Christianity (*JMN* 4:27). There is fresh force and candor in Emerson's sweeping dismissal of the "great scheme for the salvation of man" as "absolutely incredible." And this candor is not restricted to the privacy of his journals; he uses exactly the same phrase in the sermon on astronomy to which I have already alluded. Soon to send the letter that will eventually lead to his resignation, Emerson seems in these lines to be feeling an anticipatory sense of intellectual freedom. In a subsequent passage that sounds like a final farewell to the ministry, he characterizes his anticipated freedom in Enlightenment-classical terms: "I have sometimes thought that in order to be a good minister it was necessary to leave the ministry. Were not a Socratic paganism better than an effete superannuated Christianity?" (*JMN* 3:27).

To say that Emerson was excited by his new intellectual prospects is not to say, however, that it was easy for him to abandon the Unitarian ministry. As I noted in chapter 1, Emerson became ill and was unable to work during the summer of 1832 while he waited for the members of the Second Church to respond to his letter of resignation. He retreated with his brother to a country house in the White Mountains of New Hampshire, where he was so weakened by diarrhea that he could barely lift a pen. Even after the decision was finally made and Emerson resigned his position, he took a long trip to Europe in order to relax and to begin to reorient himself professionally. In his journals throughout this stressful period he repeatedly seeks inner strength in the conviction that his course of action was dictated by fidelity to "truth." On 11 August he writes:

> —A stomach ache will make a man as contemptible as a palsy. Under the diarrhoea have I suffered now one fortnight & weak am as a reed. Still the truth is not injured, not touched though thousands of them that love it fall by the way. Serene, adorable, eternal it lives, though Goethe, Mackintosh, Cuvier, Bentham, Hegel die in their places which no living men can fill. (*JMN* 4:33)

Emerson takes refuge in "the truth" here as he often does throughout this period of crisis and, indeed, throughout his life.[23] He also initiates a pattern he will follow throughout his work in representing this truth as having an existence prior to and distinct from himself. By now very close to his mature doctrine that his own moral intuitions will infallibly inform him as to whether or not he is acting or thinking in accordance with the truth, it is clear that he sees this truth as autonomous and objective. Earlier it was "a rock" to which one could cling; here it is a sort of cosmic principle, like Plato's music of the spheres—"serene, adorable, eternal." Its celestial harmonies have sounded everlastingly and will continue to do so even if all living auditors should die.

But the list of these auditors is nonetheless significant. "Goethe, Mackintosh, Cuvier, Bentham, Hegel" are conspicuously men of reason and science rather than men of faith. A great German artist-scientist, a British rationalist legal reformer, a celebrated French naturalist, an English philosopher–legal reformer who sought to demystify the tradition-bound system of British common law, and a German philosopher who saw all of history as the playing out of "Reason" properly understood—these men are distinguished by their courageous defiance of custom and prejudice in favor of the independent pursuit of rational truth. Goethe stands out most prominently because his devotion to science included a proud pagan contempt for Christianity. His aversion to comforting illusions won Emerson's highest regard throughout his life. He is quoted just a few weeks later in support of Emerson's argument against the notion of an afterlife as a motive for virtue. And in 1850 he makes it onto Emerson's very short list of *Representative Men,* where, as we will see, he joins Plato, Napoleon, Montaigne, and Shakespeare in giving the book a decidedly unchristian tone. Bentham also stands out because Emerson will later dismiss his utilitarianism as a "stinking philosophy." Emerson's invocation here of this archrationalist suggests all the more clearly that at this point he sees his struggle in Enlightenment terms—as one of reason versus prejudice, nature versus tradition.

During the trip to Europe that followed his official resignation from the Second Church, Emerson began to articulate his new vocation in scientific terms. "I will be a naturalist," he declares after visiting the Jardin des plantes in Paris. And while traveling from Liverpool to London during the same European retreat he applies the language of Newton to the motions of the spirit: "As the law of light is 'fits of easy transmission and reflection,' such is also the soul's law" (*JMN* 4:86). It should thus be possible, he infers, to bring mathematical precision to moral philosophy: "What is this they say about wanting mathematical certainty for moral truths? I have always affirmed they had it."[24] It is not incidental, then, that upon returning to Concord Emerson initiated his new career as a popular lecturer with a series on science. In this way he decisively asserted the primacy of a critical Enlightenment outlook over the traditional Christian orthodoxy that formerly claimed his professional allegiance. But he remained in the business of cultural-symbolic exposition. Just as in his early notebooks we saw him begin to develop the symbolism of "America" to provide inspirational orientation toward an enlightened future, he here draws upon the discourses of geology, protoevolutionary biology, and chemistry to provide orientation toward a distinctively Enlightenment conception of origins:

> We have come to look at the world in quite another light from any in which our fathers regarded it . . . it is found that it is itself a monument on whose surface every age of perhaps numberless centuries has somewhere inscribed its history in gigantic letters—too deep to be obliterated—but so far apart, and without visible connection, that only

the most diligent observer—say rather—an uninterrupted succession of patient observers—can read them. (*EL* 1:28–29)

At certain epochs, convulsions occur to which the changes which we witness bear no comparison. Once it would appear, the whole globe was in a state of vapor; afterwards of fusion; afterwards of solid; then broken up; and such action of waters and fire upon it as to crumble and mix the rocks to form soils; mountain chains were raised—blown up like a blister for several thousand miles together by fire underneath. (*EL* 1:31)

In fine, the conclusion at which in general geologists have arrived, is, that there had been repeated great convulsions of nature previous to the present order of things; that we now stand in the fourth succession of terrestrial animals; that after the age of reptiles, after that of paleotheria, after that of mammoths and mastadons, arrived the age in which the human species together with some domestic animals governs and fertilizes the earth peaceably; and that the present races are not more than five or six thousand years old. (*EL* 1:32)

Clearly, Emerson is still thinking about history as he moves into his first mature phase as a writer. In these first public lectures the planet earth is represented as both itself intrinsically historical and its own astonishing archive. As his use throughout this lecture of terms such as "sublime," "prophesied," and "a thousand thousand ages" suggests, Emerson knows himself to be in territory usually claimed by religious symbolism. Eons are surveyed, and a sublime effect is achieved as the mind balks at comprehending processes of such temporal magnitude. Emerson conjures world-eating conflagrations and the enormities of geological "deep time." One might find a Miltonic-Ovidian resonance in the image here of Earth as a kind of protean behemoth perpetually but imperceptibly shedding layers of rocky skin and reabsorbing the crumbling scales into its ever-convulsive innards. But there is pointedly no suggestion of any Christian millennial turning point or apocalyptic telos. Such revelations as may be at hand will not be given all at once to a nation of the righteous, but only slowly, across generations and national boundaries, to "an uninterrupted succession of patient observers," each building on the work of his or her predecessors. The diction here, its vast imaginative scale notwithstanding, is objective, cool, empirical, scientific. In a similar formulation later in the same lecture, Emerson will characterize these metamorphoses as "slow and secular," precisely, it would seem, in order to distinguish their organic evolutionary character from the extrinsic shocks of Judeo-Christian messianism. And the same sense of "secular" cosmic gradualism is reinforced in the next lecture by its fine evocations of the awesome, implacable, planet-carving capacities of flowing water: "As the operations of Nature are restricted by no limits of time the minute changes of every moment make vast revolutions in the course of ages so that the earth presents now no resemblance to its ancient appearance. And the immense effect of the incessant fall of waters for so many ages is apparent enough in the deep lines which they have cut into every part of the crust of the earth" (*EL* 1:55).

Thus, Emerson may be said to initiate what will become a career-long strategy of tapping into geological or astronomical deep time as a secular substitute for Christian *kairos*. His discovery of the imminent availability of the sublime consciousness of deep time — "these wonders are brought to our own door" (*E&L* 48) — is an important source of the abundant ecstatic energies of Emerson's early phase. And he continues verbally to solicit deep time to flow through and permeate his subsequent writing, providing much of this work's underlying progressive thrust as well as generating its tone of continuing astonishment. We might thus revise Walter Benjamin even as we borrow his phrasing: for Emerson, "the historical progress of mankind" is not a march "through homogenous, empty time" but is rather, to use one of Emerson's favorite words, an "abandonment" to the immense onwardness of deep time. Jets from this vast current, rather than Benjamin's "chips of messianic time," "shoot through" the rapids of Emerson's fluent prose.[25] But by so pointedly calling its processes "secular," Emerson frees this conception of time from the prohibitions and mystifications that are typically associated with the sacred, and thus claims it as a resource for liberal empirical consciousness.

Hans Blumenberg goes to some length to point out the obstacle presented to the emergence of such secular scientific consciousness by traditional religious strictures both against pure curiosity for its own sake (theory) and against profane practical applications of knowledge (technique). In the former case the scientist presumed to wish to know what only God could know, and in the latter he presumed to subordinate divine creation to human ends. "The early-modern renewal of the pretension to unrestricted theoretical curiosity turned against the exclusion of pure theory, and of the pure happiness that was bound up with it, from the realm of what could be reached in this world, just as it turned against the medieval God's claim to exclusive insight into nature as His work." In the writings of Galileo and Kepler, two of Emerson's most frequently listed intellectual heroes, Blumenberg adds, "the problematic of theoretical curiosity, which had depended on the idea of the world as a demonstration of divine power, and of human stupor as the corresponding effect, is paralyzed by the idea that knowledge is not a pretension to what is unfathomable but rather the laying open of necessity."[26] The remaining two lectures in Emerson's Science series, "The Uses of Natural History" and "The Naturalist," are a kind of primer for the inculcation of precisely such attitudes of secular-scientific self-assertion. Among the many benefits of the study of natural history that he lists in these lectures Emerson significantly includes the two following. First, such contemplation is the highest of pleasures, both aesthetic and theoretical, unto itself: "The beauty of the world is a perpetual invitation to the study of the world. Sunrise and sunset; fire; flowers; shells; the sea—in all its shades, from indigo to green and gray, by the light of day, and phosphorescent under the ship's keel at night" (*EL* 1:6). Second, the study of natural history is supremely useful: "It is the earth itself and its natural bodies that make the raw materials out of which we construct our food, clothing, fuel, furniture, and arms. It is the Naturalist who discovers the virtues of these bodies and the mode of converting them to use" (*EL* 1:11–12). Pumped water, ventilated chimneys, refined sugar, glass, cloth, paint, dyes, brass, silver, iron, gold, fabric, drugs, fruits, and condiments: these are just a few of the materials for the use of which, Emerson points out, we are indebted to the study of natural history, not to mention the two most important sources of energy for the already burgeoning industrial revolution—steam and coal.

He elaborates most tellingly on this last: "And so it happens that these vast beds of fuel so essential to man's comfort and civilization, which would have been covered by the crust of the globe forever from his knowledge and use, are thus brought up within reach of his little hands; and a great work of Nature in an antiquity that hath no record—namely the deposit and crystallization of antediluvian forests, is made to contribute to our pleasure and prosperity at this hour" (*EL* 1:34). Here, as throughout the Science series, Emerson shows himself to be neither fundamentally antihistorical nor containable within the categories of historical secularization. It would be hard to overstate the importance of coal as the principal energy source for the industrial revolution that was "taking off " in Great Britain exactly at the time Emerson wrote these words. Eric Hobsbawm tells us that Britain's output of coal "trebled from 15 million tons to 49 million tons" between 1830 and 1850.[27] By linking this extraordinary recent increase of human power to the recesses of deep time, Emerson folds his era's apparent departure from human history into the larger currents of cosmic history. And by celebrating the distinctively worldly benefits of this history for "man's comfort and civilization," "his knowledge and use," "[his] pleasure and prosperity at this hour," Emerson clearly articulates a secular and liberal outlook. It is not for time's transcendent mystery but for its contribution to ordinary human well-being that he expresses gratitude. Indeed, he here strikingly initiates what will become a lifelong project of providing this new kind of secular liberal society with gratitude-inducing symbolic orientation, in this case toward its primordial origins. To use a technological metaphor befitting the context, Emerson here forges a kind of verbal pipeline through which deep time may flow from its sublime primordial depths into and through the seemingly profane artifacts and conveniences of modern life. The hope is indeed for a kind of sanctification— we wash our "little hands," as it were, in time's infinite waters. But the source of blessing is the opposite of the transcendent or the messianic: it comes spontaneously from the belly of the earth and bends immensely to the variety of human needs and designs.

3

Reason II, Virtue

Nature *(1836)*

Emerson's use of the title *Nature* is usually taken in a Romantic sense as signifying the phenomena of the nonhuman environment. He invites this interpretation when he defines "nature" in these terms in his introduction—as "essences unchanged by man; space, the air, the river, the leaf " (*E&L* 8). But Emerson also alerts us that he intends the word in a broader, more "philosophical" sense. In this meaning, he asserts, "nature" means the human as well as the nonhuman environment—everything beyond our own subjectivity, including the manifold products of human labor. And he follows the Greeks and their Enlightenment heirs when he declares that in order to achieve real knowledge about nature in this sense we must first cast a critical eye on inherited explanations of it:

> Our age is retrospective. It builds the sepulchres of the fathers. It writes biographies, histories, and criticism. The foregoing generation beheld God and nature face to face, we, through their eyes. Why should not we also enjoy an original relation to the universe? Why should we not have a poetry and philosophy of insight and not of tradition, and a religion by revelation to us, and not the history of theirs? Embosomed for a season in nature, whose floods of life stream around and through us, and invite us by the powers they supply to action proportioned to nature, why should we grope among the dry bones of the past, or put the living

generation into masquerade out of its faded wardrobe? The sun shines to-day also. There is more wool and flax in the fields. There are new lands, new men, new thoughts. Let us demand our own works and laws and worship. (*E&L* 7)

It is fitting that Emerson began his career as an independent, secular writer with this remarkable passage because it is primarily a declaration of philosophical seriousness—a commitment, as it were, to Enlightenment.[1] Those disinclined to take Emerson seriously as a philosopher would tend to read this paragraph either as a statement of pragmatic will or as a piece of pure Romantic egoism.[2] They would see the demands for "newness," "originality," for something of "our own," as purely contingent and ungrounded—the self-authorizing assertion of pragmatic or Romantic selfhood. But if we keep in mind the Enlightenment context I described in chapter 2, the passage can be seen more accurately as a rhetorically potent refiguration of the basic classical antinomy between nature and tradition. "Retrospectiveness," "the sepulchres of the fathers," "biographies, histories and criticism," "the foregoing generations," "tradition," "the dry bones of the past," "the faded wardrobe [of the past]"; all of these terms suggest the somber weight of what Leo Strauss calls "the ancestral." "An original relation to the universe," "a poetry and philosophy of insight," "a religion by revelation to us," "floods of life," "the shining sun," "new lands, new men, new thoughts," "our own works and laws and worship"; all of these suggest the fresh claim of what Strauss calls "the natural."[3] The natural perspective may be said to be "fresh" not only in the Romantic sense, which implies rejuvenation of the senses by the perception of graceful, untamed forms, but also in the Enlightenment-classical sense, which implies knowledge of things as they are in themselves prior to the imposition of traditional frameworks of understanding. The language of unmediated knowing is just as important here as the language of sensual renewal; "beholding God face to face," "a poetry and a philosophy of insight," and "a religion by revelation to us" are essential to the general aura of "newness." To "enjoy an original relation to the universe" is at once to revel in enhanced sensibility and to have knowledge of origins—of things as they were before they were distorted by custom and tradition, of things in the pure primordial state that Wallace Stevens was to call "everearly candor."[4] Throughout Emerson's writing, Romantic evocations of perceptual renewal always carry this additional Enlightenment connotation.

As befits an Enlightenment moral philosopher writing in a Romantic vein, Emerson addresses himself in the above passage not only to a deep inner longing for contact with the absolute but also to an objective moral standard. The force of Romantic self-assertion in this passage is sufficiently strong that it is easy to overlook the presence within it of the basic classical definition of virtue, "action proportioned to nature."[5] In calling upon individuals to liberate themselves from subservience to custom and tradition, Emerson is not advocating disrespect for authoritative standards per se. On the contrary, in the pattern of classical and Enlightenment thought, he seeks to replace reverence for ancestral norms with reverence for natural norms—norms based on disillusioned knowledge of the true order of things. This is the burden of the last sentence of this paragraph: "Let us demand our own works and laws and worship." It is tempting to emphasize the phrase "our own" here and thus to interpret this sentence as a call to unbounded subjectivity. But the prior phrase "action proportioned to nature" functions precisely to counterbalance such a one-sided reading. In its context, all three terms of this last sentence retain an external, objective point of reference. "Worship" implies attention to something outside of and greater than oneself. "Laws" suggests stable and objective principles of order. And "works" here implies not unchecked or arbitrary self-assertion or expression but virtuous action—ethical behavior guided by respect for natural laws, limits, and principles.

The first paragraph of *Nature* thus follows a two-level Enlightenment pattern of argument that corresponds to the two levels of Enlightenment thought I sketched in the foregoing chapter. First, most generally, Emerson's argument is structured by the fundamental Enlightenment-classical antinomy between nature and tradition. Second, at the same time as Emerson makes a strong rhetorical case in favor of replacing the authority of tradition with the authority of nature, he attempts to provide some definition or description of nature as a standard. At this second stage he follows the counter-Lockean strain of Enlightenment thought described in chapter 2. He seeks insight into nature not by means of piecemeal Cartesian analysis, which he later calls "understanding," but rather by an intuitive grasp of its structure as an orderly whole, an intellectual leap he attributes to "reason." The terms with which he expresses this intuitive grasp are poetic and evocative rather than rigorous and logical. In this passage, for example, he characterizes nature as "embosom[ing]," as "floods of life [that] stream around and through us," and as a grand organic process, implacably regular and self-renewing. Such poetic formulations do not imply pure subjectivity. On the contrary, the simple, matter-of-fact tone of these last sentences is meant to suggest commonsense observation. The sun shines and the crops grow according to their own distinctive and timeless rhythms, independently of the perceiving subject. Indeed, the stable and ongoing balance of the natural order provides an objective measure by which the subject may assess the ethical value of his or her actions. To act virtuously is to act in a manner "proportioned" to this larger dynamic whole.

The rest of *Nature* repeatedly plays out varieties of this two-level Enlightenment pattern. To start chapter 1, Emerson returns again to the first level of argument, making the general case for nature against tradition, custom, and convention: "To go into solitude, a man needs to retire as much from his chamber as from society. I am not solitary whilst I read and write, though nobody is with me. But if a man would be alone, let him look at the stars. . . . One might think the atmosphere was made transparent with this design, to give man, in the heavenly bodies, the perpetual presence of the sublime" (*E&L* 9). "To go into solitude" is for Emerson, as it was for Rousseau and would be for Thoreau, a gesture of philosophical seriousness. It implies, in the first gesture of detachment, a temporary severance of the social ties of custom and convention in an effort to gain perspective on the values they enforce, a rejection of the hurry and bother of social and professional interaction in favor of a slower, more introspective, and deliberate manner of living. To then "retire from one's chamber," in the second gesture of detachment, is to raise the philosophical stakes still further. Having removed oneself from society, one is now urged also to sunder one's connection to the past as represented by the activities of reading and writing. The goal is a state of unprejudiced contemplation. Here as in the journal passage discussed in chapter 2, to "look at the stars" is a trope for philosophizing, for inquiring independently into the laws of the cosmos. Such independence of mind implies a degree of irreverence toward traditional or merely conventional views—what Wallace Stevens was to call "the old descriptions of the world."[6] But again Emerson insists that this does not require a rejection of the attitude of reverence altogether. Rather, the philosopher transfers his feelings of reverence from the world as described by tradition and myth onto the world as seen by the unprejudiced eye. In these lines as in so much of his work Emerson uses Romantically charged rhetoric to enlist a religious intensity of feeling in support of an Enlightenment philosophical outlook.

Emerson uses the same strategy in the extended trope with which he concludes this paragraph: "Seen in the streets of cities, how great they are! If the stars should appear one night in a thousand years, how would men believe and adore; and preserve for many generations the remembrance of the city of God which had been shown! But every night come out these envoys of beauty, and light the universe with their admonishing smile" (*E&L* 9). Like the opening passage of *Nature* examined above, this passage is built on the classical opposition between nature and tradition. A truly open-minded, open-eyed contemplation of nature, Emerson argues here, should yield transcendent emotions of praise and wonder. Such exalted perceptions are at the root of religious traditions, but nature's prodigality is so great that formal structures of remembrance are not necessary. Indeed, Emerson implies that traditional religious structures inhibit people from discovering the full sublimity of the world around them. A vision of the "city of God" is available on any night in the streets of any ordinary city; one need only lift up one's eyes to participate in a perpetual sacrament of self-renewal.[7] Emerson uses the Augustinian term "city of God" to do complex work here; it at once evokes intense religious feeling and comments ironically on the rigid Roman Catholic and Calvinist orthodoxies that Emerson believes historically to have stifled or misdirected the innate human need for worship. Here he attempts to tap Augustinian religious intensity for the praise of a more rationally credible cosmos.

Seen rationally, this cosmos, as I have already suggested, has the structure of an orderly whole:

> When we speak of nature in this manner, we have a distinct but most poetical sense in the mind. We mean the integrity of impression made by manifold natural objects. It is this which distinguishes the stick of timber of the wood-cutter from the tree of the poet. The charming landscape which I saw this morning, is indubitably made up of some twenty or thirty farms. Miller owns this field, Locke that, and Manning the woodland beyond. But none of them owns the landscape. There is a property in the horizon which no man has but he whose eye can integrate all the parts, that is, the poet. This is the best part of these men's farms, yet to this their warranty-deeds give no title. (*E&L* 9)

Here, in the first of many similar passages, Emerson brings together the two patterns of Enlightenment argument we have been tracing, at once establishing a basic opposition between nature and convention and figuring nature as an orderly whole. He does so primarily by invoking two

levels of law. On the one hand, a conventional or "positive" law, represented by "warranty-deeds," assigns this field to Miller, that field to
Locke, and the woodland beyond to Manning. This is a utilitarian law of
parts and particulars that assigns value to things according to their immediate usefulness. On the other hand, a broader law that Emerson associates with "nature" governs the scene as a whole. This law grants the
right of "property" on the basis of philosophical intuition. Those who
see things only according to convention and custom are granted com-
mensurately partial possessions—the woodcutter's "stick of timber,"
Miller's field, and Manning's woodland. The "poets" who see according
to nature, who can "integrate all the parts," are granted commensu-
rately whole properties—the "tree," the "landscape," and the full sweep
of the "horizon." If there were any doubt, Emerson makes clear in the
final sentence that the natural law holds pride of place in his hierarchy
of values.

In the famous paragraph that follows, Emerson vividly represents
the momentary fulfillment of these high philosophical aims. To understand it thoroughly it is necessary to review the full trajectory of this
long passage. For the purposes of commentary I have broken it up into
three distinct sections:

> 1. To speak truly, few adult persons can see nature. Most persons do not
> see the sun. At least they have a very superficial seeing. The sun illumi-
> nates only the eye of the man, but shines into the eye and the heart of
> the child. The lover of nature is he whose inward and outward senses
> are still truly adjusted to each other; who has retained the spirit of in-
> fancy even into the era of manhood. His intercourse with heaven and
> earth, becomes part of his daily food. (*E&L* 10)

> 2. In the presence of nature, a wild delight runs through the man, in
> spite of real sorrows. Nature says,—he is my creature, and maugre all
> his impertinent griefs, he shall be glad with me. Not the sun or the sum-
> mer alone, but every hour and season yields its tribute of delight; for
> every hour and change corresponds to and authorizes a different state
> of the mind, from breathless noon to grimmest midnight. Nature is a
> setting that fits equally well a comic or a mourning piece. (*E&L* 10)

> 3. In good health, the air is a cordial of incredible virtue. Crossing a
> bare common, in snow puddles, at twilight, under a clouded sky, with-
> out having in my thoughts any occurrence of special good fortune, I
> have enjoyed a perfect exhilaration. I am glad to the brink of fear. In
> the woods, too, a man casts off his years, as the snake his slough, and at

whatsoever period of life, is always a child. In the woods, is perpetual youth. Within these plantations of God, a decorum and a sanctity reign, a perennial festival is dressed, and the guest sees not how he should tire of them in a thousand years. In the woods we return to reason and faith. There I feel that nothing can befall me in life,—no disgrace, no calamity (leaving me my eyes,) which nature cannot repair. Standing on the bare ground—my head bathed by the blithe air, and uplifted into infinite space,—all mean egotism vanishes, I become a transparent eye-ball; I am nothing; I see all; the currents of the Universal Being circulate through me; I am part or particle of God. The name of the nearest friend sounds then foreign and accidental: to be brothers, to be acquaintances,—master or servant, is then a trifle and a disturbance. I am the lover of uncontained and immortal beauty. In the wilderness, I find something more dear and connate than in streets and villages. In the tranquil landscape, and especially in the distant line of the horizon, man beholds somewhat as beautiful as his own nature. (*E&L* 10)

Emerson begins the first passage above by candidly embracing a Platonic hierarchy. "Seeing the sun" is Plato's principal trope for apprehending philosophical truth. Emerson then transposes the Platonic metaphor into Rousseauian or Wordsworthian terms, aligning classical-philosophical knowing with Romantic innocence. Wordsworth's "Intimations Ode," perhaps the exemplary statement of Romantic Platonism, resonates clearly through these lines.[8]

Having again established the superiority of natural to conventional seeing, Emerson then turns again to a definition of nature in the second quote, in which nature is again characterized principally as a grand and comprehensive orderly whole. Stoicism stands firmly in the background of these sentences. Whether he takes it from Shaftesbury or from the ancient writers themselves, Emerson here clearly invokes a Stoic conception of nature as a grand compensatory order in which all human pains and losses are somehow finally balanced out. A deep sense of joy—"a wild delight"—accompanies one's apprehension of this larger pattern. The joy comes in part from the discovery that one's pains and losses have not been for nothing, that they have been part of one's education in the order of the whole. There is also joy in the perception of the harmonious fit between humans and nature, a sense of comfort and belonging—"he is my creature," Nature says, almost maternally, of man.

In this manner Emerson draws directly on the counter-Lockean Enlightenment tradition sketched above, focusing on the attunement of the self to the greater whole of which it is a part. And in a manner characteristic of the Romantic extension of this tradition, Emerson also implicitly expands the concept of attunement to a level of broad cultural utility. Nature is not only the great whole by reference to which one may achieve spiritual integration and solace, it is also a storehouse of symbols that correspond to every particular mood or motion of one's deeper self. Emerson implies that nature may thus successfully perform the role unsuccessfully performed, for example, by the secular statues placed by the French revolutionaries in the cathedral of Notre Dame. Nature, he suggests, provides an imaginatively adequate set of substitutes for the rich corpus of traditional Christian symbolism. Rightly understood and employed, natural symbolism may thus bolster the symbolic thinness of post-Christian Enlightenment culture. Like the traditional genres of comedy and tragedy, nature supplies a framework of symbolic meaning that enables us to understand and to accept our place within a greater social, political, or cosmic whole.[9] But unlike traditional dramas, which often derive much of their authority from appeals to time-honored mores and conventions, nature's symbolic order can only be apprehended by the fresh and full exercise of the mind's faculties of original reception, intuition, imagination, and synthesis — the faculties, that is, that together comprise Emerson's counter-Lockean conception of "reason."

Emersonian reason achieves its highest realization in the third passage. Describing his famous epiphany, Emerson weaves together the two levels of Enlightenment argument we have been discussing. The Romantic rhetoric of childhood again cuts against the weight of age and the past: "In the woods too, a man casts off his years." And the moment of gnosis is figured precisely in terms of liberation from convention, especially from such conventional categories of identification as profession, family, social relation, rank, or locale: "In the wilderness, I find something more dear and connate than in streets and villages." "Woods" and "wilderness" function in these lines in much the same way that "solitude" did in the passage analyzed above: they signify an atmosphere hospitable to philosophical seriousness. It is only in a locale as yet unmarked by custom and convention that one may truly "return to reason and faith." The word "dear" suggests intimate familial affection, and the word "connate" literally suggests "born with" and thus, presumably, linked by common origins, by blood. To say that the wilderness is "more dear and connate" than blood relations is to emphasize that real philosophical knowing, "the return to reason," requires an uprooting of the self from those ties most honored by tradition, custom, and convention. This emphasis on uprooting is enhanced by the giddy, unballasted, vertiginous feel of the "bathed head . . . uplifted into infinite space." And the following, too-often-overlooked phrase, "all mean egotism vanishes," completes a pattern of detachment and self-emptying that is more ascetic than imperial.

Of course, Emerson's claim to "reason" in this passage is complicated by his explicit connection of reason to "faith." But by now we have seen enough of Emerson's struggles with religious orthodoxy to recognize that in this context "faith" suggests not uncritical assent to traditional dogma but rather the innate need of the soul to place itself affirmatively in relation to a larger whole. Worshipful integration of the self into a greater order is precisely the burden of much of the rest of the passage at hand. Immediately preceding the sentence on "reason and faith," Emerson figures the woods as a strange but splendid realm in which he finds himself surprisingly at home. Having only recently uprooted himself, as we have seen, from his familiar place of origin, Emerson can be only "a guest" in this new locale. But the language here suggests that Emerson, like Odysseus at the court of Alkínoös, has wandered into a kingdom of exemplary wholesomeness and balance. In the woods he finds an atmosphere at once of expansiveness and control, festivity and formality, ostentation and dignified reserve. The crucial term is "decorum," a word suggesting proper regard for form and context, a due sense of what is fitting and appropriate, even in one's smallest actions. It suggests a subtle and thoroughgoing orientation of one's entire sensibility to an implicit, underlying order. And in the sentence immediately following the phrase "reason and faith," Emerson again makes clear that the name for this underlying order is "nature": "Nothing can befall me in life . . . which nature cannot repair." To grasp and understand this comprehensively balanced whole is at once an intellectual, spiritual, and aesthetic experience. It requires the exercise not only of "reason and faith," as we have seen, but also of aesthetic sensitivity. Once again Emerson places himself firmly in the line of counter-Lockean Enlightenment thinkers, for many of whom aesthetic perception was itself a form of knowing. "The distant line of the horizon" marks at once the boundary of an integrating whole, the geometrical outline of an intelligible idea, and the graceful curve of a beautiful form.

Having thus eloquently set in motion a two-level pattern of Enlightenment argument in his grand initial overture (the introduction and chapter 1), Emerson devotes the central chapters of *Nature* (chapters 2 through 5) to extending this argument through various spheres of knowledge and experience—from agriculture and natural history to economics, technology, aesthetics, history, law, politics, physics, music, architecture, and, not least important, ordinary domesticity. While continuing to deploy the rhetoric of natural newness against the weary burden of the ancestral as he did in the introduction and chapter 1, Emerson uses chapters 2 and 3 to describe the structure of nature as a set of fluid and interpenetrating orderly wholes.

In the short second chapter, entitled "Commodity," Emerson starts by figuring nature in general as a vast interlocking network of services for man. "Steady and prodigal provision . . . [is] made for his support and delight . . . Beasts, fire, water, stones, and corn serve him. . . . All the parts incessantly work into each other's hands for the profit of man" (*E&L* 12). We see here again Emerson's pervasive tendency to view nature in terms of orderly wholes. In this case he sketches its most far-flung pattern— "the endless circulations of the divine charity." In the next and penultimate paragraph of this short chapter he draws an analogy between this grand system and the broad array of human technological contrivances:

> [Man] no longer waits for favoring gales, but by means of steam, he realizes the fable of Aeolus's bag, and carries the two and thirty winds in the boiler of his boat. To diminish friction, he paves the road with iron bars, and mounting a coach with a ship-load of men, animals, and merchandise behind him, he darts through the country, from town to town, like an eagle or a swallow through the air. . . . The private poor man hath cities, ships, canals, bridges, built for him. He goes to the post-office, and the human race run his errands; to the book-shop, and the human race read and write of all that happens, for him; to the courthouse, and nations repair his wrongs. (*E&L* 12-13)

It is surprising to encounter this paean to technology and industrialism early in a book entitled *Nature*. Romantic nature writers, including Emersonian transcendentalists such as Thoreau, tended to set nature and industrial technology in opposition. Emerson's sweepingly affirmative analogizing of nature and technology compels us to recognize again that he intends the word "nature" in a sense much broader than we usually associate with Romanticism. To include in a description of "nature" all the institutions and machinery of modern mobility and trade — roads, trains, cities, ships, canals, bridges, post offices, shops — is again to associate the word as much with Enlightenment science as with Romantic flora and fauna. Here Emerson not only invokes a full-fledged Enlightenment conception of historical progress ("how is the face of the world changed from the era of Noah to that of Napoleon!" [*E&L* 13]) but explicitly draws out the classical-liberal political implications of this conception. As did Adam Smith and Enlightenment liberals in general, Emerson suggests here that "the private poor man" is the ultimate beneficiary of technological advances. The choice of the word "private" is important. Classical liberalism may well be characterized as that political philosophy that gives paramount importance to the private sphere. It is explicitly dedicated to preserving and enhancing the dignity, comfort, and freedom of private life. Emerson uses the phrase "private poor man" in a broad historical sense to connote not strictly the impecunious but rather the nonpolitical liberal citizen per se — the nonmartial, nontheocratic, nonaristocratic, even noncivic individual of modern commercial societies. This is only the first of many times in his work that Emerson strikes a strong classical-liberal note by giving rhetorical precedence to the exclusively private individual over larger social collectivities. And these political undertones are sounded more emphatically in the final sentence of this chapter as Emerson concludes by explicitly invoking a value second only to privacy in the hierarchy of bourgeois liberalism — that of free labor.[10] "This mercenary benefit," he writes, referring to the material advantages provided by technology, "is one which has respect to a farther good. A man is fed not that he may be fed, but that he may work" (*E&L* 13).

In the next chapter, "Beauty," Emerson turns away from "mercenary benefits" toward what he calls "nobler wants." By thus elevating the discussion, Emerson appears happily to leave behind the base concerns of political economy. But Emerson's writing is itself shaped by the same pattern of compensatory wholeness that he finds everywhere in nature. From the broad holistic philosophical perspective that the essay attempts to inculcate, the "nobler wants" of beauty can be seen to relate to the "mercenary" needs of commodity in much the same way that thesis relates to antithesis in a Hegelian synthesis; they are the constituent contraries of a larger dialectical unity. When Emerson turns to the "nobler wants" of the aesthetic, he is not departing completely from the historical-political. He is rather looking for that which may spiritually complement and complete the economic and commercial developments he celebrated in the previous section. This is why, in starting this next chapter on beauty, he italicizes the observation that natural forms "give us a delight *in and for themselves*" (*E&L* 14). Natural forms, he wishes to emphasize, are *not* commodities. They are spiritually useful to human beings: "To the body and mind which have been cramped by noxious work or company, nature is medicinal and restores their tone" (*E&L* 14). But their value cannot be reduced to this usefulness: "Nature satisfies by its loveliness, and without any mixture of corporeal benefit" (*E&L* 15). Emerson is acutely aware of the great material improvements procured for the "poor private man" by the technological and economic progress of Enlightenment-liberal civilization. But he is also acutely aware of a dangerous tendency within this civilization to reduce all values to a stark calculus of economic utility. By holding up the beauty of natural forms as a value "in and for itself," he is attempting to resist this reductive tendency in a civilization to which he gives wholehearted assent at almost every other level. Just as his contemporary, Tocqueville, believed that liberal-democratic societies needed religion to counter their tendency toward moral mediocrity, Emerson here implies that liberal-democratic societies need an appreciation of beauty for its own sake to counter their tendency toward reification, commodification, and other forms of utilitarian instrumentalism. The special value of our rare moments of pure aesthetic beholding is that they leave no psychic space for base calculations of advantage: "I see the spectacle of morning from the hill-top over against my house, from day-break to sun-rise, with emotions which an angel might share" (*E&L* 15).

Emerson divides his chapter on beauty into three parts, which we may label phenomenological, moral, and intellectual. In the first part he loosely follows Kant in arguing that the human mind is constructed in such a way that it naturally arranges the objects of its perceptions into formal wholes: "By the mutual action of [the eye's] structure and of the laws of light, perspective is produced, which integrates every mass of objects, of what character so ever, into a well colored and shaded globe, so that where the particular objects are mean and unaffecting, the landscape which they compose is round and symmetrical" (*E&L* 14). In other words, the mind spontaneously produces orderly wholes out of its encounter with the materials of experience. Emerson offers as evidence for this claim two exquisitely perceived descriptions of natural scenes in all their phenomenological specificity: "The long slender bars of cloud float like fishes in the sea of crimson light. From the earth, as from a shore, I look out into that silent sea. I seem to partake its rapid transformations: the active enchantment reaches my dust, and I dilate and conspire with the morning wind" (*E&L* 15). In the following passage he recalls "the calm, last evening, of a January sunset":

> The western clouds divided and subdivided themselves into pink flakes modulated with tints of unspeakable softness, and the air had so much life and sweetness that it was a pain to come within doors. What was it that nature would say? Was there no meaning in the live repose of the valley behind the mill, and which Homer or Shakespeare could not re-form for me in words? The leafless trees become spires of flame in the sunset, with the blue east for the background, and the stars of the dead calices of flowers, and every withered stem and stubble rimed with frost, contribute something to the mute music. (*E&L* 15)

The writing here is fine enough to register both the pressure of the mind's impulse to find form and the dispersed recalcitrance of brute phenomena. It does so by describing subtly differentiated phenomenological perceptions in an idiom that is at one level objectively precise and, on a quiet second level, symbolically coherent. On the first level, the opening sentence of the second passage ("The western clouds . . .") is a piece of pure lyrical receptivity worthy of Wordsworth. On the second level, the words "modulated" and "unspeakable" participate in an associative pattern of conceptual tension between form and formlessness that runs through the paragraph as a whole. "Unspeakable" joins with "repose," "leafless," "dead calices," "withered stem and stubble," and "mute" to suggest nature's resistance to formal articulation, her sphinxlike silence, her mortal elusiveness. "Modulated" joins with "say," "meaning," "Homer," "Shakespeare," "background," and "music" to suggest the countervailing human need to arrange the welter of perceptions into intelligible forms, whether syntactic, semantic, narrative, dramatic, epic, visual, lyrical, or musical. Of course, formlessness finally gives way to form here, or we would have nothing to discuss. But Emerson does manage to interpose an interval of uncertainty between the moment of initial perception and the subsequent imposition of intelligible order. Silence remains a real possibility as the speaker begins somewhat urgently to press the landscape for speech: "What was it that nature would say? Was there no meaning?" The repeated interrogative suggests a degree of real uneasiness. Emerson turns anxiously to Homer and Shakespeare as the most powerful resources he knows by which to "re-form" raw experience into verbal order.

This anxiety is ultimately resolved as the paragraph moves toward its conclusion. In the now familiar counter-Lockean pattern, the discrete phenomenological particulars are gathered into a resonant poetic whole. The observer of this spectacular morning, we recall, begins in a condition of granulated fragmentation—as "dust." But then, like Adam taking life from God's breath, he "dilate[s] and conspire[s]" with the beauty of this scene, transformed into a new state of confident wholeness. He is then able to assume imaginative command of a comprehensive symbolic cycle: "The dawn is my Assyria, the sun-set and moon-rise my Paphos," and so on. The same pattern is played out more subtly in the third passage as the enigmatic silence of the scene is delicately worked into a subtle winter harmony: "The leafless trees become spires of flame in the sunset." By yoking the visual phenomenon of frosted stubble with one of the elemental concepts of poetic sound, "rime" performs a rich conceptual and sensual "rhyming" of its own. Its dual action performs on a smaller scale the work of resonant compression that the paragraph as a whole performs as it gathers a wide range of perceived phenomena—"leafless trees," "blue east," "dead calices of flowers," and "withered stem[s]"—into the tense paradoxical unity of a series of juxtaposed conceptual opposites—"unspeakable" and "saying," "live" and "repose," and, summing up the rest, "mute" and "music." "Mute music" and the other tense verbal combinations form precisely the sort of dialectical wholes that, Emerson believed, structured nature at every level. The complex pattern of his rhetoric thus mimics the complex pattern of nature as he understood it. To Emerson, however, the complexity of these patterns did not render them obscure. What Cartesian or Lockean "understanding" could never grasp was readily available to Emersonian "reason"—to moral and metaphysical intuition, to unconscious inspiration, to poetic imagination, to prayer, even to proverbial common sense.

The larger pattern of nature was also readily accessible to virtue. In the second section of "Beauty" Emerson argues that moral goodness and natural beauty work together like the foreground and background of a fine painting. We already noted in our analysis of the first paragraph of the introduction that Emerson quietly invoked the primary classical definition of virtue—"action proportioned to nature." In these later paragraphs on moral beauty Emerson develops the aesthetic implications of this definition:

The high and divine beauty which can be loved without effeminacy, is that which is found in combination with the human will. Beauty is the mark God sets upon virtue. Every natural action is graceful. Every heroic act is also decent, and causes the place and the bystanders to shine. We are taught by great actions that the universe is the property of every person in it. Every rational creature has all nature for his dowry and estate. It is his, if he will. He may divest himself of it; he may creep into a corner, and abdicate his kingdom, as most men do, but he is entitled to the world by his constitution. In proportion to the energy of his thought and will, he takes up the world into himself. (*E&L* 16)

The earlier phrase, "action proportioned to nature," suggests harmony, attunement, balance, analogy, even symmetry. To greater and lesser degrees, all of these terms have aesthetic connotations; they imply repeated, matching, or at least similar patterns. In the above sentences Emerson attempts to make these correspondences explicit. In yet another version of what we have seen him do so often, here he figures virtue as an integral part of a larger whole. Moral acts are performed in accordance with the fundamental structure of nature and thereby partake of nature's inherent beauty. Emerson suggests that in virtuous actions Nature's underlying pattern is played out in richer, redoubled harmonies or, to use visual terms, in vaster, more radiant emanations.

This form of Emersonian analogizing should be familiar enough by now not to surprise us. What should surprise us are the subtle political connotations he works into the pattern. A close look at the passage above reveals a string of terms rich with associations to the liberal political order in which Emerson lived: "property," "rational," "dowry," "estate," "will," "kingdom," "entitled," "constitution." Taken together, the political, economic, and legal connotations of these terms evoke what we might call the fundamental liberal inheritance. When Emerson says "the universe is the property of every individual in it" or that "every rational creature has all nature for his dowry and estate," he is offering a characteristically romantic and rhetorically robust version of the doctrine of natural right. He appears to depart from Jefferson's relatively restrained formulations by making the grandiose claim not that all men have certain rights by nature but that each individual has a right to "all of nature," to "the universe." But if we keep in mind Emerson's conviction that nature was a kind of synecdoche, that the essence of nature as a whole was present and intelligible in any one of its parts, we can take these statements to mean that a right to any property or any liberty was

equivalent to a right to all of it.[11] Because the whole grand order of nature was discernible, as another of Emerson's poetic heirs would put it,
"in a spear of summer grass," the whole grand order of nature could be
readily possessed by any individual capable of thought and labor and
virtuous action.[12]

Emerson further develops the liberal undertones of this passage by
playing on the word "constitution." Having asserted that all human beings have a natural right to "the universe," he then acknowledges, in fittingly legal terms, that they also have the freedom to forfeit this right.
Emerson uses "constitution" here primarily in the sense of a person's
character or make-up—"the energy of his thought and will." But the
larger political connotations of "constitution" come into play in relation
to the many legal-political terms that surround it. Earlier in this sentence, Emerson uses the word "kingdom" with some historical irony as
a name for the rich legacy of natural right to which "every rational creature" is heir in a liberal democracy. According to the Enlightenment-
liberal view of history, which underwrote the liberal doctrine of natural
right, "constitutional" polities emerged precisely as a progressive improvement upon monarchical polities, that is, "kingdoms." This is the
implicit historical logic of the Declaration of Independence. By using
the term "kingdom" of nature, Emerson quietly echoes the Declaration
by associatively conjuring both the axioms of natural right and the long
historical burden of monarchical-aristocratic suppression of these rights.
He picks up on the Declaration's claim that the kingdom (of George III)
in which the colonists found themselves living was not the kingdom
to which they were entitled as rational beings. In relation to "kingdom," then, the word "constitution" takes on its full historical-political
significance—as the principal means by which natural rights were finally secured. What Emerson seems to be suggesting by invoking natural right and by playing on the double meaning of "constitution" in a
section of his essay devoted to moral beauty is that "constitution" in the
personal, moral sense has important implications for "constitution" in
the public, political sense. By conjoining these two levels of meaning,
Emerson refigures in his own distinctive fashion the reciprocal argument
familiar from Montesquieu and the writings of the founders—that the
spirit of the laws shapes the character of the people, but the character of
the people also shapes the spirit of the laws. The success of liberal democracy, in other words, depends as much on the virtue of its citizens as
on the wisdom of its legislators. The legal "constitution" of the nation

derives its strength and stability in part from the moral "constitution" of the people.

To speak of "virtue," democracy, and the American founding all together in this fashion is to raise the question of classical republicanism. And this question becomes more inevitable as we read further in the paragraph we have been discussing. After establishing analogies between beauty, morality, and politics, Emerson goes on to provide a long list of historical exemplars:

> When a noble act is done—perchance in a scene of great natural beauty; when Leonidas and his three hundred martyrs consume one day in dying, and the sun and moon come each and look at them once in the steep defile of Thermopylae; when Arnold Winkelried, in the high Alps, under the shadow of the avalanche, gathers in his side a sheaf of Austrian spears to break the line for his comrades; are not these heroes entitled to add the beauty of the scene to the beauty of the deed? When the bark of Columbus nears the shore of America;— before it, the beach lined with savages, fleeing out of all their huts of cane; the sea behind; and the purple mountains of the Indian Archipelago around, can we separate the man from the living picture? Does not the New World clothe his form with her palm-groves and savannahs as fit drapery? Ever does natural beauty steal in like air, and envelope great actions. When Sir Harry Vane was dragged up the Tower-hill, sitting on a sled, to suffer death, as the champion of the English laws, one of the multitude cried out to him, "You never sate on so glorious a seat." Charles II, to intimidate the citizens of London, caused the patriot Lord Russel[l] to be drawn in an open coach, through the principal streets of the city, on his way to the scaffold. "But," his biographer says, "the multitude imagined they saw liberty and virtue sitting by his side." (*E&L* 16–17)

In the 1960s and 1970s, the historiography of the American founding underwent a drastic and now very influential revision. On the basis of his reading of hundreds of political pamphlets from the revolutionary period, Bernard Bailyn argued that the ideology of the revolutionary leaders was based less on Lockean liberal principles than it was on classical-republican terms and concepts derived from the writings of Bolingbroke, Trenchard and Gordon, Algernon Sydney, and a number of other writers from the "Atlantic Republican" tradition.[13] While both the Lockean and the classical-republican traditions were essentially democratic, the latter was far more communitarian, nostalgic, and conservative in spirit. Where Lockean liberalism emphasized individual rights, property, contract, the virtues of commerce, tolerance, and the protection of the private sphere, classical republicanism emphasized democratic participation, sacrifice, patriotism, public duty, and civic virtue—in general, the subordination of the individual's private, selfish interests to the interest of the polis or patria as a whole.[14] Furthermore, where Lockean liberalism saw commerce as conducive to prudence, good manners, and the breakdown of provincial prejudice, classical republicanism viewed commerce suspiciously as a source of moral corruption—as conducive to divisive economic inequalities and an enervating preoccupation with luxury and material ease.[15]

This "republican revision," as it has come to be called, generated much debate. On one side, the historian Gordon Wood seconded Bailyn in stressing the importance of classical-republican ideology in his influential account of *The Creation of the American Republic.* And the political theorist Michael Sandel has more recently invoked this tradition in attempting to revive the spirit of community and civic responsibility in American political life.[16] On the other side, scholars such as Thomas Pangle, Isaac Kramnick, and John Patrick Diggins have sharply questioned the republican revision, raising doubts about the historical accuracy of Bailyn's and Wood's claims and suggesting, in any case, that there are resources within Lockean liberalism to address the important moral and civic concerns of communitarian political theorists such as Sandel.[17] Scholars such as Joyce Appleby and David Ericson have taken a third, more moderate position, arguing that classical republicanism must be understood as one pole within the larger and historically more influential discourse of classical, or Lockean, liberalism.[18] They argue that the founders and other decisive shapers of the American political tradition such as Lincoln were essentially Lockean liberals at the core, but that in times of perceived need they drew upon the sterner moral rhetoric of classical republicanism to elicit feelings of national cohesiveness and a sense of shared purpose. Pangle, initially a severe critic of the republican revision in his role as an intellectual historian, moved toward this middle position in his role as a cultural critic. In *The Ennobling of Democracy,* he called upon American intellectuals to address what he saw as a crisis of confidence in the basic values of our society by rediscovering the bracing moral vision of the classical-republican portion of our heritage.[19]

I sketch this historiographical debate at this juncture of my reading of *Nature* because I believe the long passage quoted above raises the question of Emerson's sense of his own and his country's political origins.

Upon first reading, the brief genealogy of political virtue provided by Emerson in this passage seems to be far more classical republican than classical liberal in its moral tone. Almost all of the instances of great virtue to which Emerson alludes are acts of public self-sacrifice. Leonidas epitomizes the Spartan ethic of self-abnegation and solidarity as he leads the three hundred in their fatally heroic stand against the Persian hordes at Thermopylae. Arnold Winkelried, Harry Vane, Lord Russell, Socrates, Phocion, and Jesus are similarly selfless in giving up their lives in the service of their states, nations, city-states, or humankind as a whole. It would be hard to imagine a list of heroes standing in starker contrast to the liberal emphasis on the private pursuit of self-interest. Indeed, the predominant tone of civic heroism, patriotism, martial valor, and martyrdom that pervades this passage cuts strongly against the soft, bourgeois, individualistic, and commercial ethos of classical liberalism. We would seem here to be in the republican territory of Rousseau rather than the liberal territory of Locke, Montesquieu, and Hume.

But one can also discern a subsidiary current of countervailing liberal feeling in the passage above. Emerson starts by quoting Sallust: "All those things for which men plough, build, or sail, obey virtue" (*E&L* 16). After a corroborating quotation from Gibbon, he then provides the sequence of civic martyrs in roughly chronological order—from the classical Leonidas through the late medieval Winkelried to the early modern figures Harry Vane and Lord Russell. He also includes Columbus in this list at the appropriate historical interval, although Columbus does not really fit the profile of self-sacrifice. And at the conclusion of the list, just after quoting Lord Russell's biographer, Emerson turns from the public to the private sphere: "In private places, among sordid objects, an act of truth or heroism seems at once to draw to itself the sky as its temple, the sun as its candle" (*E&L* 17). With this passage as its conclusion, the sequence as a whole can be seen to follow a recognizable historical trajectory. It has moved from the classical-republican polis (Leonidas), to the late medieval emergence of nation-states (Winkelried), to the Renaissance discovery of the New World (Columbus), to the early modern struggle for rights and constitutional self-government (Harry Vane and Lord Russell), to what Emerson sees as the contemporary freedom, dignity, and potential for moral excellence of the ordinary private individual. It is not incidental that Emerson's last two martyrs here are the English Whig heroes Harry Vane and Lord Russell, because the passage as a whole may be accurately described as a capsule version of the "Whig" or "liberal" interpretation of history summarized in chapter 1. It is important to establish this connection here because it adds force to the current of liberal feeling that runs beneath the generally republican tone of the long passage above. Classical republicanism in the eighteenth and nineteenth centuries was, as I have suggested, fundamentally nostalgic and conservative in its attitude toward history. It looked suspiciously on those developments of modern life such as finance capitalism, urbanization, commercialization, technology, and professional mobility that seemed to have the effect of uprooting people from traditional homogeneous communities. Classical liberals such as Hume or Adam Smith, by contrast, viewed with optimism the same broad historical trends that classical republicans viewed with fear. They saw the expansion of commerce and industry, the growth of cities, the spread of free markets, the improvement of technology, and greater personal mobility as decisive agents in the slow emancipation of the great mass of human beings from their long history of ignorance, illness, prejudice, and servitude. In this passage, Emerson implicitly invokes this liberal-historical optimism by presenting his summary in the form of a progressively unfolding narrative. He does not look back nostalgically to Leonidas and Sparta as an ideal to which we must return; he presents the classical republic as the beginning of a long progression of which we are now the beneficiaries. Thanks in part to Winkelried, Columbus, Harry Vane, and Lord Russell, ordinary people may now achieve a moral dignity equivalent to that of Leonidas. One can be truthful and thus heroic even "in private places, among sordid objects."

Emerson condenses this sweeping minihistory even further in the summary that concludes this section:

> A virtuous man is in unison with her [Nature's] works, and makes the central figure in the visible sphere. Homer, Pindar, Socrates, Phocion, associate themselves fitly in our memory with the geography and climate of Greece. The visible heavens and earth sympathize with Jesus. And in common life, whosoever has seen a person of powerful character and happy genius, will have remarked how easily he took all things along with him,—the persons, the opinions, and the day, and nature became ancillary to a man. (*E&L* 17)

Here the same broad trajectory we traced above is simplified into three stages: classical, Christian, and modern. Emerson again moves from the public and heroic ethos of Homer, Pindar, Socrates, and Phocion to the unassuming private world of an anonymous "person" of modern "common life." Christianity plays a transitional role in reorienting human beings from the martial and civic values of classical Greece to a more inward-looking modernity. Emerson again describes this general pattern of development in a positive, optimistic tone. And again, as has been true throughout *Nature,* he expresses his affirmation in the counter-Lockean terms of orderly wholes. As we have seen him do in his introduction to *Nature,* in his chapter on commodity, and in the first "phenomenological" section of this chapter, in these historical sketches Emerson figures his distinctive conception of liberal-political virtue as an integrated, harmonious, balanced, and therefore aesthetically pleasing relationship of part to whole—of individual to nature. The virtuous individual lives "in proportion" to nature, in conformity to her laws. What is important to notice and keep in mind, however, is that Emerson's preoccupation with integrating parts into wholes does not lead him, as one might expect, to embrace classical republicanism's communitarian conception of virtue. As my analysis of the historical sketches above illustrates, in *Nature* Emerson draws on classical republicanism in much the same manner that Appleby and Ericson have suggested that Jefferson and most of the other founders did—as a resource for civic inspiration contained within and transcended by the larger, more optimistic, more progressive, more cosmopolitan, and more individualistic historical perspective of Enlightenment liberalism.

In the third and last section of "Beauty" Emerson adds a discussion of "intellectual" beauty to the discussions of "phenomenological" and "moral [political]" beauty that I have already reviewed. Because this section shares a focus on epistemological issues with the final three chapters of *Nature* (6, 7, and 8) I will reserve commenting upon it until I take up these chapters. For the same reason I will also now skip over chapter 4, "Language." This allows me to move directly to chapter 5, "Discipline," which I believe follows logically from the discussion of moral (political) beauty I have just examined. In conclusion, I will then take up together the epistemological concerns of chapter 4, the final part of chapter 5, and all of chapters 6, 7, and 8.

Emerson's short discussion of "Discipline" in chapter 5 of *Nature* states powerfully a crucial but recently overlooked aspect of his philosophy. Because of the optimistic tone of much of Emerson's writing, it is easy to miss the action within it of a stern and remorseless moral mechanism. Like the Hindu and Persian poets, the Greek tragedians, Plutarch,

Dante, and many others among the countless moralists whom he was fond of reading, Emerson believed that the universe was constructed in such a way that personal moral choices put grand cosmic forces into motion. Base, evil, or even merely narrowly selfish choices elicited fateful punishment, while good choices earned commensurate rewards. The form of retribution or compensation was not always immediately or superficially obvious, but one's ultimate misery or happiness was inevitably the product of one's own moral will or the lack of it. For Emerson, the most palpable effects were psychological. He had faith that good actions helped to build reservoirs of strength, assurance, and well-being at the deeper inner levels of a person's character, while bad actions corroded and undermined one's selfhood. It was not radical subjectivism but rather the clarity and consistency of this transcultural moral meta-principle that led Emerson to insist so emphatically that each individual was the author of his or her own destiny.

Here as elsewhere in his thought, Emerson's grounding in the classics played an important role.[20] Although Emerson is rarely given credit for a tragic sensibility, the moral principle I have been describing had something in common with the respect for natural limits that Greek tragedy sought to inculcate.[21] Like the Greek tragic authors and the Stoic philosophers, Emerson believed that human beings lived in a grand, exquisitely balanced, but implacably severe moral cosmos. Virtue for Emerson, as for Plato and the Stoics, required aligning one's actions with the principles of this cosmos. The reward for such attunement was nothing less than a harmonious, contented inner life. The failure to observe these principles, on the other hand, brought inner discord, anxiety, guilt, even madness. From Homer to Plutarch, classical literature is filled with anecdotes about people whose heedlessness brings on the wrath of the gods in the form of psychic suffering. Emerson read these anecdotes not as artifacts of a historically remote culture but rather as narrative testimony of a living moral truth. To Emerson's mind, the counter-Lockean Enlightenment had improved upon Calvin by rediscovering the rationally intelligible moral cosmos of the Greeks, particularly the Stoics. His optimism came in large part from his joyful apprehension of the metaphysical transparency of this cosmos. But along with classical metaphysical clarity came classical moral severity. Emerson never tired of reminding his audiences that knowledge of the moral law was cause at once for great joy and great caution.

Emerson did not himself need to specify or codify the content of the moral law because he believed it was amply illustrated in the literature not only of the Greeks but of all cultures that had left a written record. Emerson believed that world literature, especially religious literature, at once reflected and contributed to the formation of what he saw as a universal moral sense. The Greek tragedians and moralists, the Hebrew prophets, Confucius, the authors of the Indian wisdom books, Jesus, Hafiz, Dante, Milton, Benjamin Franklin, and countless anonymous authors of folk proverbs all seemed to agree that the difference between right and wrong was intuitively evident to all reasonable people. Abstruse theories were unnecessary. Moderation and pursuit of one's more generous inclinations lead to happiness, while excess, selfishness, and heedlessness of the right lead to sorrow. In his own personal life Emerson had seen one of his brothers brought to emotional collapse by the relatively mild sin of excessive professional and scholarly zeal.[22] And he himself suffered from a bout of mysterious blindness partially attributed to stress.[23] One feels something of the weight of these encounters with existential limits as well as the youthful deaths of his first wife and two younger brothers from tuberculosis when Emerson observes ominously of nature in the sixth and seventh paragraphs of "Discipline," "she pardons no mistakes. Her yea is yea, and her nay, nay. . . . [Her] dice are always loaded" (*E&L* 27).

In the central and strongest paragraphs of "Discipline," Emerson argues that the moral law is not only plainly visible in every detail of the natural world but is worked by experience into the deep fabric of human feeling:

> All things are moral; and in their boundless changes have an unceasing reference to spiritual nature. Therefore is nature glorious with form, color, and motion, that every globe in the remotest heaven; every chemical change from the rudest crystal up to the laws of life; every change of vegetation from the first principle of growth in the eye of a leaf, to the tropical forest and antediluvian coal-mine; every animal function from the sponge up to Hercules, shall hint or thunder to man the laws of right and wrong, and echo the Ten Commandments. (*E&L* 28)

> The moral law lies at the center of nature and radiates to the circumference. It is the pith and marrow of every substance, every relation, and every process. All things with which we deal preach to us. (*E&L* 29)

It would be difficult to imagine a more sweeping, thoroughgoing, and confident statement of moral foundationalism. It is passages like this, and there are many similar ones throughout Emerson's opus, that lead me to disagree so strongly with West, Bloom, Poirier, and other postmodern commentators. Far from "transgressive" (West), "cheerfully amoral" (Bloom), or convinced of "the futility of [the] search for truth, values, and exaltations" (Poirier), Emerson declares himself here as the enthusiastic prophet of a universal, objective, and eminently wise moral law.[24] This law is not only central and self-subsistent, it is pervasive throughout nature, and as such it is eminently knowable. Having already represented nature in general as a network of overlapping orderly wholes, Emerson places the moral law as the common structuring principle — the metaphysical fiber, as it were — that binds nature's many parts together. Because all the various areas of human endeavor and inquiry are similarly grounded in the moral law, they are all analogously organized. It is not incidental that Emerson uses the word "every" a total of nine times in the two paragraphs from which these quotes were taken. The moral law as he understands it is emphatically universal in its application.

Emerson not only proclaims the ubiquity of the moral law in these two paragraphs, he also indicates how we come to know it. This is the function of a pervasive idiom of absorption, reception, and interiority. By using such terms as "center," "pith," "marrow," "impregnate," "sink into," "penetrate," "sponge," and "deep source" (*E&L* 29), Emerson emphasizes his conviction that morality is not principally a matter of analytical reasoning. As was the case for his Scottish-influenced preceptors, moral response for Emerson was more a function of deep feeling than of abstract ratiocination. This is also why he uses the terms "sense" and "sentiment" in these paragraphs. In becoming moral we do not master a code, a set of rules, or even a Kantian process of moral reasoning. By observing nature and by learning from our own experiences, we develop a sixth sense, an intuition, a feeling "in our bones." The process is one of slow organic infiltration and internalization rather than of mental mastery. The moral law "scents the air," "grows in the grain," "impregnates the waters of the world," and thus "is caught by man and sinks into his soul." We learn "firmness" from "the sea-beaten rock," "tranquility" from "the azure sky," "industry, providence, and affection" from "the brutes," and "self-command" from "the phenomenon of Health" (*E&L* 29). As we grow up and have more contact with a world suffused with moral meaning, we slowly become more morally sentient.

The tone is mostly celebratory here, but the underlying severity of which I have spoken is implicit in terms such as "law" itself, "right and wrong," "thunder," "Ten Commandments," "prophet and priest,"

"David and Isaiah," and "pith and marrow" (*E&L* 28–29). Emerson has moved far from the Calvinism of his forebears, but he has retained its moral intensity.[25] There is no question here of a willful God's arbitrary damnation. But Emerson makes it clear that he has not lapsed into moral laxity, relativism, or even pragmatism. A thinker so thoroughly convinced of the pervasively moral construction of the universe is unlikely to counsel transgression. Indeed, for Emerson the moral law was so deeply worked into the fabric of nature that painful retribution was as certain as the pull of gravity, the sequence of the seasons, or the kickback, as he later put it, of a fired gun.

The sternest of the many stern moments of "Discipline" is found in the only two paragraphs that touch on politics. In the third paragraph Emerson sketches a brief etiology of what he calls "the common sense," or "the Hand of the mind" (*E&L* 26). He first evokes a general quality of mature competence—of daily practical effectiveness in the mundane world. Roughly equivalent to what classical moralists called "prudence," it is a capacity for foresight, careful weighing of means and ends, and accurate tallying of moral costs and benefits. As with other lessons of the moral law, this characteristic is only acquired by much painful experience. "What tedious training," he writes, "day after day, year after year, never ending, to form the common sense; what continual reproduction of annoyances, inconveniences, dilemmas; what rejoicings over us of little men; what disputing of prices, what reckonings of interest" (*E&L* 26). Emerson then broadens his argument dramatically by suggesting that this important moral quality is especially well inculcated by the liberal institution of private property:

> The same good office is performed by Property and its filial systems of debt and credit. Debt, grinding debt, whose iron face the widow, the orphan, and the sons of genius fear and hate;—debt, which consumes so much time, which so cripples and disheartens a great spirit with cares that seem so base, is a preceptor whose lessons cannot be foregone, and is needed most by those who suffer from it most. Moreover, property, which has been well compared to snow,—"if it fall level to-day, it will be blown into drifts to-morrow,"—is the surface action of internal machinery, like the index on the face of a clock. Whilst now it is the gymnastics of the understanding, it is hiving in the foresight of the spirit, experience in profounder laws. (*E&L* 26–27)

Emerson here renders in his own idiom two standard arguments of classical-liberal political morality. John Locke, David Hume, Adam

Smith, Benjamin Franklin, and John Stuart Mill, to name a few, believed that one of most valuable effects of liberal laissez-faire capitalism was that it forced its participants to become disciplined. They believed that in order to compete, survive, and flourish in the unforgiving rough and tumble of the marketplace, one had no choice but to develop virtues of prudence, frugality, orderliness, moderation, and self-control. The unequal accumulation of property characteristic of liberal-capitalist societies was for them the inevitable fallout of the differing levels of skill, diligence, and virtue that individual players brought to the game. Far from evidence of injustice or immorality, the acquisition of wealth was a sign of moral superiority. In the first of what would be many similar statements over the course of his career, Emerson here emphatically endorses this tough-minded outlook.[26]

The moral logic of laissez-faire liberal capitalism appealed to Emerson on several levels. For one, it suited perfectly his distinctive tendency to think in terms of analogies and dynamic orderly wholes—a tendency of which we have by now seen numerous examples. Emerson's imagination could not resist the vivid analogy between, on the one hand, his own conception of nature as a grand dynamic cosmic order benignly governing all human experience and, on the other hand, the Smithian concept of an "invisible hand" working behind the scenes to guide a vast array of economic processes and institutions toward maximum productivity and efficiency.[27] For Emerson, such analogies were never merely verbal accidents. On the contrary, he believed that they reflected underlying metaphysical truths. The fact that a clear analogy could be drawn between his own metaphors for the natural order and the Smithian metaphor for the economic order suggested to Emerson that both metaphors were probably on target; they probably both provided accurate figurative representations of how things really are. The aptness of the analogy suggested not merely a happy linguistic accident or shared ideological interests but rather kindred insights into what Emerson would call elsewhere "the power and order at the heart of things." This is the significance of the snow-property passage quoted above.

The analogy implies that property is "natural" on two levels. First, on a local, particular level, it is like snow in its susceptibility to concentrated accumulation. It tends, one might say more simply, to pile up. Second, on a broader level, property is like nature in its general structure. Like all natural phenomena for Emerson, property is essentially symbolic; it is a concrete material manifestation of an underlying moral-metaphysical order. In my discussion just above of Emerson's conception of the moral law, I suggested that he believed that human fates were somehow the expression of a remorseless moral-metaphysical mechanism. Here Emerson suggests that property is similarly structured: it is "the surface action of internal machinery, like the index on the face of a clock." This broad mechanistic analogy is no less significant than the preceding snow analogy. By figuring property as analogous to nature on both a phenomenological and a deep structural level, Emerson implies that the possession of property is more than merely the result of a given individual's luck or success in the scramble for resources. It is evidence of obedience to nature's laws, which is the basis of moral virtue. To find oneself in debt is morally edifying because it forces one to begin to face up to precisely the harsh, exacting, unforgiving moral laws of which I have spoken. To overcome debt, to stay in the black, to acquire some property is to demonstrate that one has come to understand and to accept these harsh laws and to discipline oneself accordingly. Just as in the Puritans' Calvinist cosmos material wealth was a sign of salvation, in Emerson's liberal cosmos the acquisition and retention of a relatively large amount of property is evidence of one's mastery not only of the laws of the economic game but of the moral laws of nature herself. It is no accident that Emerson uses the word "foresight" here. The term "foresight of the spirit" suggests the preeminent classical-liberal virtue of prudence—precisely that impish Franklinian virtue wherein economic shrewdness and moral self-discipline are fruitfully joined together.

Emerson's class position played a part in predisposing him toward this conception of the morally educative value of property. As the son of the polished and socially well-connected minister of Boston's First Church, Emerson grew up among the New England Federalist elite. Although the Reverend William Emerson never achieved the material wealth of the many lawyers, merchants, and statesmen to whom he ministered, he was their social equal. He dined with the Adamses; he was a personal friend of the president of Harvard; he served as the chaplain of the state legislature; and he was esteemed as a moral and cultural leader. He did leave his wife and five boys in severely straitened circumstances when he died prematurely in 1811. But four of the Emerson boys managed to complete the Harvard education and make the professional contacts necessary to maintain their standing as part of the Northeast's powerful cultural and economic aristocracy. In the Emerson boys' generation this generally meant Whig rather than Federalist

politics, but the consciousness of elite social position and elite responsibilities for leadership remained constant—along with elite condescen-
sion toward the unwashed masses then emerging behind Andrew Jackson as a new and—to the Emersons—frightening political force.[28]

So when Emerson speaks of the moral benefits of property we must
keep in mind that he is speaking in part as a member of the propertied
class. Although his family had struggled to make ends meet and his own
genius had been temporarily "crippled and disheartened" by the burden of teaching school to help pay for his brothers' educations, the experience of debt was softened for him by advantages alien to the many
whom "grinding" debt's "iron face" was driving toward a fundamental
reshaping of the American political landscape.[29]

The above paragraph in praise of "property and its filial systems
of debt and credit" thus reflects a degree of political "conservatism"
on Emerson's part. But it is necessary to define this word very carefully.
The moral defense of capitalism expressed periodically throughout
Emerson's opus is clearly consistent with the ruggedly individualistic
outlook of American conservative thought running from Alexander
Hamilton through John Quincy Adams to Abraham Lincoln, Calvin
Coolidge, and Ronald Reagan.[30] The many young businesspeople who
have drawn on Emerson for moral support in their quest for success in
the capitalist marketplace have not thereby distorted the spirit of his
thought. But from a larger historical perspective, the question must be
raised regarding the extent to which this mainstream American ideology of individualism, free markets, competitive striving, and upward
mobility may be appropriately understood as "conservative." On the
whole, the major theorists of classical-liberal political thought have seen
their project as dedicated to emancipatory change rather than to the
preservation for their own sake of time-honored customs, traditions,
and authorities. Irving Kristol has observed of Adam Smith that he was
proud to count himself as among his generation's most progressive,
forward-looking, undogmatic, and generously sympathetic men.[31] The
same may certainly be said of Locke, Montesquieu, Hume, Franklin,
James Madison, Wilhelm von Humboldt, Benjamin Constant, Mill, or
Tocqueville. While most of these thinkers recognized the value of social
stability, civic order, meaningful moral authority, and generational continuity, they generally invoked these principles as checks on overly rapid
change rather than as dogmatic bulwarks against change per se. For all
of them, as for Emerson, the capitalist free market—"property and its

filial systems of credit and debt"—was understood principally as an agent of progress and liberation. It was a solvent of the feudal chains that for so long had prevented the unaffiliated "private poor man" from exercising his energies and talents to improve the material conditions of his life. It was a vast and dynamic force that held out the hope of unprecedented levels of economic well-being for ordinary people. And they believed that even as capitalism broke the chains of feudal social bondage it would help to form softer, more supple, but ultimately stronger social ties based not on enforced servitude but rather on mutual interest, politeness, prudence, and cosmopolitan civility. It is a paradox of American economic and political history that the system that American "conservatives" have sought to conserve has been revolutionary in its broadest historical effects. Emerson's *Nature* and much of his subsequent writing is indeed "conservative," but only in this paradoxical American sense. His is a moderate, progressive, liberal conservatism fundamentally at odds with the nostalgic, reactionary conservatism of, say, Joseph-Marie de Maistre, the later Thomas Carlyle, or John Calhoun. Indeed, as we shall see in a later chapter, Emerson's most highly developed and explicit political ideas were formulated in direct opposition to the conservative outlook of Calhoun (and his various disciples) during the national debate over slavery in the 1850s.

Most of the remaining epistemological sections of *Nature* are devoted to celebrating the liberation of man's faculties by means of their attunement to nature's permanent laws. To summarize broadly, we can say that in these sections Emerson situates the knowing self at the nexus of an overlapping set of analogously structured orderly wholes. Language, the explicit subject of chapter 4 and a major subtopic of chapters 6 and 8, provides the symbolic ligature of interconnection between these various spheres of experience. Poetic metaphor especially has the power to articulate a vast and intricate network of analogies between the self and nature. Emerson characterizes these analogies not in the manner of contemporary poststructuralists as contingent constructions of particular cultures but rather in the idealist manner of Coleridge or Plotinus as evidences of an underlying metaphysical order. "It is easily seen that there is nothing lucky or capricious in these analogies," he writes, "but that they are constant, and pervade nature" (*E&L* 21). The faculty by which we apprehend these pervasive analogies, Emerson suggests, is akin to the faculty by which we dream, or pray, or meditate, or read, or write poetry. It is an intuitive, imaginative, and associative faculty awakened in us by an open-minded attentiveness to natural phenomenon, to literature of every stripe, and, perhaps most importantly, to ordinary experience. Emerson explicitly distinguishes this faculty from the strictly methodical and analytical faculty employed in empirical science, but he retains for it the honorific name we usually associate with scientific pursuits—"reason." By expanding the meaning of this term in *Nature* to include a wide range of mental activities usually deemed to be less than rational, Emerson attempts to claim for his own intuitive approach a place in the long legacy of Western rationalism. And he remains confident throughout that the most exalted aims of this tradition are readily within his and his readers' grasp. Toward the end of chapter 6, for example, he reiterates without rhetorical fanfare the same bold claim for which the "transparent eyeball" passage is so famous. "We apprehend the absolute," he writes with calm declarative assurance. "As it were, for the first time, *we exist*" (*E&L* 37).

In the concluding paragraph of *Nature* Emerson revisits several of what I have suggested are the most important thematic sites of the essay as a whole:

> So shall we come to look at the world with new eyes. . . . For you is the phenomenon perfect. What we are, that only can we see. All that Adam had, all that Caesar could, you have and can do. Adam called his house, heaven and earth; Caesar called his house, Rome; you perhaps call yours, a cobler's trade, a hundred acres of ploughed land; or a scholar's garret. Yet line for line and point for point, your dominion is as great as theirs, though without fine names. Build, therefore, your own world. As fast as you conform your life to the pure idea in your mind, that will unfold its great proportions. A correspondent revolution in things will attend the influx of the spirit. (*E&L* 48)

Perhaps the most striking thing about reading *Nature* in 2009, I would suggest in closing, is just how little "vexed" or "precarious" it feels. On the contrary, one senses in reading it something akin to what one senses in reading Homer, Sophocles, Dante or Milton. Here at the late date of 1836 is an example of an author who lived in what György Lukács called an "integrated civilization."[32] Here is an author for whom the inner ideal and the historical reality of his political community are still commensurate. Here is an author who without reservation commanded a rich and coherent body of symbols and concepts that he deployed in the full confidence that they affirmed and extended the best values of his political-cultural community. The fact that this community is still in many ways our own gives this work a special poignancy and a special relevance.

4

Property, Culture

The Philosophy of History (1836–1837); Human Culture (1837–1838); Human Life (1838–1839); The Present Age (1839–1840); "The Divinity School Address" (1838); "History" (1841); "Compensation" (1841)

The distinctive eloquence and scope of Lord Acton's account of the history of liberty helped us to frame Emerson's sense of history in the foregoing chapters. But Acton's version has idiosyncrasies beyond its imposing Englishness. His Catholicism, for one thing, causes Acton to downplay the significance of the Reformation, which he associates principally with a variant of early modern absolutism. But most nineteenth-century liberals, Hegel not least among them, singled out Luther's great revolt as the principal deliverer of modern liberty—"the all illuminating sun which followed the dawn at the end of the Middle Ages," whose "essential content," grounded in "the old and well-tried *inwardness of the German people*" and discovered by a "simple monk," was that "human beings are by nature destined to be free."[1] Acton's Catholic spirituality also caused him to minimize economics. He only grudgingly grants the importance of commerce and emerging capitalism to the advancement of liberty, acknowledging the special contributions of Hume, Adam Smith, and Macaulay in highlighting these factors but rejecting their point of view as too narrowly materialistic. Acton thus aligns himself with the Burkean side of what J. W. Burrow describes as a Victorian-Whig historical tradition divided between a Scottish-influenced "modern" school and the longer-headed Burkean adherents of the organic-Saxon myth.[2] For the purposes of this chapter it is now necessary to briefly fill out the Burkean with the Scottish "modern" strain of Victorian Whiggism because Emerson's early essays and lectures characteristically weave both of them, along with no little Protestant inwardness, together.

England and the English were the heroes of modernity for Hume, Smith, and the Scots, as they would come to be for Acton, but rather because the revolution of 1688 ensured the economic liberties of the emerging middle classes than because of the ancient constitution or a primordial Saxon instinct for freedom. The stark contrast between the "opulent," "polite," "commercial" civilization of postsettlement Edinburgh or Glasgow, on the one hand, and the impoverished, violent, and increasingly desperate culture of the traditional agrarian Highlands, on the other, gave eighteenth-century Scottish intellectuals a sharp sense of historical progress and a secure belief in the progressive benefits of capitalism and "doux commerce." For them, most importantly, the main vehicle of progress was the evolution of an abstract idea of property. This was most clearly formulated in a four-stage conception of human history, the original authorship of which seems to have been a matter of private dispute, but which provides the common underlying narrative schema of no less a set of historical works than David Hume's *Essays: Moral, Political, and Literary* (1779) and *The History of England* (1786); William Robertson's *History of Scotland* (1759), *A View of the Progress of Society in Europe* (1769), and *History of America* (1777); Adam Ferguson's *An Essay on the History of Civil Society* (1767); Lord Kames's *Historical Law Tracts* (1758) and *Sketches of the History of Man* (1774); John Millar's *An Historical View of the English Government* (1803) and *The Origin of the Distinction of Ranks* (1779); Adam Smith's *Lectures on Jurisprudence* (1978) and *An Inquiry into the Nature and Causes of the Wealth of Nations* (1776); and Edward Gibbon's *The History of the Rise and Fall of the Roman Empire* (1776).[3] We know for certain that Emerson read Hume, Robertson, Smith, and Gibbon in his early, intellectually formative years.[4] (Some scholars at the time and recently have judged Robertson to be the most widely read historian in America from 1800 to 1820.)[5] And Emerson's Unitarian teachers at Harvard certainly read Ferguson as well.[6]

According to Scottish "conjectural" history, human beings have advanced naturally over time from (1) hunting and gathering to (2) herding, (3) farming, and (4) commerce as their means of subsistence. Corresponding to this progression, and to some extent enabling its transformations, has been a crucial evolution of the concept of property. In the first "savage" hunter-gatherer phase there was, strictly speaking, no abstract conception of property at all but merely a basic notion of immediate, concrete, and temporary "possession." Entirely immersed in the present, the most primitive Amerindian, according to the Scots, thought no further than the foodstuff he or she could physically hold and devour or the wild animal he or she could immediately kill and eat. In the second phase, herding societies were said to begin to develop an abstract notion of property insofar as they understood tamed animals to be owned by a given herdsman if these animals would physically return to him when lost or stolen. This conception was then taken an important step further when symbolic marking of herds made it possible to associate a given animal with an "owner" regardless of distance or estrangement. Agricultural societies advanced further still to the extent that a given farmer's land could be understood to be his own even while he was not farming it or living contiguously with it, and in some cases a farmer could "alienate" his land in the form of trade or sale. Finally, in the fourth, "commercial" stage, rational division of labor exponentially multiplied human productivity, and stable and trustworthy laws made it possible for now abundant properties, including land, to be unrestrictedly abstracted and "alienable" in the form of "credit notes and bills of exchange."[7] Only then did human societies achieve the comparatively astonishing levels of "opulence" characteristic of the major cities of eighteenth-century Western Europe and North America. And with such increased general levels of "opulence" came increased general levels of freedom and dignity and even general morality and intelligence. For each individual to have property of his or her own and the freedom to exchange it, invest it, or add to it as he or she saw fit, Adam Smith argued, was the only sure antidote to the morally abominable but historically commonplace practice of slavery, not to mention the only slightly less demeaning forms of feudal servitude. And for a person to learn to reckon with symbolic representation in the form of money was to begin to develop the capacity for abstract cognition of many kinds, including philosophical, moral, and scientific speculation, or artistic production and appreciation. Starting in the newly emergent towns of the early modern era, "commerce and manufactures gradually introduced order and good government, and with them, the liberty and security of individuals, among the inhabitants of the country, who had before lived in an almost continual state of war with their neighbors, and of servile dependency on their superiors."[8] In short, for Smith and the authors of the Scottish Enlightenment, an abstract conception of property was the principal catalyst of human progress.

Four series of public lectures Emerson gave from 1836 to 1840—The Philosophy of History (1836–1837), Human Culture (1837–1838), Human Life (1838–1839), and The Present Age (1839–1840)—at once assume and expound a version of this Anglo-Scottish liberal-progressive conception of history, including its special emphasis on property. Indeed, this large group of lectures as a whole, delivered over a four-year period, has a striking historical coherence and completeness, and thus can be seen as an important stage in the distillation and refinement of Emerson's own historical outlook. He raises to a higher level of clarity the liberal sense of history we saw him beginning to develop in his first notebooks and in *Nature*, and thus secures the liberal orientation underlying the early essays and addresses.

The titles of the first two series themselves may be taken as a further clarification of Emerson's historical vocation: starting with the publication of *Nature* (1836), he had begun trying to develop a "culture," a network of affectively commanding concepts and symbols, appropriate to what he has come to understand as his society's new and distinctive position in—and beyond—"history." He thus covers a lot of ground in these lectures, including some now-familiar favorite topics. To start with, he calls for more psychologically intimate forms of history writing: "Is number the only preference; war the only association; and battle the only crisis?" (*EL* 2:9). He notes the parallel progressive currents of cosmos, society, and individual: "The upward movement in society dating from the beginning of the world and including in it, as a concert of a thousand tongues, every inspired man, and every beneficent revolution, has for its end to teach the Doctrine of the Soul: Who it is that lives this human life and to what end?" (*EL* 2:14). He celebrates the shift from martial to commercial values: "[Trade] makes peace and keeps peace," "it sharpens the faculties and stimulates the pulse. It mingles all nations in its marts" (*EL* 2:160–61). And he tries to arrive at a new progressive definition of culture: "Culture in the high sense does not consist in polishing and varnishing, but in so presenting the attractions of nature that the slumbering attributes of man may burst their sleep and rush into day" (*EL* 2:216). But there is a central historical red thread running through all of these and drawing them together. For Emerson as for Hegel, the English, American, and French revolutions of the seventeenth and eighteenth centuries, and the ongoing liberal revolutions of the nineteenth century, all portend a profound, world-historical shift in the structure of human societies. Whereas for most of human history the good of the individual had been subordinated to the interests of the society as a whole, now the concept of rights has reversed this tendency and given the individual decisive legal priority over the collective:

> An attentive observer will easily see, by comparing the character of the institutions and books of the present day, with those of any other former period—say of ancient Judea, or the Greek, or Italian era, or the Reformation or the Elizabethan age of England—that the tone and aims are totally changed. The former men acted and spoke under the thought that a shining social prosperity was the aim of men, and compromised ever the individuals to the nation. The modern mind teaches (in extremes) that the nation exists for the individual; for the guardianship and education of every man. (*EL* 2:213)

For Emerson, the advent of societies based on rights is the moral-social equivalent of the Copernican revolution in astronomy. A long-hidden moral truth has been disclosed, and nothing is the same thereafter. The individual no longer revolves around the society, but rather society revolves—at a safe distance—around the individual, and the effects are liberating for both. "The individual finds his being not impoverished or curtailed on any side. For him the world expands in the glory of the first morning" (*EL* 2:173). "The individual heart faithful to itself is fenced with a sacred palisado not to be traversed or approached unto, and is free forevermore. And out of the strength and wisdom of the private heart shall go forth at another era the regeneration of society" (*EL* 2:186).

The imagery of "fence" and "palisado" is significant here. It anticipates the close of "The American Scholar," where Emerson proclaims: "The dread of man and the love of man shall be a wall of defence and a wreath of joy around all" (*E&L* 71). The same type of language crops up frequently, if more prosaically, in Locke. "As much land as a man tills, plants, improves, cultivates, and can use the product of, so much is his property," Locke writes in one crucial and characteristic passage of "The Second Treatise." "He by his labor does, as it were, *enclose* it from the common." Well-established laws and sound judges are then necessary, Locke writes, "to determine the rights, and *fence* the properties" of men who have thus emerged from the state of nature into civil society.[9] And in *A Letter Concerning Toleration* Locke speaks of "settl[ing] the just *bounds*" that lie between the "business of civil government" and "that of religion."[10] I do not mean to suggest that Emerson directly borrowed his "fence" metaphors from Locke but rather that the similar emphasis indicated by the shared symbolism helps to confirm the already strong likelihood of Locke's influence. The fence imagery reveals Emerson's perhaps unconscious assent to the "negative" character of the Lockean conception of rights with its principal concern, as Isaiah Berlin, among others, has noted, to set limits to the activities of government rather than to enlist political power in the service of "positive" moral ends.[11] Emerson's use of "fence" metaphors also expresses his perhaps unconscious assent to a Lockean tradition for which, as many scholars have noted, the right to property is the foundation of all the other rights. As Guido de Ruggiero put it some eighty years ago: "Property is a natural right of the individual, independent of the State, because it represents his most immediate field of action without which his formal independence and autonomy would be wholly empty. Only so far as he is an owner of property is he self-sufficient and able to resist encroachment by other individuals and the state."[12] Or, as Richard Pipes put it more recently, "The notion of 'inalienable rights,' which has played an increasing role in the political thought and practice of the West since the 17th century, grows out of the right to property, the most elementary of rights. One of its aspects is the principle that the sovereign rules but does not own and hence must not appropriate the belongings of subjects or violate their persons—a principle that erected a powerful barrier to political authority and permitted the evolution first of civil and then of political rights."[13]

. Emerson is therefore on solid Lockean liberal ground throughout these early lectures, as he takes the right to property as the starting point of an ever-widening virtuous circle. He begins with an unmistakably Lockean definition—"property is merely the obedience of nature to human labor" (*EL* 2:73–75)—and then expounds upon the multiple radiating benefits of a free and authentic engagement in this foundational relationship. Through honest labor an individual not only generates the material provision necessary for physical survival, satisfaction, and perhaps prosperity, but in the process discovers both his world and himself: "It is in the happy marriage of the faculty to the object that both are for the first time made known to us" (*EL* 2:113). One learns the laws of the universe in the microcosm of one's own métier: "The absolute balance of Give and Take: the doctrine that everything has its price; and that if not that price is paid, not that thing but something else is obtained; and that it is impossible and absurd to get anything without its price" (*EL* 2:127). And by action in obedience to these laws one establishes and begins to strengthen one's own identity: "In the gratification of his petty animal wants, he is taught, he is armed, he is exalted" (*EL* 2:115). Emerson has not moved so far from his roots in Calvinism as to lose touch with its work ethic or its emphasis on vocation. Indeed, it is an underappreciated feature of Emerson's writing as a whole that, from early to late, it offers a sustained hymn in praise of labor. In one of many exhortations in these early lectures he celebrates "the heroism of a calling": "A true-hearted man exerting himself earnestly in that mode he can, seeing his increase of power in his craft and the manifold benefits flowing out of it, comes to love his work for its own sake" (*EL* 2:124).

As the Calvinists well knew, such devotion to work yields tangible rewards. A person who is free to do what she or he loves is likely to do it better and more efficiently than someone who is merely maintaining family status or following in her or his parents' footsteps. "It is incredible what amounts of strength and wit that once slept inactive, and went to the grave unknown, are now strained to the utmost for the equal benefit of the workman and of society," Emerson writes. And thus "the present day is marked, as we have already had occasion to say, by the immense creation of property" (*EL* 2:160–61). Energetic, disciplined, efficient labor yields not only self-esteem but surplus. Surplus may be sold for profit or traded. Profits may be reinvested in better tools or technology, yielding greater efficiency and more surplus, which is then more widely traded, and so on. Trade across cultural or national borders increases international familiarity and thus decreases prejudice. "The growth of the property party destroys the war party and invites the arts and the embellishment of peace" (*EL* 2:73–75). Tolerance and commerce replace hostility and warfare. Thus, with the lever of work, the entire agrarian and martial feudal-aristocratic civilization is upended. And upon the foundation of work-earned property, a new industrial and commercial bourgeois-liberal order is established. "The constant progress of civilization of course tends to leave the individual at greater liberty: the policy of all governments is to unfetter trade. This serves among other good purposes mainly these; to make men acquainted with each other by commerce; and to make labor attractive, by allowing each to do what he can, and therefore what he likes best. The immense expansion of commerce since the discovery of America has wrought a signal revolution on the barbarous as on the Christian world" (*EL* 2:128).

For Emerson, as for the Scots, an abstract conception of property made progress possible. But for Emerson, as for most nineteenth-century liberals, the right to property had a conservative aspect as well. The fifth lecture of the series on the philosophy of history, entitled "Politics," is one of the most sustained political statements of Emerson's entire career, and in the context of Jacksonian democracy it can only be read as conservative:

> It is plain that there are two objects for whose protection government exists, 1. Persons, 2. Property. (*EL* 2:70)

> In a theory of government, this principle lies at the foundation, that property should make the law for property, and persons the law for persons. But to embody this theory in the forms of a government is not easy. For persons and property mix themselves in every transaction. . . . In fact, the nature of human society does so inextricably mix these two interests, that it becomes necessary that the same government, the same King, Council, Bench, Senate, House, should administer both; and the rightful distinction demanded is that the proprietors of the nation should have more elective franchise than nonproprietors. It was a Spartan maxim, "Call that which is just, equal, not that which is equal, just." (*EL* 2:72)

It is important to be clear about exactly what Emerson is proposing here. He begins again with the orthodox Lockean axiom that government exists for the protection of people and property. He then argues that, because people who own substantial amounts of property have more at stake in the state than those who do not, the former should have more votes than the latter. However shocking to our current democratic sensibilities, this idea was by no means novel within the transatlantic liberal tradition. A property qualification for the franchise was implicit in Locke, axiomatic for eighteenth- and nineteenth-century English Whigs, and held firmly in the nineteenth century even by "radical" middle-class "Manchester liberals" such as Richard Cobden.[14] In France at exactly this time François Guizot, the prime minister and intellectual leader of the governing moderate "Doctrinaire" liberals, vigorously opposed universal suffrage on similar grounds of protection of property.[15] And the American founders had taken pains to build electoral safeguards for the propertied class into the federal Constitution of 1789. The election of Andrew Jackson as president in 1828 under newly instituted federal laws of universal manhood suffrage and Jackson's continuing symbolic dominance of American politics up to the Civil War have been widely understood to represent a broad popular rejection of the rule of the propertied Virginia and Massachusetts elite. Emerson does not presume here to entirely roll back the Jacksonian revolution—he allows the continuation of universal manhood suffrage. But in the moderate manner of American Federalist or European aristocratic liberalism he does seek to counterbalance and mitigate democracy's potentially dangerous effects on matters of economic policy by granting extra votes to property owners.

It is hardly a realistic proposal for electoral reform, and I do not propose to take it as such. However, Emerson believed in it enough to include it verbatim in the essay entitled "Politics" in *Essays: Second Series* (1844), and it does reveal something important about his general political orientation in these years. As I detailed in my introduction, a long and distinguished line of political interpreters of Emerson has sought to assimilate him to the point of view of twentieth-century social democratic liberalism, which has its roots in nineteenth-century European socialism. The most distinguished recent contributor to this tradition, Sacvan Bercovitch, has even suggested that the early Emerson came "*to the edge* of class analysis" before falling back on his liberal roots in his later work.[16] And Michael Gilmore argues similarly that Emerson passed through "an anti-market" stage between 1837 and 1843 before "becoming an apologist for commercial and industrial capitalism."[17] But this lecture was delivered in 1838, in the midst of Emerson's so-called radical early stage, and it is hard to imagine a clearer repudiation of the egalitarian spirit of Jacksonianism, which was itself rather safely liberal by comparison to emerging European socialism. Emerson is indeed engaged in class politics here, but only of a conservative-liberal American Whig variety entirely in keeping with his own elite upper-middle-class status and akin to the cautious aristocratic liberalism of Hamilton or Madison in the United States, or Guizot in France, or to the middle-class liberalism of Cobden in England. Indeed, the position Emerson takes in the paragraphs above accords directly with that of his first intellectual milieu—the conservative-liberal Unitarian Whigs as described by Daniel Walker Howe: "The Liberal clergy of the Congregational establishments in New England had been traditional opponents of both 'levelism' and 'tyranny,' and defenders of mixed 'Aristocrato-Democratical' government. And so the antebellum Unitarians generally supported such devices as bicameral legislatures in which one house represented people and the other, properties' interests."[18]

To put Emerson in this conservative-liberal company, however, is not to say that he was oblivious to the potential spiritual dangers of the liberal valorization of property. Bercovitch, Gilmore, and the social democratic readers in general are not entirely off-base in calling our attention to Emerson's occasional scathing criticisms of what he saw as a kind of all-devouring materialism in antebellum American life. "Things are in the saddle, and ride mankind" is only the most catchy of many statements in which Emerson warns his readers of a real tendency in capitalist society toward what Marxists call the "reification" of all relationships.[19] And Carolyn Porter is right to point out that Emerson's underlying sense of "reality as an active process" (an intuition, she points out, he shared with Marx) inevitably came into painful friction with capitalism's apparent tendency to reduce all processes and ultimately all subjective being into consumable objects.[20] Even in the midst of one of his most triumphant celebrations of commerce as an agent of world-historical emancipation in "The Young American," for example, Emerson acknowledges this problem: "This is the good and this the evil of trade, that it would put everything into market, talent, beauty, virtue, and man himself" (*E&L* 221). But where Porter sees Emerson's resistance to reification as ultimately vitiated by his adoption of the liberal categories of the hegemonic capitalist class, I would suggest that Porter's Marxist radicalism allows a too-narrow range of legitimate resistance. Like his friends Carlyle and Thoreau, Emerson was profoundly attuned to the dangers of the potential commodification of consciousness in a commercial culture governed by what Carlyle himself had dubbed "the cash nexus." And, like Tocqueville, Emerson feared the insidious ordinariness and pervasiveness of this mentality in a mass democratic society. He understood that in a world flooded with readily acquired things it was all too easy for people to begin to imagine reality itself as a thing. And to be thus unable to contemplate a person, a place, or time itself from any point of view other than its material-economic utility was for Emerson the grimmest spiritual poverty. But Emerson also understood that free markets and private property were essential to the still fledgling emancipation of Western society from the thousand-year stranglehold of a tiny aristocratic elite. Therefore, just as the Federalist founders, whom Emerson never ceased to admire, sought "a republican remedy for the diseases most incident to republican government," Emerson sought a liberal remedy to the problems, of which reification is one, intrinsic to liberal society.[21] Just as Madison and Hamilton looked to the large size of the American republic as a counterpoise to the historical tendency of small republics to be destroyed by faction, or to the judiciary branch as a counterpoise to the legislative, or to the Senate as a counterpoise to the House of Representatives, so Emerson looked to the spiritually elevating power of what he called "culture" as a counterpoise to the spiritual diminishments of the capitalist marketplace.

It is for this reason that Emerson so frequently has recourse to the language of property at crucial moments in his best early writing, as when in *Nature* he says: "There is a *property* in the horizon which no man has but he whose eye can integrate all the parts" (*E&L* 9), or when in "Self-Reliance" he says that in works of genius "our own rejected thoughts . . . come back to us with a certain *alienated* majesty" (*E&L* 259), or when in "Experience" he says so darkly of the loss of his son: "I seem to have lost a beautiful *estate*" (*E&L* 473). I will discuss each of these passages in their full contexts below; I cite them here preliminarily only as a few prominent instances of a pervasive pattern of diction. Emerson seems to use the word "property" at every opportunity in his early work, as well as an array of more or less closely associated terms such as "proper," "propriety," "debt," "credit," "dowry," "estate," "possession," "plantation," "warranty," "deeds," "kingdom," "dominion," "own," "right," "thine," "mine," "my," "has" (in the sense of ownership), "alienate," "joint-stock company," "trustee," "poverty," "fortune," "compensation," and "wealth." And he uses many of these terms in more than one sense at a time and in differing senses in different contexts. These multiple resonances are then further multiplied by the rich and complex historical legacy of the word "property" itself. From its earliest modern days the word has tended to draw to itself a wonderfully suggestive and reflexive set of associated terms. Richard Tuck has shown in detail how the modern idea of natural rights evolved over centuries out of the complex circular interplay between the Latin legal concepts of "ius," initially a narrowly drawn positive "right" or permission to do or demand a specific thing, and "dominium," translated as "property," with the strong connotations of "dominion" or "sovereignty" and indicating ownership in the broader negative sense of exclusive control. Over time, Tuck writes, "all of a man's rights, of whatever kind, were to come to be seen as his property," and ownership of property, as we have already observed, came to be seen as the foremost of his rights. Thus, "property . . . ," Tuck writes, "[began] an expansion towards all the corners of man's moral world."[22]

The attraction of this intricate idiom for Emerson should by now be apparent. Emerson's writing as a whole consciously situates itself within the long historical narrative sketched by Scottish liberalism in which an increasingly abstract conception of property is understood to be the decisive agent of human progress. And he lived and wrote in a time and place where property of every kind was being pursued with unprecedented energy and success by an unprecedented number of people at every level of society. "The Revolution," Gordon Wood reminds us, "did not merely create a political and legal environment conducive to economic expansion; it also released powerful popular entrepreneurial and commercial energies that few realized existed and transformed the economic landscape of the country."[23] As I have tried to show, Emerson had a profound appreciation of the world-historical emancipating significance of these changes. And yet he was also seriously attuned to the dangers of reification contained therein. This dual awareness cut out for him the special dual work of culture in a modern liberal-capitalist society. On the one hand, his writing had to continue to proclaim the liberal revolution—to announce, honor, and verbally enact the emancipation entailed in the movement from feudal-aristocratic to liberal-democratic-capitalist conceptions of property, rights, and personhood. On the other hand, his writing had to counter the incipient ossification and degradation of these ideas due to a pervasive spirit of callous, calculating instrumentalism. He sought, in other words, at once to celebrate the liberal conception of property and to bring the idea to a further but no less liberal stage—a stage of yet higher, subtler, more ethical, and more intimate abstraction that might be best called existential. In order to carry out this dual task, as we will now see, Emerson made elaborate and often dazzling use of an extraordinary array of property words in all their remarkably rich, often dual, sometimes dueling connotations. He found in the idiom of property a highly charged and accessible vocabulary that could resonate simultaneously on existential, epistemo-logical, ethical, and historical levels and that could, when necessary, register duality and ambivalence on each.

The ultimate effect may be best suggested by a perhaps unlikely blend of Stanley Cavell and Hegel. Emerson and Thoreau hold an important place in Cavell's work because, as he puts it, they convey more deeply than Wittgenstein and Austin the underlying intuition of ordinary-language philosophy of "our intimacy with existence, or intimacy lost"—that "our relation to the world's existence is somehow closer than the ideas of believing and knowing are made to convey."[24] Cavell does not himself make the connection, but his formulation names precisely the primary significance of the language of property in Emerson's work: it is, as I hope the following readings will show, a supple and many-shaded metaphor for a distinctive conception of "intimacy with existence." For Emerson, the language of property and ownership, deployed with all due subtlety and nuance, does what the ideas of believing and knowing fail to do. If it is not quite right to say that we "believe" we exist or that we "know" we exist, it is perhaps more accurate to say that we "have property in" existence in some way too fine for deeds or titles or conventional philosophical argumentation to convey. Such phrasing has the additional advantage not only of a degree of hortatory empowerment but also of a greater appeal insofar as it addresses distinctively property-minded listeners and readers at the intimate level of their most ordinary daily concerns. And this is where Hegel becomes relevant. For Hegel property is the necessary material incarnation of the spiritual reality of liberal freedom—the body, as it were, containing and expressing the individual's historical soul. Emerson's long study of history had led him to conclude similarly that liberalism's protection of the individual from the collective had finally made it possible for more than just a very few to fulfill their humanity in this sense. Emerson plays so richly on the idiom of property, as we will now see, in order to raise the possibility of intimacy with existence as a realization of the history of liberty in the realms of ordinary feeling and consciousness.

Our first example comes from among Emerson's first published paragraphs. "There is a *property* in the horizon," he writes in chapter 1 of *Nature*, "which no man has but he whose eyes can integrate all the parts" (*E&L* 9). I have discussed this phrase in some detail in the foregoing chapter on *Nature* as one of many instances in which Emerson represents knowledge as the intuition of an orderly whole—"integrat[ing] all the parts." It nonetheless warrants another look here to note the several levels of significance in his use of the word "property" to characterize such knowledge. On the first level Emerson is suggesting that the holistic perception of the beauty and order of the landscape is a form of moral/intellectual/spiritual wealth no less valuable than the literal legal ownership of any of the farmlands that comprise the view. He does not seek to disparage or subvert the commercial value of the farmers' property/land, but he does seek to make his readers aware of the availability of a higher, subtler, less easily commodified way of relating to it. And he adds another important nuance by playing gently on the scientific connotation of "property," as when we refer to the "properties" of a given substance or element, as Emerson himself does later on in the essay when he lists some of the "propert[ies] of matter—its solidity or resistance, its inertia, its extension, its figure, its divisibility" (*E&L* 26). This quasi-scientific connotation serves to remind the reader that Emerson does not regard such ephemeral apprehensions of consciousness to be purely subjective: what one perceives in integrating all the parts within a given horizon is an objective "property" of the world in the sense of being one of its constitutive phenomena—a modality, however momentary, of its being. He calls such holistic perception a form of "property" here precisely in order to include it in the continuum of the liberal narrative of the history of liberty in which the institution of private property plays such an important part, but he is trying at the same time to push that narrative a step further. The passage as a whole is thus a vivid instance of Emerson carrying out the dual liberal-cultural work we see him at the same time assigning himself in his early lectures.

Later in the essay Emerson makes a claim for property in "virtue" precisely analogous to the one we have just seen him make for property in what we might call rational perception: "Beauty is the mark God sets upon virtue. Every natural action is graceful. Every heroic act is also decent, and causes the place and the bystanders to shine. We are taught by great actions that the universe is the property of every individual in it. Every rational creature has all nature for his dowry and estate. It is his, if he will" (*E&L* 16). As we noted in commenting on these lines in chapter 3, the philosophy here would seem to be unreconstructed Platonism. Truth, beauty, and virtue are all functions of the alignment of the human mind with an underlying metaphysical order. But Emerson rather oddly uses the word "property" to characterize the individual's relationship to this order. Plato would not have characterized it this way. That Emerson does so is consistent with his larger liberal-historical cultural project on several levels. To start with, he shows that he knows his audience well. Just as a good preacher tries to draw upon language related to the daily life of his congregation, Emerson here uses the term "property" to appeal to the quotidian concerns of a pragmatic, middle-class, Yankee readership even as he seeks to lift their minds beyond the quotidian. The term also bespeaks Emerson's constant awareness of history. For Emerson the very existence of his Yankee audience and the secular literary form of his own address to them have specific historical significance. Both are products of the history of liberty as he understood it—a history in which the emergence of a right to property plays a decisive role. Once again, in keeping with Emerson's dual conception of his cultural mission, the sentence cuts two ways. To say that "we are taught by great actions that the universe is the property of every individual in it" is not just a way of making an essentially Platonic claim interesting to middle-class folks and hopefully thereby refining their sense of property. It is also a substantial revision of Plato in light of the history of middle-class liberty. It holds with Plato that there is an underlying metaphysical order to the universe, of which truth and beauty and virtue are reflections, but it implies most un-Platonically that history has made alignment with that order available to all human beings. And, more un-Platonically still, it implies that material "property" is somehow expressive or symbolic of such an alignment—a very large claim indeed for the epistemological, aesthetic, and moral importance of this idea. Which brings us, finally, to the expressive effectiveness of Emerson's phrasing. To say "the universe is the property of everyone in it" is to arrest the reader's attention by a kind of explosive spatial paradox in which the infinite expanse of "universe" seems to push gigantically against the boundedness and containment of "property." It makes so great a claim for property as to threaten to shatter the boundaries of the concept from within—precisely the sort of dual message Emerson sought to send.

The idiom of property comes up at other moments in *Nature,* as when Emerson refers to natural creation in general as the "plantations of God," or when, as I have discussed in the preceding chapter, he writes at length about the salutary moral discipline instilled by the harsh economic laws of the marketplace—"the good office . . . performed by Property and its filial systems of credit and debt" (*E&L* 26). But the two most striking instances are more ambiguous. In the fourth section, entitled "Language," Emerson again uses the term "property" in connection with his own idiosyncratic Platonism: "Man is conscious of a universal soul within or behind his individual life, wherein, as in a firmament, the natures of Justice, Truth, Love, Freedom, arise and shine. This universal soul, he calls Reason: it is not mine, or thine, or his, but we are its; we are its Property and Men" (*E&L* 21). And property is the governing metaphor of much of the stirring concluding paragraph of the book as a whole:

> Nature is not fixed but fluid. Spirit alters, moulds, makes it. The immobility or bruteness of nature, is the absence of spirit; to pure spirit it is fluid, it is volatile, it is obedient. Every spirit builds itself a *house;* and beyond its *house,* a world; and beyond its world, a heaven. Know then, that the world exists for you. For you is the phenomenon perfect. What we are, that only can we see. All that Adam *had,* all that Caesar could, you *have* and can do. Adam called his *house,* heaven and earth; Caesar called his *house,* Rome; you perhaps call yours, a cobler's trade, a hundred acres of ploughed land; or a scholar's garret. Yet line for line and point for point, your *dominion* is as great as theirs, though without fine names. Build, therefore, your own world. . . . The *kingdom* of man over nature, which cometh not with observation,—a *dominion* such as now is beyond his dream of God,—he shall enter without more wonder than the blind man feels who is gradually restored to perfect sight. (*E&L* 48)

I will start off by discussing the latter passage, which is more rhetorically elaborate. The subject is the self's possible relationship to nature, and Emerson represents our options in a three-stage reiterated pattern of hierarchically ordered types of ownership. In the first stage we move "up" from "fixed" to "fluid" in the first sentence, from "alter" to "mould" to "make" in the second, from "brute nature" to "spirit" in the third, and from "house" to "world" to "heaven" in the fourth. In the second stage the pattern is reversed, and we spiral "down" from Adam/heaven and earth to Caesar/Rome to you/a cobbler's trade, a hundred acres, or a scholar's garret. And in the third stage we turn and again move "up" across three sentences from "garret" to "dominion" to "kingdom" to a yet higher "dominion" that lies "beyond his dream of God." Emerson could hardly make more vivid his hope to raise his readers to an expanded, intensified, and more spiritual conception of property. The elaborate rhetorical form of this passage enacts precisely the expansive movement intended by Emerson, and its prominent rhetorical position at the conclusion of his first major work supports my claim as to the overarching importance of this general aim in Emerson's early writing as a whole. Once again, Emerson uses the terminology of property both to resoundingly affirm this fundamental liberal value and to resist its reification by rendering it maximally "volatile" and "fluid."

But if Emerson wants his readers to approach nature as a form of property in this expanded sense of the word, what are they to make of his preceding suggestion that they are themselves Reason's "Property and Men"? In light of the repeated efforts we have seen Emerson make in *Nature* and elsewhere to break out of an overly rigid, Cartesian subject-object conception of reason, it is not so difficult to grasp his main point in the sentences above, namely, that reason is not "a thing" possessed by any given individual—"it is not mine, or thine, or his, but we are its." But why use the language of property to advance the contrary point? Does not thinking of ourselves as Reason's "Property and Men" raise a similar problem of reification, but now with subject and object reversed, so that the individual himself or herself becomes an owned thing? I think the answer again lies in Emerson's desire to retain the value of property even as he attempts to expand its meaning. He uses the word "property" as a metaphor here as so often elsewhere because, despite its difficulties, it serves to connote a uniquely intimate and intense quality of relationship between self and world. And at the same time the associations to its literal legal meaning evoke the specific political-historical developments that to his mind had uniquely begun to make it possible at least in principle in the United States for most human beings to pursue such gratifying existential contact.[25] He thus uses the word for its literal, historical, and more loosely evocative existential associations all at once, and directs some of the latter connotations against the encroaching rigidities of the first two levels of meaning.

What is thus a significant motif in *Nature*, and had been gradually crystallizing in the early lectures, becomes the central concern of three of Emerson's most important early works—"The Divinity School Address," "History," and "Compensation." All three employ the apparently paradoxical strategy of countering reified forms of consciousness by means of an expanded conception of property and ownership, with all the dualities that this entails.

This pattern is perhaps most evident in "The Divinity School

Address." The speech breaks down quite simply into two parts, in the first of which Emerson beautifully sketches his own vibrant vision of Christian spirituality and morality, and in the second of which he laments the failures of "historical Christianity" to live up to this ideal. Emerson's understanding of the source of the failures is not surprising: in the best radical Protestant tradition he attributes a tepid spirit in the churches to an excessive preoccupation with formalities—routinized observance rather than freshly inspired inward encounters with God's word and God's creation. "The manner in which [Jesus's] name is surrounded with expressions, which were once sallies of admiration and love, but are now petrified into official titles, kills all generous sympathy and liking" (*E&L* 81). Emerson's proposed correctives were nothing short of shocking to many of his listeners at the time. Against self-abnegating forms of devotion that seem to require that (1) "you shall not be a man even, you shall not *own* the world" (*E&L* 81, italics mine, as in the following numbered passages), Emerson counters as follows:

2. That which he venerates is still his *own*, though he has not realized it yet. (*E&L* 76)

3. [*I*]*n the soul* of man there is a justice whose retributions are instant and entire. He who does a noble deed is instantly ennobled. He who does a mean deed, is by the action itself contracted. . . . *If a man is at heart just, then insofar is he God;* the safety of God, the immortality of God, the majesty of God do *enter into* that man with justice. If a man dissemble, deceive, he deceives himself, and goes out of *acquaintance with his own being.* . . . See how this rapid *intrinsic* energy worketh everywhere. . . . By it, a man is made the *Providence to himself.* (*E&L* 76–77)

4. That is always best which *gives me to myself.* . . . That which shows *God in me*, fortifies me. That which shows God out of me, makes me a wart and a wen. (*E&L* 81)

5. The time is coming when all men will see, that the gift of God to the soul is not a vaunting, overpowering, excluding sanctity, but a sweet, natural goodness, a goodness like *thine and mine*, and that so invites *thine and mine* to be and to grow. (*E&L* 82)

6. Now do not degrade the life and dialogues of Christ out of the circle of this charm, by insulation and peculiarity. Let them lie as they befell, alive and warm, *part of human life, and of the landscape, and of the cheerful day.* (*E&L* 82)

7. The spirit only can teach. Not any profane man, not any sensual, not any liar, not any slave can teach, but only he can give, who *has;* he only can create, who is. (*E&L* 83)

8. In how many churches, by how many prophets, tell me, is man made sensible that he is an infinite Soul; *that the earth and heavens are passing into his mind; that he is drinking forever the soul of God?* Where now sounds the persuasion, that by its very melody imparadises my heart, and so affirms its *own* origin in heaven? (*E&L* 84)

Possessive terms and phrasing are pervasive. The word "own" shows up four times—in passages 1, 2, 3, and 8. Passage 3 uses four different terms indicative of possession or ownership—"intrinsic," "in the soul," "at heart," and "himself." "Myself " appears in passage 4; "thine and mine" are both used twice in a chiastic construction in passage 5. The word "of " is used in its possessive sense four times—thrice in passage 6 and once in passage 8. The verb "has" is used in its possessive sense in passage 7, and the possessive pronoun "his" occurs in passage 8. The associative play is in several instances very intricate, and striking throughout.

To start with, Emerson launches his critique with a claim of affront at the current church's efforts to inhibit ownership. He equates not being permitted to "own the world" with not being permitted to "be a man," which amounts to saying that in order to be human one must "own" property in some sense of the word. Much depends, of course, on which sense of the word, but that is left provocatively unclear. Given the impossibility of literally "owning the world" in the familiar legal-economic sense, it is logical to infer that Emerson does not have this meaning primarily in mind. And indeed, in the rest of the address, Emerson shows little interest in his listeners' relationship to lands, houses, clothing, or money. But he does show a great deal of intense interest in their relationship to morality and to God, and he persists in using the language of ownership to evoke what he sees as a possible but as yet unachieved intimacy in these relationships. The most audacious formulations occur in passages 2 ("That which he venerates is still his own") and 3 ("If a man is at heart just, then insofar is he God"). It is no wonder that some of the more orthodox listeners took offense at these phrases. In trying to counter what he sees as a pattern of reification (though he would not himself have used this word) in which God and morality come to be treated as sacred ritual objects hived off and isolated from ordinary human experience, Emerson here seems altogether to obliterate the boundary between human individuality and the divine. From an orthodox point of view he might as well have said that the human self *is* God, and it is instructive to put the question to these passages: does Emerson not equate the self with God when he says "that which he venerates is still his own" or "if a man is at heart just, then insofar is he God"? The answer, I think, is ultimately "no," but the passages achieve an important part of their purpose by begging this question. Although to "own" a thing or to "have" an idea "at heart" is not to "be" that thing or idea, ownership and "having at heart" are nonetheless forms of relationship so close as to approach and even sometimes to slowly blend into identity. This is why Emerson elsewhere in his writing is so fond of playing on both the economic and the scientific sense of the word "property"—as both a thing owned and as a quality or characteristic definitive of an object. It might not be strictly accurate to say of Emerson as has been said of Locke that for him to be is to have, but it would be fair to say that Emerson was perpetually fascinated by the relationship between being and having and took every opportunity to play the concepts off of each other. Although for Emerson it is not true that you are necessarily part of what you have, it is true that what you have is in some significant sense part of you. Locke would say that you have assimilated it into yourself by "mixing" your labor with it. Emerson here uses a wide range of metaphors to express how the self internalizes God and "Justice": from direct ingestion ("drink[s] forever his soul"), to a kind of permeation ("the earth and heavens are passing into his mind"), to gentle organic assimilation ("a sweet, natural goodness . . . that so invites thine and mine to be and to grow"), to reception of a gift ("gives me to myself"), to the transportations of eloquence ("the spirit only can teach"), and finally to the most relaxed and incidental inclusion ("part of human life, and of the landscape, and of the cheerful day"). In an effort to counteract what he saw as the reified deadness of Unitarian preaching and worship Emerson thus uses the language of ownership and possession in these passages to bring self, God, and morality together as intimately as possible without entirely collapsing their identities into one another. And the consonance of this idiom of ownership with the enormous acquisitive energies of the moment was not incidental. Emerson does not say to the assembled Harvard Divinity School students that the church they are inheriting has lost contact with God because the society they serve is too preoccupied with commerce; he says in effect that this church has lost contact with God because its leaders do not pursue spiritual ownership with the same vast avidity with which the society as a whole pursues coarser forms of possession.

In "The Divinity School Address" Emerson thus oddly attempts to transport emancipated acquisitive energy from the commercial to the religious sphere, and to refine both in the process. And this unusual intracultural directionality takes the speech out of any simple schema of secularization. In reply to the self-posed question "What in these desponding days can be done by us?" Emerson replies with yet another series of verbal gestures of internalization and self-ownership: "We have contrasted the Church with the Soul," he writes. "In the Soul, then, let the redemption be sought" (*E&L* 88). As the paragraph continues he exhorts his listeners to insist "on [their] *own* knowledge of God," "[their] *own* sentiment" (italics mine). And he repeats the noun "soul" so often (four times) that one hears the resonance of its secular homophone— "sole"—in the background of the programmatic advice at which he finally arrives, a Kantian Enlightenment admonition to "go alone" (*E&L* 88). The transition from Christian "soul" to Kantian "sole" indicates a process of secularization in the sense that it reflects Emerson's participation in a larger cultural-historical shift from religious to secular frames of reference. But it does not fit into secularization theory because traditional religion does not function as modernity's cultural unconscious here, secretly dictating apparently secular behavior and expression according to the deep structures of a repressed religious past. On the contrary, part of what is extraordinary about "The Divinity School Address" is the candid absence of nostalgia with which it announces and embraces a conviction that liberal-individualist modernity will outstrip historical Christianity and the "cultus." What it enacts is emphatically not an unconscious repetition of its Puritan past but, as in "The Lord's Supper," a fully conscious though not unregretful valediction.

A cultural anthropologist, if we may take Clifford Geertz as representative, would probably regard the symbolic denudation implicit in Emerson's farewell in "The Divinity School Address" as ultimately untenable. From an anthropological perspective, strictly rational "go[ing] alone," however ennobling the admonition may sound, is too difficult for such social and symbol-using animals as human beings. Noting children's love of stories and adults' love of novels and theater, Emerson himself acknowledges in his journals the necessity of "imagination in education": "We must have symbols" (*JMN* 10:15). And indeed, we know from his early journals and *Nature* that Emerson does not intend the cultural-symbolic impoverishment that comes in the wake of the rational rejection of historical Christianity to become a permanent state of being. As I have suggested, the main aim of *Nature* as a whole was to present the full array of natural phenomena—sky, stars, sea, seasons, and so on—as a substitute for Christian symbolism no less adequate to the deepest and most various psychological needs of self and society. In "History," the first essay in Emerson's first book of essays, he adds all of human history to all of nature as a source of symbols numerous and varied enough to more than compensate for the increasingly evident obsolescence of the Bible. "Every history should be written in a wisdom which divined the range of our affinities and looked at facts as symbols" (*E&L* 256).

At the risk of oversimplifying, it may be said that "History" is principally made up of two contrasting verbal motifs. On the one hand, it is pervaded throughout by language and imagery of fluidity, mutability, and metamorphosis: "Time dissipates to shining ether the solid angularity of facts" (*E&L* 240); "Nature is a mutable cloud, which is always and never the same" (*E&L* 242); "The adamant streams into soft but precise form before it, and whilst I look at it, its outline and texture are changed again. Nothing is so fleeting as form; yet never does it quite deny itself " (*E&L* 242); "The Gothic cathedral is a blossoming in stone" (*E&L* 246); "The transmigration of souls is no fable" (*E&L* 251); "What is our life but an endless flight of winged facts or events?" (*E&L* 251). And, to emphasize the point further, Emerson everywhere enacts verbal metamorphoses in brief lists of associated but distinct nouns: "Egypt, Greece, Rome, Gaul, Britain, America" (*E&L* 237); "camp, kingdom, empire, republic, democracy" (*E&L* 237); "crabs, goats, scorpions, the balance, and the waterpot" (*E&L* 238); "Solomon, Alcibiades, Catiline" (*E&L* 238) to present just a few examples of the essay's most pervasive syntactic pattern.[26] He thus supports frequent general assertions of what might be called ontological fluidity—"Genius watches the monad through all his masks as he performs the metempsychosis of nature" (*E&L* 242)—with illustrative sequences of particulars: "Babylon, Troy, Tyre, Palestine" (*E&L* 240); "locust, elm, oak, pine, fir, and spruce" (*E&L* 246); "Aesop, Homer, Hafiz, Ariosto, Chaucer, Scott" (*E&L* 251). The reader is thus put into the position of Odysseus holding Proteus, a figure Emerson refers to three times in this essay. We focus briefly on each term in the sequence, imagining each shape, place, or person for a moment before it dissolves into "shining ether." But as long as we manage to maintain flexible but firm attention, Proteus reappears in another new form, from locust to elm to oak and so on. The effect of fluidity is worthy of Woolf or Proust. The idea of history is thus relieved of all the ponderous and alien heaviness of accumulated fact and suffused instead with the intimate, elusive lightness and delicacy of time passing.

At the same time, Proteus is only one example of the essay's preoccupation with forms of "holding," especially "ownership" and "property": "I am the *owner* of the sphere / Of the seven stars and the solar year" (*E&L* 236); "He that is once admitted to the right of reason is made a freeman of the whole *estate*" (*E&L* 237); "All its *properties* consist in him" (*E&L* 237); "*Property* also *holds* of the soul . . . and we first *hold* to it with swords and laws" (*E&L* 238); "We honor the rich, because they have externally the freedom, power, and grace which we feel to be *proper* to man, *proper* to us" (*E&L* 239); "Those old worships of Moses, of Zoroaster, of Menu, of Socrates . . . they are *mine* as much as theirs" (*E&L* 250); "The advancing man discovers how deep a *property* he has in literature" (*E&L* 250); "out of the human heart go, as it were, highways to the heart of every object in nature, to reduce it under the *dominion* of man" (*E&L* 250, all italics mine). The prominence of this secondary motif necessarily begs the question of its relation to the primary one. How is it possible to "own," to "have property" in an intrinsically ephemeral historical world that ceaselessly sheds its skin and changes its shapes before our very eyes? How does one go about "holding" Proteus in this sense? The answer to this question is the deep subject of the essay. Just as *Nature* concerns itself not only with what we know of the "not me" but how we know it, "History" concerns itself not only with the meaning of the past but with how we come to understand or read it. Thus, more than any other of Emerson's works, "History" is about reading, the central avocation and most abiding pleasure of his long life. And, not surprisingly, it offers a rich and complex phenomenological treatment of this theme, in which the language of property plays a crucial part.

For Emerson, all of history is present as a kind of collective unconscious in the mind of every individual. As with Proust's madeleine, each particular book serves to activate a chain of associated memories, but in this case the links reach ultimately to all of humanity's common past. Seen in this way, reading becomes a form of expanded possession of the self as world historical, a textually mediated consciousness of all of history as the expression of the full range of one's own latent powers and potentials. Thus, the global history of liberty and Emerson's own personal liberation from tradition are intertwined. This is valuable property indeed, but it cannot be secured by locking it into any reified system, structure, or object. As I suggested above, Proteus must not be held too tightly. Emersonian reading achieves an expanded selfhood as a benefit of its openness, suppleness, and suggestibility—the mutual permeability of the boundaries of its consciousness and the texts it takes up. Like Keats entering into the being of the sparrow on the sill through "negative capability," the Emersonian reader takes possession of all of history by continuous local and temporary fits of spontaneous empathic projection. "A painter," he writes, "told me that nobody could draw a tree without in some sort becoming a tree; or draw a child by studying the outlines of its form merely—but, by watching for a time his motions and plays, the painter enters into his nature, and can then draw him at will in every attitude" (*E&L* 244).

Emerson provides a striking formulation and a moving image of this distinctive conception of history as property very early on in the essay. In the context of discussing what he calls "Unconscious Nature" as "the grandeur of man" he writes:

> *Property also holds of the soul,* covers great spiritual facts, and instinctively therefore we at first hold to it with swords and laws and wide and complex combinations. The obscure consciousness of this fact is the light of all our day, the claim of claims; the plea for education, for justice, for charity, the foundation of friendship and love, and of the heroism and grandeur which belong to acts of self-reliance. It is a remarkable fact that we always read as superior beings. . . . All that Shakespeare says of the king, yonder slip of boy that reads in the corner feels to be true of himself. (*E&L* 238, italics mine)

The phrase "Property also holds of the soul" could serve as a gloss for the entire cultural project I have been attempting to describe. Lockean fence imagery surrounds the "property" here—"hedges it round," "holds to it with swords and laws." But what it protects is eminently inward, abstract, intimate, private, ephemeral—nothing even so portentous as an act of worship or philosophical critique, merely the play of a boy's imagination as he reads. But the content of the boy's imagining is quietly world historical and revolutionary. In the freedom of his solitude he is able to open himself up to possession by a text, and those moments of possession abruptly erase from the ledger of his feelings a thousand years of culturally encoded feudal-aristocratic deference and subordination. Thus, Emerson seeks here to lift and extend the concept of property into the realm of spontaneous consciousness while retaining its political-historical resonances, and he does so in a deliberately ambiguous manner. He could simply have said, "The soul also holds property," and this would have sufficed to outline in general terms what would become a pervasive tenet of all of Emerson's work—that there are immensely valuable but generally overlooked immaterial forms of ownership in what we *have to ourselves* in the private and inward activities of consciousness and perception. Seeing especially, but also other forms of sensing as well as feeling, thinking, praying, knowing, reading, and remembering, are for Emerson infinitely self-renewing sources of spiritual wealth no less real than land, houses, or money in the bank. But to have said simply that "the soul also *holds* property" would have suggested a reified conception, like the first-stage "primitive" conception as the Scots understood it—property as something empirically concrete and verifiable. By contrast, the phrase "property *also holds of* the soul" enacts the abstract, ephemeral, and perhaps unpredictable character of these forms of owning even as it strongly asserts their legitimacy.

An inescapably abstract word—"truth"—is unstated but tacitly necessary to the intelligibility of this formulation. We wouldn't say Emerson "holds of " the ball or "holds of " baby Waldo, but we might say that a quality of roundness "holds true of" the ball or a quality of sorrow "holds true of " Emerson after little Waldo died. And Emerson has raised the level of abstraction higher still by inverting the usual order of subject and object: the soul here, after all, neither "holds" nor "holds of " property but rather "property" "holds of " the soul. To put it this way makes property the subject and soul the object: the soul is owned or possessed, as it were, by property. We know Emerson to be capable of saying something like this in his caustic mode, as in the aforementioned "Things are in the saddle, and ride mankind." But neither tone nor context supports such an interpretation here. It seems more likely that, as he often does, Emerson is here evoking and playing upon the associative links between "holding," "possession," "property," and "truth." We need look no further than the famous "transparent eyeball" passage in *Nature* for evidence that, to Emerson, the deepest knowledge may involve an element of unconscious "possession" in the sense of being taken over temporarily, occupied, as it were, by the being, in this case divine, of the object to be known: "all mean egotism vanishes . . . I am part or particle of God" (*E&L* 10). He says something similar in "The Method of

Nature" when he writes: "There is a Life not to be described or known other than by possession. . . . There is the incoming or the receding of God: that is all we can affirm" (*E&L* 122). For Emerson, in other words, in the new stage of history that his writing announces the concept of property will be expanded to include seeing, feeling, knowing, and especially reading as high and fluid inward forms of "possession" of which the self is both subject and object.

But even such abstract property has a price, and that is the subject of "Compensation," the last of the essays we will here discuss in full. As with "History" and "The Divinity School Address," the basic structure of "Compensation" may be briefly described. Emerson begins by providing an anecdotal example of the outlook he wishes to critique—a minister who urges in a sermon that the righteous will be compensated in the next life by receiving in greater abundance the benefits that sinners seem so often to reap in this one. Emerson charges him with preaching a crudely reified conception of divine justice—"deferring to the base estimate of the market" (*E&L* 286). But, as in the previous instances, Emerson counters such reified "market" consciousness not by rejecting the market per se but by more subtly appropriating its vocabulary. He spends roughly the first half of the essay refiguring his by-now-familiar insistence that no particular thing can be understood separately from the larger whole of which it is a part. And he argues that, from the largest holistic perspective, the rewards of virtue and the punishments of vice must be seen to be immediate, imminent, and instantaneous. "Justice," he writes, "cannot be postponed." The advantages that the sinner appears to have gained by his sin are not ultimately true benefits because they have been obtained without initiating their recipient into any knowledge of the underlying principle of moral existence. To characterize this principle Emerson then shifts, at roughly the midway point of the essay, into a sharp market idiom. "In nature nothing can be given," he writes. "All things are sold" (*E&L* 292). Terms such as "payment," "property," "debt," "tax," "benefit," "price," "earn," "gain," and "riches" take over thereafter. Here are just a few of a great many possible examples:

> What will you *have*? quoth God; *pay* for it and *take* it.—Nothing *venture*, nothing *have*. . . . Who doth not work shall not eat. . . . If you put a chain around the neck of a slave, the other end fastens itself around your own. (*E&L* 293)

The *borrower* runs in his own *debt*. Has a man *gained* anything who has received a hundred favors and rendered none? (*E&L* 295)

A wise man will extend this lesson to all parts of life, and know that it is the part of prudence to face every claimant, and *pay* every just demand on your time, your talents, or your heart. Always *pay;* for, first or last, you must *pay* your entire debt. (*E&L* 295)

Human labor, through all its forms, from the sharpening of a stake to the construction of a city or an epic, is one immense illustration of the perfect compensation of the universe. The absolute *balance* of *Give* and *Take*, the doctrine that everything has its *price*, —and if that *price* is not *paid*, not that thing but something else is obtained, and that it is impossible to get anything without its *price*—is not less sublime in the columns of a *leger* than in the *budgets* of states, in the laws of light and darkness, in all the action and reaction of nature. (*E&L* 296)

A certain moral-ideological fastidiousness in response to Emerson's affinities for the language of the marketplace has prevented most critics, their own bourgeois status notwithstanding, from fully registering the important cultural-symbolic work it performs. To draw again upon Blumenberg's conceptualization of the transition from religious to secular culture, Emerson's account of ever-imminent metaphysical "compensation" here may be said to "occupy the position" formerly held generally by the Christian idea of ultimate reward for the righteous in the hereafter. In the particular variant pertinent to Emerson, this took the form of the Calvinist drama of depravity, grace, and redemption. The symbolism in each case serves to provide the members of its community with fundamental moral-practical orientation—with sufficient reassurance or fear that acting or not acting according to collective norms will prove personally rewarding or destructive in the long run. Calvinism notoriously stages a high-intensity struggle in which a combination of delicious but exquisitely mystified assurance and systematically induced metaphysical anxiety whipsaws the psyche into raptures of rigorous compliance. Emerson's liberal cultural system is ultimately no less invested in fostering a work ethic equal to the demands of (ever-more) modern capitalism, but that is where the similarity ends. Where Calvinist "compensation" is endlessly deferred, otherworldly, eschatological, messianic, and extrinsic, Emerson's is imminent, worldly, secular, "natural," and available. Where the Calvinist system thus depends on mystification, Emerson's language here aims for an almost arithmetical simplicity, perspicuity, and accessibility: "Thou shalt be paid exactly for what thou hast done, no more, no less.—Who doth not work shall not eat. . . . The law of nature is, Do the thing, and you shall have the power: but they who do not do the thing have not the power" (*E&L* 293, 296). Where the Calvinist system bases its appeal on the authority of the Bible and addresses a particular sectarian tribe, Emerson's system is based on what he believes to be universal experience as reported by a cosmopolitan mixture of Greek philosophers, Hindu poets, and ordinary people, and it addresses, in principle, all human beings: "Experienced men of the world know very well that it is best to pay scot and lot as they go along" (*E&L* 295); thoughtful consumers learn that "what we buy in a broom, a mat, a wagon, a knife, is some application of good sense to a common want" (*E&L* 296); conscientious laborers understand that "the cheat, the defaulter, the gambler, cannot extort the knowledge of material and moral nature which his honest care and pains yields to the operative" (*E&L* 296). And countless generations of ordinary folk have distilled this stark moral empiricism into vivid proverbs: "Tit for tat; an eye for an eye; a tooth for a tooth; blood for blood; measure for measure; love for love.—Give and it shall be given you. . . . What will you have? quoth God; pay for it and take it" (*E&L* 293).

As this diction makes clear, Emerson seeks to retain something of the inexorability of Calvinist judgment but none of its aura of mystery and deferred doom. The verbal curve from Old Testament vengeance to New Testament mercy—from "an eye for an eye" to "love for love"—is an arc of moral progress and expresses a part of Emerson's ever-present historical optimism. And the larger property connotations of "pay," "take," and "have" move historically beyond both Testaments altogether. They blend historical hope, moral realism, a classical sense of existential finitude, rational perspicuity, and, last but not least, individualist acquisitive license in a secular, pragmatic, and not entirely untragic sense of reality that can only be called liberal. It is a sense of reality that can only be acquired through intensive work, but it is consistent with the phenomenological aspect of liberalism we have seen Emerson developing in these early essays that the actual property thus to be gained through labor is not entirely contained in things. How does one measure what is gained inwardly from devoting the time and energy necessary to master a craft or a profession, train one's body, lay down railroad tracks, learn a subject, develop a skill, or see a difficult project through? Self-esteem is only part of it. No less important is the insight into the difficult malleability of self and world. Both can be shaped, but only through hard choices, focus, persistence, and expense of time. These are perhaps rather ordinary virtues, but Emerson was all the more drawn to them as such, and he assigned them no ordinary praise. He calls what we gain from them "wisdom" and, in a phrase that elegantly synthesizes material, ethical, and abstractly ontological conceptions of property, "proper additions of being" (*E&L* 300).

It is tempting to conclude our discussion on this high note. But just three years after the publication of the book of essays containing "History" and "Compensation" in 1841, Emerson published another (1844) that included "Experience." Dealing in part with the death of his five-year-old son in 1842, this essay presents by far the darkest moments in Emerson's entire oeuvre, and many scholars have taken it as marking the beginning of a sober and chastened "late" phase. In its most painful passage, we must acknowledge, Emerson turns again to the language of property:

> In the death of my son, now more than two years ago, I seem to have lost a beautiful *estate,*—no more. I cannot get it nearer to me. If tomorrow I should be informed of the *bankruptcy of my principal debtors, the loss of my property* would be a great inconvenience to me, perhaps, for many years, but it would leave me as it found me,—neither better nor worse. So it is with this calamity: it does not touch me: some thing which I fancied was a part of me, which could not be torn away without tearing me, nor enlarged without *enriching* me, falls off from me, and leaves no scar. It was caduceus. I grieve that grief can teach me nothing, nor carry me one step into real nature. (*E&L* 472–73)

I have argued in the preceding pages that Emerson uses the language of ownership as a metaphor for what Stanley Cavell calls "intimacy with existence" and that in doing so his early writing extends the Scottish liberal narrative of progress as a function of increasingly abstract ideas of property. And yet here Emerson very pointedly uses the language of property to complain of what he experiences as a lack of intimacy in his grief: he is distressed to find that he feels the loss of his son no more deeply than he would feel the loss of "a beautiful estate" or the default of his debtors—"I cannot get it nearer to me." Rather than directly contradicting my argument, these lines actually give it a deeper psychological intensity. Just as Freud suggests that words with "primordial," deep-psychological resonance often take on "antithetical meanings" as

a result of our underlying ambivalences, so words of primordial significance for liberal culture, such as "property," are likely to take on con-
flicted meanings in the consciousness of one of its strongest prophets. It
is consistent with his by now long-standing tendency to affectively associate property and intimacy that Emerson here draws again on the language of property to represent what he experiences as a crisis of intimacy. Indeed, it adds poignancy to his understated plaint. For Emerson,
to revert to this entirely reified conception of property as an external
object is akin to saying, "Everything that I once held dear now seems
without value." Or, as we also feel in a state of mourning, "I have lost
not only this particular beloved person but with him or her the capacity
to love at all." Throughout Emerson's early writing, as we have seen,
property was a name not only for beautiful estates or profits from interest but for an inward achievement of human freedom—for a fluid, ever-
ongoing, and intimately personal interchange of consciousness and
world. It is a measure of his grief that in losing Waldo he believed he
had lost his prized capacity to thus make the world his own. It is a measure of his resilience that even in this essay, as we will now see, he re-
covers this capacity so largely.

5

Reason III, Skepticism

"Experience" (1844)

There is little dispute about the robustly affirmative character of Emerson's early writing. Scholars agree that in *Nature* Emerson expresses an expansive philosophical, cultural, and political optimism. They agree further that this optimism carries through his immediately subsequent addresses and essays, including "The American Scholar" (1837), "The Divinity School Address" (1838), "The Method of Nature" (1841), and *Essays: First Series* (1841). But thereafter, it is argued, Emerson's bright morning mood began to darken. The great essay "Experience," published in *Essays: Second Series* (1844), is understood by many to signal the beginning of a drastic, lifelong contraction of Emerson's vision.[1] Commentators now regularly invoke an accepted distinction between "early" and "later" Emerson, with "Experience" marking the transition from Emerson's ecstatic youthful declamations of transcendence to the sadder, more skeptical, and more conservative musings of an older writer who emphasized "acquiescence" to inescapable existential limits.[2]

One of the aims of this chapter is to suggest a revision of this standard narrative. Examined closely, I argue, the essays most often cited as exemplary of Emerson's darker "later" stance reveal a substantial underlying continuity of outlook with his earlier work. And this later outlook is no less fundamentally affirmative of what I have been calling

Enlightenment-liberal values. The author of "Experience" was no less confident than the author of *Nature*, "Self-Reliance," and "Compensation" that, by exercising "reason" as he understood it, human beings were capable of moving from false traditional opinions about the world to autonomous apprehension of stable, universal, and eternal truths. The content of these truths was consistent with Cartesian and Newtonian science, but, again, the chief means of disclosure was not Cartesian method. In "later" as in earlier Emerson, the highest truths were vouchsafed to an integrative moral, aesthetic, and analogical faculty of consciousness that accurately related parts to wholes under the emotional guidance of a moral feeling that Emerson called variously "the sentiment of virtue," "the moral sentiment," or "the moral sense." Following Coleridge, Emerson named this composite faculty "reason."[3] In the "later" no less than in the "early" work, Emerson celebrates the capacity of "reason" thus romantically redefined to orient the self appropriately in relation to the greater social, natural, and cosmic wholes of which it is a part. "Experience" broaches new ground only in making explicit the skeptical process by which Emerson had long since arrived at this important redefinition of reason. The nature of the change between "early" and "later" Emerson, then, is better understood as one of growth, maturation, and refinement rather than of resignation, contraction, or, least of all, radical departure. There is undoubtedly a tone of increased worldliness and more emphasis on moderation in the later work, but this is part of a ripening and sharpening of Emerson's convictions rather than a fundamental revision of them.

I do not deny that in important passages of "Experience" Emerson gives unprecedented expression to a profound sense of disorientation, disconnection, and fragmentation. But for each of the prominent moments of psychic contraction in this essay, there are corresponding and no-less-significant moments of recovery and assurance. To a considerable extent, it is by recourse to the moral sense and its "rational" intuition of a universal moral law that Emerson rallies his psychic forces and reclaims a confidently integrated relationship to nature and society. Thus what appear to be moments of "fatalism" and "acquiescence" in "Experience," I argue, are better read as slightly more stark reformulations of the moral severities we have already seen sternly asserted in the "Discipline" section of *Nature* and intricately woven through the exhilarations of "Self-Reliance" and "Compensation." Far from pessimistic, they are confident and at times ecstatic reaffirmations of the moral principle that gives so much of Emerson's writing its distinctive moral backbone. The early Emerson had already declared that the tune of self-reliance is played on an "iron string"; the later Emerson merely plucks this taut wire more distinctly and more often. If it sometimes sounds excessively harsh to us, to Emerson its piercing lucidity occasioned a complex emotion Nietzsche would later call "tragic joy."

Experience," I realize, is not usually read as a joyful essay. On the contrary, the mood of psychic disconnection, alienation, and unreality with which it begins is generally and rightly viewed as the darkest moment in Emerson's writing. But it is easy to exaggerate the gloom of the work as a whole by focusing too narrowly on its ominous beginning. Viewed in its entirety, "Experience" is actually evenly balanced between what we might call "dark," "negative," or "skeptical" passages and more "positive," "affirmative," or hopeful statements. Of twenty-five total paragraphs, eleven are generally "negative" in their outlook, eleven are generally "affirmative," and three are transitional moments of recovery. The essay as a whole is clearly divided into two analogous recuperative movements of feeling that may be pictured as a capital *U* and a lowercase *u*. The first is longer in both descent and ascent, moving down the left side of the *U* through tropes of psychic disorientation and disconnection from paragraphs 1 through 6 ("Sleep lingers all our lifetime about our eyes" [*E&L* 471]; "Dream delivers us to dream, and there is no end to illusion" [*E&L* 473]), rallying briefly at paragraph 7 ("When virtue is in presence, all subordinate powers sleep" [*E&L* 476]), then continuing downward to a nadir of despair at the *U*'s bottom curve in paragraph 9 ("But is this not pitiful? Life is not worth the taking, to do tricks in" [*E&L* 477]). The speaker then rallies, turns, and ascends up the *U*'s right arm through a sequence of more affirmative passages from the end of paragraph 10 ("Something is learned too from conversing with so much folly and defect" [*E&L* 477]) to paragraph 17's climactic statement of affirmation, integration, and final elated expansiveness ("Suffice it for the joy of the universe, that we have not arrived at a wall, but at interminable oceans" [*E&L* 486]). The second, small *u* then repeats more concisely the entire pattern of the first, descending precipitously down the left arm from paragraphs 18 to 20 ("It is very unhappy, but too late to be helped, the discovery we have made, that we exist" [*E&L* 487] to "How long before our masquerade will end its noise of tamborines, laughter, and shouting, and we shall find it was a solitary performance?" [*E&L*

489]), reaching both a suicidal nadir and turning point at the bottom of the u's curve in paragraph 21 ("And yet is the God the native of these bleak rocks" [*E&L* 490]) before ascending steadily in mood to the affirmative close of the essay in paragraph 25 ("—there is victory yet for all justice" [*E&L* 492]). To my mind, the "descending" rhetoric of disintegration and the "ascending" idiom of reintegration are roughly equivalent in verbal intensity and evocative power. The second, more concise arc of feeling is somewhat less intense at both emotional poles than the first, recapitulating the vertiginous initial movement in a more measured, muted, and presumably wiser key. But the carefully weighed balance of the essay as a whole, along with the important fact that it concludes on the high end of an ascending emotional arc, gives it a satisfying final effect of resolution and affirmation. As at the end of a tragedy, there is a feeling of enhanced understanding and acceptance at the end of "Experience"—a sense that, by facing up to some of the darker sides of human existence without succumbing to hopelessness, one has strengthened one's grasp of reality.

I deliberately choose the term "grasp of reality" because this is precisely what is at issue in "Experience." Can an individual consciousness make contact with anything outside of itself? Can the self know other selves? Can we know objects as they are in themselves? Can we grasp outside "reality" at all, or are we hopelessly locked in deluded solipsistic self-reference? Scholars now generally agree that in the early and middle 1820s, the years immediately following his graduation from Harvard, Emerson underwent a protracted struggle with the thought of David Hume, the great Scottish Enlightenment skeptic who answered all but the last of these questions in a witheringly logical negative.[4] Indeed, Emerson's embroilment with Hume grew so intense during those years that his aunt Mary Moody, perhaps his closest intellectual confidante, worried that his mind had been permanently contaminated, "so imbued with his [Hume's] manner of thinking that you cannot shake him off."[5] Aunt Mary's observation was, as often, uncannily acute. It is clear from "Experience," "Montaigne," and "Illusions," published twenty, twenty-five, and forty years, respectively, after Aunt Mary made this remark, that Emerson never entirely "shook off" the formidable specter of Hume. These essays are centrally and seriously preoccupied with the fundamental skeptical doubts about the connection of ideas to objective reality that Hume famously raised in *A Treatise of Human Nature* (1739) and *An Enquiry Concerning Human Understanding* (1772).

But these essays also prove Emerson to have become a subtler and more sophisticated reader of Hume than his aunt. It was characteristic of religious sensibilities like Aunt Mary's to view Hume almost exclusively as a figure to be feared, as a nihilistic atheist who represented the worst intellectual heresies of the Enlightenment. But Emerson, as I have been suggesting, was himself sufficiently a product of the Enlightenment to arrive finally at a more sympathetic and nuanced relationship to the thought of this representative Enlightenment figure. In the final analysis, Emerson rejected Hume's epistemological skepticism by recourse to a characteristically counter-Lockean blend of Scottish moral-sense realism and Kantian-Coleridgean transcendentalism. But, like Thomas Reid and Dugald Stewart, Emerson came to view his great skeptical antagonist with the utmost respect. We have already noted Emerson's youthful sympathy with Hume's critique of the Christian doctrine of miracles. As his thinking matured, Emerson's sympathies with aspects of Hume deepened further. Even as he struggled to find a way out of the perplexities Hume posed, Emerson, like Kant, came to see what Hume himself never doubted—that his critiques performed a potentially valuable constructive role in demonstrating the limitations of a certain conception of rationality, that only by learning the limits of reason could one begin to exercise reason responsibly, realistically, accurately, and constructively. For Hume as subsequently for Kant, reason's first task was the chastening of reason. Like the major writings of Hume and Kant, "Experience" appears at first to have purely destructive implications as it spirals down the steeply descending slope of its first constitutive arc of feeling, but, as in the works of Hume and Kant, one finds that an initial descent prepares the way for a surprising recovery. "Experience" shares with the work of both these Enlightenment thinkers the broad constructive aim of making possible a more truly reasonable philosophy by first showing Cartesian-Lockean reason its limits. Like Hume and Kant, Emerson came to see skepticism as a necessary initial stage in philosophical awakening and a crucial component of any mature philosophy. He came to see skepticism as the indispensable solvent agent in a dialectical progression of thought that moved from dogmatic traditionalism to an untenable Faustian rationalism, and from there to the open, modest, and potentially fuller and more accurate apprehension of reality made possible by the skeptical chastening of both tradition and reason too narrowly conceived.[6] "Experience" is a figurative and lyrical account of this complex progression.

"Where do we find ourselves?" Emerson had asked to start the essay. He has not yet found an answer as he here begins his second paragraph by amplifying the initial note of disorientation:

> If any of us knew what we were doing, or where we are going, then when we think we best know! We do not know today whether we are busy or idle. At times when we thought ourselves indolent, we have afterwards discovered, that much was accomplished, and much was begun in us. All our days are so unprofitable while they pass, that 'tis wonderful where or when we ever got anything of this which we call wisdom, poetry, virtue. We never got it on any dated calendar day. 'Tis the trick of nature thus to degrade today; a good deal of buzz, and somewhere a result slipped magically in. Every roof is agreeable to the eye, until it is lifted; then we find tragedy, and moaning women, and hard-eyed husbands, and deluges of lethe, and the men ask, "what's the news?" as if the old were so bad. . . . So much of our time is preparation, so much is routine, and so much retrospect, that the pith of each man's genius contracts itself to a very few hours. (*E&L* 472)

We remain lost, but Emerson now begins to suggest that the specific cause of our confusion is a mistaken conception of knowledge. A fundamental epistemological error leads to a series of failures in self-knowledge: we fail to understand our own capacity for creative work ("In times when we thought ourselves indolent"); we fail to understand our own capacity for insight, expression, or goodness ("'tis wonderful where or when"); we fail to understand our capacity for moral excellence ("all martyrdoms looked mean"); and we fail to appreciate the value and dignity of our own daily endeavors ("Our life looks trivial"). The picture is bleak, and it gets bleaker as the paragraph goes on to evoke extreme suffering ("tragedy and moaning women"), a blank traumatized toughness ("hard-eyed husbands and deluges of lethe"), and a soul-killing routinization ("So much of our time is preparation, so much is routine, and so much retrospect"). It is important to note, however, that Emerson does not categorically condemn us to these harsh conditions. He suggests, as I have said, that much of this diminished and mechanical state of being is the result of a mistaken conception of knowledge: we don't know ourselves *"then when we think we best know."* He does not thus suggest that we are incapable of knowing, going, or doing. On the contrary, he clearly acknowledges that "much is begun in us" despite our confusion, that we unconsciously possess "something of wisdom, poetry, virtue," and that we are capable of moral heroism. The problem is that we are out of touch with the intuitive and preconscious sources of these capacities. We attempt to impose crude and inappropriate external categories on spontaneous moments of inner illumination: "We never got it on any calendar day." As in the first paragraph, where we were briefly made aware of an undercurrent of positive feeling, we are here allowed fleetingly to wonder whether we may yet correct our mistake and learn not only to know but to know when and how we know.

Emerson plants such seeds of hope intentionally, and they yield epistemological fruit later in the essay. But things must get worse before they get better. Before offering any suggestions as to how we might correct the errors under which we labor, Emerson spends most of the next eight paragraphs, with the exception of a brief reprieve in paragraph 7, tallying the full extent of our ignorance and susceptibility to illusion. This long descent might be described as Emerson's haphazard and idiosyncratic version of what were known in classical skepticism as "modes." The modes were general categories of skeptical argumentation formulated and listed by Sextus Empiricus, a synthesizer and proponent of the "academic" school of Greek skepticism.[7] According to Sextus, a rational person should be led to a position of fundamental uncertainty about his or her capacity to know things "as they are absolutely and in their own nature" by considering ten fundamental propositions about the heterogeneity and instability of human consciousness.[8] "That things appear differently to different kinds of people" (mode 2), for example; or that circumstance and disposition affect the way different people perceive things (mode 4); or that things are always perceived relative to other things, and there is no way of arriving at an absolute point of view (mode 8); or the sheer variety of divergent customs, laws, ways of life, and mythical beliefs (mode 10)—such considerations led Sextus to argue that we must suspend judgment (*epochē*) with regard to all fundamental or dogmatic philosophical claims.[9] Emerson makes no effort to be thorough and systematic in the manner of Sextus, but he draws on emotionally evocative figurative language to raise similar philosophical doubts. From paragraphs 3 to 9 he presents a kind of poetic and impressionistic survey of those features of human consciousness and human existence that most persistently obstruct our efforts to know with certainty our world as it really is.

Emerson provides his own rubrics for these obstructions in the essay's concluding summary: "Illusion, Temperament, Succession, Surface, Surprise, Reality, Subjectiveness—these are the threads on the loom of time, these are the Lords of Life" (*E&L* 491). As with the modes of Sextus, each of these headings (with the exception of "Surprise" and the anomalous "Reality") corresponds roughly to a different aspect of Emerson's skepticism. But where Sextus coolly enumerates his arguments as stages on the way to an ultimate state of almost Buddhist philosophical detachment (what he calls "arataxia"), Emerson's procedure is disorderly, fragmentary, and fraught with evident personal anguish. There is a sense of crisis and real peril as Emerson evokes a psychic condition of bereavement, profound isolation, and a sort of panicky numbness. Here, as throughout his writing, Emerson gives the lie to T. S. Eliot's contention that the Romantics were incapable of integrating thought and feeling, that "they thought and felt in fits."[10] In these darkest passages of "Experience," Emerson succeeds in representing skepticism not as a remote academic theory but as a deeply felt affliction of the whole self.

The observation of human blindness and weakness is the result of all philosophy," David Hume remarks in *An Enquiry Concerning Human Understanding*.[11] Emerson is so lucid in these paragraphs on the subject of human blindness and weakness that one wonders how he could ever have been optimistic, and if he would ever be again. "There is no power of expansion in men," he summarizes wearily, and the ecstasies of *Nature* seem far away. But as we read on we find that they are not irretrievable. No sooner does Emerson touch bottom at the end of paragraph 9 ("Life is not worth the taking, to do tricks in") than he begins in paragraph 10 to recover a broader perspective and to build toward a climactic affirmation in paragraphs 15 through 17. Dante was one of Emerson's favorite writers, and the pattern of descent and ascent in "Experience" is reminiscent of the structure of *The Divine Comedy*. In "Experience" as in "The Inferno," the author-pilgrim learns from a predecessor-guide that the way down leads to the way up. For Dante, the guide was Virgil. For Emerson, it was David Hume. The great Enlightenment doubter who led Emerson down into the morass of skepticism also showed him the first steps out of the swamp and up toward the stars.

Recent scholarship has greatly enriched our understanding of Hume's thought. In his own time and through much of the nineteenth and twentieth centuries, Aunt Mary's response to Hume was typical; as I have said, he was regarded for the most part as a subversive nihilist, a nay-saying atheist whose skepticism led only to the abyss.[12] Norman

Kemp Smith provided an important corrective to this view in 1905 by drawing attention to the more affirmative "naturalist" dimension of Hume's thought, and Richard Popkin, David Fate Norton, and Donald Livingston have since developed impressively sophisticated modifications of Kemp Smith's revision.[13] For all of their differences, Kemp Smith, Popkin, Fate Norton, and Livingston agree in two important respects: they all grant the destructive intent of Hume's critique of reason, yet they also all maintain that, for Hume, the skeptical subversion of reason did not lead inevitably to nihilism. On the contrary, they argue that in deconstructing reason Hume aimed principally to clear a space for a range of "natural" beliefs. Hume had indeed sought to show that there is no coherent rational basis for belief in the existence of natural objects, or in the principle of causation, or even in the basic principles of morality, but he had also recognized that ordinary life nonetheless requires human beings to believe in these things. Nature in her benevolence had thus provided human beings with a sort of instinctive conviction that, for example, the objects in their environment exist independently of perception, or that one billiard ball will always move another upon collision, or that it is wrong to kill or enslave other human beings. Since Hume shared with Shaftesbury, Hutcheson, and his friends in the Scottish "common sense" school a confidence that nature had entrusted the most essential tasks of environmental adaptation, socialization, and moral behavior to intuitive feeling rather than to analytical reasoning, he remained untroubled by the larger implications of his own skepticism. Skepticism was powerless to disorient ordinary people in their most fundamental activities or beliefs, Hume maintained, because none of these were ultimately dependent, strictly speaking, on reason. With his own feet firmly planted on the solid ground of "common life," Hume sought only to undermine what he saw as the fanatical delusions of dogmatic religionists and the hubristic pretensions of philosophers and men of science. For Hume, the fact that reason could not account for the most basic constituents of human experience did not negate the validity of experience but rather sharply indicated the limits of reason. And yet to understand these limits of reason required the exercise of a particular kind of skeptical reason. Indeed, a salutary awareness of reason's inadequacy in the face of experience was precisely the positive lesson of skepticism, the substance of what Livingston calls Hume's "Pyrrhonian illumination." Livingston writes:

> From the perspective of Pyrrhonian doubt the philosopher can see for the first time the magnificent, philosophically unreflective order of common life in opposition to whatever order is constituted by autonomous philosophical reflection and with an authority all its own to command belief and judgment. We recognize that we are determined to make judgements and have beliefs about reality within this order no matter what the dictates of philosophical reflection might be. And yet recognition of the peculiar authority of the common life is dependent upon a philosophical process of working through philosophical incoherence to the point where we are thoroughly convinced of the force of the Pyrrhonian doubt.[14]

I quote Livingston's account of Hume's "Pyrrhonian illumination" in full because I believe that "Experience" turns on precisely such a complex skeptical gnosis. Having reached the first and most important of the essay's two emotional-rhetorical nadirs at the end of paragraph 9, Emerson devotes the next eight paragraphs, as I have said, to a gradual recovery—a steady emotional-rhetorical ascent that builds toward a sweeping affirmation in paragraph 17. The philosophical basis of this recovery is closely akin to the commonsense or "naturalist" dimension of Hume as it has been characterized by Kemp Smith, Popkin, Fate Norton, and especially Livingston.

Like Hume, Emerson in the first several of these paragraphs responds to skepticism not by direct counterattack but rather by shifting ground. Like the naturalist Hume and his commonsense compatriots, Emerson turns to common life and especially to common morality as a source of truths that somehow stand outside of skepticism's reach. But skepticism remains valuable to Emerson, as it did to Hume, as the catalyst of the philosophical process by which this fresh apprehension of common life and common morality is achieved. One could say that Emerson here synthesizes Hume and the common sense school in an attempt to retain the genuine insights of skepticism within a broader and more affirmative philosophical perspective. Of course, Emerson then goes far beyond both Hume and the Scots in an affirmative direction, arriving finally at his own idiosyncratic transcendentalism. Where Hume is content to draw upon the perspective of common life principally to highlight the narrow boundaries of reason's relevance, Emerson ultimately draws upon the vantage point of common life to rehearse his ambitious reconceptualization of reason altogether—the expanded counter-Lockean and transcendental conception of reason for which he had laid the groundwork in his earlier writing. But this is getting ahead of our argument. The full force and scope of Emerson's recovery emerge most clearly if we carefully examine this part of "Experience."

The ascending emotional-rhetorical arc to which I have been referring has three main parts, of which the first two may be discussed together. From the turn at the despondent base of the *U* in paragraph 10, "Experience" moves quickly from a brief intimation in paragraph 10 of the need for a perception of the whole to a sustained discourse in paragraphs 11–14 on the common life and "the middle way." The basic argument of the first part, paragraph 10, is already familiar to us from our analysis of *Nature:*

> Of course, it needs the whole society, to give the symmetry we seek. The party-colored wheel must revolve very fast to appear white. Something is learned too from conversing with so much folly and defect. In fine, whoever loses, we are always of the gaining party. Divinity is behind our failures and follies also. The plays of children are nonsense, but very educative nonsense. So it is with the largest and solemnest things, with commerce, government, church, marriage, and so with the history of every man's bread, and the ways by which he is to come by it. Like a bird which alights nowhere, but hops perpetually from bough to bough, is the Power which abides in no man and no woman, but for a moment speaks from this one, and for another moment from that one. (*E&L* 477)

This is the intuition of the whole that we have already seen to be the foundational act of Emerson's counter-Lockean conception of reason. In this instance it serves not to integrate observed particulars into an overarching perceptual order but rather to establish the need for a larger perspective within which the long, preceding catalog of "failures and follies" might be rendered constructive and meaningful. Speaking simply, Emerson here could be said to begin to counter his own skepticism by adopting the attitude of "learning from one's mistakes." This is what he is getting at in the decisively declarative statement by which he characteristically takes possession of that which he seeks: "Something is learned too from conversing with so much folly and defect." Emerson's aim is to find a way to incorporate into a larger ordered whole the painful experiences and insights that lead him toward skepticism. The special difficulty in this case is that skepticism by nature militates against the establishment of any such stable and comprehensive perspective. It is in an effort to find a foundation for a larger vision that will somehow accommodate the negations of skepticism that Emerson turns toward what Hume called "common life."

The next four paragraphs offer a sustained celebration of common life. Skepticism seems compelling on a strictly theoretical plane, Emerson suggests here, but most of our existence continues with little regard for theories. If "contact" with objective reality is what we seek, we may have it in abundance simply by energetically engaging in the most ordinary worldly activities: "But what help from these fineries or pedantries? What help from thought? Life is not dialectics" (*E&L* 478). Invoking the immediacy and spontaneous forcefulness of physical labor, basic appetites, and even biological impulse, Emerson in these paragraphs (most of which I have not quoted) champions a kind of rough-and-ready vitalistic know-how over the effete and "tremulous" paralysis bred of too much abstraction. "Intellectual tasting of life," he says, "will not supersede muscular activity. If a man should consider the nicety of the passage of a piece of bread down his throat, he would starve" (*E&L* 478). He makes the same point with a travel metaphor in the next paragraph: "The great gifts are not got by analysis. Everything good is on the highway" (*E&L* 480). And he makes the same point yet again in commercial and legal terms in the paragraph after: "Whilst the debate goes forward on the equity of commerce, and will not be closed for a century or two, New and Old England may keep shop" (*E&L* 481). Emerson's language is sharper and more various than Hume's, but at this point he employs a precisely analogous strategy for countering skepticism. He marshals his seemingly inexhaustible supply of tropes all to evoke precisely what Livingston described as the "magnificent, unreflective order of common life." For Emerson as for Hume, this unreflective order points the way out of skepticism not by refuting its logic but by indicating the rather narrow boundaries of logic's domain. Stretching out amply beyond logic's polar preserve, Emerson reminds us, lies the fecund and diverse but unexplored terrain of what he calls variously "the mid-world" (*E&L* 481), "the equator of life" (*E&L* 480), or "the middle region of our being" (*E&L* 480). This is the familiar landscape of the ordinary, with its gentle climate of "moderate goods" (*E&L* 480) and "small mercies" (*E&L* 479), its easy, irregular, "potluck" pace (*E&L* 479), its reliable intimacies of "wife, babes, and mother" (*E&L* 480), its accessible splendors in "the commonest books" (*E&L* 480), and "nature's pictures in every street, sunsets and sunrises everyday" (*E&L* 480). As is usually the case in Emerson, there is a compensation at work. For every moment of skeptical alienation, absence, and ghostly unreality endured earlier in the essay, we now begin to find compensatory glimmers of wholeness, vitality, and ontological presence.

The most influential contemporary scholarship, as I have suggested, has tended to interpret passages like these as prototypes of Jamesian pragmatism.[15] The language itself makes it easy to see why. "Life is not dialectics." "Do not craze yourself with thinking, but go about your business anywhere." "Life is not intellectual or critical, but sturdy. Its chief good is for well-mixed people who can enjoy what they find, without question." "I accept the clangor and jangle of contrary tendencies." "So many things are unsettled which it is of the first importance to settle,—and, pending their settlement, we will do as we do." William James himself could easily have written any of these sentences. They exude James's characteristic impatience with scholastic hairsplitting and his relish for unmediated sensuousness and heterogeneity. The last sentence especially takes precisely that tone of "insouciance" toward philosophy's perennial big questions that Richard Rorty sees as definitive of pragmatism.[16]

But such affinities must be placed in the balance with that substantial portion of Emerson's work that runs directly counter to the pragmatist point of view. The latter-day Platonist, the metaphysician, the thinker of "the oversoul" who continued in however novel a fashion to search out eternal, unchanging, and absolute principles undergirding the phenomenal world—contemporary "pragmatist" commentators tend to downplay or simply to ignore these Emersonian personae, particularly in his later work, and to focus exclusively on protopragmatist moments such as the ones quoted above. In doing so they significantly reduce and distort Emerson's general position. The sentences above and the paragraphs (10–14) from which they were taken must be seen as part of a larger argument, as one stage in a complex progression of thought and feeling that the essay as a whole seeks to represent. That complex whole undeniably contains a pragmatist moment. But this moment is preceded, followed, and generally outweighed by other moments of very different, and in many cases contrary, philosophical coloring. In particular, contemporary pragmatist commentators fail to consider the extent to which Emerson's "pragmatism" in "Experience," as throughout his work, is bolstered by intimations of a metaphysically subsistent moral law. In the introduction to *Consequences of Pragmatism*, Rorty makes it clear that pragmatism is emphatically opposed in general to nineteenth-century "transcendentalism" and in particular to the "intuitive realist" conviction that there are "common elements" or shared moral intuitions "built into the vocabularies of Homeric warriors, Buddhist sages, [and] Enlightenment scientists."[17] Notwithstanding Emerson's occasional pragmatic-sounding utterances, there can be little question that from early to late he occupied the "transcendental" side of nineteenth-century debates between positivists and transcendentalists, and that an important aspect of his transcendentalism consisted in the belief that a clear set of universal moral principles could be both intuited by the moral sense and distilled from the epic and prophetic literatures of the vast range and variety of human cultures, past and present. Emerson's general solicitude for moral-metaphysical support keeps his work as a whole firmly outside of pragmatism's resolutely antimetaphysical parameters.

Emerson first hears what he calls the "whisper" of moral metaphysics in "Experience" at an advanced stage of his initial descent. Toward the end of paragraph 7, under the category of "temperament," Emerson considers with horror the nineteenth-century version of behaviorist psychology, which saw human personality as a set of predictable responses to given physiological stimuli. "Theoretic kidnappers and slave-drivers," he labels the proponents of this view, "they esteem each man the victim of another, who winds him round his finger by knowing the law of his being, and by such cheap signboards as the color of his beard, or the slope of his occiput, reads the inventory of his fortunes and character" (*E&L* 475). In an effort to counter what he sees as the intolerable reductionism of this outlook, Emerson invokes the incalculable freedom of the moral will. Like Kant, he suggests that it is ultimately the capacity for disinterested moral action, or "virtue," that distinguishes human beings from beasts: "Into every intelligence there is a door which is never closed, through which the creator passes. The intellect, seeker of absolute truth, or the heart, lover of absolute good, intervenes for our succor, and at one whisper of these high powers, we awake from ineffectual struggles with this nightmare. We hurl it into its own hell, and cannot again contract ourselves to so base a state" (*E&L* 476). The concluding promise of this passage proves premature. It is not until three paragraphs later that the speaker begins fully to awaken from the burden of the essay's skeptical nightmare. But it is nonetheless crucial that the speaker characterizes the "high power" that brings about this awakening as a kind of moral-metaphysical attunement. This sentence William

James could never have written. For him, as for contemporary antifoundationalists, such hankering after "absolute truth" and "absolute good" is precisely the problem with philosophy. By contrast, Emerson attributes nothing less than his willingness to continue living to the same moral-metaphysical intuitions that Rorty explicitly wishes to "suppress," "extirpate," or "eradicate."[18]

And these intuitions continue to play a crucial role in the subsequent "common-life" passages upon which the essay as a whole pivots. The primary importance of these passages, as I have already suggested, is epistemological. Like Hume, Emerson sinks his toes into the dirt of daily life principally as ballast for his tendency to drift off into a kind of impermeable skeptical bubble. But interlaced with his celebration of the ordinary is a complementary discourse that can only be described as moral. Throughout these four pivotal paragraphs, some of which I have previously quoted and analyzed, Emerson persistently invokes his version of the classical doctrine of the mean:

> Life itself is a mixture of power and form, and will not bear the least excess of either. . . . Since our office is with moments, let us husband them. Five minutes of today are worth as much to me, as five minutes in the next millennium. Let us be poised, and wise, and our own, today. Let us treat the men and women well: treat them as if they were real: perhaps they are. . . . Without any shadow of doubt, amidst this vertigo of shows and politics, I settle myself ever the firmer in the creed, that we should not postpone and refer and wish, but do broad justice where we are, by whomsoever we deal with, accepting our actual companions and circumstances, however humble or odious, as the mystic officials to whom the universe has delegated its whole pleasure for us. . . . I compared notes with one of my friends who expects everything of the universe, and is disappointed when anything is less than the best, and I found that I begin at the other extreme, expecting nothing, and am always full of thanks for moderate goods. . . . If we will take the good we find, asking no questions, we shall have heaping measures. The great gifts are not got by analysis. Everything good is on the highway. The middle region of our being is the temperate zone. We may climb into the thin and cold realm of pure geometry and lifeless science, or sink into that of sensation. Between these extremes is the equator of life, of thought, of spirit, or poetry,—a narrow belt. (*E&L* 478–80)

Emerson's assimilative powers were prodigious. And in no area of inquiry were they so vastly exercised as in moral philosophy. The ethical wisdom that Emerson offers here is in good part the product of independent reflection on his own experience. But it is also in good part the distillation of more than two thousand years of Western religious and philosophical literature, ranging from the oracular fragments of the pre-Socratics to Plato's dialogues, Aristotle's ethical treatises, the works of the Stoics, Plutarch, Montaigne, Cudworth, Hutcheson, Hume, Pope, Samuel Johnson, Richard Price, the Scottish common sense school, Adam Smith, Benjamin Franklin, and William Ellery Channing. It hardly needs stating that Emerson was also steeped in the Hebrew prophecies, the New Testament, and Augustinian-Protestant theology. But I deliberately omit the major texts of the Judeo-Christian tradition here because these passages, for all their synthetic breadth, remain pointedly Hellenic rather than Hebraic. Emerson never became bitterly anti-Christian in the manner of Nietzsche; on the contrary, he remained committed to what he saw as the ethical truth of Christianity throughout his life. But in passages like these, one begins to see why Nietzsche felt an affinity with this Yankee aphorist. As in much of Nietzsche's writing, the prevailing moral framework informing these statements is classical rather than Christian. Far from selflessness, meekness, or ascetic self-abnegation, the emphasis in this section of "Experience" is on a kind of sturdy Aristotelian balance—a prudent, self-confident competence that manifests itself not in humility but in magnanimity, not in self-sacrifice but in "broad justice" (*E&L* 479). Like many of his recent Enlightenment predecessors, Emerson derived a devotion to moderation and the middle way not only from Aristotle and Plato but also prominently from Plutarch, Seneca, Marcus Aurelius, and the Stoic tradition in general. The Stoic voice is most audible in these passages in the talk of "indifferency," "going about your business," "filling the hour," and the "skillful handling" of convention. There is also a touch of the Epicurean-Lucretian "this-worldliness" so admired by Nietzsche in Emerson's emphasis here on "the strong present tense," "husbanding" the moment, and "living the greatest number of good hours." "Five minutes of today," Emerson declares in an uncharacteristically overt dig at Christian otherworldliness, "are worth as much to me, as five minutes in the next millennium." And he sustains a distinctively classical hauteur even as he turns his attention to that most Christian of ethical topics—the "other." "Treat the men and women well," he quips, "treat them as if they were real: perhaps they are." The wry tone puts us a long way away from "Blessed are the poor in spirit," and the aristocratic bite grows sharper yet as Emerson counsels the reader to find consolation for the "coarse[ness] and frivol[ity]" of his companions in the knowledge that even they must ultimately pay "homage" to true superiority (*E&L* 479).

But to be unchristian in this classical sense was not, as Nietzsche well knew, to be morally soft. Nor was it, as Nietzsche also knew, to be metaphysically ungrounded. The same stern moral standard, the same sinewy "iron string," runs through these passages as ran through *Nature*, "Self-Reliance," and the other early essays. Now as then, Emerson preaches a version of the doctrine of the mean that is flexible and pragmatic but rooted in the very nature of things, and as such utterly inescapable and unrelenting—"a coat woven of elastic steel," as he puts it in "Montaigne," "stout as the first, and limber as the second" (*E&L* 696). This is well illustrated by juxtaposing this section's most overtly anti-Christian passage with its closing paragraph:

> The mid-world is best. Nature, as we know her, is no saint. The lights of the church, the ascetics, Gentoos and Grahamites, she does not distinguish by any favor. She comes eating and drinking and sinning. Her darlings, the great, the strong, the beautiful, are not children of our law, do not come out of the Sunday School, nor weigh their food, nor punctually keep the commandments. If we will be strong with her strength, we must not harbor such disconsolate consciences, borrowed too from the consciences of other nations. We must set up the strong present tense against all the rumors of wrath, past or to come. . . .
>
> Human life is made up of the two elements, power and form, and the proportion must be invariably kept, if we would have it sweet and sound. Each of these elements in excess makes a mischief as hurtful as its defect. Everything runs to excess: every good quality is noxious, if unmixed, and, to carry the danger to the edge of ruin, nature causes each man's peculiarity to superabound. Here, among the farms, we adduce the scholars as examples of this treachery. They are nature's victims of expression. You who see the artist, the orator, the poet, too near, and find their life no more excellent than that of mechanics or farmers, and themselves victims of partiality, very hollow and haggard, and pronounce them failures,—not heroes, but quacks,—conclude very reasonably, that these arts are not for man, but are disease. Yet nature will not bear you out. Irresistible nature made man such, and makes legions more of such, every day. You love the boy reading in a book, gazing at a drawing, or a cast; yet what are these millions who read and behold, but incipient writers and sculptors? Add a little more of that quality which now reads and sees, and they will seize the pen and chisel. And if one

remembers how innocently he began to be an artist, he perceives that
nature joined with his enemy. A man is a golden impossibility. The line
he must walk is a hair's breadth. The wise through excess of wisdom is
made a fool. (*E&L* 481–82)

Just as we saw so often in our analysis of *Nature,* the first of these paragraphs is built upon an opposition between two conceptions of law. On
the one hand, there is the traditional or conventional law of "the
church"—the law of "sainthood," of "the ascetics," of "Gentoos and
Grahamites," of "Sunday School," "the commandments," of "discon-
solate consciences," and "the rumors of wrath." On the other hand,
there is nature's law. This is the law of "the mid-world" or of common
life as it has been evoked in the two foregoing paragraphs. It is the law of
"eating, and drinking, and sinning," of "the great, the strong, the beautiful," of those who "are strong with [Nature's] strength," of "the strong
present tense." By rejecting the former principle (the law of tradition) in
favor of the latter (the law of nature), Emerson invokes the same fundamental Enlightenment-classical antinomy that structured *Nature* and the
earlier essays.

But it is fair, in this case, to ask whether Emerson does not simply
opt for the easier of the two principles. Is he not merely suggesting that
our consciences would trouble us less often if we simply adopted a less
restrictive, more "natural" code of behavior? The "natural" standard
does sound a lot more pleasant, even a bit licentious, especially when
Emerson says that Nature "comes eating and drinking and sinning." Do
not these lines support the "liberated" image of Emerson that I have
been arguing against? The allusion to the New Testament in this key
sentence helps us to see why not. Jesus says, "The son of man comes eating and drinking" in Luke 7:34 in part to differentiate his new law of the
spirit from the old Pharisaic law of the letter. Emerson shrewdly invokes
this precedent here in order to perform a complex rhetorical task with
maximum economy. He paradoxically alludes to Christ in an effort to
appropriate Christ's moral authority for his own critique of Christian
morality. Just as Christ criticized a Judaic tradition that had become
bloodlessly legalistic, Emerson implies, so he now must criticize a Christian tradition that has become similarly abstract and lifeless. Thus
Emerson not only clarifies the nature of his complaint but also reassures
his audience of his own moral seriousness. "Don't misinterpret me,"
Emerson signals his readers. "Like Jesus I use provocative language to

subvert the old law, but my aim is not subversion for its own sake. Like Jesus I speak in the name of a higher and better law that is no less rigorous or demanding in its own way." There is a firm standard of virtue in the new dispensation, Emerson reassures us, but its demands cannot be met by self-denial and the observance of ritual, by "punctuality" and "weighing one's food." On the contrary, obedience to nature's law requires courage, independence of spirit, and a bit of gusto. It requires the fortitude to resist convention and tradition in the name of a higher truth. We saw earlier that Kant's principal general term for such qualities was "maturity"; Emerson's favored word in this passage is "strength." It is not incidental that a writer so steeped in the classics should use the word "strength" three times in an effort to suggest an alternative to Christian morality. For Plato and Aristotle, as for Plutarch and the Stoics, the concept of virtue was always closely associated with the idea of strength.[19]

But even if we possess all the requisite strengths, the second paragraph quoted above reminds us that nature's standard is never easy to meet. Nature's law, as it turns out, is not only very exacting, it is also elusive at times. The paragraph starts out, familiarly enough, with yet another idiosyncratic Emersonian formulation of the doctrine of the mean. The imperative, here again, is on balance, moderation, and "proportion." Even those who are philosophically mature enough to resist tradition and convention should only do so when it is necessary and appropriate. "Power" must show due regard to "form." Virtue lies in a natural "sweetness and soundness" rather than in ideological vigilance. But Emerson then complicates his own argument. First he cites the "hollowness" and "partiality" of scholars as examples of the "noxiousness" that results from focusing too exclusively on abstract pursuits. He says that a one-sided devotion to the intellect leads to "quackery" and "disease." Then he seems to contradict himself yet again by suggesting that nature itself fosters such excess. "Irresistible nature made man such," he writes, alluding to the "haggard" artists, "and makes legions more of such, every day." How does this statement fit together with what preceded it? How can Emerson persistently invoke nature in support of an ethic of moderation, balance, and "the mid-world" yet at the same time affirm happily that this very same nature makes "legions" of men such that they are destined obsessively to pursue narrowly specialized professions that will inevitably warp and deform them? How, to put it in Emerson's terms, can "nature join with his enemy"? Is nature not bound by its own laws?

The answer to this question lies in the lesson of skepticism, and it brings us to the next and climactic phase of "Experience" as a whole. Emerson is comfortable here saying apparently contradictory things about nature because he has already absorbed skepticism's hard teaching about the severe limitations of human logic or human rationality narrowly conceived. Emerson turned his attention to the "the midworld" in the first place, we must remember, in an effort to shake himself free of the paralysis brought on by skepticism's withering logic. To his and his readers' relief, he found that logic only pertained to a small portion of human experience. In the uncritical territory of common life there was much to be done, much to be enjoyed, and even, if one revised one's conception of knowing, much to be known. These discoveries were recorded in a tone of slowly increasing confidence and clarity as the essay moved from its skeptical nadir at paragraph 10 to its current middle height at paragraph 14. At this middle point, Emerson is confident enough to allow nature to exceed and even to explode the classical moral categories by which he was coming to understand it because he has learned the danger of clinging too rigidly to any set of preordained categories. He acknowledges that there does seem to be a natural moral order that favors balance, proportion, and moderation in all things. But he also notes that for creatures as limited as human beings, it is necessary to be moderate even in one's conviction in the value of moderation: "The wise through excess of wisdom is made a fool." When nature seems to violate its own law, we must have faith that it does so in the service of a salutary larger purpose, however inscrutable at the moment. Having first rejected Christian ethics in favor of a classical naturalism, one could say, Emerson now brings back a kind of secularized Christian metaphysics by figuring nature in Protestant terms. Like the Calvinist God, Emerson's Nature provides "images and shadows" by recourse to which we may ascend to some inkling of her ultimate will, but we must never presume that she is constrained in any way by our necessarily limited conceptions.[20] This is not, strictly speaking, a skeptical stance; to apprehend that nature exceeds our categories is, after all, to apprehend something about nature. Before Copernicus knew exactly what the new model of the heavens should be, he presumably apprehended something that told him that the old model was inadequate. But for Emerson, as for Copernicus, Calvin, and Hume, there remains an important skeptical moment within a larger intuitive-realist confidence—the moment in which established categories or time-honored conventions or traditional assumptions are cast into doubt. This is why in the ecstatic and climactic paragraphs that follow, Emerson explicitly incorporates skepticism into his proclamation of a new kind of knowledge and a new way of knowing.

Emerson is not generally regarded as a deliberate craftsman. He wrote quickly, in fits of inspiration. His many family obligations and his busy lecture schedule did not generally leave him time to weave and reweave his verbal artifacts with the intricate symbolic artistry of, say, Thoreau. It is thus all the more remarkable to read carefully paragraphs 15 through 17 of "Experience" and to discover how subtly, precisely, and thoroughly they revisit, refigure, and attempt to resolve the fundamental issues of the essay. The strategy is basically dialectical. Having initially posited a skeptical thesis followed by what I have called a "common life" antithesis, Emerson now attempts to synthesize a larger ordered whole that somehow both contains and transcends these constitutive parts.

Paragraph 15 begins more or less where paragraph 14 leaves off, with a commonsense doctrine of the mean as the basis of an alternative to skepticism: "How easily, if fate would suffer it, we might keep forever these beautiful limits, and adjust ourselves, once for all, to the perfect calculation of the kingdom of known cause and effect. In the street and in the newspapers, life appears so plain a business, that manly resolution and adherence to the multiplication-table through all weathers, will insure success" (*E&L* 482). This is a significant step beyond the anxiety and uncertainty with which the essay began. Rediscovery of the discipline of the mean has reoriented Emerson; it has restored a sense of structure, order, and intelligibility to his experience. His statement of confidence in the mathematics of "cause and effect" suggests that he has also at last moved decisively beyond Hume's most fundamental skeptical doubts. But Emerson also deliberately overstates his case. In speaking of "perfect calculation" and "adherence to the multiplication-table," he makes it sound as if he has already forgotten the principal lesson learned from his engagement with skepticism—that we must not be too eager to reduce our experience to narrowly rational categories. But he has not actually forgotten. By again leaning toward one extreme he has rather set himself up rhetorically for the first stage of a remarkably powerful reformulation of this essay's central skeptical wisdom, its ambitious climactic synthesis of blindness and insight:

But ah! presently comes a day, or is it only a half-hour, with its angel-whispering—which discomfits the conclusions of nations and of years! Tomorrow again, everything looks real and angular, the habitual standards are reinstated, common sense is as rare as genius,—is the basis of genius, and experience is hands and feet to every enterprise,—and yet, he who should do his business on this understanding would be quickly bankrupt. Power keeps quite another road than the turnpikes of choice and will, namely, the subterranean and invisible tunnels and channels of life. (*E&L* 482)

This "angel-whispering" has been heard once before in "Experience"— in the passage cited above where Emerson rejected naturalist determinism by reference to humanity's distinctive metaphysical hunger, its seemingly innate hankering for "absolute truth" and "absolute good." Metaphysical intimations perform an analogous task here in upsetting Emerson's own tendency to settle into what we might call a determinism of the middle way. Common sense and moderation, "the habitual standards," are invaluable, Emerson acknowledges; they are "the basis of genius" and "the hands and feet to every enterprise." But we must not rely on them exclusively. We must not rest content with pragmatism. We must trust our deeper intuitions when they tell us that there is a higher kind of knowledge, a larger and more fundamental moral-metaphysical insight that will not yield itself to the strictly pragmatic mind. To attune ourselves to this transcendent principle or "Power," we need to retain a bit of skeptical openness even as we move beyond skepticism. Only when commonsense reverence for "beautiful limits" remains skeptically mindful of the limits of its own commonsensical position are we open to the intense apprehension of fundamental reality that Emerson calls "surprise."

Emerson's concept of "surprise" is necessarily somewhat elusive. It becomes considerably less so, however, if we notice how carefully Emerson represents it. At this late stage of "Experience" Emerson characterizes "surprise," with remarkable exactitude, as the precise compensatory counterpart of the skeptical negativity with which the essay began. The very first sentences of "Experience," we recall, found us alone and stranded, lost on a stairway "in a series of which we do not know the extremes," wishing to proceed one way or the other but too drunk from Lethe's cup to remember which way to go. A few paragraphs later Lethe's waters had seeped into everything, rendering all objects "sliding," "lubricious," and "evanescent." And, as the essay descended further in mood and tone, Emerson memorably characterized our "slippery" epistemological and moral condition: "We may have the sphere for our cricketball, but not a berry for our philosophy. Direct strokes she never gave us to make; all our blows glance, all our hits are accidents. Our relations to each other are oblique and casual." But now, as the essay nears the top of its counterbalancing rhetorical ascent, Emerson casts a similarly uncertain situation in a positive light:

> Life is a series of surprises, and would not be worth taking or keeping, if it were not. God delights to isolate us every day, and hide from us the past and future. We would look about us, but with grand politeness he draws down before us an impenetrable screen of purest sky, and another behind us of purest sky. "You will not remember," he seems to say, "and you will not expect." All good conversation, manners, and action, come from a spontaneity which forgets usages, and makes the moment great. Nature hates calculators; her methods are saltatory and impulsive. . . . We thrive by casualties. Our chief experiences have been casual. The most attractive class of people are those who are powerful obliquely, and not by the direct stroke. . . . Theirs is the beauty of the bird, or the morning light, and not of art. In the thought of genius there is always a surprise, and the moral sentiment is well called "the newness," for it is never other, as new to the oldest intelligence as to the young child,—"the kingdom that cometh without observation." In like manner, for practical success, there must not be too much design. . . . Every man is an impossibility, until he is born; every thing impossible, until we see a success. The ardors of piety agree at last with the coldest skepticism,—that nothing is of us or our works,—that all is of God. (*E&L* 483)

Emerson thus executes a deft conceptual and figurative pivot. Where in the essay's first paragraph our past and future pathways up "the stair" were ominously obscured by the darkness of "Sleep," here the limits imposed upon our memory and foreknowledge are suffused with light— "an impenetrable screen of purest sky, and another behind us of purest sky." Our vision is blocked in both scenarios, but what was a dark source of deep anxiety in the opening passage has here become luminous and lovely, even sublime. The phrase "screen of purest sky" performs the difficult dialectical task of associatively linking limitation with transcendence. Similarly, the same obstacles to "contact" that at first so deeply frustrated Emerson are here celebrated as the "casualties" by which we "thrive." Again, the ominously mortal connotations of "casualty" are dialectically absorbed into a broader vitalistic embrace. And the same may be said of "direct stroke," a phrase that is directly transported from paragraph 4. Where initially "direct strokes" were lamented as an unattainable immediacy—"Direct strokes [nature] never gave us to make; all our blows glance, all our hits are accidents," here they are cheerfully forgone in favor of a capacious epistemological nonchalance: "The most attractive class of people are those who are powerful obliquely, and not by the direct stroke."

This passage as a whole may be said to initiate a large-scale affirmative reappropriation of the same fundamental existential and epistemological limits the discovery of which initially pushed Emerson toward despondency. Where at the beginning of the essay obstructions to knowledge were symptomatic of a generally abject condition of lostness and disorientation, they are here refigured as nature's way of keeping our minds in a state of salutary openness. An awareness of the severe limitations of our capacity for knowledge need not lead us to despair, Emerson argues here, because the inspirations of "genius" and the intuitions of the moral sentiment occur outside of these narrow boundaries. Indeed, we should be exhilarated by the discovery of the limitations of rationality because our reliance on "design" and "calculation" inhibited the activity of these more potent inner resources. "Genius" and "the moral sentiment" are associated with "newness" because they cannot be anticipated or planned for in a programmatic rational way. Seen from this perspective, the limits of rationality become thresholds of moral-metaphysical insight. What was crisis at the beginning of the essay has now become opportunity. "Deluges of lethe" have here become refreshing waters.

The accommodation of skepticism becomes Emerson's explicit focus as the essay reaches the summit of its major ascending arc. Paragraphs 16 and 17 of "Experience" contain some of Emerson's most ecstatically affirmative writing:

> So is it with us, now skeptical, or without unity, because immersed in forms and effects all seeming to be of equal yet hostile value, and now religious, whilst in the reception of spiritual law. . . . Do but observe the mode of our illumination. When I converse with a profound mind, or if at any time being alone I have good thoughts, I do not at once arrive at satisfactions, as when, being thirsty, I drink water, or go to the fire, being cold: no! but I am at first apprised of my vicinity to a new and excellent

region of life. By persisting to read or to think, this region gives further sign of itself, as it were in flashes of light, in sudden discoveries of its profound beauty and repose, as if the clouds that covered it parted at intervals, and showed the approaching traveller the inland mountains, with the tranquil eternal meadows spread at their base, whereon flocks graze, and shepherds pipe and dance. But every insight from this realm of thought is felt as initial, and promises a sequel. (*E&L* 484–85)

Fortune, Minerva, Muse, Holy Ghost,—these are quaint names, too narrow to cover this unbounded substance. . . . In our more correct writing, we give to this generalization the name of Being, and thereby confess that we have arrived as far as we can go. Suffice it for the joy of the universe, that we have not arrived at a wall, but at interminable oceans. Our life seems not present, so much as prospective; not for the affairs on which it is wasted, but as a hint of this vast-flowing vigor. (*E&L* 485–86)

The most common understanding of the complementarity of skepticism and faith suggests simply that skepticism shows reason its limits and faith steps in to fill the void. This is the "fideistic" view of Tertullian, Erasmus, Pascal, Hume, or Kierkegaard. While Emerson's position in "Experience" resembles "fideism" to some extent, it is substantially different in at least one very important respect. For fideists, skepticism and faith continue to occupy opposite conceptual poles even as the former yields to the latter. Having arrived via skepticism at a conviction of reason's inability to provide satisfactory answers to a range of fundamental questions, the fideist accepts by faith the truth of the answers supplied by a given religious orthodoxy. In Emerson, by contrast, skepticism and "faith" as he understands them never cease to interpenetrate each other. They are both contained within a dialectical conception of "reason" wherein an inclination to doubt never entirely negates the capacity for intuitive certainty. At no point does Emerson's understanding of the limitations of rationality compel him to advocate consent to a given orthodoxy. But neither does Emerson's sense of the limitations of orthodox faith at any point compel him to advocate a narrow or strictly secular rationalism. This is what allows him to declare so many times that his position is "new." It is neither a radical Enlightenment deflation of religious belief per se nor a nostalgic Romantic reversion to religious tradition. It is an effort to somehow distill and synthesize the element of truth in both of these philosophical-historical moments.

In the lines quoted above, Emerson's words are carefully chosen and arranged to both announce and enact a form of knowledge that incorporates skepticism—a form of knowing made possible by the acceptance of a degree of unknowing. In characterizing "the mode of our illumination" Emerson emphasizes indirectness, irregular and unpredictable pursuit of fugitive intimations, a rhythmic pattern of halting uncertainty followed by sudden overwhelming epiphany. These spontaneous "flashes of light," he implies, only come to those who have learned the limits of the "direct stroke," those who do not insist too rigidly on a preconceived analytical protocol. At the beginning of the essay, we recall, in the first sentences of the second paragraph, Emerson lamented that we do not know "what we [are] doing, or where we are going, then when we think we best know." The implication was that we possess much virtue and knowledge, but we do not know that we possess them because we are looking for them in the wrong places. What we conventionally think of as knowledge is only a relatively superficial form of it. Now, at this late stage of the essay, at the climax of its principal ascending trajectory, we have at last learned what we do and can know by confronting the extent of what we do not and cannot know. Skepticism has taught us not to expect too much from abstract logic and analysis and has thus freed us up to attend to the deeper knowledge disclosed by intuitive and initially unconscious processes of "opening," "arrival," and "beholding."

To Emerson's delighted "surprise," the "opening" at which he "arrives" is nothing less than absolute metaphysical ground. What he "beholds" there is nothing less than the fundamental, all-encompassing, and divine reality that constitutes the universe as a whole and underlies all experience. Emerson ranges through a broad array of timeless religious metaphors in an effort to capture and evoke the character of this "unbounded substance." He speaks with infectious rapture of "Chance," "the miracle of life," "a musical perfection," "the Ideal," "august magnificence," "the life of life," "the sunbright Mecca of the desert," "Fortune," "Minerva," "Muse," "Holy Ghost," "ineffable cause," "water," "air," "fire," "love," "vast-flowing vigor" (*E&L* 485), and, simply, "Being" (*E&L* 486). He also gives special place to a Pauline-Christian idiom of rebirth in characterizing the transformative effect on him of this insight. "What a future it opens!" he writes. "I feel a *new* heart beating with the love of the *new* beauty. I am ready to *die* out of nature, and be *born again* into this new yet unapproachable America I have found in the West" (*E&L* 485, italics mine). Emerson brings together such a vast range of Christian and non-Christian discourses here—pre-Socratic Greek, Platonic, Chinese, classical Latin, Christian Latin, Islamic, and, not least important, Western Enlightenment—in an effort to suggest the transcultural universality of the principle he is naming. And, as if this were not expansive enough, for the first time in the essay he attaches specific historical and political significance to his argument. In imagining "America" as the nation historically destined to overcome nationhood by embodying and carrying forward this cosmopolitan moral-metaphysical principle, he again enlists his distinctive Romantic epistemology in the service of an Enlightenment political vision.

Perhaps because the language of these passages is not strikingly original, they have not generally earned the fame of the "transparent eyeball" section of *Nature*. But the contact claimed is every bit as fundamental and every bit as exalted, and it is all the more valuable for being so hard won. For in "Experience," unlike in *Nature*, Emerson has taken the time, as he suggests in "Montaigne," to "count and describe [the] doubts and negations" (*E&L* 702). It has proven a difficult but cathartic exercise. At the apex of the ascending leg of the essay's first and more important arc of feeling, having "done justice to [negation's] terrors" (*E&L* 703), Emerson proclaims himself nonetheless confident and whole, nonetheless optimistic and worshipful.

The second of the two arcs of feeling in "Experience," as I have suggested, reiterates on a smaller scale the cathartic *U* pattern of the first. It is thus not necessary to trace its entire trajectory, but it is nonetheless helpful to conclude my discussion by noting and commenting upon what I take to be the three most important passages of this minor second movement. By drawing relevant thematic connections to the first movement, I shall be able at once to review, to extend, and to complete my account of the structure and substance of the essay as a whole.

The three passages I have in mind occur in paragraphs 18, 21, and 25, respectively. Picturing the section as a whole as a lowercase *u*, these passages may be said to occupy the apex of the left leg, the base curve, and the concluding apex of the right leg, respectively. They thus plot the general trajectory of the movement, beginning with the following mordant statement: "It is very unhappy, but too late to be helped, the discovery we have made, that we exist. That discovery is called the Fall of

Man. Ever afterwards, we suspect our instruments. We have learned that we do not see directly, but mediately, and that we have no means of correcting these colored and distorting lenses which we are, or of computing the amount of their errors" (*E&L* 487).

From here, as in the first section, the discussion descends steadily through an extended figurative commentary on subjectivity. This time, however, Emerson restricts himself for the most part to one subtopic of this broad category—solipsism. He pursues this topic to its reductive nadir at the end of paragraph 21, where he compares all human striving for objective knowledge to a kitten's fruitless, solitary pursuit of her own tail: "A subject and an object," he writes, "—it takes so much to make the galvanic circuit complete, but magnitude adds nothing. What imports it whether it is Kepler and the sphere; Columbus and America; a reader and his book; or puss with her tail?" (*E&L* 489). But again, as in the first movement, no sooner does Emerson reach this despondent low point than he begins to turn himself around. The second passage initiates this recovery: "And yet is the God the native of these bleak rocks. That need makes in morals the capital virtue of self-trust. We most hold hard to this poverty, however scandalous, and by more vigorous self-recoveries, after the sallies of action, possess our axis more firmly. The life of truth is cold, and so far mournful, but it is not the slave of tears, contritions, and perturbations. It does not attempt another's work, nor adopt another's facts" (*E&L* 490).

From this turn Emerson builds slowly to the affirmative concluding paragraph of the essay, whose great first sentences must be read in connection with the final sentences of the preceding paragraph:

> People disparage knowing and the intellectual life, and urge doing. I am very content with knowing, if only I could know. That is august entertainment, and would suffice me a great while. To know a little, would be worth the expense of this world. I hear always the law of Adrastia, "that every soul which had acquired any truth, should be safe from harm until another period."
>
> I know that the world I converse with in the city and in the farms is not the world I think. I observe that difference, and shall observe it. One day, I shall know the value and law of this discrepance. (*E&L* 491–92)

Despite their chastened tone, all three of these passages lay claim to a kind of knowledge. Emerson speaks in the first passage of "the discovery we have made" and of what "we have learned." In the second passage he invokes a "main lesson of wisdom," which, again, he claims "to have learned." And in the third passage, somewhat confusingly, Emerson first proclaims the near-impossibility of "knowing" and then tells us something he "knows."

To understand the nature of this knowledge is to understand the affirmative cast of "Experience" as a whole. We have already laid the groundwork for such understanding in examining Emerson's struggle with skepticism in the first part of the essay. The claim here in the concluding second movement is essentially a reformulation of what I earlier called a skeptical gnosis or a Pyrrhonian illumination. It is not knowledge of a given fact or principle but rather knowledge about the "fallen" condition of knowledge itself, an awareness of the limits of Cartesian rationality, that prepares Emerson for more profound intuitive forms of knowing. The first part of this process is plainly described in the first passage, where Emerson declares simply, "We have learned that we do not see directly, but mediately, and that we have no means of correcting these colored and distorting lenses which we are, or of computing the amount of their errors." Just as we saw him do in the concluding sections of the first movement, Emerson here claims one kind of certainty even as he disclaims another; he admits severe limitations to "our" capacity for knowledge, but this admission is itself presented as a secure piece of wisdom. He proclaims confidence, in other words, in having acquired knowledge of the limitations of knowledge. For all its negativity, this is still a substantial improvement upon his condition at the start of the essay. He has moved from subjective delusion and disorientation to a lucid and objective knowledge of limits. In much the same sense that Henry Adams would later negatively describe his own formidable education as a series of progressively higher stages of awareness of his own ignorance, Emerson here announces in negative terms a substantial step forward in his philosophical growth.

The second passage describes further progress. Having raised the ominous specter of solipsism in the intervening paragraphs, Emerson grants in the sentences I have quoted that there is an important degree of truth in the solipsist's argument. We are indeed inescapably alone in some fundamental existential sense, Emerson acknowledges, and we do incorrigibly impose our own puny perspective on the people and things we encounter. Such a situation is indeed "bleak," "poor," "cold," and "mournful." But to face up to this "poverty" honestly and to accept its conditions is to give oneself access to nothing less than "wisdom," "truth," "virtue," stability, self-knowledge, and even a "God." It is to "recover" one's selfhood. These are not trivial rewards. They have long been Emerson's highest philosophical aims. For Emerson, to understand that his condition is limited is not necessarily to limit his desire for understanding. The use of the word "axis" is telling here, because, like the "iron string" of "Self-Reliance," it suggests stability within motion. To suggest that our "poverty" may provide an "axis" is again to suggest that knowledge of the limitations of knowledge is itself a stable, even a foundational, form of knowledge. It is the epistemological equivalent of psychological individuation. "To know [his] own from another's" is "bleak" and "mournful" in the same way that separating from his parents is painful for a child. But it is similarly essential to a mature grasp of reality.

And a mature grasp of reality is precisely what "Experience" finally wishes to claim. The first three sentences of the last paragraph of "Experience" are short in length and modest in tone. Unlike the concluding paragraphs of the first movement, they profess no ecstatic metaphysical insights. But they do make a remarkably strong and subtle assertion of what we might call psychoepistemological maturity. And they do so in carefully chosen words that manage aptly to distill the positive wisdom of "Experience" without reducing its subtlety or complexity. In the concluding sentences of the penultimate paragraph quoted above, Emerson wryly restates the principal aim of the essay in terms that again decisively distinguish his project from pragmatism: "People disparage knowing and the intellectual life, and urge doing," he writes. "I am very content with knowing, if only I could know." Knowledge is here unambiguously defended as a high and sufficient aim in itself. Indeed, in dramatic contrast to pragmatist "insouciance," knowledge for its own sake is said to be a prize worth any price. Following such a preface, Emerson's next sentence emerges as profoundly ambitious. "*I know*," he writes to begin the next paragraph, "that the world I converse with in the city and in the farms is not the world I *think*" (italics mine). In using the phrase "I know" at this precise juncture, Emerson quietly lays claim to all the rewards of knowledge he has just wistfully sketched. Even though the form of his knowledge is negative—"the world . . . is not the world I *think*"—it is nonetheless knowledge, nonetheless a bit of truth, and as such may stand as "august entertainment," "sufficiency," and "safety from harm."

And if we reflect on the substance of the knowledge Emerson claims here in the context of the essay as a whole, we cannot but conclude that these sentences announce with appropriate modesty the achievement of real and lasting wisdom. In short, for Emerson to say that he knows that the outside world is not the world he thinks is to say that he has gained an invaluable degree of perspective on the subjective distortions, distances, and delusions that tricked and at times terrorized him in the body of the essay. In Freudian terms one could say that Emerson has finally consented to heed the reality principle; he has eschewed infantile fantasies of omnipotence, adolescent narcissistic projections, and any number of adult complexes and defensive evasions. He has taken an important step beyond childish or neurotic unreality toward a fuller and more realistic acceptance of the world as it is. In more general terms one can say simply that in accepting the difference between the world and what he *thinks* Emerson has laid the foundation of both personal and political sanity.

6

Limited Government

*"Man the Reformer" (1841); "Lecture on
the Times" (1841); "The Conservative" (1841);
"The Transcendentalist" (1842); "The Young
American" (1844); "Politics" (1844);
"New England Reformers" (1844)*

For most of "Experience" Emerson focuses inward, training a
withering gaze on the foundations of his own selfhood. But in the
essay's concluding sentences he looks out to a larger social world. From
a mature epistemological perspective, the achievement of which constitutes the central psychic drama of "Experience" as a whole, Emerson
delivers in closing a nuanced, carefully weighed statement on politics:

> But I have not found that much was gained by manipular attempts to
> realize the world of thought. Many eager persons successively make
> an experiment in this way, and make themselves ridiculous. They ac-
> quire democratic manners, they foam at the mouth, they hate and
> deny. But far be from me the despair which prejudges the law by a pal-
> try empiricism,—since there never was a right endeavor, but it suc-
> ceeded. Patience and patience, we shall win at the last. . . . We dress
> our garden, eat our dinners, and these things make no impression, are
> forgotten next week; but in the solitude to which every man is always

returning, he has a sanity and revelations which in his passage into new
worlds he will carry with him. (*E&L* 492)

Addressing himself to an ideological climate both at home and abroad
in which utopian-socialist political theories and experiments were pro-
liferating, Emerson here takes up a moderate stance on the general issue
of social reform.[1] If our personal sanity depends upon "observing the
difference" between abstract ideality and the recalcitrant concrete otherness of the objective world, he infers, it follows that the health of societies will benefit from an analogous dose of skeptical caution.[2] He thus
emphatically rejects utopian social engineering ("manipular attempts to
realize the world of thought") while endorsing the political pursuit of
moral intimations ("there never was a right endeavor, but it succeeded").
The privateness of the private sphere must be protected, he implies, for
this "solitude to which [we are] always returning" is both the haven of
our "sanity" and the oracular ground of new insights. But if a political
program is duly respectful of our inner freedom and duly attuned to the
moral intuitions that arise in this inviolable space, then it is salutary to
labor in its behalf, and it will eventually succeed. The tone is explicitly
not "despairing" but rather forward-looking in a balanced, realistic, and
resilient manner. In essence, Emerson recognizes the need for social
change, but he advocates slow, piecemeal, organic change unfolding in
an open-ended fashion from secure moral principles—"patience and
patience, we shall win at the last"—rather than any thoroughgoing radical transformation ideologically imposed from on high.[3]

Emerson articulates this moderate moral progressivism not only in
these concluding sentences of "Experience" but in the broad pattern of
the many overtly political statements he made throughout the 1840s and
1850s. On the one hand, Emerson's response in the 1840s to the efflorescence of utopian theories and experiments was persistently skeptical in
the manner of the passage above. In "Man the Reformer" (1841), "Lecture on the Times" (1841), "The Conservative" (1841), "The Transcendentalist" (1842), "The Young American" (1844), "Politics" (1844), "New
England Reformers" (1844), and in his generally tepid responses to the
revolutionary uprisings he witnessed in Europe in 1848, we find what
might be described as an antiutopian corollary to the important aspect
of "Experience" that stresses the limits of Cartesian rationality. If it
is impossible for the individual consciousness to attain complete analytical mastery over the "evanescent" and "slippery" objects of its own

experience, Emerson infers in these addresses, there is no reason to believe that collectivities comprised of such individuals should fare any better. On the other hand, Emerson's response to the slavery issue in the mid- and late 1840s and the 1850s was persistently and profoundly morally idealistic. In "An Address . . . on . . . the Emancipation of the Negroes in the British West Indies" (1844), "Anniversary of West Indian Emancipation" (1845), "Antislavery Speech at Dedham" (1846), "Address to the Citizens of Concord" on the Fugitive Slave Law (1851), "The Fugitive Slave Law" (1854), "Lecture on Slavery" (1855), "Speech at a Meeting to Aid John Brown's Family" (1859), "John Brown" (1860), "The President's Proclamation" (1862), and "Fortune of the Republic" (1863), Emerson may be said to draw a natural rights corollary to that aspect of "Experience" that found an antidote to psychic disorientation in the intuition of an objectively subsistent moral law.[4] Just as the anguished individual selfhood in "Experience" reorients itself by recourse to universal moral principles, so Emerson exhorted an increasingly anguished America in the late 1840s and throughout the 1850s to find its bearings by a renewed dedication to the "self-evident" foundational political truth of natural rights. For Emerson, natural rights were the direct political analogue of the moral law—similarly knowable by all sane human beings possessed of a moral sense, similarly essential to societal health and wholeness, and similarly dangerous to transgress. In these two clusters of addresses we can observe Emerson arriving at his political maturity by striking a balance between two positions that might initially seem antithetical—on the one hand, an often caustic antiutopian skepticism, and on the other hand, a fervent commitment to the principle of natural rights as the absolute moral-metaphysical foundation of a just political order. In thus moving between political realism and natural rights foundationalism, I will argue, Emerson weaves together in his own distinctively eclectic way two prominent conceptual strands of liberal political thought.

A healthy degree of skepticism toward utopian schemes has characterized the modern liberal political tradition throughout its history. At its outset, as Leo Strauss and his students have shown and as I have already mentioned, Locke's epochal solution to the problem of religious factionalism in seventeenth-century England depended in large part on a dramatic deflation of the classical conception of the ethically ennobling purposes of political life.[5] Taking a page from the realism of Hobbes and Machiavelli, Locke based his political theory not on a vision of how virtuously human beings might behave at their best but rather on how selfishly they observably do behave at their most ordinary. Having witnessed the havoc wreaked throughout Europe by religiously inspired political zealots, Locke was willing to purchase tolerance, institutional stability, social harmony, and individual rights at the price of communal cohesion, moral exaltation, and martial rigor. Such a tough-minded trade-off implied an underlying skepticism about the viability of perfectionist political schemes per se—a skepticism that has characterized mainstream liberal thought ever since. In seeking principally to keep people from harming one another rather than to help them become more virtuous, Locke established the fundamentally "negative" libertarian orientation that Benjamin Constant, Isaiah Berlin, and others have identified as the central defining feature of modern liberal politics.[6]

Of course, there have been important exceptions within the modern liberal tradition to its own generally antiutopian temper. In the late eighteenth century radical French prophets of reason and progress such as Condorcet foresaw "the achievement of a society in which all the natural evils are suppressed and the immemorial human follies—war, tyranny, intolerance—abolished."[7] Radical English contemporaries of Condorcet such as Thomas Paine and William Godwin harbored similarly exalted hopes. Benthamite radicals carried the utopian torch in the first half of the nineteenth century, planning for the systematic reconstruction of British society in accordance with the stringently rational postulates of the "felicific calculus." And many today argue that a sluggish and intrusive welfare-state Leviathan is the unwieldy offspring of early-twentieth-century "revisionist" liberalism's ill-advised utopian departure from orthodox classical liberal principles of limited government. But it is nonetheless accurate to hold with John Gray that the liberal tradition has been on the whole more "meliorist" than utopian.[8] Liberals have tended optimistically to believe that wise political arrangements will have the long-term historical effect of gradually reducing human misery and liberating human potentials. But liberals have also been quick to insist that the first building block of such wise political arrangements must be a due distrust of any concentration of political authority itself, however high-minded the professed aims of its agents.[9]

Within the broad corpus of liberal theory, Gray has pointed out, it is preeminently in the political and economic writings of David Hume,

Adam Smith, their American Federalist offspring, and their twentieth-century disciple F. A. Hayek that we find due consideration given to the facts of human fallibility. Hamilton and Madison follow their Scottish teachers primarily in voicing a degree of residual Calvinist moral pessimism; it is because human beings are irremediably morally flawed, because they are possessed by an insatiable lust for dominance, that it is necessary to impose legal limits upon what they may do, especially when they hold power.[10] It would be difficult to overstate the importance of this fundamental Augustinian insight to the American liberal tradition; it is the principal source of the deeply ingrained wariness of centralized political authority that arguably preserved the United States, Britain, and in turn Western civilization as a whole from the cataclysmic totalitarian hubris that convulsed much of the world in our century. But residual Augustinianism is not, I think, the most important legacy of Scottish liberalism for Emerson, who with regard to innate depravity managed, after all, to travel a long way from his New England Calvinist roots. The important political connection to be drawn between Emerson and the Scots has more to do with epistemological than with moral fallibility. And the best guide to the fallibilist epistemology of Scottish liberalism is F. A. Hayek.

We have seen how in "Experience" a Humean/Kantian skeptical chastening of the Cartesian conception of knowledge opened the way to the speaker's discovery of a different kind of knowing. Having reluctantly accepted that "the great gifts are not got by analysis," the speaker found to his delighted "surprise" that they may better be had by spontaneous activity and a kind of patient intuitive openness. Adding to his surprise, the speaker also finds that such intuitive knowing is not strictly the privilege of poets in solitude or prophets speaking in tongues. His eyes cleansed by skepticism, the speaker notices that the performance of even the most ordinary concrete tasks often depends upon a kind of quick, intuitive knowing inaccessible to plodding analysis: "In like manner, for practical success, there must not be too much design. A man will not be observed in doing that which he can do best. There is a certain magic about his properest action, which stupefies your powers of observation, so that though it is done before you, you wist not of it" (*E&L* 483). By giving up on an initially rigid attachment to abstract rational "design," Emerson's speaker here gives himself access to a vast hidden reserve of tacit knowledge and practical know-how. "Do not craze yourself with thinking," he summarizes, with a disparaging glance at the utopian experiment at Brook Farm, "but go about your business anywhere. Life is not intellectual or critical, but sturdy" (*E&L* 478).

The wisdom of Smithian political economy, Hayek has argued, stems from an analogous chastening of Cartesian epistemology. According to Hayek's account, utopian-socialist planned economies were bound to founder for the same reason that the speaker of "Experience" initially foundered—an excessive and unviable confidence in the capacity of Cartesian analysis to impose a preconceived rational design on an irreducibly spontaneous, multifarious, fluid, and unpredictable human reality. And, for Hayek, free-market economies were likely to flourish for at least one of the same reasons that the speaker of "Experience" eventually flourishes—a flexible, open-ended readiness to draw upon the various and often tacit resources of ordinary practical know-how and decentralized local knowledge. Through Hayek, then, we can see a way in which Emerson was not only a Lockean liberal but also a Humean liberal, and a liberal à la Montaigne.[11] Emerson was inclined skeptically to limit government rather than to entrust it with transformative utopian powers, not only because he wished to guard a sacrosanct open space for individuals but also because he believed that no central mind or group of minds could ever know enough or know the right sort of things to successfully design an entire society according to a preconceived plan. If he could not himself force his own experience into such systematically knowable order, he concluded, there was no reason to believe that an entire society could or should do so. In rejecting "manipular attempts to realize the world of thought," the above paragraph from "Experience" concisely expresses a crucial political inference that Emerson drew from his complex accommodation of Humean skepticism. For Emerson, as implicitly for Hume and Adam Smith and explicitly for Hayek, "the impossibility of socialism [was] an epistemological impossibility."[12]

Hayek coined a term for the type of utopian political epistemology he opposed: "constructivist rationalism." According to Gray's concise definition, "constructivism" is "the error that the order we discover—in nature, in our minds, and in society—has been put there by some designing mind."[13] Despite the persistent efforts of Western philosophers since Plato, Hayek argued, the larger natural, mental, and social orders in which human beings participate cannot accurately be understood by analogy to human artifice. The most fundamental processes of human evolution, human consciousness, and human interaction are irreducibly spontaneous, complex, contingent, concretely manifold, and locally distinctive. While it is possible to arrive at accurate inductive generalizations about the rules that obtain in any of these various spheres of experience, such rules cannot be intelligibly harmonized or manipulated in advance by the universal mind or will of any philosopher-king, rational God, elite body of experts, or state bureaucracy. Modern political constructivism posed an ominous threat to human freedom and human flourishing, Hayek argued, by hubristically ignoring these inescapable epistemological limits. To entrust an implausibly benevolent and impossibly omniscient centralized political authority with planning and supervising a perfectly harmonious, egalitarian, and cohesive society was not only historically naive, it was objectively untenable. The excessive constructivist reliance on "design" and its concomitant blindness to the intrinsic dynamism, wisdom, and loveliness of human spontaneity would result not only in the economic but also in the mental, moral, and aesthetic impoverishment of its subjects. The citizens of a constructivist regime would not only lack choices in the supermarket, in professional pursuits, and in forms of self-expression but also lose touch with the rich and various moral, intellectual, and aesthetic resources tacitly contained within long-standing "prerational" local traditions and practices. Ultimately, as the grim history of the Soviet Union and its satellites proved, a regime based on a "rationally constructivist" theory of human social order was bound first to dislocate, deracinate, and destroy its subjects, and then to destroy itself.

Hayek's conception of constructivism is helpful for our purposes because the utopian theory that held the most fascination for idealistic New Englanders in the early 1840s, including many of Emerson's friends, fits the definition perfectly. The Frenchman Charles Fourier, having first exhaustively anatomized, enumerated, and labeled every species of human passion and all possible passionate intermixtures in an elaborate taxonomy of emotions, then calculated the exact number of human character types necessary to populate an ideally attractive, industrious, cohesive, and pleasurably engaged community. The number was 810. Multiplying by two for gender, Fourier concluded that the optimally efficient socioeconomic unit, for which he adopted the aptly militaristic term "phalanx," must contain exactly 1,620 men, women, and children. He developed a "minutely detailed organization plan," complete with precise charts, tables, and schedules, to govern every contingency in the busy daily lives of this happy vanguard.[14] Believing that all human labor and social life should be governed by "attraction," Fourier ingeniously mixed and matched tasks, types, and timetables to provide in advance for the satisfaction of the 1,620 "phalansterians" every imaginable economic, social, and sexual wish. The ensuing high morale combined with rational streamlining and vast economies of scale, he argued, would make his phalanxes many times more productive and prosperous than dispirited, disorganized, and wastefully competitive capitalist social groupings. He sketched the vast Versailles-like structures and surrounding Edenic acres that would house and feed his blissful cohorts and looked sanguinely ahead to the time when "a global federation of two million phalanxes would supplant existing states and governments."[15] Informed throughout by a whimsically naive confidence in preconceived abstract design, Fourier's approach, which he called "social science," would be better classified as constructivist rationalism run amok.

Mocked and largely dismissed in France, Fourier's ideas found in Albert Brisbane an able and energetic American proselytizer. Such is the force of human credulity that in the decade after 1842 nearly thirty model phalanxes were founded throughout New England, New York, and the northern Midwest.[16] The most famous and influential of these was located at Brook Farm, Massachusetts, where a number of Emerson's friends and disciples reorganized their own previously established utopian community according to Fourierist principles and increasingly offered their services as publicists and spokespeople for the national Associationist movement. Emerson saluted his friends' imagination and generosity of spirit, but he notoriously declined to join the effort. And in a *Dial* article of July 1842 entitled "Fourierism and the Socialists" he made his objections emphatically clear:

> In spite of the assurances of its friends, that it was new and widely discriminated from all other plans for the regeneration of society, we could not exempt it from the criticism which we apply to so many projects for reform with which the brain of the age teems. Our feeling was, that Fourier had skipped no fact but one, namely, Life. He treats man as a plastic thing, something that may be put up or down, ripened or retarded, moulded, polished, made into solid, or fluid, or gas, at the will of the leader; or, perhaps, as a vegetable, from which, though now a poor crab, a very good peach can by manure and exposure be in time

produced, but skips the faculty of life, which spawns and scorns system and system-makers, which eludes all conditions, which makes or supplants a thousand phalanxes and New-Harmonies with each pulsation. (*E&L* 1207)

Emerson's tone is mocking, but a twenty-first-century reader will hear in his words an ominous forewarning about the danger of collective bewitchment by the totalizing false promise of Cartesian constructivism. Emerson here arrives by broad intuitive leaps at the same fundamental insight that twentieth-century liberals such as Isaiah Berlin, Václav Havel, and F. O. Hayek distilled from vast and bitter historical experience. His stance is a characteristically loose blend of Romantic vitalism and Kantian moral principle, reverently invoking "Life" as an ultimate value and implicitly invoking the categorical imperative in warning against Fourier's readiness to "treat man as a plastic thing." Berlin turned similarly to Kant to draw a moral from the tragic story of twentieth-century utopian overreaching: "Out of the crooked timber of humanity," he tirelessly quoted the Enlightenment sage, "no straight thing was ever made."[17] And Havel could have been directly paraphrasing the skeptical vitalism expressed by Emerson above when in "What I Believe" he wrote: "The attempt to unite all economic entities under the authority of a single monstrous owner, the state, and to subject all economic life to one central voice of reason that deems itself more clever than life itself, is an attempt against life itself."[18] Emerson in his darkest hours could not have begun to imagine the horrors that were matters of grim fact to Berlin and Havel. But it nonetheless speaks well of Emerson's basic political intuitions that they accord so closely with the sober maxims of these most sane, sophisticated, and humane witnesses of the tragic history of the twentieth century. In so clearly grasping and rejecting the inhuman drift of utopian constructivism Emerson displays a realistic historical-political instinct. It is a moderate, undogmatic, profoundly liberal instinct, the seeds of which were planted by Emerson's youthful reading of Montaigne, Locke, Montesquieu, Hume, Smith, Burke, and the American founders, and which came to full fruition in "Experience" as he reckoned forthrightly with the tendency of his own overreaching mind to tyrannize both its objects and itself. Emerson places himself in the liberal tradition, in other words, by successfully transferring the difficult wisdom of "Experience" from the personal to the political sphere. On the basis of his own inner experience he concludes that constructivist rationalism can only have a deadening and distorting effect on human subjects because it will inevitably uproot them from the intimate, organic, and spontaneous sources of their energy, feeling, creativity, and insight.

The seven political addresses and essays that Emerson wrote in the early 1840s are all founded upon the basic conceptual opposition thus powerfully articulated at the conclusion of "Experience" and in his brief critique of Fourier. "Man the Reformer," "Lecture on the Times," "The Conservative," "The Transcendentalist," "The Young American," "Politics," and "New England Reformers" are unified in broadly favoring what one might call an "individualist moral organicism" over a socialist political constructivism. As Emerson states in "Politics," "The State must follow and not lead the character and progress of its citizens" (*E&L* 559). This broad "major" argument is built out of two constitutive subsidiary themes that appear and reappear with varying frequency, length, and emphasis among these seven works. These two themes may be labeled as the "sacrosanct Lockean boundary" and the "priority of virtue." Since the repetition of these themes would make it redundant to discuss each essay or address in turn, and since no single work contains all of the significant subsidiary arguments, it will be best to proceed thematically, reviewing each of these several constitutive aspects of Emerson's mature position as it is developed in the works in which it appears.

Emerson clearly shared in the broadly "negative" Lockean orientation of modern liberalism. His work as a whole might well stand as the preeminent cultural exfoliation of a "rights-based" American legal regime in which a set of constitutionally established individual liberties "trump" all other interests, including, importantly, the democratically expressed will of the community. We have already noted Emerson's pervasive defensiveness of an open preserve of free intellectual, artistic, and even moral space in which the individual should be subject to no will other than his or her own. The verbal demarcation of this space is his most characteristic political gesture. At every opportunity Emerson poeticizes the primordial boundary of Lockean liberalism. He retreats behind this boundary in pursuit of self-communion: "To go into solitude, a man needs to retire as much from his chamber as from society" (*Nature, E&L* 8). He sharpens this boundary as he achieves solitary elation: "The name of the nearest friend sounds then foreign and accidental, to be brothers, to be acquaintances, master or servant, is then a trifle and a disturbance" (*Nature, E&L* 10). He claims this boundary as protection for the pursuit of truth: "In silence, in steadiness, in severe abstraction, let him hold by himself . . . happy enough, if he can satisfy himself alone that this day he has seen something truly" ("The American Scholar," *E&L* 64). He explicitly links culture and science to politics along the trajectory of this boundary: "Free should the scholar be, free and brave. Free even to the definition of freedom, 'without any hindrance that does not arise from his own constitution'" ("The American Scholar," *E&L* 65). He bemoans the dissolution of this boundary in mass democratic society: "The doctrine of inspiration is lost; the base doctrine of the majority of voices usurps the place of the doctrine of the soul" ("The Divinity School Address," *E&L* 79). And in these threatening conditions he takes it upon himself wherever possible to rhetorically redraw this boundary: "What I must do is all that concerns me, not what the people think" ("Self-Reliance," *E&L* 263); "I shun father and mother and wife and brother when my genius calls me" ("Self-Reliance," *E&L* 262); "These are the voices which we hear in solitude, but they grow faint and inaudible when we enter the world" ("Self-Reliance," *E&L* 263); "Society is everywhere in conspiracy against the integrity of every one of its members" ("Self-Reliance," *E&L* 263); "We must go alone. I like the silent church before the service begins better than any preaching" ("Self-Reliance," *E&L* 272); "High be his heart, faithful be his will, clear his sight, that he may in good earnest be doctrine, society, law to himself, that a simple purpose may be to him as strong as iron necessity to others" ("Self-Reliance," *E&L* 274).

Perhaps the single most elegant of Emerson's countless figurations of this Lockean boundary comes toward the end of "The American Scholar": "We will walk on our own feet; we will work with our own hands; we will speak our own minds," he declares movingly in the concluding paragraph. "The dread of man and the love of man shall be a wall of defence and a wreath of joy around all" (*E&L* 71). By representing the same boundary as ambivalently charged with both "dread" and "love," as both "a wall of defence" and "a wreath of joy," Emerson is here able to connote at once the "negative" scaffolding of Lockean-liberal rights and the "positive" potential for human flourishing thereby protected. "The dread of man" infers the Augustinian-Christian and Hobbesean pessimism about human nature that, as I suggested earlier, so deeply informs liberalism's manifold checks on political power. "The love of man" evokes the more optimistic Enlightenment aspect of liberalism that sees all human beings as sacred vessels of natural rights and that looks toward the emancipation of hitherto untapped human potentials. Emerson's language characteristically seeks to connect theory to feeling at both levels, suggesting that the emotional tone of a liberal culture will be necessarily nuanced, shaded, complex, and creatively tense. On the one hand, his imagery suggests, liberal societies will be inherently defensive, fearful, and cautious; each individual will warily guard his or her freedoms from encroachment by others or by the state.[19] But at the same time liberal societies will also be optimistic, open, dynamic, expansive, and forward-looking: the foundational legal limit imposed by a truly liberal regime will raise individuals' hopes by the same stroke with which it defuses communal solidarity. This liberal vision is sufficiently ambivalent to stop short of utopianism, but its positive charge is emotionally potent. No sooner will the "wall of defence" be made secure than it will transform itself into "a wreath of joy."

Both faces of this liminal structure, the "wall" and the "wreath," present themselves at different moments throughout Emerson's political addresses and essays of the early 1840s. But the "defensive" or "negative" side clearly takes precedence, as we will see in the following passages from "Politics," "New England Reformers," and "The Young American":

> Whenever I find my dominion over myself not sufficient for me, and undertake the direction of him also, I overstep the truth, and come into false relations to him. . . . [W]hen a quarter of the human race assume to tell me what I must do, I may be too much disturbed by the circumstances to see so clearly the absurdity of their command. Therefore, all public ends look vague and quixotic beside private ones. For, any laws but those which men make for themselves, are laughable. . . .
>
> Hence, the less government we have, the better,—the fewer laws, and the less confided power. ("Politics," *E&L* 567)

> I confess, the motto of the Globe newspaper is so attractive to me, that I can seldom find much appetite to read what is below it in its columns, "The world is governed too much." So the country is frequently affording solitary examples of resistance to government, solitary nullifiers, who throw themselves on their reserved rights; nay, who have reserved all their rights; who reply to the assessor, and to the clerk of court, that they do not know the State; and embarrass the courts of law, by nonjuring, and the commander-in-chief of the militia, by non-resistance. ("New England Reformers," *E&L* 593)

Yes, Government must educate the poor man. Look across the country from any hill-side around us, and the landscape seems to crave Government. The actual differences of men must be acknowledged, and met with love and wisdom. These rising grounds which command the champaign below, seem to ask for lords, true lords, *land*-lords, who understand the land and its uses, and the applicabilities of men, and whose government would be what it should, namely, mediation between want and supply. . . . There really seems a progress towards such a state of things, in which this work shall be done by these natural workmen; and this, not certainly through any increased discretion shown by the citizens at elections, but by the gradual contempt into which official government falls, and the increasing disposition of private adventurers to assume its fallen functions. Thus the costly Post Office is likely to go into disuse before the private transportation-shop of Harnden and his competitors. The currency threatens to fall entirely into private hands. Justice is continually administered more and more by private reference, and not by litigation. We have feudal governments in a commercial age. It would be but an easy extension of our commercial system, to pay a private emperor a fee for services, as we pay an architect, an engineer, or a lawyer. If any man has a talent for righting wrong, for administering difficult affairs, for councelling poor farmers how to turn their estates to good husbandry, for combining a hundred private enterprises to a general benefit, let him in the county-town, or in Court-street, put up his sign-board, Mr. Smith, *Governor*, Mr. Johnson, *Working king*. ("The Young American," *E&L* 224–25)

In these passages as in much of his political commentary Emerson's rhetorical oppositions line up neatly on either side of what I have been calling the "primordial Lockean-liberal boundary." On the "outside" we find a familiar set of libertarian targets: taxation, state coercion ("control" and "interference"), paternalism ("undertaking for another"), remote centralized power ("a man who cannot be acquainted with me"), bureaucrats ("clerks of court" and "assessors"), militarism ("the commander-in-chief of the militia"), state services ("the costly Post Office"), legalism ("litigation"); politicians ("*Governor*"), feudal-aristocratic privilege ("lords"), and mass democracy ("a quarter of the human race assume to tell me what I must do"). On the "inside" we find a no-less-familiar list of libertarian-liberal preferences: private conscience ("my right and wrong"), autonomy ("self-control"), self-government ("any laws but those which men make for themselves, are laughable"), limited government ("the less government we have, the better," "the world is governed too much"), "dissent," "Free Trade," "rights," "revolution," natural aristocracy ("true lords"), localism ("native skill, native talent"), and private rather than public services. Here, as everywhere, Emerson exaggerates for rhetorical effect, so we need not take his radically anti-nomian assertion of legal individualism as a considered practical pro-posal. And here, as everywhere, Emerson's instincts remain moderate and undogmatic, so that his general distrust of government does not com-pel him to resist the burgeoning movement in support of public schools. "Yes," he acknowledges plainly enough, with a nod to his friend and fel-low New Englander Horace Mann, "Government must educate the poor." (Elsewhere he takes a similarly nonlibertarian position on the question of public provision for the indigent.) But there can be little ques-tion in general as to the strong libertarian-liberal emphasis of these pas-sages as a whole, an emphasis made all the sharper by Emerson's almost exclusively "negative" vocabulary of political agency. "*Abstain* from what is unfit," he warns, *do not* "*overstep* the truth," *refrain* from "force" and "blunder," *limit* to oneself the desire for control, "*resist* governors," "*re-serve* rights," commit yourself to "*non-juring*," "*non-resistance*," and "*nullifi-cation*," exercise "*contempt*" for "official government," observe principles of "*no control*" and "*no interference*" (italics mine). Political life is thus figured here in clearly negative terms, and Emerson goes on to represent politi-cal progress in history as a process of negation. The movement from the feudal to the "commercial age" is marked by the professional demystifi-cation of social roles and the commercial debunking of inherited titles of rank: he calls for "Emperors" to be hired on a "fee for service" basis, and the obscure and anonymous "Mr. Johnson" is temporarily employed as a "working king." The tone here is light; the proposals are whimsically far-fetched; and the overall effect is one of deflation. But the aim of this de-flation is consistent with the serious liberal-historical revaluation to which Emerson's work as a whole is dedicated—the shifting of power, prestige, and authority from the public to the private sphere.

But what, then, it is fair to ask, about the "wreath of joy"? I suggested that Emerson's liberalism has a "positive" dimension, a vision of how human beings would thrive and prosper under a properly delimited Lockean regime. How is human flourishing and human excellence pre-sented in this set of political essays and addresses? The answer takes us into the second of the subthemes listed above (the priority of virtue), and it may be generally stated by analogy to a point I made in my initial chapters about the Enlightenment roots of Emerson's concept of self-reliance. In his early works, I argued, Emerson championed "thinking for oneself" not out of proto-postmodern subjectivism but rather out of an Enlightenment conviction that free critical inquiry was the only way to arrive at real truths. His defense of "negative liberty" in the political sphere has a similarly positive rationale. Emerson everywhere insists on a firm barrier against political interference in the private moral lives of citizens neither out of a proto-postmodern desire to protect or promote license nor out of any Mandevillean calculation of the beneficial public effects of private vice but rather out of a conviction that free agency is a necessary precondition for the flowering of true virtue. Just as his British counterpart John Stuart Mill argued in *On Liberty* that authentic self-realization is impossible if an individual's range of choices is arbitrarily restricted by the political enforcement of social custom, so Emerson believed that the attainment of true virtue is impossible if an individual's access to the voice of his or her own conscience is obstructed by the artificial political imposition of social norms. Unlike Mill, of course, Emerson never states this view as a formal logical proposition, but it is clearly implicit in his manner of speaking about virtue throughout his opus.

Without counting, it is safe to say that "virtue" stands along with "truth" as one of the most commonly used nouns in Emerson's writing. It is hard to think of a single address or essay in which the term is not invoked, and it occupies crucial turning points in many of Emerson's most important works, including not only the political pieces here at hand but also *Nature*, "The Divinity School Address," "Self-Reliance," "Experience," "Montaigne," and the essays in *The Conduct of Life*. And yet Emerson seems to take the concept of virtue almost entirely for granted. He tirelessly exhorts his readers to pursue virtue, drawing moral axioms from what seems to be the entire range of the world's religious and ethical literature. But he never pauses to explain, define, or defend the concept, and he never provides anything like a list or a ranking of virtues. On the contrary, Emerson seems certain that his audience knows exactly what this word means and why it is important. His refusal to theorize or systematize virtue even as he so energetically celebrates it is itself revealing about Emerson's understanding of this quality. Emerson never tries abstractly to define virtue for the same reason that he believes governments should never try artificially to impose it. For Emerson as for Hutcheson, Reid, Stewart, Hume, and Adam Smith, virtue is preeminently a matter of organic, intuitive, and spontaneous feeling. As such it is powerfully inimical to systematic definition or legal control. Human beings at all times and all places, Emerson believes, are innately possessed of what his Scottish Enlightenment predecessors called "the moral sense" or "the moral sentiment." Gut instinct, a visceral response of attraction or revulsion, dictates the moral worth of a contemplated action. Emerson's confidence in the vividness and accuracy of this innate moral sense is the chief basis for his underlying optimism about human nature and human history. From the beginning to the end of his career and at every stage in between Emerson followed the Stoics and the Scots in affirming the self's capacity for a profound kind of double attunement—an introspective attunement to an inner emotional monitor that is itself sharply attuned to the underlying balance and rightness of nature.

The best way for government to foster virtue, then, is to preserve and protect a free private space in which "the voices which we hear in solitude" can make themselves understood. For Emerson, it is in this way that the "negative" restraint of Lockean liberalism contributes to "positive" moral ends. Like Montesquieu or Burke in somewhat different connections, Emerson believed that the positive moral tone of the liberal state developed out of a reciprocal structure in which wise, moderate, and well-adapted laws gave expression to the indigenous moral character of a particular people—character that was then reinforced in turn by the spirit of the laws. But Emerson pushed this analysis farther in an individualist direction than Montesquieu or Burke, insisting repeatedly and eloquently throughout these essays that the character of any collective "people" is itself only the sum of the particular moral personalities of each of its constituent members. Emerson continues to counter utopian constructivism in these essays, in other words, by finding a host of different ways of saying that personality is prior to politics, that virtue and other forms of human excellence cannot be mechanically produced by ingenious and efficient institutions but must rather grow up slowly, freely, and unpredictably from the inner depths of individuals:

> For the origin of all reform is in that mysterious fountain of the moral sentiment in man, which, amidst the natural, ever contains the supernatural for men. ("Lecture on the Times," *E&L* 160)

> The man of ideas, accounting the circumstance nothing, judges of the commonwealth, from the state of his own mind. "If," he says, "I am selfish, then there is slavery, or the effort to establish it, wherever I go.

But if I am just, then is there no slavery, let the laws say what they will. For if I treat all men as gods, how to me can there be such a thing as a slave?" ("Lecture on the Times," *E&L* 164)

Instead of that reliance, which the soul suggests on the eternity of truth and duty, men are misled into a reliance on institutions, which, the moment they cease to be the instantaneous creations of the devout sentiment, are worthless. ("The Conservative," *E&L* 187)

Republics abound in young civilians, who believe that the laws make the city, that grave modifications of the policy and modes of living . . . may be voted in or out. . . . But the wise know that foolish legislation is a rope of sand, which perishes in the twisting; that the State must follow, and not lead the character and progress of the citizen. . . . The law is only a memorandum. We are superstitious, and esteem the statute somewhat: so much life as it has in the character of living men, is its force. ("Politics," *E&L* 559)

Governments have their origin in the moral identity of men. ("Politics," *E&L* 566)

The wise and just man will always feel that he stands on his own feet; that he imparts strength to the state, not receives security from it. ("The Young American," *E&L* 227–28)

The argument of all these passages is clear and consistent. Emerson establishes a firm distinction between the fine-tuned moral inwardness of individuals and the crude external apparatus of collective statecraft, and he assigns to the former the burden of responsibility for shaping the character of society. In "Man the Reformer" the organically transformative power of "principles" is said to outlast any kind of social engineering—the transient artificial constructions of the political "carpenter," "engineer," or "chemist" (*E&L* 147). In "Lecture on the Times" "persons" are given power over "facts," the "strong man" is said to be able to "redeem" and "replace" institutions (*E&L* 155); "love" is said to be more potent than "multitudes," "circumstances," "money," "party," or "government" (*E&L* 162); and "the origin of all reform" is unambiguously located in "that mysterious fountain of the moral sentiment in man" (*E&L* 160). Similarly, in "The Conservative" we are advised to rely on "truth and duty" before "institutions" and on "character," "genero[sity]," "great[ness]," "brave[ry]," "virtue," "honor," and "labor" before "conventions," "parliaments," and "law" (*E&L* 187–89). And the same fundamental priority is reasserted in "Politics": "governments," "statutes" (*E&L* 566), and "the State" (*E&L* 560) are said to derive all of their authority and vitality from "the character and progress of the citizen" (*E&L* 559) and his or her "thought," "culture," and "aspiration[s]" (*E&L* 560).

This line of argument is familiar to twenty-first-century American readers as a standard part of "conservative" ideology. Prominent twentieth-century American conservatives from Calvin Coolidge to Ronald Reagan to William Bennett and William Kristol have similarly emphasized virtue, personal responsibility, and private initiative as alternatives to what they perceive as an unhealthy reliance on an ominously expanding federal government. But, from a larger historical perspective, it is possible to see that there is nothing inherently conservative about this position per se, and certainly nothing fundamentally conservative about Emerson's adoption of it. If we define conservatism broadly as an outlook that insists on deference to established traditions and authorities, then we must accept that the imperative to restrict the moral authority of political institutions and to thereby increase the moral agency of freely choosing, rational, and autonomous individuals is not inherently conservative. While Emerson shares twentieth-century American conservatives' libertarian wariness of government, he does not share their frequent deference to ancillary authorities. As we have seen, he left the church in which he was raised on a matter of intellectual principle; he despised the militaristic imperialist jingoism of "manifest destiny" and "Indian removal"; he consistently attacked the moral shallowness and callousness of emerging big business even as he celebrated its emancipatory economic dynamism; he went to considerable lengths to support and encourage Margaret Fuller and other feminist critics of male dominance; and, as we shall see in the next chapter, he vehemently opposed the traditionally racist political-economic structure of the American South.

In all of these respects Emerson was rather consistently "liberal" in the larger historical sense of the word; he overlaps with contemporary "conservatism" only where this ideology is itself fundamentally liberal. This is especially true of the priority he gives to private virtue. Emerson sounds like a twentieth-century American conservative in this regard only to the extent that twentieth-century American conservatism is candidly classically liberal. The common ground is not a shared conservative deference to traditional authorities but rather a shared libertarian distrust of politically imposed morality and a shared interest in locating alternative moral resources in the private sphere. At this stage Emerson emerges as far more individualistic than contemporary conservatives. Because of his confidence in the moral sentiment he did not need to look to secondary institutions to foster virtue; he needed only to teach men and women to heed their own deeper moral intuitions. "I bring it home to the private heart," he declares tellingly in "The Conservative."

Emerson's emphasis on the priority of virtue, then, should serve not so much to align him with the contemporary Right as to remind contemporary progressive liberals of a moral dimension of their heritage the neglect of which threatens to impoverish their position. There is nothing inherent in the ideology of progressive liberalism that should prevent it from appealing inspirationally, as Emerson does, to the special moral responsibility borne by private individuals in a liberal-democratic society.[20] One can support an activist role for government in the areas of public education, civil rights, labor, health care, welfare, the protection of the environment, and the regulation of big business and still recognize that the character of American society depends most fundamentally on the cumulative moral decency of individual citizens making free choices in the privacy of their daily lives. Emerson joins with a range of inspiring left-liberal leaders in refusing to cede this important moral ground to the right. John Stuart Mill, no conservative, put the case as follows in *On Representative Government:* "If we ask ourselves on what causes and conditions good government in all its senses, from the humblest to the most exalted, depends, we find that the principal of them, the one that transcends all others, is the qualities of the human being composing the society over which the government is exercised."[21] Martin Luther King, Jr., demanded of his followers not only extraordinary measures of Christian compassion but also the near-heroic discipline of nonviolence. And Václav Havel, who describes himself as a man "whose heart [is] . . . slightly left of centre," insists repeatedly on the pervasive importance of a rigorous inner standard of personal moral virtue among individual members of liberal-democratic societies.[22] He writes:

> As ridiculous or quixotic as it may sound these days, one thing seems certain to me, that it is my responsibility to emphasize, again and again, the moral origin of all genuine politics, to stress the significance of moral values and standards in all spheres of social life, including economics,

and to explain that if we don't try, within ourselves, to discover or redis-
cover or cultivate what I call "higher responsibility," things will turn out
very badly indeed for our country.[23]

There is no evidence that Havel has read Emerson, but this sentence
and the following could stand on their own as an adequate gloss of
Emerson's conception of the role of virtue in a liberal culture: "As in
everything else, I must start with myself . . . [and remember that] there
is only one way to strive for decency, reason, responsibility, sincerity,
civility, and tolerance, and that is decently, reasonably, responsibly, sin-
cerely, civilly, and tolerantly."[24]

The progressive orientation of Emerson's liberal morality is further
confirmed by the specific nature of the two virtues he singles out in
these political addresses. I said earlier that Emerson does not enumerate
or rank the virtues he so persistently invokes, but in these pieces he does
seem to emphasize two above the others: work and love.

Emerson most intensively advocates the virtue of work in several
crucial paragraphs in "Man the Reformer." Skeptical about the feasibil-
ity of the currently popular utopian idea that all members of a given society should share the burden of manual labor, he nonetheless finds
broad moral-educational value in the notion of everyone occasionally
getting their hands dirty:

> When I go into my garden with a spade, and dig a bed, I feel such an
> exhilaration and health, that I discover that I have been defrauding my-
> self all this time in letting others do for me what I should have done
> with my own hands. But not only health, but education is in the work. Is
> it possible that I who get indefinite quantities of sugar, hominy, cotton,
> buckets, crockery ware, and letter paper, by simply signing my name
> once in three months to a cheque in favor of John Smith and Co. Trad-
> ers, get the fair share of exercise to my faculties by that act, which na-
> ture intended for me in making all these far-fetched matters important
> to my comfort? It is Smith himself, and his carriers, and dealers, and
> manufacturers, it is the sailor, the hidedrogher, the butcher, the negro,
> the hunter, and the planter, who have intercepted the sugar of the
> sugar, and the cotton of the cotton. They have got the education, I only
> the commodity. (*E&L* 140)

> Hence it happens that the whole interest of history lies in the fortunes
> of the poor. Knowledge, Virtue, Power are the victories of man over his

necessities, his march to the dominion of the world. Every man ought to have this opportunity to conquer the world for himself. Only such persons interest us, Spartans, Romans, Saracens, English, Americans, who have stood in the jaws of need, and have by their own wit and might extricated themselves, and made man victorious. (*E&L* 141–42)

In Hegel's grand and dark "master-slave" theory of history it is the slave's capacity for work that enables him eventually to turn the tables on the master and to win not only emancipation but recognition and self-fulfillment. "Only the Slave," Alexandre Kojeve writes, "can transform the World that forms him and fixes him in slavery and create a World that he has formed in which he will be free. And the Slave achieves this only through forced and terrified work carried out in the Master's service. To be sure, this work by itself does not free him. But in transforming the World by this work, the Slave transforms himself too. . . . And thus in the long run all slavish work realizes not the Master's will, but the will—at first unconscious—of the Slave, who—finally—succeeds where the Master—necessarily—fails."[25] Emerson's treatment of the psychological, historical, and educative value of work in the passage above is broadly similar to Hegel's but different in one very important and illuminating respect. Speaking from the point of view of a perceptively anxious "Master," Emerson worries that his middle-class distance from essential labor confines him within an abstracted, alienated, and reified relationship to the concrete world, thereby depriving him of a fundamental set of "antagonistic" experiences necessary for full human development. Because his relatively comfortable social position allows him to pay others to do the most unpleasant and physically demanding tasks, Emerson frets, he will never be forced to develop the strength, skill, patience, resourcefulness, and resilience such work demands. He will remain "puny" and "protected," while the worker grows "good-humor[ed]," power[ful]," "strong and learned," "supple," "mighty," and "prevailing" (*E&L* 141). Here as throughout his writing Emerson echoes Hegel in thus attributing essential self-formative and self-transformative powers to work. These resonances then reach further to Marx's appropriation of Hegel as Emerson projects this idea onto a broad historical canvas and gives historical preeminence and momentum to those peoples who have been forced to learn the hard but empowering lessons of labor. Marx would surely have found Emerson's list of "poor" peoples odd ("Spartans, Romans, Saracens, English,

Americans"), but the notion of labor as an emancipatory force in human history would nonetheless have been broadly sympathetic, as would the generously progressive orientation of the passage as a whole. But Marx would also have been quick to point out the crucial ideological difference between Emerson's and his own Hegelian conception of labor: in these passages as throughout his writing Emerson's frame of reference remains firmly bourgeois, liberal, and individualistic. Emerson's sympathy and support for "poor" peoples was no doubt sincere, Marx would have granted, but it was inadvertently undermined by his more fundamental commitment to the notion of work as a means of *individual* self-culture. Even as Emerson appropriately frets about his alienated condition as an atomized bourgeois individual parasitically feeding off the fruits of others' labor in a capitalist economy, Marx would point out, he can only imagine a thoroughly atomistic and bourgeois solution to the problem: the middle-class or upwardly mobile individual must improve himself or herself by independently finding a way to include a little manual labor in his or her routine: "A man must have a farm or a mechanical craft for his culture" (*E&L* 140). Emerson thus advocates manual labor not as a means of achieving radical solidarity with the working classes but as a means by which the ambitious private soul may come into instructive contact with the reality of nature and thereby grow toward his or her own distinctive spiritual fulfillment. He looks not toward the betterment of what Marx called the "species-being" but rather toward enhanced individuality: "the prosecution of his love, the helping of his friend, the worship of his God, the enlargement of his knowledge, the serving of his country, the indulgence of his sentiment" (*E&L* 141).

It is possible, of course, to see this individualist conception of the self-educative value of labor in a more positive light. Contrasting Emerson's commitment to *Bildung* with the Hegelian collectivism of Marx is only meant to highlight Emerson's thoroughgoing liberalism; we are not thus compelled to take on Marx's antiliberal bias. If we take Emerson on his own terms and attempt sympathetically to place his conception of work within the context of the "liberal sense of history" discussed earlier, we retain access to its original emancipatory spirit. According to the liberal-historical schema, we should recall, the transition from the feudalistic Middle Ages to capitalistic modernity, from inherited privilege to "careers open to talent," from the servitude of the masses to majority rule, from monarchical-aristocratic tyranny to bourgeois freedom, hinges upon what Nietzsche called a "transvaluation of all values" at the center of which was the value of work. In the era of aristocracy and servitude, to put it perhaps too simply, a person's status depended largely on how little he or she needed to work. In the era of liberal modernity, by contrast, a person's status depends largely on the kind, quantity, and quality of the work he or she is capable of doing. Emerson was acutely aware of the extent to which he himself, his upwardly mobile middle-class audiences, and American society in general were products and beneficiaries of this great transformation, and this liberal-historical consciousness implicitly informs his commitment to the educating and liberating power of labor. For Emerson as for the Puritans, Benjamin Franklin, Abraham Lincoln, Horatio Alger, Booker T. Washington, and countless millions of immigrants escaping to America from semifeudal conditions around the globe, disciplined and energetic labor was valued as nothing less than a historically revolutionary force—a force to which every healthy individual had access. It was the most concretely available, realistic, and effective means by which a human being could dramatically alter his or her situation both materially and spiritually, even to the extent of total self-transformation. Slavery and the institutional exclusion of women and minorities from meaningful work were hateful to Emerson in good part because they undermined this most fundamental liberal-historical hope.

When freedom and opportunity for self-improvement through work were accompanied by a communal spirit of Christian charity, Emerson believed, liberal-democratic societies could be not only "negatively" stable and fair but positively just and lovely and inspiring. At a few surprising moments in these works, of which the following is one example, Emerson offers his vision of an ideal future society:

> An acceptance of the sentiment of love throughout Christendom for a season, would bring the felon and the outcast to our side in tears, with the devotion of his faculties to our service. See this wide society of laboring men and women. We allow ourselves to be served by them, we live apart from them, and meet them without a salute in the streets. . . . Let our affection flow out to our fellows; it would operate in a day the greatest of all revolutions. It is better to work on institutions by the sun than by the wind. The state must consider the poor man, and all voices must speak for him. Every child that is born must have a just chance for

his bread. Let the amelioration of our laws of property proceed from the concession of the rich, not from the grasping of the poor. Let us begin by habitual imparting. ("Man the Reformer," *E&L* 148–49)

Another error of the postmodern tendency to read Emerson through Nietzsche is made clear in such passages. Nietzsche admired Emerson's aphoristic prose, his affinity for the classics, and his cheerful Hellenic freedom from Christian resentment, meekness, and pessimism. But, unlike Nietzsche, Emerson never rejected Christianity outright. He dispensed with Christian metaphysics, but he remained committed throughout his life to what he saw as the timeless truths of Christian ethics—precisely those principles of love, tolerance, and compassion upon which Nietzsche heaped so much brilliant scorn. Although his idiom is relatively secular, Emerson's political morality in these passages is every bit as Christian as that of John Winthrop, Jonathan Edwards, or William Ellery Channing. Like these great American Protestant moralists, Emerson looked to Christian charity to provide a communitarian counterpoise to the atomizing and divisive effects of a competitive capitalist system—a system to which he elsewhere repeatedly affirms his allegiance.

But again, to thus invoke Christian virtue in a political context is not necessarily to be as politically conservative as Winthrop or Edwards. Emerson's vision of a society infused by Christian love is derived to some extent from Puritanism and evangelical Protestantism, but it looks progressively forward rather than conservatively backward. Indeed, it looks forward most strikingly to the "beloved community" so powerfully evoked in the twentieth century by Martin Luther King, Jr., in his calls for political and social reform. In "Politics" Emerson expresses surprise and regret that "there never was in any man sufficient faith in the power of rectitude, to inspire him with the broad design of renovating the State on the principle of right and love." More than a hundred years later the eloquent black minister from Atlanta sounds like the man Emerson had been looking for:

And so at the center of our movement stood the philosophy of love. The attitude that the only way to ultimately change humanity and make for the society that we all long for is to keep love at the center of our lives. . . . Love in this connection means understanding, redemptive good will . . . an overflowing love which is purely spontaneous, unmotivated, groundless and creative. . . . Whether we call it an unconscious process, an impersonal Brahman, or a Personal Being of matchless power and infinite love, there is a creative force in this universe that works to bring the disconnected aspects of reality into a harmonious whole.[26]

King echoes Emerson here not only in proposing love as the basis for a truly just society but in enlisting the cosmos itself for support. Like Emerson, he places his hope not principally in constructivist institutional design but rather in the "spontaneous" and "creative" flow of awakened moral feeling. For both, in other words, authentic moral renewal would effect dramatic political change, but the latter would ultimately prove hollow without the former.[27]

7

Natural Rights, Civil Society

"An Address . . . on . . . the Emancipation of
the Negroes in the British West Indies" (1844)

The libertarian addresses and lectures discussed in the previous chapter were not the only important political statements Emerson made in the early 1840s. On 1 August 1844 he spoke out decisively against slavery in a substantial address delivered to the women of Concord as part of their annual celebration of the anniversary of black emancipation in the British West Indies. As we will see, the speech is consistent in many ways with the foregoing set: in primarily asserting a natural right to liberty as the inviolable first principle of justice, Emerson here maintains a "negative" libertarian emphasis; in honoring the former slaves' capacity for labor, he continues to celebrate the transformative power of work; and, as we saw him do in parts of "Man the Reformer," he also infuses this speech at many moments with strong communal moral feeling best described as secularized Christian love. But it is nonetheless appropriate to treat "Address . . . on . . . the Emancipation of the Negroes in the British West Indies" separately because, as recent scholars have come increasingly to recognize, it opens a crucial new phase of Emerson's work. Starting with this address in 1844 and continuing through "The Fortune of the Republic" in 1863, Emerson's numerous public antislavery statements stretch an "iron string" of piercingly articulated liberal principle through the entire second half of his career. In doing so they provide a taut moral-metaphysical ligature for the distinctively rich rhetorical-symbolic imagining of liberal culture embodied in the aggregate of Emerson's major later works as a whole— *Representative Men* (1850), *English Traits* (1856), and *The Conduct of Life* (1860). In this chapter I lay the groundwork for a new assessment of the later work by closely reading Emerson's first, most ambitious antislavery address in the broad historical context provided by David Brion Davis's monumental studies of New World slavery and its abolition.

As befits the complexity of its subject, Davis's great trilogy— *The Problem of Slavery in Western Culture* (1966), *The Problem of Slavery in the Age of Revolution* (1975), and *Slavery and Human Progress* (1984)— is Janus-faced. On the one hand, Davis's rich account of the intellectual backgrounds of both slavery and its successful critique in the West is implicitly optimistic about human moral agency in history. Viewed from the largest historical perspective, these studies suggest, the wonder about New World slavery is not that, for all its horrors, it ever existed but rather that, for all its horrors, it ever ended. Human beings, Davis points out, have been bought, sold, and exploited in a great many societies throughout history. The use of bondsmen and -women in ancient Egypt, Greece, and Rome is well known. But slaves were also present in many more recent, if less familiar, societies, including those "around the edges of Medieval Europe" and in a vast international trade on the Black Sea and the Mediterranean from the thirteenth to the late fifteenth century.[1] In none of these communities, many of them highly developed, cosmopolitan, and "progressive," was the morality of this practice ever questioned. As late as 1750 the Atlantic slave trade and the large-scale slave plantations of the southern United States, the Caribbean, and South America were more or less taken for granted by Western governments, churches, and intellectuals. And yet by the 1880s the slave trade and slavery itself had been almost entirely eradicated in the West. Scholars adduce a wide range of factors contributing to this remarkable change. Davis himself, as we will see, argues that it was in no small part the agency of a distinct formation of Anglo-liberal culture, powerfully informed both by radical Protestantism and certain strains of the Enlightenment, that brought about the abrupt and astounding ending of human slavery in the Western world. But however one comes to understand its causes, Davis writes, there can be little doubt that the outlawing of slavery in early- and mid-nineteenth-century England and America was "a stupendous transformation," "a momentous turning point in the evolution of man's moral perception, and thus in man's image of himself."[2]

But Davis declines to accept the cosmically optimistic accounting for this transformation offered by many of the Anglo-liberal agents themselves. Especially in the latter two volumes of the trilogy Davis calls into question what had become an almost axiomatic Anglo-liberal attribution of slavery's demise to the providential efficacy of the nebulous but benign metahistorical design of "progress"—a design in which imperial England played a favored role. Davis points out that England had been no less eager than other "progressive" European powers to enter into the slave trade to begin with and had profited no less splendidly from its iniquitous returns. And he notes that many of the English leaders who cited progress in opposition to the moral backwardness of the slave trade seemed to feel no similar compunction about the only marginally less brutal exploitation of imperial subalterns around the globe or class subalterns in their own cities. Indeed, Davis goes so far as to suggest that the linking of antislavery with progress functioned as a kind of hegemonic mystification whereby both the local and global economic predations of the English merchant class could be not only shielded from moral critique but actually sanctified as quasi providential. This suggestion has stirred no little controversy, but it is beyond the scope of this book to try to resolve it. For now I will draw on Davis's more admiring account of the morally transformative achievement of antislavery activism to further open up the multiple dimensions of Emerson's liberalism as we find it so stirringly distilled in his address.

For Davis, changing attitudes about slavery were ultimately rooted in changing ideas about sin. As of 1834, for almost two millennia since the writings of St. Augustine, Roman Catholicism had explained and accepted the ubiquity of human bondage as a worldly manifestation of the underlying spiritual truth of universal human fallenness. Captivity of bodies in society was a vivid concrete symbol of the human soul's intrinsic captivity to sin—a kind of cringing ambulatory image of all persons' inner moral powerlessness. One effect of this outlook was that slaveholders in Roman Catholic societies tended to intermingle readily and openly with their slaves (Protestants mingled with their slaves, to be sure, but less openly and candidly); in God's eyes Catholics knew themselves to be on the same lowly plane as their servants. But first in offshoots of the Protestant Reformation and then in certain strains of the Enlightenment, a new perspective began to develop.

Luther and Calvin, with their stern emphases on original sin and innate depravity, largely accepted the traditional Augustinian view. But when radical perfectionist and millenarian groups such as the followers of Thomas Muntzer, Ranters, Hussites, Anabaptists, and, especially in the English-speaking world, Quakers began in the sixteenth and seventeenth centuries to look for the full realization of God's kingdom on this earth, they began also to look for the imminent apocalyptic end of human servitude, both spiritual and social. These groups did not lack a robust conception of sin, but they drew on biblical imagery of the apocalypse to separate sin out from human nature per se and to "hypostasize" it in a demonized figure of the Antichrist, with whom there must be no quarter and who would finally be defeated, it is important to note, on the stage of human history itself.[3] Thus inimical to compromise and hostile toward European societies still structured by finely graded social hierarchies, these groups tended to marginalize themselves by withdrawing into separatist enclaves. Most did not survive, with the important exception of the Quakers, who fashioned a distinctive blend of perfectionist moral intensity, social accommodation, and the Protestant work ethic into a viable and economically highly successful subculture.[4] For many years between the founding of the sect by George Fox in 1652 and the end of the eighteenth century, the Quakers made their peace with slavery as they did with many other institutions of which they tacitly disapproved. Indeed, some of their most successful merchants profited handsomely from trading slaves. And the constitution of the state of Pennsylvania, strongly inflected by Quaker values, nonetheless included a harsh slave code. But the perfectionist Quaker conscience remained uneasy, and it spoke up sharply, if sporadically, in statements such as George Fox's 1657 letter "To Friends Beyond Sea That Have Blacks and Indian Slaves"; William Edmundson's "general letter" of 1676 from Newport, Rhode Island, to Quakers in slaveholding societies; the Germantown antislavery petition of 1688; George Keith's 1693 "Exhortation & Caution to Friends Concerning Buying or Keeping of Negroes"; John Hepburn's *The American Defence of the Christian Golden Rule* of 1715; Elihu Coleman's 1733 *A Testimony Against that Antichristian Practice of Making Slaves of Men*—"the first attack on slavery," Davis informs us, "to receive official approval from a Quaker meeting"; and, finally, the eccentric, anguished, but finally prophetic publications and agitations of Ralph Sandiford (1693–1733) and Benjamin Lay (1681–1760). No one of these publications affected the slave trade or slavery in general in the short term, though they may have helped check the rod of particular Quaker masters. But they and the broader "inner light" orientation of Quaker culture did help to keep alive a profound and ultimately world-historical moral intuition. The essential content of this principle was unitary and unambiguous—Christ's radical insistence on the equal dignity, value, and freedom of all human beings. But it had a dual emotional charge—on the one hand, a wrathful prophetic wariness that long-accepted cultural practice might nonetheless harbor great evil, and, on the other hand, a joyous millennial confidence that human beings were capable of permanently expunging such evil from both their private hearts and their public acts. In time both modes would become typical of abolitionist discourse.

If sectarian and Quaker influence thus moved gradually from fringe peripheries to the center, Davis's second important source of antislavery thought projected its influence outward to multiple peripheries from one of the European epicenters of higher learning—Cambridge University. The Cambridge Platonists of the later seventeenth century helped to undermine the traditional Augustinian-Calvinist justifications for slavery by providing a sophisticated optimistic alternative to Calvin's (and Hobbes's) pessimistic account of an inherently slavish human nature. Scholars such as Benjamin Whichcote and Ralph Cudworth drew on Plato himself, Renaissance Neoplatonism, and emerging natural science to argue contra Calvin that human beings were not innately depraved dupes of their own inescapable blindness and lust but rather superbly moral and rational creatures innately capable of finely attuning their minds and their actions to an orderly, intelligible, and benign universe. Moreover, as I pointed out in my discussion of *Nature*, these scholars managed to avoid the reductions, alienations, and epistemological paradoxes of Cartesian and Lockean rationality by developing a holistic conception of reason characterized by the affective intuition of orderly wholes. "For a man cannot open his eye, nor lend his ear," Whichcote wrote, "but everything will declare more or less of God."[5] Thoughtful Anglican ministers who were excited by the discoveries of Galileo and Newton but inhibited by the severities of Calvinist orthodoxy readily adapted their theology to an outlook equally open to the empirical truths of science, the revelations of scripture, and the mystical presence of God in the cosmos. The thought of these so-called latitudinarians had an impact on every level of Anglo-Protestantism, from High Church to Low. When pressed to explain how there could be so much evil in the world if human beings were so nobly fitted to an over-arching order, the latitudinarians arrived at the argument that the human race as a whole was like an intelligent child being led gradually toward greater understanding and responsibility. God used history as an instrument for progressively educating human reason and conscience by allowing his creatures to make moral mistakes, learn from them, and correct them in the future. It took no great leap to come to see slavery as one such edifying error. The fiery exhortations in the mid-eighteenth century of emergent Wesleyan Evangelicalism (a vast mass movement itself not entirely untouched by latitudinarian rationality) impelled many to take this leap. Thus, increasingly in the later eighteenth and early nineteenth century it became possible for sincere mainstream Protestants of every stripe in both England and America to come to believe that slavery's hard lesson had been learned and to join hands with their sectarian coreligionists in calling for its end.

Another important outgrowth of Cambridge Platonism that would contribute to antislavery opinion, Davis points out, was the enormously influential "moral sentiment" strain of the Scottish Enlightenment. Notwithstanding their readiness to question custom and tradition, Davis argues, Enlightenment thinkers in general were not uniformly antislavery. But the Scots' debt to Francis Hutcheson's theory of moral sentiments predisposed them to opposition along predictable lines. As Hutcheson and Adam Smith both argued, the repugnance felt by most sentient and fair-minded adults when they witnessed or learned of the cruelties inflicted upon the slaves—whether in their capture, their transport, or their disciplining—was sufficient evidence of the immorality of the institution. The capacity for such revulsion, moral-sense thinkers argued, was instilled in us by God to help us quickly and decisively to distinguish wrong from right, and in this case the message was clear. Smith argued that American Southerners and other slaveholders must have had similar feelings but were inhibited from admitting them by defensive pride. Smith also showed the residual influence of Cambridge Platonism when he argued that by turning people away from what was after all a woefully inefficient economic institution, these negative feelings attuned people to their true economic interests. Smith's and his friend Hume's contributions to classical liberal thought were, needless to say, immense and multifaceted, and they helped, among many other things, to draw out antislavery intimations that remained ambiguous and implicit in the cautious writings of Locke and the Whig libertarian tradition. On the other side of the Atlantic their moral-sense orientation, as Garry Wills has demonstrated, found eternal eloquent enshrinement in Jefferson's Declaration of Independence, the original draft of which was explicitly antislavery.[6] The further dissemination of moral-sense thought via the works of Rousseau into popular late-eighteenth-century sentimental literature in Europe and America also helped to cultivate among the educated a susceptibility to "tender" emotions of sympathy for the sufferings of the downtrodden—feelings to which, in time, abolitionist writers and speakers readily and effectively appealed. And as the eighteenth century turned into the nineteenth, the "sentimental" revaluation reached yet larger fruition in the pan-European cultural revolution of Romanticism. In each instance, Davis again stresses, the granting of moral authority to spontaneous emotion had optimistic implications for general theories of human nature. To say that spontaneous feeling tells the self important truths about the world is to suggest that the self is inherently attuned to the good, a claim directly at odds with Augustinian and Calvinist ideas of innate depravity and thus also at odds with the long-standing traditional defense of slavery. This revaluation of feeling in many areas of life, from the arts to domesticity to religious observance, was therefore making it increasingly possible for people to regard slavery not as an externalized metaphor of all men's and women's inner impotence but as an alien external imposition upon their manifold inward potentials. For almost two millennia, Davis summarizes with an aphorism, it had been understood that "sin was slavery"; by the end of the eighteenth century it was becoming increasingly commonplace in the English-speaking world to believe that "slavery was sin." This was in good part due to an emerging Romantic-evangelical synthesis of a sustained dialectic between Anglo-Protestantism and the (especially Scottish) Enlightenment.

Anyone who has read the preceding chapters will find these antislavery sources familiar. They are also among the principal sources of Emerson's thought in general. Emerson included a lecture on George Fox in his 1835 series entitled Biography; he recognized an affinity between the Quaker doctrine of the inner light and his own faith in spontaneous intuition; and he long admired Quaker independence, simplicity, inwardness, and moral intensity. The influence of Cambridge Platonism is also everywhere apparent, as we have seen, in Emerson's emphasis on rational attunement to a finely calibrated cosmic order. We have found the Scottish Enlightenment idea of moral sentiment at the heart of much of Emerson's writing; indeed, it is arguably the cornerstone of his entire intellectual edifice. We have noted his repeated refigurings of Adam Smith's invisible hand. We have read "Experience" as a sustained and productive dialogue with David Hume. We have traced the great extent to which, from his youth, Emerson's outlook was shaped by the Whig-libertarian sense of history. And though he was no fan of Rousseau, we have acknowledged that Emerson was an important American conduit of European Romanticism as a whole. So, despite its standing as a new departure for Emerson, we should not be disappointed to find little that is radically new in the intellectual armature of his address on emancipation. On the contrary, what we find here and throughout the antislavery speeches is rather a distillation and clarification of many of Emerson's long-standing liberal themes—the preeminent value of reason, history as the progress of freedom, natural rights as the political corollary of the moral law, moral sense in citizens as the source of social cohesion, ambivalence toward commerce—formulated with fresh moral urgency and a new sense of social commitment. The cultural and intellectual sources that he shared with the antislavery movement had long since predisposed Emerson to believe that he lived, to repeat Davis's phrase, at "a momentous turning point in the evolution of man's moral perception," and it is a fair description of his lifelong literary project to say that he had long sought to provide an accordingly new and historically apposite verbal image of "man himself." But even as he gracefully aligned the public and political orientation of the abolitionists with his own more privately focused liberal vision, Emerson found that vision significantly sharpened and enhanced.

But we should not draw the lines of influence and continuity too smoothly. Emerson admired the sectarian intensity of Quakers and Abolitionists, but in the address on emancipation, as elsewhere in his work, his Enlightenment commitments prevent him from invoking any supernatural agent of salvation assisting from outside of history. At the same time, as I have stressed throughout, Emerson's roots in Puritanism caused him to look for more robust symbolic orientation than Enlightenment skepticism and empiricism alone could provide. So in this speech we will again find Emerson delicately and decorously navigating what might be called the symbolic problematic of secularization—the modern cultural need, as Blumenberg puts it, to "occupy the positions" of religious symbols without reinstalling the worldview they represented. A subtle but profound shift in symbolic orientation was required, after all, to secure the transition from "sin as slavery" to "slavery as sin"—intricate rhetorical work for which long experience had trained Emerson well. But to perform this task adequately first required, among other things, a full recognition on Emerson's part that he was now (and had in fact long since begun) preaching to a new kind of collectivity. "Sin is slavery" was a personal psychological message traditionally addressed to a knowable community, a rooted and intimate parish or congregation every face and family member of which the priest or minister knew and expected to continue to know for many years, and whose moral frame of reference was local and provincial. "Slavery is sin," by contrast, is a large-scale historical-political message implicitly invoking a diffuse, supralocal, cross-cultural, even global community whose boundaries are uncertain and most of whose members will always remain personally unknown to the speaker. A notion of "civil society" as a real social entity distinct from the state but reaching beyond traditional face-to-face communities had long been implicit in Emerson's discursive practice and in many of the libertarian arguments presented in the political speeches discussed in the previous chapter. But Emerson first becomes fully self-conscious of civil society in this speech, and the idea remains prominent in all his subsequent work. Indeed, next to the moral-political principle of natural right, Emerson's dawning discovery of the full merit and power of civil society is the most important theme of this address and of the anti-slavery speeches as a whole.

The speech begins with two incongruous verbal gestures. The first assumes a grand distance and situates the outlawing of slavery in the West Indies within the largest possible horizon:

> We are met to exchange congratulations on the anniversary of an event singular in the history of civilization; a day of reason; of the clear light; of that which makes us better than a flock of birds and beasts; a day which gave the immense fortification of a fact,—of gross history,—to ethical abstractions. (*AW* 7)

Several of Emerson's characteristic liberal emphases are already present here and handled with the usual, seemingly effortless, symbol-making finesse. We have already traced back to his earliest notebooks an effort to understand his own moment in relation to human history as a whole. That ambition has not faded. Indeed, he assays it afresh when he identifies the date of black emancipation in the West Indies as a kind of epiphanic crux, a radiant turning point in relation to which the entire "history of civilization" may be seen, at last, in a morally intelligible pattern. But it is explicitly a secular epiphany, even as it seems to manifest a quasi-religious aura. It is "a day of reason," not of messianic shock, a day "of the *clear* light" (italics mine) of human intelligence, not the blinding light of the divine. A kind of incarnation is celebrated, but it is human moral intuitions rather than a divine word that are given historical flesh. And the redeemed community could not be any less sectarian: it is the human community per se, as defined only against morally nonsentient "birds and beasts."

Emerson then almost immediately counterbalances the Apollonian aplomb of this beginning with a protracted vacillation between further self-assertion and ingratiating self-censure:

> I might well hesitate . . . to undertake to set this matter before you . . . but I shall not apologize for my weakness. . . . Therefore I will speak,— or, not I, but the might of liberty in my weakness. . . . If any cannot speak, or cannot hear the words of freedom, let him go hence,—I had almost said, Creep into your grave, the universe has no need of you! But I have thought better: let him not go. . . . Let us withhold every reproachful, and, if we can, every indignant remark. . . . If there be any man who thinks the ruin of a race of men a small matter, compared with the last decoration and completions of his own comfort[,] . . . I think, I must not hesitate to satisfy that man, that also his cream and vanilla are safer and cheaper, by placing the negro nation on a fair footing, than by robbing them. (*AW* 7–8)

It is very unusual for Emerson to reveal so much uncertainty in this way. His more common manner of dealing with conflicting feelings or ideas is to express both opposing impulses with maximum rhetorical zest at distinct moments and to allow the reader to try to resolve them. Here, the reflexive self-checking betrays a degree of real confusion on his part as to where to draw the lines of community with regard to the slavery debate. Should he rhetorically exclude his many proslavery compatriots ("let [them] go hence"), dismissing them as not worthy of life ("creep into your grave, the universe has no need of you")? Or should he include them in the implied discursive community ("let [them] not go") and attempt to persuade them by appealing rationally to their larger self-interest ("his cream and vanilla are safer and cheaper")? Having stepped beyond his usual topics and occasions, Emerson is not exactly sure to whom he is speaking, or to whom he should speak. In its largest ramifications this is a profound question about American national identity that would continue to vex Emerson and the country as a whole in all the years leading up to the Civil War. How should the American community be bounded and defined? Should it include or exclude slaves? Or former slaves? Or slaveholders? The perfectionist William Lloyd Garrison had already begun symbolically to exclude proslavery voices from his imagined community by insisting upon immediate northern secession. If the sinners wouldn't leave the room, Garrison insisted, the pure would have to "come out." Emerson was uneasy as yet with Garrison and his followers, though he would move closer to their position in the 1850s in the wake of the Fugitive Slave Act. For now, Emerson attempts to accommodate the incipient conflict by a protracted performance of a kind of awkward verbal civility. It is of the essence of civility and of civil society, as Edward Shils points out, to "postulate that antagonists are also members of the same society, that they participate in the same collective self-consciousness."[7] It is consistent with a commitment to civility that, even as Emerson does not downplay his antagonism to the values of the slaveholders (he suggests that they are vermin who should crawl back underground), he hems and haws and reverses himself and invites them to stay and listen to his address. He thus makes a genuinely civil effort to maintain a strained but distinctively liberal social bond—the same bond that Lincoln would also assiduously strive to preserve.

The theme of civil society becomes even more prominent over the next several paragraphs as Emerson builds toward the speech's first climax. Adam Seligman, an important voice in the reinvigoration of the concept of civil society over the past two decades, implicitly includes Emerson in its history when he gives Scottish Enlightenment moral-sense thought a crucial role. For Seligman, modern civil society theory can be broken down into two general viewpoints, pro and con. Liberals from Locke to Kant to Tocqueville to Václav Havel, ever anxious about centralized government power, are innately friendly toward the idea of a sphere of social existence "exist[ing] beyond the realm of the state."[8] To them, a healthy network of "uncoerced" associations—whether familial, commercial, professional, religious, ideological, or otherwise— seems good not only because it provides men and women with a variety of freely chosen forms of social connection and fulfillment but also because such groups' jealousy of their autonomy provides checks against state power.[9] In the paradigmatic case of a free press, an institution of civil society plays an overtly monitoring role in relation to the state: "The more I consider the independence of the press in its principal consequences," as Tocqueville put it, "the more am I convinced that in the modern world it is the chief and, so to speak, the constitutive element of liberty."[10] Marx and Marxian-Hegelians, on the other hand, are innately hostile toward a conception of social existence that by definition prevents men and women from recognizing what these thinkers saw as their rational identity as part of a universal human community. "Civil" or "bourgeois" society, according to Marx, is inherently fragmented, partial, and exploitative: man acts within it only "as a private individual, regards other men as means, degrades himself into a means and becomes a plaything of alien powers."[11] The special contribution of the Scottish moral-sense thinkers, Seligman suggests, was to have anticipated the concerns about social cohesion expressed in Marx's critique, to have recognized their salience, and to have laid the moral-philosophical groundwork for a liberal response. Liberals such as Adam Smith were no less worried than Hegel or Marx about the centrifugal tendencies of liberal-capitalist societies toward alienation, atomization, ennui, and reification. But a blend of Protestant transcendentalism, moral sentiment psychology, and what I have called counter-Lockean rationality in their conception of human nature, Seligman argues, allowed the Scots to believe that individuals left to the open spaces of civil society were not thereby merely tossed to the economic winds.

At the founding core of Protestantism had been Luther's ferocious resentment of the church's institutional interference with the individual's relationship to God. Herein lay the religious roots of the classical-liberal wariness of centralized power. However urbane the Scottish liberals may have become regarding specific articles of belief, they were decidedly culturally Protestant in this respect. On the other hand, at the core of their moral sentiment psychology was a conviction that human individuals are possessed from birth by a set of powerfully gregarious feelings that orient them instinctively toward social wholeness and, by extension, moral goodness. Crucial among these feelings was a never-sated need for social approval that ensured that individuals could never achieve fulfillment outside of social networks. As we have seen, the Scots also believed that these same feelings were partly constitutive of a holistic rationality that allowed individuals to intuitively grasp and contribute to the larger orders of society, history, and nature. Paramount among these, as we have also seen, was the overarching order of natural law, which took precedence over all local systems of positive law and tied each individual human being to the human community per se. This tension between residual Protestant individualism and "natural" moral-sense sociability predisposed the Scots toward the middle-ground concept of civil society. As latter-day Calvinists, they took it for granted that human beings had a lust for power and domination; thus, the state was still to be feared and carefully proscribed. But because they also believed that human individuals carry a rich endowment of social, moral, and even rational affections into all their relationships, civil society for the Scots was not the cold, empty, value-neutral zone of stark instrumentalism feared by Marx and his followers. On the contrary, for the Scots to speak of "civil" society was not just a terminological way of distinguishing a realm of relatively "soft" interaction from the ultimately violent undercurrents of state-enforced association. "Civil" society referred to a complexly peaceable, trustful, tolerant, neighborly, and constructive moral sphere, implicitly governed by the emotionally embedded promptings of natural law. As Seligman puts it, for the Scots "the public arena of exchange and interaction—the realm of civil society—is not simply a 'neutral' space of market exchange where already-fully-constituted individuals meet to exchange property and develop commerce, manufacturing, and the arts. It is itself an ethical arena, in which the individual is constituted in his individuality through the very act of exchange with others. . . . [M]oral sense (now divorced from its theological source) stands at the core of the image of civil society. Its source is a natural benevolence which we must recover from within."[12]

Seligman's account of the Scottish moral-sense contribution to the modern liberal concept of civil society is directly relevant to Emerson's address on emancipation. Emerson constructs the first half of the speech as a narrative in which feelings of moral repugnance toward slavery slowly spread through the networks of English civil society and ultimately find legal institutionalization. The sequence—from ordinary moral feeling to law—is important, so Emerson carefully marks the stages. He begins by presenting his own moral outrage as a model:

> From the earliest time, the negro has been made an article of luxury to the commercial nations. So has it been, down to the day that has just dawned on the world. Language must be raked, the secrets of slaughterhouses and infamous holes that cannot front the day, must be ransacked, to tell what negro-slavery has been. These men, our benefactors, as they are the producers of corn and wine, of coffee, of tobacco,

of cotton, of sugar, of rum, and brandy. . . . I am heart-sick when I read how they came there, and how they are kept there. Their case was left out of the mind and out of the heart of their brothers. (*AW* 9)

Emerson speaks here both as an ordinary man of strong moral feeling and as a moral leader. He successfully links the colloquial immediacy of "heart-sick" with the rhetorically formal parallelisms of "how they came there, and how they are kept there" and "out of the mind and out of the heart" to give the matter both direct emotional appeal and high moral seriousness. Then he goes to some lengths to evoke the same intensity of feeling in his listeners or readers:

> Conscience rolled on its pillow, and could not sleep. . . . [I]f we saw the whip applied to old men, to tender women; and, undeniably, though I shrink to say so,—pregnant women set in the treadmill for refusing to work, when, not they, but the eternal law of animal nature refused to work;—if we saw men's backs flayed with cowhides, and "hot rum poured on, superinduced with brine or pickle, rubbed in with a corn-husk, in the scorching heat of the sun;" if we saw the runaways hunted with blood-hounds into swamps and hills; and, in cases of passion, a planter throwing his negro into a copper of boiling cane-juice,—if we saw these things with eyes, we too should wince. They are not pleasant sights. The blood is moral: the blood is anti-slavery: it runs cold in the veins: the stomach rises with disgust, and curses slavery. (*AW* 10)

In this passage Emerson powerfully evokes what might be called the emotional physicality of moral reason. The diction is emphatically physical and sensual, and the rhetorical structure emphasizes an act of sensory perception. In an effective deployment of anaphora Emerson uses the phrase "if we saw" four times at the beginning of four long conditional clauses, each of which contains vivid images of bodies in pain— "old men" and "tender women" whipped, "pregnant women set in the treadmill," "men's backs flayed," "hot rum poured on," "runaways hunted," a "negro" thrown "into a copper of boiling cane-juice." He builds suspense by withholding the result of these grimly accumulating conditionals until the very last word of a 112-word periodic sentence— "*wince*." The verb strikes us first as anticlimactic, as does the subsequent statement ("they are not pleasant sights"), and both serve in this way to acknowledge the difference between the sufferings of the actual victims and whatever sympathetic pain an observer might feel. But this does not diminish the importance here of reflexive sympathetic feeling. Emerson chooses "winc[ing]" and "the stomach ris[ing] in disgust" as the long-delayed verbs to emphasize an involuntary and therefore inescapable moral-physical response. He imbues the "impartial spectator" of Adam Smith's *Theory of the Moral Sentiments* with a nervous system. Even from the double distance of imagined witnessing Emerson seeks to establish an intimate physical connection between the bodies of the slaves and the bodies of his listeners or readers.[13] With admittedly far different degrees of intensity, both suffering slave and "wincing" reader react physically to the lacerations of the lash and the sting of rum and brine. Similarly, when Emerson concludes by saying that "the blood is moral," he means primarily to reiterate the general point that human beings respond in a primordial physical manner to gross violations of the moral sense. But he reinforces this on a more intimate secondary associative level as the word "blood" again makes a bodily link between what is shed by the whip or smelled by the hounds and the deep-flowing, moral-physical consciousness of the observer. As small and brief as a "wince" or a wave of "disgust" or a chill in the blood might be in comparison to the sufferings of the slaves, such moral reflexes affirm an elemental human bond that could become the basis for a better kind of society. It is consistent with Emerson's interest in the history of liberty as a history of feeling that he pays careful attention to feelings such as these. Indeed, if Norbert Elias is right that civilization advances by raising "the threshold of disgust," Emerson may be seen here in the process of training liberal citizens by at once modeling and evoking a higher revulsion.[14]

But high moral feelings are not restricted to people of high social or political standing. It is significant that the gradual mobilization of civil society that leads finally to the abolition of slavery in the West Indies begins now, in Emerson's account, with obscure ordinary people. "Well, so it happened," he writes in the sentence immediately following those quoted above; "a good man or woman, a country-boy or girl, it would so fall out, once in a while saw these injuries, and had the indiscretion to tell of them. The horrid story ran and flew; the winds blew it all over the world" (*AW* 10). Emerson then takes pains over the next five pages to provide a factual account of the years-long process by which antislavery sentiment moved from the feeling hearts of decent citizens, to the heroic purposes of dedicated activists, to the reluctant decisions of high court judges, to the halls of Parliament, and then back down, as it were, to the effects of the law on the planters and the (former) slaves themselves. He evokes the weight of conservative inertia; the countervailing force of radical perseverance; the gradual effectiveness of boycotts, petitions, public debates, government reports; the decency of fair-minded conservatism turned; the intricate compromises of the legal implementation of social change; the stratagems of noncompliance; the unintended consequences; the slowness at every stage of legal and government machinery. More than any other of Emerson's essays or speeches, this one is tied to the complex factual texture of historical events and their many and various actors. We hear briefly about the modest and charitable Doctor Sharp, who initially seeks merely to help a maimed slave. We learn more about his driven brother, Granville Sharp, one of the heroes of antislavery, who studies English law for two years on his own in order to advance the injured slave's appeal not to be returned to a master who beat him nearly to death with a pistol. We are made acquainted with the conflicting inclinations of the reluctant Lord Mansfield, who tries to get the case dismissed but is ultimately compelled by conscience to announce a righteous and momentous decision. We are told also about the small brotherhood of six Quakers, who initiate the long process of translating the principle implicit in Lord Mansfield's legal ruling into national legislation. High-profile politicians like Wilberforce, Pitt, Fox, and Burke play their part in dramatic public debate. And we learn about the fair-minded colonial governor Lionel Smith, who is associated with the West Indian planters but rules against his friends when they take advantage of the temporary apprenticeship provision to try to preserve the old system.

Emerson includes all these facts and personages here in part because they are inherently compelling and dramatic. But, more importantly, he does so because they are constitutive of what he has discovered to be a crucial component of his subject. "An Address . . . on . . . the Emancipation" is primarily about the progress of a great moral-political principle—natural rights—in history: "The history of mankind interests us only," Emerson writes, "as it exhibits a steady gain of truth and right" (*AW* 8). But in researching this topic Emerson has found that this "steady gain" is only made possible by the multidimensional, many-leveled, intersubjective agencies of a diffuse and disparate civil society. Thus, a substantial portion of the speech is dedicated to an effort to represent the complex historical reality of this notoriously amorphous entity, especially insofar as it is porous to moral feeling. We have seen that from his earliest notebooks Emerson was interested in the history of moral feeling. This is the sole instance in his work where we find him actually trying to write such history.

The rationale for Emerson's uncharacteristically long factual excursus becomes clearer still in relation to the paragraphs immediately following it. The accounts of the "reception" by the West Indian slaves of the news of emancipation are the climax of the essay. The first emancipation bill, which included provisions for a four-to-six-year transition stage of apprenticeship, pronounced the slaves "free, and discharged of and from all manner of slavery" as of 1 August 1834:

> The reception of it by the negro population was equal in nobleness to the deed. The negroes were called together by the missionaries and by the planters, and the news explained to them. On the night of the 31st of July, they met everywhere at their churches and chapels, and at midnight, when the clock struck twelve, on their knees, the silent, weeping assembly became men; they rose and embraced each other; they cried, they sung, they prayed, they were wild with joy, but there was no riot, no feasting. I have never read anything in history more touching than the moderation of the negroes. Some American captains left the shore and put to sea, anticipating insurrection and general murder. With far different thoughts, the negroes spent the hour in their huts and chapels. (*AW* 15)

Similarly, the day of 1 August itself, according to the commissioners of the antislavery society whom Emerson quotes, "was like a Sabbath. Work had ceased. The hum of business was still; tranquility pervaded the towns and country":

> At Grace Hill, there were at least a thousand persons around the Moravian chapel who could not get in. For once the house of God suffered violence, and the violent took it by force. At Grace Bay, the people, all dressed in white, formed a procession, and walked arm in arm to the chapel. We were told that the dress of the Negroes on that occasion was uncommonly simple and modest. There was not the least disposition to gaiety. Throughout the island, there was not a single dance known of, either day or night, nor so much as a fiddle played. (*AW* 16)

And the tone of response is similarly grave four years later, when finally "the shackles dropped from every British slave":

> The manner in which the new festival was celebrated, brings tears to the eyes. The First of August, 1838, was observed in Jamaica as a day of

thanksgiving and prayer. Sir Lionel Smith, the governor, writes to the British Ministry, "It is impossible for me to do justice to the good order, decorum, and gratitude, which the whole laboring population manifested on that happy occasion. Though joy beamed on every countenance, it was throughout tempered with solemn thankfulness to God, and the churches and chapels were everywhere filled with these happy people in humble offering of praise." (*AW* 18)

These passages, including Emerson's carefully chosen quotation of a firsthand account, carry a heavy symbolic burden. They must somehow do symbolic justice to a revolution in moral history every bit as profound as the Copernican revolution in science. This is the unique historical moment when the "stupendous transformation" Davis speaks of was brought to a focus and made irrevocable. Human society would never be the same hereafter. As we have seen him do before, Emerson attempts to rise to the occasion by tapping into the residual sacred resonances of Christian religious symbolism but in the service of a distinct modern worldview—a value system differentiated from traditional Christianity precisely, in part, by its rejection of the principle of slavery in both self and society. Using terms such as "sabbath," "festival," "solemn," and "procession," Emerson and his source imbue this annunciation of freedom with a quality of holy stillness and decorum, a kind of awed hush appropriate to a birth or a death or the arrival of a god—the sort of occurrence that alters the character of everything that follows it. One is reminded of T. S. Eliot's invocation of "the still point of the turning world" in *Four Quartets,* his great poetic meditation on self, time, and God(s).[15] For Eliot, the human experience of time only becomes intelligible, and thus tolerable, as a result of the Incarnation—God's gracious entrance into history. Emerson, as I have suggested, is also commemorating a kind of incarnation here, but it is moral feeling that crystallizes into real presence from within society and history, not a messiah impinging from without. The preceding pages of historical detail about this-worldly processes of civil social change are meant to assure that listeners and readers understand this, even if the liberated slaves do not. And the human provenance of this transformation is subtly reinforced in several instances by the way in which Emerson situates the slaves in relation to their churches. In the first passage above, for example, he tells us that "when the clock struck twelve, on their knees, the silent, weeping assembly became men; they rose and embraced each other." Though this event does represent a transcendence of history as previously ordered, and this scene occurs within a church, there is no transcendence of the human condition but rather only a rising to fully possess it. The slaves do not stay on their knees to receive God's grace; they lift themselves up from their knees to own their full humanity. They become "men," not angels or gods. Similarly, in the second passage above it is significant that the slaves carry their joy and dignity into the churches, not out from them. At the suggestively named "Grace Bay" they form a procession outside and file in. They bring a new kind of secular grace into the church with them.

Many people, especially the planters themselves, had understandably feared physical violence—an anarchic interval of "insurrection and general murder"—between the termination of the old slave system and the establishment of free labor. Emerson was clearly moved by the absence thereof, and the passages above emphasize the peacefulness of the transition. The first emancipation bill of 1834, he notes, was announced on a Friday. On that day and the weekend that followed the freed slaves gathered together, embraced, prayed, and quietly rejoiced. The following Monday they went peacefully back to work. The more radical bill of 1838 met with a similarly restrained response. The colonial governor of Jamaica was astounded by what he describes above as "good order, decorum, and gratitude." "The manner in which the new festival was celebrated," Emerson adds, "brings tears to the eyes." No doubt there is more than a little Anglo-colonialist paternalism to go with the sheer relief in these statements and the others quoted above. But something larger is also at stake for Emerson. His burgeoning respect for civil society depends in part, as we have seen, on his confidence that human interaction outside of the control of the state is nonetheless governed by an innate natural law encoded in spontaneous moral sentiment. The orderly behavior of the freed slaves, temporarily released from a long-standing system of brutal domination and with every reason to wreak vengeful havoc, confirms that the inward and implicit "natural" law has indeed kicked in and that it conduces to civility rather than permitting revenge. We read just a few sentences later of the freed population building "churches, chapels, and schools" (*AW* 19). And we read passages from a speech given in 1840 by the new governor of Jamaica that characterizes the new citizens in the following terms: they are "as free, as independent in their conduct, as well-conditioned, as much in the enjoyment of abundance, and as strongly sensible of the blessings of liberty, as any that we know of in any country" (*AW* 19). Almost overnight, in other words, spontaneous moral sentiment has ensured that the liberated slaves have become capable and conscientious participants in civil society. The latent violence of the situation surfaces only briefly when, in the immediate aftermath of emancipation, some freed slaves seem to have forced their way into a Moravian chapel. But even here it is unclear exactly what occurred: the account merely invokes without further explanation a notoriously enigmatic line from scripture: "The kingdom of heaven suffereth violence, and the violent bear it away" (Matthew 11: 12). Whatever violence may have occurred at this scene, Emerson does not seem disturbed by the intimation. On the contrary, he seems to find it fitting that the freed slaves should have directed their anger not at their former oppressors but at the house of symbols that in many complex ways reinforced the oppression. He welcomes the implication that a symbolic structure must now be seized, repossessed, and reoriented. This is the sort of cultural-symbolic rather than physical aggression to which Emerson had long since committed himself. The emphasis, in any case, is again on the solidarity and strength the Negroes now bring "violently" into the church with them rather than any gift from God bestowed within. As Emerson puts it later in the essay, "this event was a moral revolution. The history of it is before you. Here was no prodigy, no fabulous hero, no Trojan horse, no bloody war, but all was achieved by plain means of plain men, working not under a leader, but under a sentiment" (*AW* 26).

The civil avoidance of a cycle of revenge also obviates associated cycles of guilt. One of the most striking aspects of Emerson's symbolism of historical rebirth in this address is the general absence within it of any compulsion to assign fault and to exact penance. He is by no means ignorant of the brutality of the slave system. I have already quoted passages where he feelingly details some of the worst abuses. He indicates more than once that he is aware of the endemic sexual violence. And in this address he makes a special point of saying that he does not believe that the motivation behind enslaving human beings was purely economic: "I think experience . . . shows the existence, beside the covetousness, of a bitterer element, the love of power, the voluptuousness of holding a human in his absolute control" (*AW* 17). This is as close as Emerson gets to identifying a principle of evil in the world. But he nonetheless resists casting the planters as devils and nowhere calls for their punishment. On the contrary, in this and other speeches he is supportive of the idea of providing financial compensation to the former slave owners for the value of their lost assets. The reasons for this go deeper than Emerson's irenic temperament or even his reverence for the liberal value of private property. He steers clear of the language of guilt and atonement for reasons perhaps similar to those that lead the freed slaves to decline to take revenge. It would entail a return to the violent past rather than a departure from it. Emerson knew personally from his own inner struggles what Davis learned from historical study: ideas of sin and ideas of slavery are psychologically linked. Thus, Emerson seeks in this speech and throughout his work to find an alternative, less punitive—psychologically as well as socially emancipated—symbolic language. In his more generalizing statements he unfailingly emphasizes the optimistic and progressive rather than the tragic aspects of this anniversary. He arrives, for example, in the closing paragraph of the speech as a whole at the following summation: "Seen in masses, it cannot be disputed, there is progress in human society. There is a blessed necessity by which the interest of men is always driving them to the right; and, again, making all crime mean and ugly. . . . The sentiment of Right, once very low and indistinct, but ever more articulate, because it is the voice of the universe, pronounces Freedom" (*AW* 33). Or, as he more briefly puts it at the beginning of a shorter speech given on the same anniversary the next year, "this occasion seems one of hope, not of sorrow and distrust" (*AW* 35).

It is illuminating, by contrast, to read the last line of Garrison's "First Anniversary Editorial" in the *Liberator*: "We are guilty—all guilty—horribly guilty."[16] Emerson explicitly distances himself from this self-punishing approach in a revealing pair of journal entries several years later:

> Everything hastens to its judgment Day. The merriest poem, the sweetest music rushes to its critic. From Calvinism we shall not get away. See how sedulously we plant a pair of eyes in every window to overlook our comings and goings. (*JMN* 10:94)

> Garrison accepts in his speech, all the logic and routine of tradition, and condescends to prove his heresy by text and sectarian machinery with a whole new calendar of saints. What a loss of juice & animal spirits & elemental force. (*JMN* 10:94)

By summer of 1847, roughly the date of these entries, Emerson was in full public support of Garrison's goal of abolition; the address on the emancipation is sufficient evidence of that. But here he confesses to finding Garrison's symbolic methods all-too-familiarly depressing and inadequate. In essence, Emerson here charges Garrison with adhering too closely to one model of secularization: the great crusader unconsciously replays the traditional Calvinist symbolic order in a new setting rather than finding new symbols that will occupy the positions of the old ones but evoke appropriately new feelings and values. Garrison may have changed the main characters ("a whole new calendar of saints"), but Emerson perceives that the structure of feeling thus endorsed is still essentially the same. It is harsh, punitive, censorious, and ultimately eschatological in its orientation, referring all events to an ultimate extrahistorical assignment of value ("everything hastens to its judgment day"). The psychic cost in vitality, spontaneity, affirmative energy—"juice & animal spirits & elemental force"—is as high as ever.

Emerson begins the second half of the address on the emancipation by returning, in a kind of ritual circling, to its opening statement: "I said, this event is signal in the history of civilization." Once again he places the occurrence in the widest possible span of secular time and confirms its symbolic importance therein. "Signal" is finely chosen to suggest the multiple ways in which this new symbol will work. As all such cultural markers do, it gives primordial orientation to a self "thrown," to borrow Heidegger's metaphor, into the otherwise uncharted sea of time. Henceforth the anniversary of emancipation in the West Indies will be a kind of beacon light, visible from all directions for a great distance, and it will provide a reference point, a sense of direction, a way to measure movement, transforming the blank expanses of time into the narrative pattern of history. The pattern in this case is a progressive one, and thus this "signal" event will also be a "sign" of a specific set of liberal-progressive values and ideas, as well as a means of disseminating them. Prominent among those ideas, we have seen, in addition to rights per se, is the liberal concept of civil society. Emerson branches out from the word "civilization" in this first sentence and uses the word "civility" no fewer than six times, and the word "civil" once, in the latter section of the speech. Indeed, the entire latter half of the speech may be characterized as a broad reflection on the phenomenon of civil society as Emerson has observed it in action in the distinctive English and American responses to what Davis calls "the problem of slavery." Emerson here celebrates civil society, as we will see, chiefly as an agency of collective moral reflection and self-correction.

But in order to celebrate the capacity of liberal society for moral self-correction, Emerson must first show how liberal society has morally failed. On this point this speech pulls no punches. The first very long paragraph of the second half of this address contains some of the harshest criticism anywhere in Emerson's writing of the failings of Anglo-American liberal-capitalist culture:

> Our culture is very cheap and intelligible. Unroof any house, and you shall find it. The well-being consists in having a sufficiency of coffee and toast, with a daily newspaper; a well-glazed parlor, with marbles, mirrors and centre-table; and the excitement of a few parties and a few rides in a year. Such as one house, such are all. (*AW* 19)

> There have been nations elevated by great sentiments. Such was the civility of Sparta and the Dorian race, whilst it was defective in some of the chief elements of ours. That of Athens, again lay in an intellect dedicated to beauty. That of Asia Minor in poetry, music, and arts; that of Palestine in piety; that of Rome in military arts and virtues, exalted to a prodigious magnanimity. . . . Our civility, England determines the style of, inasmuch as England is the strongest of the family of existing nations, and as we are the expansion of that people. It is that of a trad-ing nation; it is a shopkeeping civility. . . . We peddle, we truck, we sail, we row, we ride in cars, we creep in teams, we go in canals—to market, and for the sale of goods. The national aim and employment stream into our ways of thinking, our laws, our habits, and our manners. The customer is the immediate jewel of our souls. (*AW* 19, 20)

> It was or it seemed the dictate of trade, to keep the negro down. We had found a race who were less warlike, and less energetic shopkeepers than we; who had very little skill in trade. We found it very convenient to keep them at work, since, by the aid of a little whipping, we could get their work for nothing but their board and the cost of whips. What if it cost a few unpleasant scenes on the coast of Africa? That was a great way off. . . . If any mention was made of homicide, madness, adultery, and intolerable tortures, we would let the church-bells ring louder, and the church organ swell its peal, and drown the hideous sound. The sugar they raised was excellent: nobody tasted blood in it. (*AW* 20)

Emerson condenses into these passages several of the most searching, se-rious, and persistent charges voiced against liberal-capitalist civilization during the first century of its emerging dominance. First, it is narrowly and dispiritingly materialistic, as Thomas Carlyle, among many others, charged, in its conception of human flourishing: "The well-being consists in having a sufficiency of coffee and toast." Second, its obsession with material objects, as Marx initially argued and György Lukács subsequently extended, causes its subjects to think of the world and others only as objects: "The national aim and employment stream into our ways of thinking, our laws, our habits, and our manners." Third, it produces a numbingly uniform and herdlike mentality, as Tocqueville and Nietzsche suggested: "Such as one house, such are all." Fourth, it is spiritually mediocre, unpoetic, and uninspired, as Tocqueville and Nietzsche also charged, fostering subjects void of spirit or passion: "There have been nations elevated by great sentiments. . . . Our civility . . . is a shopkeeping civility." Finally, it is outright iniquitous and hypocritical, as Marx most prominently asserted, gaining great wealth for a lucky few by heartless exploitation of working-class and subject peoples around the globe and congratulating itself at the same time for moral superiority: "It was or it seemed the dictate of trade, to keep the negro down."

It is a formidable set of criticisms, and Emerson is clearly not just going through the dialectical motions in sketching them. The bite of his language suggests that he has personally felt the element of truth in each charge. And yet elsewhere in this speech, as throughout his work, Emerson remains an eloquent champion of the same civilization that he here characterizes as "cheap," superficial, banal, predatory, petty in spirit, and hypocritically self-righteous. How, it is fair to ask, does he sustain this contradiction? How can he continue to celebrate a way of life about which he also harbors such damning reservations? Part of the answer lies in the antiutopian temper we saw on display in the last chapter. Emerson may dislike, in certain moods, many aspects of liberal-capitalist civilization, but he dislikes even more the inhuman schemes thus far proposed and/or pursued as alternatives. And, like such liberal theorists as Kant, Mill, Habermas, and John Rawls, Emerson finds great promise of improvement in the very fact that liberal principles allow him to give public voice to such serious criticisms. "[T]hat his errors are corrigible," John Stuart Mill writes in *On Liberty*, "[is] the source of everything respectable in man either as an intellectual or as a moral being." But for Mill it was only by means of free public conversation that corrigible errors could be identified to start with: "He is capable of rectifying his mistakes by discussion and experience. Not by experience alone. There must be discussion to show how experience is to be interpreted."[17] For similar reasons, each of these theorists, with distinctive emphases and in some cases with the support of elaborate theoretical apparatus, gives great importance to what may be called the critical discursive dimension of liberal-democratic civil society. Taking for granted the Scottish-liberal axiom that life in civil society is everywhere suffused by moral sense, each theorist argues in his own way that the imperatives of self-government, combined with the liberal principle of free public discussion, institutionalize and thus secure an ongoing public practice of collective moral-rational self-assessment, clarification, and correction. Since the members of liberal-democratic polities must collectively decide for themselves which constitutional-legal arrangements and policies are best, they must engage public conversations, variously mediated, that require them to step mentally beyond their own narrow sphere of interests and enter imaginatively into the situations and points of view of others in their society, especially the weak and disenfranchised. Even if only to continue to ensure their own freedom to pursue their own interests in their own way, the citizens of a liberal democracy are thus compelled, in other words, to think and converse in earnest about the common good. The implicit rules and norms and aims of such conversations in and of themselves elicit a high level of moral rationality. As Rawls puts it, "Since the exercise of political power itself must be legitimate, the ideal of citizenship imposes a moral, not a legal, duty—the duty of civility— to be able to explain to one another on those fundamental questions how the principles and policies they advocate and vote for can be supported by the political values of public reason. This duty involves a willingness to listen to others and a fairmindedness in deciding when accommodations to their views should reasonably be made." For these thinkers, life in civil society has not only the morally neutral "negative" libertarian advantages of independence from the state but also potentially the morally bracing and uplifting benefits of activating its participants' highest, most humane, and most cosmopolitan conceptions of equity, fairness, and justice. To again quote Rawls, a theorist not given to rhetorical embellishment, "the political values realized by a well-ordered constitutional regime are very great values and not easily overridden, and the ideals they express are not to be lightly abandoned."[18]

It is thus significant that, in the second half of the address on the emancipation, Emerson gives what he calls the "stately spectacle" (*AW* 22) of public reason the decisive role. The speech had reached its nadir of moral complaint at the conclusion of the first half, when Emerson imaginatively linked the cheap sweetener on his kitchen tables with the forced labor of African captives in the West Indies: "The sugar they raised was excellent: nobody tasted blood in it" (*AW* 20). One cannot help but respond with revulsion to the implied image of a crimson stain of blood spreading slowly through soon-to-be-ingested white granules—and this was exactly Emerson's aim. For him, as we have seen before, such disgust was a reflex of the moral sense, and the "An Address . . . on . . . the Emancipation," like "Experience," turns precisely on the activation of this faculty: "But unhappily, most unhappily, gentlemen, man is born with intellect, as well as with a love of sugar, and with a sense of justice, as well as a taste for strong drink" (*AW* 20–21). With even the smallest bit of education and cultivation the awakened moral sense begins to cry out against the injustice of slavery, and a long process of liberation is set in motion.

Most of the rest of the address is then given to celebratory comment on the extended public discussion in England of the legality and morality of slavery in the West Indies. Emerson is greatly impressed by many aspects of this process and moves with characteristic rhetorical swiftness among multiple levels, but it is possible to distinguish four broad areas of strong approval. First, he admires most effusively the high plane of civility and moral principle on which the conversation was generally conducted. He characterizes the tone as "patient" (*AW* 22), "generous" (*AW* 23), "magnanimous" (*AW* 23), and "elevat[ed]" (*AW* 26). He notes that the debates were held at an appropriate distance from the interested parties, namely, the planters (*AW* 23). And he is intensely gratified to find that the debates occasioned frequent eloquent invocations of the most fundamental moral-legal maxims of the culture: "The bare enunciation of the theses, at which the lawyers and legislators arrived, gives a glow to the heart of the reader."

To Emerson's mind, any process is good that thus refreshes a community's consciousness of its foundational moral-legal principles. He believes that in this case it has had a beneficial ripple effect throughout society, so that now "the popular discussion . . . of every question" makes reference to "the absolute standard" (*AW* 28). Second, with underlying principles thus clarified, he is then even further impressed that the detailed empirical evidence relevant to the particular issue at hand was aired and examined in a careful, thorough, and rigorous manner. Leading politicians took the trouble to read closely through a bulky government report. Ample time—"months and years" (*AW* 22)—was provided for debate and discussion on the floor of Parliament: "Every argument was weighed, every particle of evidence was sifted, and laid in the scale" (*AW* 22). Third, he also approves that these rational procedures occurred openly and publicly in accessible venues and media, with opportunity for input by informed citizens. Finally, despite the necessary publicity and the conclusive role ultimately played by politicians in official legislative forums, it is also of great importance to Emerson that the entire process took its impetus from the private sphere. When at last compelled by the tide of public opinion, the politicians acted, in Emerson's view, properly. But it was the tidal force of civil society, not political leadership, he asserts, that was ultimately decisive in bringing about this epochal change: "The stream of human affairs flows its own way, and is very little affected by the activity of legislators. What great masses of men wish done, will be done. . . . There are now other energies than force, other than political, which no man in future can allow himself to disregard. There is direct conversation and influence" (*AW* 28).

It is difficult to know, of course, whether Emerson's account of how the West Indian slavery debate unfolded in England is strictly accurate. He derived it largely from Thomas Clarkson, who, needless to say, had his own angle of interest.[19] But, again, for our purposes, the strict historical accuracy of Emerson's representation of events is less important than his manifestly liberal construction of them. Emerson's sketch of the processes of civil society involved in the outlawing of slavery in the West Indies is necessarily general, impressionistic, intuitive, selective, abbreviated, and secondhand. But it is nonetheless striking how closely the processes it sketches accord with the prescriptions of some of the most rigorous theorists in the modern liberal tradition. Emerson's account might be fairly paraphrased as follows: in a legally well-delimited process of public reason (Rawls) and open civil debate (Mill) governed by implicitly universal norms of rational consensus (Habermas), the great universal Kantian legal-moral imperative (to treat all human beings as ends rather than means), which had been tacitly understood in English legal culture for centuries, was reanimated, rearticulated, and efficaciously reapplied. A grievous and morally shocking injustice afflicting an entire race of human beings was thus brought to an end. Emerson's rhetorically stirring language thus may be said to make an emotionally inspiring symbol of liberal procedures for which these more cautious and logical thinkers laid out the rules. His speech elaborates a symbol that is everywhere resonant of a progressive sense of history and that gives historical specificity and focus and concreteness, a rallying point if you will, to the hope for a progressive universal realization of the core liberal principle of natural right.

I do not wish to argue that Emerson participated knowingly in any variant of the often rather technical "public reason" strain of modern liberal theory, nor am I suggesting that he made any distinctive theoretical contribution to it. I submit rather that the contemplation of the abolition of slavery in the West Indies confirmed in Emerson a long-held liberal hope similar to the one more rigorously and systematically developed by "public reason" liberals such as Kant, Mill, Habermas, and Rawls. Slavery was not only hateful in itself to Emerson; it was a metonymy for everything else, as we saw above, that he found morally deficient in liberal capitalism. But at the same time the successful abolition of slavery in the West Indies symbolized no less vividly the astounding real-world effectiveness of the institutional provision within Anglo liberalism for a process of genuine public criticism, empirical disclosure, review, and testing against the principles of justice implicit in its laws and/or founding documents. If slavery could be eradicated by the procedures of public reason, then so, in time, Emerson had cause to hope, could the many other failings of his society.[20]

8

Empiricism

Representative Men *(1850)*

In his *An Area of Darkness* V.S. Naipaul is told "This is Pandavas' fort" when he asks about some ruins in Awantipur in Kashmir. The answer vexes Naipaul because he can see plainly that the ruins are not large enough to have served the military purposes of these ancient heroes of the Mahabharata. "This is not a fort," he says flatly. But his guide remains fixed: "It is Pandavas' fort." Naipaul's vexation grows. It frustrates and even angers Naipaul that neither his guide nor his fellow tourists seem willing to look carefully at the evidence before them. Rather than using their eyes to arrive at an empirically plausible estimation of the building's purpose, the Kashmiris are content with the stock response of local lore—"Pandavas' fort." Throughout his travel writing about South Asia, Indonesia, and the Middle East Naipaul rails against the seemingly willful blindness of members of traditional societies who thus refuse to register what he regards as simple, self-evident historical facts. He harshly criticizes these "believers" for thus denying to themselves a realistic sense of their own oppressed and impoverished conditions. Such denial condemns them, Naipaul believes, to continuing subjection and poverty.

Ernest Gellner, in his capacity as historical anthropologist of liberal modernity, takes a broader view of this matter. In *Plough, Sword, and Book*, which he offers as a latter-day contribution to the Scottish

222

Enlightenment genre of "conjectural" philosophy of history, Gellner argues in effect that the resistance to empirical facts of the sort that exasperates Naipaul in his encounters with traditional peoples indicates not willful blindness or perversity but rather a stage of human cognitive development. To use words to refer strictly to singular and distinct facts would seem to be a primordial linguistic function, but Gellner points out that such "single-stranded" empirical reference is actually a rare, idiosyncratic, and relatively recent achievement of the modern West—a cognitive-linguistic by-product of the advance of natural science and the industrial-liberal division of labor. For most of history, Gellner argues, human beings have used words in a more broadly symbolic, "many-stranded" fashion in which contextual social meanings take precedence over strict empirical reference to the world "outside" a given network of relationships. The objectively accurate age and purpose of the ruins in Kashmir, after all, matter little to the life of the villagers whom Naipaul questions. It is far more important—indeed, a matter of collective inclusion or exclusion, social life or social death—to affirm their shared reverence for the building's mythical role. Pandavas' fort may not be an empirically accurate statement, but it is nonetheless rational and coherent within its social-symbolic context. "Most of what men say, and the content of what they say," Gellner summarizes, "has no direct relationship to nature (contrary to the view of naïve theorists of language who would treat all acts of discourse as if they were experiential reports). They simply play a part in social interaction. Language is not merely rooted in ritual; it *is* a ritual."[1] We are not historians, the Kashmiris say, but we know who our gods, and thus our friends, are.

Gellner thus allows for a distinction between two historically sequential—traditional versus modern or agrarian versus industrial—conceptions of truth. It is instructive in this regard, he argues, that the English word "true" connotes loyalty as well as correctness. The first meaning corresponds to a culturally relative conception of symbolic truth as what Gellner calls "Shared Concept Affirmation": on this model the villager's statement that the temple is a thousand years old is "true" insofar as it exhibits loyalty to the general norms, values, and concepts that govern his society. The second meaning corresponds to a more rigorous empiricist conception of truth as "referential accuracy": it is by implicit reference to this model that Naipaul finds the Kashmiris' statement obviously and exasperatingly "untrue" in relation to the readily observable facts on the ground. This distinction is critical,

Gellner urges, to the large-scale historical self-understanding of the West. For Western societies, to have moved from feudal-agrarian traditionalism to industrial-scientific liberal modernity is to have moved not only from one means of production and its corresponding sociopolitical order to another, it is to have moved from one way of representing reality to another. The older way, though not entirely without "apertures" to the outside world, was largely a matter of the associative concatenation of networks of static, self-enclosed, religiously resonant, and often intricately interlocking concepts and symbols. The newer way, in principle radically open to nature as it unfolds itself to ever finer instruments of observation, is a matter of empirically precise rendering and correlation of an infinite number of distinct, disenchanted, disparate, but logically interrelatable facts. The passage from the former to the latter conception of truth, Gellner suggests, is the epistemological-representational crux of liberal progress. But he elegantly summarizes the oft-noted trade-offs of this advance: "From all this, one may in fact formulate a supremely important if rough law of the intellectual history of mankind: *logical and social coherence are inversely related.*"[2] He explains as follows:

> The complex and cognitively "progressive" societies, within whose internal intellectual economy cognition has become fairly well separated from other activities and criteria[,] . . . possess a high level of *logical* coherence. All "facts" can be cross-related and fitted into a single logical space. . . . At the same time, however, they generally lack *social* coherence: their moral and cognitive orders do not constitute any unity. . . . By contrast, simpler societies tend to possess a high level of social coherence. The world one inhabits and acts in is the same world as that in which one thinks, and the moral and cognitive orders reinforce and sustain each other.[3]

I begin a chapter on Emerson's *Representative Men* with this brief excursus into what might be called a progressive-historical anthropology of "truth" because it helps to illuminate a crucial but generally overlooked liberal-symbolic dimension of this book. On the first level, as I said at the beginning of the previous chapter, *Representative Men* stands with the antislavery addresses, *English Traits,* and *The Conduct of Life* as part of Emerson's mature "late" filling out of his liberal vision. *Representative Men* seeks, along with these other late works, to add fleshed-out, historically recognizable images of human flourishing to the relatively abstract, negative-libertarian bones of the antiutopian political addresses and lectures. Each of Emerson's representative men embodies important liberal values and/or virtues, which I will specify in due course. And the book as a whole traces a decidedly liberal-progressive historical trajectory, with Napoleon's muddy boots, for Emerson as again for Hegel, setting the pace forward. But on another, less-evident level the book is equally concerned with the other term in its title, not so much with exemplary "men" as with what it means to be "representative"— what it means, in modern liberal times, to be, to have, or to construct symbols. Plato, Montaigne, Shakespeare, Swedenborg, Goethe: to name the members of Emerson's pantheon in *Representative Men* is to be struck by the extent to which they are not only symbols in various ways of liberal freedom and fulfillment but also, with the exception of Napoleon, exemplary liberal symbol makers—at once liberal representatives and, as it were, liberal representers. And to read Emerson's construction of them, as we will see, is to be struck by the extent to which, their widely divergent moments and modes notwithstanding, they all seem to share a structurally similar and immensely ambitious representational project. Like Emerson himself, almost all of Emerson's representative men are centrally engaged in spanning the gap between what we may call, with Naipaul and Gellner in mind, traditional and modern conceptions of truth. They at once *affirm* a recognizable and coherent set of (liberal) concepts and *refer* capaciously and accurately to the empirical world. Indeed, in Emerson's account, each representative man attempts in distinctive ways to do exactly what Emerson seeks to do in his work as a whole: to enfold the scientific-empirical world of infinitely multitudinous particulars into a comprehensive, holistic, interlocking, and psychologically resonant verbal-symbolic order.

Observations about symbolism crop up frequently in Emerson's writing in the lead-up to *Representative Men* throughout the 1840s. In one respect this is not surprising: symbols had long been Emerson's stock-in-trade. As a young minister he had used symbols in the traditional manner as focal points for rituals of consensus by a local face-to-face community. His first major published work, *Nature*, presented land, sea, and sky itself as a grand and gorgeous symbolic text. But as Emerson's career as a lecturer began to take promising shape in the 1840s, the topic found a new focus. He became increasingly concerned in these years with questions about what sorts of symbols and what comportment toward symbolism were appropriate for the new kind of far-flung, anonymous, and essentially secular audiences and communities he was addressing.

On the broadest level of generality, Emerson often reflected during these years on what he saw as a primordial and universal human need for symbolic orientation. "A man should carry nature in his head, should know the hour of the day and the time of the year, should know the solstice and the equinox, the quarter of the moon and daily tides. The Egyptian pyramids, I have heard, were square to the points of the compass and the custom of different nations has been to lay the dead with the feet to the east" (*JMN* 9:17–18). Here Emerson approaches modern anthropology's understanding of the role of symbolism in helping human beings to situate themselves in a literal physical sense within the otherwise empty expanses of space and time. Religious symbolism (the pyramids) and empirical reference (the points of the compass) are seen here as complementary and mutually reinforcing. Emerson calls, only somewhat wistfully, for greater attunement to the planet we live on—and must die on—by means of the internalization of both symbolic and representational schemas, one laid within the other.

Symbols are no less essential, Emerson suggests in another entry, to people's inner moral or spiritual attunement and orientation: "What I want to know, is, the meaning of what I do; believing that any of my current Mondays or Tuesdays is bible /fatebook/ for me; and believing that hints & telegraphic symbols are arriving to me out of the interior eternity, I am tormented with impatience to make them out" (*JMN* 11: 180). Emerson thus again anticipates Geertz and others in noting the psychobiological benefits of adequately mapping inchoate inner experience onto an orderly symbolic structure. "Every symbol gives a new joy, as if it were a twirl of the world wheels. . . . That is the joy of eloquence, and of Chemistry. . . . The /Every/ correspondence we observe in mind and matter, gives the same joy . . . suggesting a thread older & deeper than either of these old nobilities" (*JMN* 9:352). The "joy" Emerson speaks of here is the affective register of the reassurance sent to the nervous system by a stable symbolic system. To sustain its morale, the human organism needs to believe that the world is intelligibly ordered and thus not impossible to navigate and survive in. Emerson ultimately goes so far in these years as to equate symbolism with civilization per se: "Each religion, each philosophy, each civilization, perhaps, is only the immense sequel of one exaggerated symbol" (*JMN* 9:353). But he finds little help from the customary sources as he looks for symbols appropriate to his own time and place. "I may well ask when men wanted their bard & prophet as now?" he writes. "They have a Quixote gallery of old romances & mythologies, Norse, Greek, Persian, Jewish, and Indian, but nothing that will fit them, and they go without music or symbol to their day labor" (*JMN* 10:83). "The questions that I incessantly ask myself as, What is our mythology? never come into my mind when I meet with clergymen; & what Academy has propounded this for a prize?" (*JMN* 10:109–10).

The two most important lecture series Emerson gave during these years—New England (1843–1844) and Mind and Manners of the Nineteenth Century (1848–1850)—are to some extent preparatory to an answer to these questions regarding "our mythology." Indeed, together they may be read in part as brief histories of changing cultural-symbolic practices in New England from the arrival of the Puritans to the most recent efforts of Emerson's literary-intellectual contemporaries, with an eye toward what might be the appropriate next step. "New England" begins with praise of the all-encompassing religious-symbolic consciousness of the original Puritan settlers. Emerson salutes the Commonwealth period as "one of the great epochs in the spiritual history of mankind," quoting Milton's account of London during the Long Parliament as "the mansion house of liberty" (*LL* 1:10). Nothing less than a comprehensive new cultural-symbolic framework was under construction as countless "pens and heads there [sat] by their studious lamps, musing, searching, revolving new motions and ideas wherewith to present as with their homage and their fealty the approaching reformation" (*LL* 1:10). The Puritan-emigrants carried these vast symbol-making energies across the Atlantic to North America and there drew upon them to infuse every aspect of life with higher meaning: they "raised every trivial incident to a celestial dignity" (*LL* 1:11). A tap at the window of a dying man's room was recognized as the beckoning of the angel of death; a parishioner exiting the meetinghouse during a sermon was known as a "graceless sinner"; and every new day brought new occasions, great and small, for the manifestations of divine charity. Even a catastrophic event such as the burning down of a minister's house was received as a gracious reminder of the location of the soul's true home. The good man, Emerson tells us, stood apart from the flames with some members of his church and sang, "There is a house not made with hands" (*LL* 1:12).

To thus understand the true symbolic import of each day's events, however, required access to the great code—the Bible—wherein the keys to these meanings were contained. And such access required education.

Emerson speaks with pride in these lectures of the fact that Harvard College was founded in 1636, only sixteen years after the founding of the Massachusetts Bay Colony itself. And he is no less pleased to remind his audience that the General Court of Massachusetts provided for universal public education not long thereafter—in 1647. "Many and rich are the fruits of that simple statute. The universality of an elementary education in New England is her praise and her power in the whole world" (*LL* 1:15). But education breeds independence of mind, and independence of mind leads to questioning, and questioning leads to skepticism. And thus, with regard to symbolism, Puritan New England bequeathed to its Yankee children a difficult dual legacy: "I picture New England to myself as a mother, sitting amidst her thousand churches, heir of whatever was rich, and profound, and efficient in thought and emotion in the old religion which planted and peopled this land, and strangely uniting to this passionate piety the fatal gift of penetration; a love of philosophy, an impatience of words, and thus becoming at once religious and skeptical—a most religious infidel" (*LL* 1:14).

"Passionate piety" versus "the fatal gift of penetration"; "at once religious and skeptical": the polarities contained in both pairs of terms suggest diametrically opposed responses to the authority of traditional religious symbolism. "Piety," on the one hand, implies submission to the standing symbolic order; "the fatal gift of penetration" implies exactly the opposite. The former pays heed to a set of traditionally sanctioned symbols; the latter calls such symbols into question by reference to as-yet-unaccommodated ideas, perceptions, or facts. The most characteristic symbolic practices of post-Puritan New England culture, Emerson suggests, are partial syntheses of these antitheses. The commercial marketplace, most prominently, erases the aura from all things but compels quasi-religious discipline and obedience as it gathers an almost infinite range of disenchanted facts into its intricate, all-encompassing symbolic nets. In the journal entry immediately following the one quoted above regarding the need for a new mythology, Emerson anticipates the "doubloon" episode in *Moby Dick*. He ironically seconds a satirical proposal of W. E. Channing that "there should be a magnified Dollar, say as big as a barrel head, made of silver or gold, in each village, & Col Shattuck or other priest appointed to take care of it . . . ; then we should be provided with a local deity, and could bring it baked beans, or other offerings and rites, as pleased us" (*JMN* 10:83). Political oratory, for another example, routinely invokes quasi-religious pieties and symbols, but often in the service of skeptical, self-interested, decidedly nonspiritual ends.

Most immediately relevant to Emerson's own purposes, the newly emergent but rapidly expanding lyceum movement was carving out a space for what he saw as a potentially ideal hybrid symbolic practice:

> I look upon it as a vent for new and higher communications than any to which we have been wont to listen. . . . Is it not plain that not in senates and courts, which only treat of a very narrow range of external rights, but in the depths of philosophy and poetry, the eloquence must be found that can agitate, convict, inspire, and possess us and guide men to a true peace? I look on the Lecture Room as the true Church of the coming time, and as the home of a richer eloquence than Faneuil Hall or the Capitol ever know. For here is all that the true orator will ask, namely, a convertible audience,—an audience coming up to the house, not knowing what shall befall them there, but uncommitted and will-ing victims to reason and love. There is no topic that may not be treated, and no method excluded. *Here,* everything is admissible, phi-losophy, ethics, divinity, criticism, poetry, humor, anecdote, mimicry,— ventriloquism almost,—all the breadth and versatility of the most lib-eral conversation, and of the highest, lowest, personal, and local topics—all are permitted, and all may be combined in one speech. It is a panharmonicon combining every note on the longest gamut, from the explosion of cannon to the tinkle of a guitar. . . . Here is a pulpit that makes the other chairs of instruction cold and ineffectual with their customary preparation for a delivery. . . . Here the American orator shall find the theatre he needs. . . .
>
> Here he may dare to hope for the higher inspiration and a total transfusion of himself into the minds of men. (*LL* 1:48)

Here again, as in many previously cited passages, we find Emerson can-nily negotiating the intricate problematic of secularization. On the one hand, he taps into religious terminology to confer seriousness and cul-tural authority on the lyceum movement. He envisions a "convertible au-dience" assembling before the "pulpit" of "the true church" and finding itself "inspired" and "possessed" by "higher communications." These communicants, however, raise themselves not by ingesting the body of Christ but by the more secular act of absorbing the words of the lecturer in an event of relatively commonplace linguistic transubstantiation— "a total transfusion of himself into the minds of men." Thus the Puri-tan imperative of "conversion" modulates into the decidedly secular and explicitly "liberal" form of "conversation." Hearts and minds are nonetheless changed, but the procedure is rational, dialogical, and indeterminate rather than ritualistic, prepatterned, and mystified: the audience comes "to the house, not knowing what shall befall them there, but uncommitted and willing victims to reason and love." The word "victim" evokes both archaic and Christian rituals of sacrifice, but Emerson again transposes this motif into a modern, enlightened, post-Christian key by consecrating the "victims" to "reason and love" rather than to tribal solidarity. Those who approach this altar neither are consumed by sacrificial fires nor consume the surrogate blood of the lamb but rather more modestly find themselves elevated in sentiment and enlarged in knowledge. It is consistent with the dialogical, open-ended spirit of this collectivity that no type of discourse is categorically excluded from its hearing: "Everything is admissible." And where strong rhythms were used in communal rituals to break down the boundaries between distinct selves and to meld them into what Émile Durkheim called collective effervescence, the harmony characteristic of this new pluralistic ceremonial seeks to preserve difference even as it seeks higher unities—"a panharmonicon combining every note." The relevant sociological categories here are thus not intimate, bounded, face-to-face communities and churches but rather the loose, shifting, anonymous, and porous social aggregations of civil society and nation. These "halls opened for discourse and debate," Emerson writes, shall provide "for the fact loving, and moral American" "a *national* music" (*LL* 1:48, italics mine).

The lyceum movement is thus presented as the secularized culmination of the dialectical development of cultural-symbolic practice in New England. It is crucial to the purposes of this chapter that Emerson first publicly brings together several of the figures who will eventually serve as his representative men immediately following this synthesis. In the fourth and final lecture in this New England series, entitled "Recent Literary and Spiritual Influences" (30 January 1843), Emerson touches on Plato, Shakespeare, Swedenborg, Napoleon, and Goethe in terms that directly anticipate his discussion of them in his 1850 book. Of Plato he says, "The highest minds of the race have been those who did deeply feel and enjoy the double meaning of every sensuous fact" (*LL* 1:67). Of Shakespeare he remarks how gladly we would "learn from [him] those daily facts," those "familiar circumstances," that "hodiernal economy" that we now "shun to record": "At a distance, it will appear to ourselves also what was the significance of those employments and meannesses as symbolical" (*LL* 1:68). Of Napoleon he says he "[broke] down the old

walls of language, religion, and politics" (*LL* 1:60). In Goethe he praises
the responsiveness to "every species of merit down to that of a good
stock or stone" (*LL* 1:61). And of Swedenborg he goes on at length, ex-
travagantly celebrating his capacity to transform "every trivial action,"
every "familiar fact" into "pregnant symbols" (*LL* 1:70): "The poet could
not see the poorest culinary stove, but he saw its relation to the charity
which is the foundation of nature" (*LL* 1:68); "his mythus is so coherent,
and vital, and true to those who dwell within" (*LL* 1:69). With Plato as the
great ancient precursor and Napoleon as the modern historical-political
agent, Emerson praises each of his representative-men-to-be for essentially the same reason: they all succeed in finding comprehensive symbolic richness, resonance, and meaning—worthy of the Puritans—in the
otherwise disconnected and disenchanted modern world of positive
facts. They all thus bridge the gap between traditional and modern conceptions of truth and representation in precisely the manner Emerson
hoped that the lyceum, and his own lecturing and writing, would do.
They all then were ripe for recruitment to help supply the answer to
what "our modern mythology" might be and how it might function. By
transmuting the potentially infinite and thus overwhelming raw data of
experience into accessible and manageable networks of symbolic meaning, they each help to resolve, as Emerson puts it in his next lecture series, Mind and Manners of the Nineteenth Century, "the disproportion
between the length of human life and the number of knowables and
doables" (*LL* 1:138). Later in the same series he writes: "This singular
exactness of analogy between all the parts of nature—this copula or tie
between all the sciences—has been and remains the highest problem
which men have to solve" (*LL* 1:159).

It is also significant for our purposes that this lecture contains a
sustained discussion of Carlyle. Emerson had discovered Carlyle's early
writings during the painful year of his departure from the Unitarian
ministry. It fortified him at this difficult time to encounter in the pages of
Fraser's and the *Edinburgh Review* a mind so forcefully confronting what
Emerson was discovering to be the central crisis both of his own life and
of Western humanism in the nineteenth century: how, in the wake of
the Enlightenment and its revolutions, to find or to construct a substitute for the demolished cultural-symbolic system of the Christian West?
Emerson was inspired and influenced by Carlyle's youthful determina-
tion to find symbolic sustenance and reorientation in secular literature
as represented, preeminently, by the writings of Goethe. During his trip
to Europe immediately following his year of crisis, Emerson journeyed

far out of his way to visit Carlyle at his home in rural Scotland. Their two days of elevated talk became enshrined in both men's memories as a halcyon interval of intellectual happiness and marked the beginning of a lifelong, and celebrated, correspondence.

Right from the start the Emerson-Carlyle letters were preoccupied with what both writers understood to be their anomalous position as purveyors of cultural symbolism, formerly the role of priests and ministers, in an increasingly secular age. In his very first letter, Emerson attributes the "defying diction" of Carlyle's *Sartor Resartus*, a book that in other respects he fulsomely praises, to Carlyle's isolation as a prophetic figure in profane times: "Can it be that this humor proceeds from a despair of finding a contemporary audience & so the Prophet feels at liberty to utter his message in droll sounds?"[4] It is only the first of many times in the correspondence that Emerson provocatively refers to his friend as a prophet, and Carlyle often reciprocates in kind. The bandying of this term amidst the dollars-and-cents details of publication suggests both men's self-consciousness about their ambiguous (secular or sacred? sales or souls?) cultural position. But the specific language of Carlyle's response here, in any case, reveals important differences in his way of engaging the problem:

> For you are to know, my view is that now at last we have lived to see all manner of Poetics and Rhetorics and Sermonics, and one may say generally all manner of Pulpits for addressing mankind from, as good as broken and abolished: alas, yes, if you have any earnest meaning, which demands to be not only listened to but believed and done, you cannot (at least I cannot) utter it *there*, but the sound sticks in my throat, as when a Solemnity were felt to become a Mummery; and so one leaves the pasteboard coulisses, and three unities, and Blairs lectures, quite behind, and feels only that there is nothing sacred, then, but the speech of men to believing men. *This*, come what will, has, is, and forever must be sacred, and will one day doubtless environ itself with fit modes, with Solemnities that are not Mummeries. Meanwhile, however, is it not pitiable? For tho Teufelsdrockh explains: "Pulpit! canst thou not *make* a pulpit, by simply *inverting the nearest tub*"; yet alas he does not sufficiently reflect that it is still only a *tub*, that the most inspired utterance will come from *it*, inconceivable, misconceivable to the million; questionable (not of ascertained significance) even to the few.[5]

Carlyle's remarks here parallel directly Emerson's comments above on the lyceum insofar as they situate his own literary practice at the latter end of a transition from a religious to a secular cultural context. Carlyle acknowledges having left behind the ritual formalities of "Sermonics," "Pulpits," and "Solemnities" in favor of the unceremonious simplicity of "the speech of men to believing men." Like Emerson, Carlyle asserts that such demystified speech is the only authentic mode of public address still available to serious people. But, unlike Emerson, Carlyle laments this change as a loss rather than as liberation. Where Emerson celebrates what might be called the horizontal secular openness of the lyceum ("You may laugh, weep, reason, sing, sneer, or pray, according to your genius"),[6] Carlyle retains the vertical exclusivity of the term "sacred" to characterize the sort of literature he sought to write in *Sartor Resartus* ("*This*, come what will, has, is, and forever must be sacred"). In time, Carlyle hopes, such authentic-sacred speech will find appropriate ritual reinforcement ("Solemnities that are not Mummeries"). But Carlyle is ultimately forced by his retention of the imperatives of the sacred to reverse the secularizing hope Teufelsdröckh had voiced in *Sartor Resartus:* an inverted tub, Carlyle grants dejectedly, is still "only a tub," and the speaker who ascends such a secular pulpit has no presumptive claim to the attention or assent of the public. Carlyle thus shares Emerson's sense of their historical moment and their personal vocations as defined by the general diminishment of traditional religious authority, but he is far less optimistic about the benefits thereof.

Carlyle's religious nostalgia similarly marks *On Heroes, Hero-Worship, and the Heroic in History* (1841), which in some respects provided the immediate model for Emerson's *Representative Men*. Carlyle's two most important foregoing works, *Sartor Resartus* (1833–1834) and *The French Revolution* (1837), had already established his protoanthropological conception of human social reality as pervasively symbolic. In the former the mysterious "philosophy of clothes" at which Professor Diogenes Toefelsdröckh arrives after many existential-philosophical trials turns out to be a theory of symbolism: "By symbols . . . ," we are told in the climactic chapter, "is man guided and commanded, made happy, made wretched. He everywhere finds himself encompassed with symbols." And "highest" among these, Toefelsdröckh explains, are "religious symbols"—"those wherein the Artist or Poet has risen into Prophet, and all men can recognize a present God, and worship the same."[7] It is consistent, then, that in his next major work Carlyle tells the story of the French Revolution primarily as a crisis of symbolic authority in which the desacralization of the personalities of the king and queen—living symbols and lynchpins of a vast interlocking cultural system—leads to the unraveling of French society as a whole. And it is further consistent that in subsequent works, Carlyle turns his formidable narrative and rhetorical energies to an effort to reconstitute a post-Christian, postrevolutionary symbolic order on the basis of celebratory-symbolic biographies of "heroic," authoritative men. His first substantial effort along these lines was the aforementioned *On Heroes*, derived from a series of lectures he gave in 1840 on Odin, Mahomet, Dante, Shakespeare, Luther, John Knox, Samuel Johnson, Robert Burns, Cromwell, and Napoleon. (He would subsequently devote much of the latter half of his life to multivolume biographies of Oliver Cromwell and Frederick the Great.) The book is sufficiently doctrinally heterodox to negate any imputation of a specific Christian theological agenda on Carlyle's part, but it is nonetheless religious in the more general sense that Carlyle explicitly solicits a worshipful response to the charismatic aura of the figures he writes about. Indeed, one of the most striking aspects of *On Heroes* is the proto-Durkheimean anthropological insight with which Carlyle characterizes and attempts to utilize the inspirational power, orienting purpose, and socially unifying centripetal pull of religious symbolism per se. "By him," he writes of Odin's place in the "rude Norse heart," "they now know what they have to do here, what to look for hereafter. Existence has become articulate, melodious by him; he has first made Life alive." "His view of the Universe once promulgated, a like view starts into being in all minds; grows, keeps ever growing. . . . And then consider what mere Time will do in such cases; how if a man was great while living, he becomes tenfold greater when dead. What an enormous camera-obscura magnifier is Tradition!" Of Mahomet, Carlyle similarly marvels that "the word this man spoke has been the life guidance now of one hundred and eighty millions of men these twelve hundred years." And he declines to look down upon these faithful masses: "Belief is great, life-giving. The history of a nation becomes fruitful, soul-elevating, great, so soon as it believes." Whether Norse-pagan, Islamic, medieval Catholic, or any variant of Protestant, religious symbolism gives the human creature, forlornly tossed into the sea of existence, a means of "fronting Time . . . and Eternity."[8]

The advent of print technology, Carlyle argues further in *On Heroes*, though often viewed as the beginning of the end of religious-symbolic authority, actually augmented its power:

The Church is the working recognized Union of our Priests and Prophets, or those who by wise teaching guide the souls of men. While there was no Writing, even while there was no Easy-Writing, or Printing, the preaching of the voice was the natural sole method of performing this. But now with Books!—He that can write a true Book, to persuade England, is he not the Bishop and Archbishop, the primate of England and of all England? I many a time say, the writers of Newspapers, Pamphlets, Poems, Books, these are the real working effective Church of a modern country. Nay, not only our preaching, but even our worship, is not it too accomplished by means of Printed Books? The noble sentiment which a gifted soul has clothed for us in melodious words, which brings melody into our hearts—is not this essentially, if one well understood it, of the nature of worship?

... Fragments of a real "Church Liturgy" and "body of Homilies," strangely Disguised from the common eye, are to be found weltering in that huge froth-ocean of Printed Speech we loosely call Literature. Books are our Church too.[9]

Carlyle here again unmistakably embraces a conception of secularization that sees the modern age as replaying or extending traditional religious culture by different means. Secular writers are seen as "Priests" and "Prophets" using new modes of communication. The feelings of assent they evoke in their readers are equated to "worship." The sharing of these feelings by many readers amounts to a "Church," in which writers are given exalted hierarchical standing as "Bishop and Archbishop." And literature, like religion, serves mainly to provide human beings with primordial existential orientation: "Men of letters," as Carlyle puts it in a foregoing passage of the same lecture, "are a perpetual Priesthood, from age to age, teaching all men that a God is still present in their life . . . the world's Priest[s]—guiding it, like a sacred Pillar of Fire, in its dark pilgrimage through the waste of Time."[10]

Carlyle thus does not yet, at this stage of his career, blame modernization per se for what he sees as the degraded condition of contemporary life. He blames rather a specific kind of modern mindset that he associates specifically with the eighteenth century and that he labels broadly as "skepticism." No sooner does he conclude his sacralization of secular literature in "The Hero as Man of Letters" than he turns his rhetorical energies to casting out what he sees as its particular skeptical demon—"this black malady and life foe, against which all teaching and discoursing since man's life began has directed itself." He writes: "The Eighteenth Century was a Sceptical Century; in which little word there is a whole Pandora's Box of miseries. Scepticism means not intellectual Doubt alone, but moral Doubt; all sorts of infidelity, insincerity, spiritual paralysis . . . a chronic atrophy and disease of the whole soul."[11]

In some broad respects *Representative Men* and *On Heroes* are similar. They may both be classed as Romantic efforts to reconstitute a symbolic order in the aftermath of the successful Enlightenment assault on the cultural system of the European "old regime." Both thus attempt to provide the spiritual nourishment perceived to be missing from Enlightenment materialism and its nineteenth-century utilitarian offspring. And both are historically comprehensive and inclusive—ecumenical with respect to established religious orthodoxies and eclectic with respect to nationality. They even overlap in two of their choices of heroes—Shakespeare and Napoleon. But Emerson decisively differentiates his project from Carlyle's by including first Plato and then, more importantly, Montaigne, or, as Emerson labels him, "the skeptic," in his pantheon.

Although not the strongest essay in *Representative Men*, "Plato; or, the Philosopher" establishes the book's emphases in two important respects. Emerson calls Socrates a "tyrannous *realist*," and two broad meanings of the term color everything that follows in this work. Emerson uses the word primarily in a loose philosophical sense to connote Plato's and Socrates's insistence on what is "real" as opposed to what is illusory or chimerical, as in the allegory of the cave. Socrates is a "realist" in this sense because he refuses to accept the "reality" or truth of an opinion, no matter how long or widely held, unless it can pass the test of strenuous logical-rational analysis. "The misery of man is to be baulked of the sight of essence," Emerson paraphrases, "and to be stuffed with conjectures: but the supreme good is reality; the supreme beauty is reality; and all virtue and all felicity depend on this science of the real: for courage is nothing else than knowledge: the fairest fortune that can befall man, is to be guided by his daemon to that which is truly his own" (*E&L* 646). To be a "realist" is synonymous in Emerson's mind with being a philosopher, as he makes clear also when he says that "Plato *is* philosophy, and philosophy, Plato" (*E&L* 633). By placing a symbol of philosophy per se at the beginning of *Representative Men*, Emerson gives the book as a whole a critical-rationalist, Hellenic, and thus Enlightenment orientation, in contrast to Carlyle's traditional, Hebraic, and stridently

anti-Enlightenment slant. Where Carlyle's *On Heroes* had celebrated religious belief and authority, Emerson draws upon Plato to announce
from the beginning that his symbolic system has a prominent place for
skepticism toward religious tradition and convention. Indeed, it is striking by contrast to Carlyle's work that none of Emerson's representative
men are principally associated with Christianity. Even Swedenborg, as
we will see, was important to Emerson principally as a symbolist of scientific empiricism rather than as a Lutheran mystic.

But this is not to suggest that the essay on Plato or *Representative Men*
as a whole bears no trace whatsoever of Christian influence. Emerson's
Christian-Hebraic cultural background does come prominently into
play, but as a mode of representation rather than as a body of beliefs.
Ironically, Emerson attributes to Plato a mode of realistic representation
that Erich Auerbach has taught us to see as the product of a momentous
departure from classical mimetic norms in early Christian culture.[12]
Plato's importance, Emerson argues, derives not only from the critical
rigor of his thinking but also from his distinctive skill and scope as a
writer: "He has reason, as all the philosophic and poetic class have: but
he has, also, what they have not, — this strong solving sense to reconcile
his poetry with the appearances of the world, and build a bridge from
the streets of cities to Atlantis" (*E&L* 644). Even Plato's most abstract
and "transcendental" distinctions, Emerson points out, are illustrated by
examples drawn from common life — "from mares and puppies; from
pitchers and soup-ladles; from cooks and criers; the shops of potters,
horse-doctors, butchers, and fishmongers" (*E&L* 641). And the character
of Socrates, Plato's great exemplar of virtue and wisdom, is similarly associated at every turn with the prosaic details of ordinary experience —
"a man of humble stem, but honest enough; of the commonest history;
of a personal homeliness so remarkable, as to be the cause of wit in
others . . . plain as a Quaker in habit and speech, affect[ing] low phrases,
and illustration from cocks and quails, soup-pans and sycamore-spoons,
grooms and farriers, and unnameable offices" (*E&L* 649–50). In Auerbach's account, the New Testament images of a domestic Jesus interact-
ing with humble people in their own milieu inaugurated the great tradition of realistic "mimesis" in the West precisely by breaking away from
an unwritten classical rule that reserved serious literary treatment to
aristocratic characters in public settings. But Emerson suggests here that
the strength of Plato's writings derives from their placing a "homely"
Socrates in just the same sort of humble settings, speaking the same sort

of down-to-earth language. It is beyond the scope of this book to try to resolve the literary-historical questions arising from this discrepancy. But it seems most plausible to accept Auerbach's highly regarded account and to suggest that in his essay on Plato, Emerson projects a mode of Christian realism onto a classical source, and in doing so reveals his own continuing attachment to an important aspect of Christian-Hebraic culture even as he attempts to move beyond it. He remains attached, specifically, to Christianity's comprehensive, morally egalitarian, symbolic-representational reach. Paradoxically, Emerson seeks ultimately to emulate this Christian-realist comprehensiveness in symbolizing a world otherwise released from Christian framing—a release secured in good part through the agency of classical-Enlightenment philosophical critique, here symbolized by Plato.

The inclusion of Swedenborg in *Representative Men* is also best understood in terms of the adaptation of Christian symbolic models to post-Enlightenment facts. At first glance Swedenborg seems out of place in the company of Plato, Montaigne, Shakespeare, and Goethe. A relatively obscure Swedish scientist and mystic, Swedenborg lacks the stature and sophistication of these world-historical literary-philosophical giants. Yet a bit of biographical research reveals that Swedenborg led an extraordinary life riven by precisely the split between (Christian) symbolism and empirical fact that Gellner sees as the epistemological pivot of liberal modernity and that Emerson seeks to overcome in *Representative Men* as a whole.

Born in Uppsala in 1688 into the family of an imposing scholar and minister who helped inject pietistic feeling into the established Lutheran Church of Sweden and who later became bishop of Skara, Swedenborg grew up in a household environment of fervent, evangelical religiosity. It was "an atmosphere," his biographer tells us, "in which all blessings or blows of fate, all illnesses, conflagrations, and floods were perceived as the action of either heaven or hell." As a young child, Swedenborg showed signs of inheriting his father's spiritual gifts: "From my fourth until my tenth year," he wrote years later in his *Spiritual Diary*, "my thoughts were constantly occupied with God, salvation, and the spiritual conditions of men. I often uttered things which made my parents wonder and think that angels must be speaking through my mouth." From the time of his adolescent schooling and university career, however, until he was fully fifty years old, Swedenborg showed little subsequent interest in religious matters. He devoted himself instead, with "almost inconceivable intensity," to study, publication, and practical engagement in multiple areas of natural science, especially mine engineering. Upon finishing university he traveled to England, where from 1709 to 1714 he served a remarkable self-initiated apprenticeship to some of the leading scientific minds of the era, including Newton himself, the great astronomer John Flamsteed, the mathematician Sir Edmund Halley, and John Woodward, the founder of the science of geology. He witnessed the trial for heresy of William Whiston, a charismatic pupil of Newton whose questioning of the doctrine of the Trinity cost him a professorship at Cambridge—an event characterized by Swedenborg's biographer as "the first great trial in which modern science collided with Church doctrine."[13] And Swedenborg pitted himself, unsuccessfully, against Whiston, Flamsteed, and others in the public competition for the solution of longitude.

By the time he returned to Sweden in 1714, Swedenborg's encyclopedic mind was overflowing with scientific knowledge and sketches of new technological devices. His ideas included a submarine, an air gun, a steam machine, various pumps, a water elevator, new methods for manufacturing springs, a mechanical carriage, a flying machine, a water clock, a drawbridge, and a mechanical method for reproducing silhouettes and prints. Charles XII recognized his brilliance and installed him as "assessor of mines" in 1716, an ideal position providing public prestige, flexibility, and enormous resources for continuing research. Over the next twenty-eight years Swedenborg carried out prodigious scientific and technological labors, including the planning and construction of "complicated sluice and dockworks," the calculation of the "fluctuations in water level in various lakes and watercourses," and the preparation of reports on the tin industry, trade and manufacture, the extraction, processing, and export of Swedish ores, and the expansion of Swedish paper manufacturing. He wrote a treatise entitled "On the Nature of Fire and Furnaces" and another entitled "On the Height of Water and the Strong Tides in the Primeval World." He made contributions to geometry and algebra, including a ten-volume algebra textbook, and he continued his astronomical studies. He "climbed into the mines, measured ebb and tide, pounded rock fragments from shafts and quarries, collected drift stones in the valleys and gravel from the rivers, compared the metallic traces of various ore-containing rocks, calculated the movements of the stars and the changes of the horizon." He "recorded, viewed, compared, and methodically classified everything with strict scientific self-discipline to glean the inner laws of nature."[14]

Then, in 1743–1744, while bringing to completion a comprehensive biological study entitled *The Economy of the Animal Kingdom,* Swedenborg underwent a "convulsive" religious crisis that transformed his personality. He had overwhelming personal experiences of Christ's love and found himself able to see and converse with angels and other spirits, including that of his admonishing dead father, with perfect clarity. He soon gave up all scientific ambitions and devoted the rest of his long life (he lived vigorously and sociably, largely on coffee, until he was eighty-four) to writing massive, arcane, multivolume chartings of the symbolic links between passages of scripture, inner states of mind, and material phenomena. His biographer summarizes these voluminous visionary works as follows:

> Swedenborg endeavor[ed] to work out in detail a sort of encyclopedia of correspondences. On the basis of a compilation of various passages in which the same word or image occurs, he seeks to determine its symbolic meaning or spiritual sense. For each animal, each color, each figure occurring in the Bible, a unique, definitive spiritual meaning is ascertained, which varies according to the context. . . . Thus, the animal kingdom corresponds to the realm of instincts, desires, and appetites in men, whereby a concrete meaning attaches to each species and type of animal. The same applies to the plant kingdom, which generally corresponds to our knowledge and insights, whereby the individual types of plants have a special meaning. The mineral world corresponds generally and in detail to our fixed principles. In this fashion, the whole of Holy Scripture is transformed into a complex of spiritual meanings, which are woven into a doctrine of salvation.[15]

It is hard to imagine a more vivid or psychologically wrenching illustration of the fraught Enlightenment transition from symbolic to empirical standards of reference. The three phases of Swedenborg's life, as described by Ernest Benz, are defined by his crossing and recrossing of this epistemological threshold. He begins with symbolism as a young child in his father's pietistic household, believing that all events may be interpreted as manifestations of either God-Heaven or the Devil-Hell. He then breaks away into encyclopedic empiricism in adolescence and early adulthood, energetically absorbing and applying multiple bodies of mathematical and natural-scientific knowledge. But in later adulthood he is pulled back toward symbolism in visionary writings whose encyclopedic scope encompasses the full range of his vast empirical learning. At both the beginning and the end of the trajectory stands the potent imago of Swedenborg's forbidding father, about whom Swedenborg dreamed repeatedly at the time of his religious crisis. As a young scientist Swedenborg had sustained a magnificent, if manic, rebellion against his father's authority, pushing ahead with his scientific projects in spite of the bishop's increasingly explicit objections. But in late midlife Swedenborg seems to have capitulated to the internalized voice of his father, and he surrendered thereafter to a massive psychocultural regression. It is as if at age fifty Swedenborg's psyche finally balked at the disparate, denuded, and affectively isolated postsymbolic condition to which his prodigious empirical labors had brought him, and he compensated thereafter by a no-less-prodigious effort at affective-symbolic reintegration.

Emerson does not himself speculate in *Representative Men* on the psychological roots of Swedenborg's changes. He is more interested in marking the distinct phases of the narrative, noting with disappointment the "colossal" Swede's late-life reversion to Christian orthodoxy. His use of "The Mystic" as a subtitle notwithstanding, for Emerson the work that justifies Swedenborg's inclusion in *Representative Men* is not the voluminous mystical-religious arcana but rather the book he was just finishing at the time his visionary experiences began—the aforementioned *Economy of the Animal Kingdom* (1744). Emerson was drawn to this work in good part because he shared some of its principal influences, especially the writings of those late-seventeenth-century scholars whom Charles Taylor has called "counter-Lockean deists," typified by the Cambridge Platonists. For Swedenborg as for Emerson at the time he was writing *Nature,* the holistic analogical conception of rationality developed by these thinkers seemed to provide a means of integrating disparate empirical data into an intuitively intelligible orderly whole. *The Economy of the Animal Kingdom* held nothing less than world-historical cultural importance in Emerson's eyes because he believed that it successfully drew on the associative logic of analogy to bridge the gap between symbolism and empiricism—without recourse, as yet, to a scriptural key. Emerson praises Swedenborg's mastery of the extensive empirical and mathematical researches of the day—the work of Harvey (circulation of the blood); Gilbert (magnetism); Descartes (geometry and vertical motion); Newton (gravity); Swammerdam, Leeuwenhoek, Winslow, Eustachius, Heister, Vesalius, Boerhave (anatomy). He calls the members of this latter group "unrivalled dissectors" who "had left nothing for scalpel or microscope to reveal in human or comparative anatomy" (*E&L* 667). But of greater importance to Emerson was Swedenborg's insight into the pattern of analogy that knit all of these data together. The recognition that "nature is always self-similar," that "little explains large, and large, little" gave to Swedenborg, Emerson suggests, "a capacity to entertain and vivify these volumes of thought" (*E&L* 667). "Each law of nature," Emerson paraphrases, "has the like universality; eating, sleep or hibernation, rotation, generation, metamorphosis, vertical motion, which is seen in eggs as in planets. These grand rhymes or returns in nature . . . delighted the prophetic eye of Swedenborg; and he must be reckoned a leader in that revolution, which, by giving to science an idea, has given to an aimless accumulation of experiments, guidance and form, and a beating heart" (*E&L* 670). The generous terms in which Emerson celebrates *The Economy of the Animal Kingdom* say as much about his own largest liberal-cultural ambition as they do about Swedenborg. This book was written, Emerson says, "with the highest end,—to put science and the soul, long estranged from each other, at one again. It was an anatomist's account of the human body, in the highest style of poetry" (*E&L* 671). "The earth had fed its mankind through five or six millenniums, and they had sciences, religions, philosophies; and yet had failed to see the correspondence of meaning between every part and every other part. And down to this hour, literature has no book in which the symbolism of things is scientifically opened" (*E&L* 674). To put "science and the soul . . . at one again" is yet another way of formulating the broad challenge of liberal culture as Emerson understood it. Meeting this challenge would require subsequent writers to continue to "open . . . the symbolism of things" along the lines Swedenborg's pivotal work had laid out.

The terms in which Emerson puts Swedenborg's subsequent failure to live up to his own challenge are no less self-revealing than those he used to characterize the energetic Swede's success in posing it:

> This design of exhibiting such correspondences, which, if adequately executed, would be the poem of the world, in which all history and science would play an essential part, was narrowed and defeated by the exclusively theologic direction which his inquiries took. His perception of nature is not human and universal, but is mystical and Hebraic. He fastens each natural object to a theologic notion,—a horse signifies carnal understanding; a tree, perception; the moon, faith; a cat means this;

an ostrich, that; an artichoke, the other; and poorly tethers every symbol to a several ecclesiastical sense. The slippery Proteus is not so easily caught. In nature, each individual symbol plays innumerable parts, as each particle of matter circulates in turn through every system. The central identity enables any one symbol to express successively all the qualities and shades of real being. In the transmission of heavenly waters, every hose fits every hydrant. Nature avenges herself speedily on the hard pedantry that would chain her waves. She is no literalist. Everything must be taken genially, and we must be at the top of our condition, to understand any thing rightly. (*E&L* 676)

Emerson commends Swedenborg for so profoundly registering the symbolic hunger left unsated by scientific positivism and for trying so prodigiously to assuage it. The effort alone is sufficient, in Emerson's mind, to place Swedenborg among modernity's heroes. Although Swedenborg failed to complete the job himself, he cut out for liberal civilization its most important cultural work. But to do that work successfully requires a greater admixture of the qualities of mind that Emerson will turn to next in the essay on Montaigne—suppleness, flexibility, lightness, openness, urbanity. In addition to prodigious dual capacity—abundant access to both raw data and symbols with which to map them—one needs a high degree of tact in executing the match. Montaigne could exercise such epistemological tact because as a man who found himself caught between Catholicism and Protestantism, between faith and rationality, or, more remotely, between the "old" world and the new, he understood, in a distinctively liberal way, the multiplicity, variety, and contingency of symbolic systems. He could function in the dangerous, undefined middle ground of liberal-symbolic pluralism in which the rules were not settled beforehand, balances could be abruptly tipped, exchanges could go in many possible directions, and sensitivity to contexts, even as they constantly shifted, was essential.

The essay entitled "Montaigne, or, The Skeptic" is often rightfully singled out from the others in *Representative Men* for moments of verbal brilliance worthy of Emerson's most electric early writings. "The Skeptic" is also rightfully valued for its elegantly condensed reprise and resolution of the psychoepistemological crisis of "Experience," an aspect to which we will return. But this essay also has crucial importance for any attempt to understand Emerson from a political-cultural point of view. It reveals much about Emerson's own political temperament, to start with, that he takes pains to honor a figure who stood out as liberal minded in an illiberal age. "In the civil wars of the League, which converted every house into a fort," Emerson writes admiringly, "Montaigne kept his gates open, and his house without defence. All parties freely came and went, his courage and honor being universally esteemed" (*E&L* 698). These sentences do not perhaps tell us anything we did not already know about Montaigne; but they do tell us something about Emerson as distinct from Carlyle. Emerson includes Montaigne among the exemplary men of human history in part because he holds the liberal virtues of tolerance, openness, fair-mindedness, and urbanity in the very highest regard. Like Judith Shklar more recently, Emerson perhaps sensed that the deep-seated aversion to cruelty voiced by Montaigne was the affective foundation of liberal freedom.[16] But the political-cultural significance of Emerson's inclusion of Montaigne in *Representative Men* goes further still. Whereas Carlyle's polemic against skepticism, as we saw above, was necessary to his larger effort to retrieve pre-Enlightenment religious monuments for post-Enlightenment symbolic use, Emerson's inclusion of "the skeptic" marks his awareness that the Enlightenment could not be simply elided or denied in such Romantic efforts at symbolic reconstruction. He recognizes here as throughout his work that, for all who came after it, the Enlightenment permanently changed Western human beings' comportment toward symbolism per se. And he recognizes that the great achievement of Montaigne, more than a century ahead of his time, was to have anticipated, embraced, and verbally enacted this change.

One of the most common settings of Montaigne's anecdotes is a besieged city or the ground between its walls and a besieging army. "Truly man is a marvelously vain, diverse, and undulating object," he declares in the very first essay of the first book of essays, entitled "By Diverse Means We Arrive at the Same End." And in support he cites the case of Edward, Prince of Wales, who wreaked cruel vengeance upon the conquered Limousins until he was moved abruptly to mercy by the sight of three citizens fighting with "incredible boldness" against his occupying forces, "holding out alone against the assault of the victorious army." Similarly, Emperor Conrad III granted no terms to the besieged Guelph, duke of Bavaria, beyond allowing the gentlewomen of his city to leave on foot with whatever possessions they could carry on their backs. But when the women emerged with "their husbands, their children, and the duke himself on their shoulders," the emperor "wept with delight" and "wholly subdued the bitter and deadly hatred he had borne against this duke." The extraordinary valor exhibited by Betis in defence of Gaza, on the other hand, only whetted the victorious Alexander's appetite for retribution. "Turning his anger into rage, he ordered Betis' heels to be pierced through and had him thus dragged alive, torn, and dismembered, behind a cart." So volatile and unpredictable are human beings, Montaigne suggests, that there is no categorical answer to the title question of essay 5, "whether the governor of a besieged place should go out to parley." The only thing certain is conveyed by the title of essay 6: "Parley time is dangerous." Here he relates a recent incident "in [his] neighborhood," where the French army cut the enemy to pieces "during the discussion of terms." Rejecting complaints of treachery, Montaigne says merely that "parties should not trust one another until the last binding seal has been set. Even then there is plenty of room for wariness."[17]

This reiterated scenario of siege and parley serves as an apt, three-leveled metaphor for Montaigne's protoliberal political-historical position and thus for his special political significance to Emerson. On the first level, it evokes the literal historical circumstances in which Montaigne found himself during the era of the wars of religion. At this time much of Europe, including France, had been split into warring camps of Catholics versus Protestants. Montaigne would have personally witnessed or heard firsthand accounts of a good many attacks, counterattacks, sieges, and surrenders. As a soldier-aristocrat he knew well and yet recoiled from all the blood and suffering these battles brought. His frequent reversion to such scenes of violence nonetheless suggests their almost traumatic hold on his own consciousness and on that of Europe in general. But, as Emerson makes clear, Montaigne was more than just a passive register of this bloody situation. As a tolerant, peace-loving, and socially eminent Catholic respected by both sides, Montaigne would have hosted and participated in periodic negotiations—"parleys"—between the embattled opponents. Indeed, Emerson is not mistaken in suggesting that Montaigne held open his own estate as a neutral ground of peaceable passage and diplomatic exchange—and therein lies the second level of liberal significance in these anecdotes. Roughly one hundred years after the publication of Montaigne's *Essays*, Locke's *Letter Concerning Toleration* and "The Second Treatise" showed a way out of the impasse of religious warfare precisely by proposing that all the public space of England should be treated as such open, neutral ground.

Locke drew one large national circle, in effect, around all the warring religious camps (in his case, Anglicans, Puritans, and Presbyterians as well as Catholics), and he, theoretically, instituted legal tolerance and protection within this circle for all the groups' privacy, physical safety, and even mutual interaction and cooperation. Thus the multicultural civil society distinctive to modern liberalism was born, and it looked a good deal like Montaigne's open estate or one of his anecdotal parleys, but with rules agreed upon and firmly enforced. It also looked a bit like Montaigne's uniquely open form of writing, and this takes us to the third level of the parley's liberal meaning.

I started this chapter by drawing on V. S. Naipaul and Ernest Gellner to make a distinction between traditional-symbolic and modern-empirical conceptions of truth and linguistic representation. I drew on Gellner to suggest further that the transition from truth as loyal "concept affirmation" to truth as empirical reference was a crucial step in the evolution of modern liberal civilization. We have seen how Swedenborg's life was marked by the difficulty of this epistemic change. We know also from history that figures such as Socrates, Copernicus, and Galileo, to name just a few of the most famous, risked their lives when they tried to introduce empirical data that implicitly or explicitly contradicted received symbolic accounts of reality. Montaigne's imagination so frequently reverts to the setting of the parley in his essays, I would suggest, because he found himself in a similarly dangerous situation of epistemological transition with respect to the representation of the self. The most devoted recent champion of the essay form, G. Douglas Atkins, aptly likens the spontaneous accretion of self-attuned sentences in Montaigne's essays to Paul Klee's playful self-description of his own improvisational approach as a painter—"taking 'a line out for a walk.'"[18] It does not stretch Atkins's point unduly to suggest that, just as Klee's approach broke all the established rules of pictorial representation, so fidelity to the multidirectional tugs, tangents, and reversals of his own unfolding consciousness led Montaigne beyond all the extant symbolic models for a coherent verbal picture of the self. Auerbach confirms this: "Montaigne's emancipation from the Christian conceptual schema did not—despite his exact knowledge and continual study of antique culture—simply put him back among the ideas and conditions among which men of his sort had lived in the days of Cicero or Plutarch. His newly acquired freedom was much more exciting, much more of the historical moment, directly connected with the feeling of insecurity."[19] The essay form itself as Montaigne practiced it, in other words, may be said to venture out from tradition's city of established symbols—"a thousand years old"—into the as yet symbolically uncharted no-man's-land of open-ended empirical reference and self-description. "Others form man," he wrote. "I describe him."[20] Indeed, the peregrine progressions of the essays typically move through a series of inadequate symbolic frames and arrive at an astringent, but nonetheless joyful, apprehension of the granular, fleeting, overbrimming, and symbolically uncontainable particularity of self and world. Montaigne's delightfully relaxed auto-biographical "parlez" was also a tense, high-stakes cultural-historical "parley" in this sense. He does not reject symbolism altogether but rather offers himself as a symbol of the inadequacy of all the extant networks. Ideally, symbols should not force their referents into a mold but should rather be adapted to fit the heterogeneity of what they represent: "For every foot its own shoe."[21]

Emerson's inclusion of Montaigne in *Representative Men* allows him to incorporate all three levels of the wise Frenchman's liberal significance into his new mythology. For one, Montaigne's association, however anti-thetical, with the European wars of religion allows Emerson to memo-rialize modern liberalism's precipitating historical crisis. He thus bal-lasts the optimistic cast of *Representative Men* with due consciousness of the dark pattern of religious genocide that the Lockean-liberal compro-mise was designed to avert. Second, Montaigne's distinctive dilatory gusto allows Emerson to hold up the liberal virtues of tolerance and open-mindedness not just as privative abstractions but as deeply felt and greatly enriching ways of being. And third, Montaigne's magnificent enactment in his essays of the transition from symbolic to empirical (self-)representation allows Emerson to fully own the fertile paradox im-plicit in his larger symbolic project as a whole. Its status as part of a symbolic framework notwithstanding, Emerson's essay does not shy away from that aspect of Montaigne's writing that contests the ade-quacy of any general symbolic framework to represent the complex specificity of individual experience and selfhood. Indeed, the language of Emerson's paraphrases of Montaigne repeatedly calls attention to this intrinsic disjunction:

> The Spartan and Stoic schemes are too stark and stiff for our occasion.
> A theory of Saint John, and of nonresistance, seems, on the other hand,
> too thin and aerial. (*E&L* 696)

I stand here for truth, and will not, for all the states, and churches, and revenues of Europe, overstate the dry fact, as I see it. (*E&L* 699)

It stands in his mind, that our life in this world is not of quite so easy interpretation as churches and school-books say. (*E&L* 703)

The astonishment of life, is, the absence of any appearance of reconciliation between the theory and practice of life. (*E&L* 705)

He denies out of honesty. He had rather stand charged with the imbecility of skepticism, than with untruth. (*E&L* 707)

The argument of these lines is, in part, historically specific. They assert the inadequacies of the particular symbolic systems that governed European life at the time Montaigne wrote: classical-Hellenic ("Spartan and Stoic schemes"); Christian-Hebraic ("a theory of Saint John"); feudal-aristocratic ("states"); Roman Catholic and Protestant ("churches"); and scholastic ("school-books"). On this level Emerson presents Montaigne much as he presents Swedenborg, Goethe, and Napoleon each in his turn—as a symbol of Western modernity. But Montaigne also serves in these lines as a symbol of modernity in a subtler and more radical manner unique to him among all of Emerson's representative men. For, in addition to registering Montaigne's refusal of full assent to many of the ideologies of his day, these lines and the essay as a whole also attribute to him a systematic skepticism in the strict philosophical sense of the word—a radical doubt in principle as to the reliable correspondence between word and thing, idea and reality, and, most pertinently, symbol and experience. Emerson's account emphasizes, to be sure, that such skepticism must not be mistaken for pessimism. Just as proved true for Emerson himself in "Experience," Emerson argues that Montaigne's perpetually renewed perception of a gap between word and thing yielded not lethargy or cynical disillusion but rather, as we saw above, a wise, healthy, and ever-refreshed admixture of equanimity, openness, and "astonishment." "The interrogation of custom at all points," Emerson insists, "is an inevitable stage in the growth of every superior mind, and is the evidence of the flowing power which remains itself in all changes." Thence comes the characteristic wry but affirmative tone of Montaigne's essays. Thence comes their unique way of being both perpetually inconclusive and infinitely satisfying. Thence comes what Auerbach calls their unique "calmness": "He has enough of substance and elasticity in himself, he possesses a natural moderation, and has little need of security since it always reestablishes itself spontaneously within him."[22] And thence also come the deceptive fluid strength and understated intensity of their resistance to all variants of dogmatism and symbolic enclosure.

For Emerson to have placed among his symbols in *Representative Men* a figure so pointedly inimical to symbolic representation gave his symbolic structure as a whole a strikingly modern, post-Enlightenment tilt. Emerson was too much of a Romantic, as we have seen in his journal entries and lectures, to do without symbolism altogether. But at the same time he understood the emancipating aspects of the Enlightenment too well not to embrace the cognitive advance afforded by its release of the vast world of positive facts from mystifying symbolic frames. So, just as in "Experience" Emerson arrived at a regenerated conception of knowledge by acknowledging the limits of knowledge, in "Montaigne, or, The Skeptic" he attempts, paradoxically, to establish a more apt network of symbols by acknowledging the limits of symbolism. Scholars such as John Gray and Judith Shklar have noted an affinity between skepticism and liberalism in that both attempt to be self-limiting and self-correcting out of an awareness of human fallibility. The connection holds true in relation to Emerson's construction of liberal culture in *Representative Men*. A degree of skepticism toward politics had compelled the American founders to build checks and balances and mechanisms for review into their political constitution. In the same way, Emerson's skepticism toward symbolism per se compels him to build into his symbolic system a symbol—Montaigne—of the intrinsic contingency and partiality of all such systems. Indeed, Emerson's inclusion of Montaigne is part of an attempt, perhaps quixotic, to build a set of symbols that will be constantly self-correcting and self-adjusting by reference to the "facts on the ground," recognizing that the emergence of new facts will continually exceed and outstrip the representational capacities of any symbolic system that seeks to distill and organize them. In Gellner's terms, Emerson may be said to use Montaigne, whose writing enacts the release of his own facticity from all symbolic framing, to ensure that his new symbolic system is thoroughly perforated by "apertures" to the outside world. Or, in Lacanian terms, Emerson may be said to use Montaigne to help him reconstitute the post-Enlightenment liberal "Symbolic" in such a way as to make it maximally open to the revisionary agency of the creative, experiencing subject.[23] Nietzsche once characterized Emerson as "more enlightened, more roving, more manifold, subtler than Carlyle; above all, happier."²⁴ Nowhere is the truth of this assessment so evident as in the difference in the historical self-consciousness of their respective efforts at symbolic reconstruction. Unlike Carlyle, who seeks in *On Heroes* to reconstitute premodern symbolic authority in the modern age, Emerson includes Montaigne among his heroes to signify his understanding and acceptance of liberal modernity as defined by a new, more skeptical orientation to symbolic authority per se.

Emerson's Napoleon does to the feudal-aristocratic sociopolitical frame what his Montaigne did to the medieval framings of the self: he shatters it. Napoleon, Emerson writes, "was the agitator, the destroyer of pre-scription, the internal improver, the liberal, the radical, the inventor of means, the opener of doors and markets, the subverter of monopoly and abuse" (*E&L* 742). It is hardly original on Emerson's part to thus paint Napoleon as the historical catalyst who helped bring to a boil the long-simmering opposition of the European middle classes to aristocratic hegemony. Hegel, among others, had already interpreted Napoleon in this way. But the rhetorical energy of Emerson's version is nonetheless striking. Though not without criticism of the revolutionary-turned-emperor, this is one of the most inspired essays in *Representative Men*, and it again confirms Emerson's robust bourgeois-liberal sympathies. His praises of Napoleon touch on many core nineteenth-century liberal principles: putting an end to aristocratic class exploitation; canceling the privileges of the clerisy; instituting representative government; implementing scientific and technological improvements; establishing free markets and careers open to talent.

With Napoleon as the historical wrecking ball, battering down the rotted-out social-symbolic structures of medievalism, Goethe follows after, picking up the splintered pieces, finding them worthy of serious aesthetic attention, and setting them in new, more "natural" relations. Emerson explicitly makes this connection. "I described Bonaparte," he writes, "as a representative of the popular external life and aims of the nineteenth century. Its other half, its poet, is Goethe" (*E&L* 750–51). Goethe's principal qualification for this important post was a capacity to mimetically assimilate a vast quantity of new data freshly released from the old symbolic frame:

> There was never such a miscellany of facts. The world extends itself like American trade. . . . Goethe was the philosopher of this multiplicity;

hundred-handed, Argus-eyed, able and happy to cope with this rolling miscellany of facts and sciences, and, by his own versatility, to dispose of them with ease; a manly mind, unembarrassed by the variety of coats of convention with which life had got encrusted, easily able by his subtlety to pierce these, and to draw his strength from nature, with which he lived in full communion. (*E&L* 751)

Still he is a poet,—poet of a prouder laurel than any contemporary, and, under this plague of microscopes (for he seems to see out of every pore of his skin,) strikes the harp with a hero's strength and grace. (*E&L* 752)

What new mythologies sail through his head! . . . He was the soul of his century. If that was learned, and had become, by population, compact organization, and drill of parts, one great Exploring Expedition, accumulating a glut of facts and fruits too fast for any hitherto-existing savans to classify, this man's mind had ample chambers for the distribution of all. He had a power to unite the detached atoms again by their own law. He has clothed our modern existence with poetry. (*E&L* 752)

Thus, some twenty years after he first read Wordsworth and five years before Whitman's *Leaves of Grass,* Emerson announces that he has found in Goethe the poet he had long been looking for. Goethe crosses without aesthetic loss or existential disorientation from the old symbolic to the new empirical mode of consciousness: "This man was entirely at home and happy in his century and the world" (*E&L* 760). He is uniquely able to remain open to the empirical "glut" and "miscellany" of positivist modernity while still finding beauty—the "harp"—and provisional coherencies—"new mythologies"—therein. The order he found, Emerson is careful to note, was not imposed extrinsically on the facts but rather derived imminently, in the manner of science, from the patterns the facts themselves disclosed: he "unite[s] the detached atoms again *by their own law*" (*E&L* 752, italics mine).

The key word of Emerson's essay on Goethe is "report." He uses it six times in the first three paragraphs. The task of the writer, magnificently performed by Goethe, Emerson suggests in the first paragraph, is to "*report* the doings of the miraculous spirit of life" (*E&L* 746, italics mine). Indeed, the spirit of life solicits such representation: "Nature will be *reported*" (*E&L* 746, italics mine). This "report" must strive to be mimetically accurate but will inevitably be "more than print of the seal": "It is a new and finer form of the original" (*E&L* 746). So capable a writer as Goethe will not be discouraged by the notion that some things are beyond representation: "He would *report* the Holy Ghost," Emerson writes, "or attempt it" (*E&L* 747, italics mine). "In his eyes," Emerson summarizes, "a man is the faculty of *reporting*, and the universe is the possibility of being *reported*" (*E&L* 747, italics mine). Placed in the broad historical-epistemological context we have been developing, the word seems pointedly chosen to privilege empiricism over symbolism. Emerson might well have said that "nature will be *represented*," or that "man is the faculty of *symbolizing*," or that "the universe exists to be *drawn*," or "*painted*," or "*written*," or "*imaged*," or "*interpreted*." But by repeating "*reported*" he seeks instead to downplay as much as possible the creative, reshaping agency of the mediator. As its frequent use in journalism suggests, the term connotes neutrality, objectivity, and transparency. It gives priority to the facts rather than to their representational vehicle. This is not to suggest that Emerson was blind to the inevitable transformations that facts undergo in the process of even the most careful linguistic or other mediation. We have seen him pay scrupulous dues to skepticism everywhere in his writing, and even here he acknowledges that the report will be "more than print of the seal."[25] But there are degrees of idealization, mystification, and ideological manipulation. Emerson here praises Goethe and holds him up as a model because he sought, in a scientific spirit, to minimize such distortions. In this way Goethe managed uniquely to synthesize the two liberal cultures of humanism and science, performing the symbolic work of the former in the strictly realistic or referential-representational manner of the latter.

This reading of Goethe as "reporter" is consistent with the eminent German's own late-life reflections and exhortations in *Conversations of Goethe with Eckermann*. Throughout the book Goethe repeatedly insists that poetry and painting must be realistic in the sense that they must derive their subjects from the particularities of real life, real settings, and actual occasions. "The world is so great and rich," he advises his friend Johann Peter Eckermann in one of their first conversations, "and life so full of variety, that you can never want occasions for poems. But they must be *occasioned*, that is to say, reality must give both impulse and material. . . . All my poems are occasional poems, suggested by real life, and having therein a firm foundation. I attach no value to poems snatched out of the air." Goethe similarly gives precedence to subject over style: "What can be more important than the subject, and what is all the science of art without it? All talent is wasted if the subject is unsuitable." He recommends that some contemporary poets would benefit from trying "a piece in prose" to align their vision with ordinary life and to help them to achieve an "easy, living representation." He says that painters, for similar reasons, should desist from painting a subject in artificial isolation but should include treatment of all factors contributing to that subject's unique texture and appearance. A painting of a mossy stone, for example, should register the fact that the moss is nourished not only by moisture from the nearby stream but by the stone's northerly orientation and its position under the shade of trees: "If I omit these influential causes from my picture, it will be without truth." And every detail must be treated with the utmost mimetic fidelity consistent with a comprehensible whole. In Philip Peter Roos's paintings of sheep, for example, Goethe notes how the artist clearly took pleasure in rendering the tiniest nuances of the postures and countenances of these "dull, gaping, and dreaming" beasts: "It is most wonderful how Roos has been able to think and feel himself into the very soul of these creatures, so as to make the internal character peer with such force through the outward covering." Most strikingly, Goethe advises a struggling contemporary poet to try describing his recent return to the city of Hamburg. When the man commences versifying the many feelings that arose within him as he entered the familiar gates of his home city, Goethe corrects him by pointing out that he has said nothing that would distinguish the scene from Magdeburg or Jena. "Yet what a peculiar city is Hamburg! and what a rich field was offered him for the most minute description, if he had known or ventured to take hold of the subject properly." This poet does not lack talent or imagination, Goethe declares, but he can only be "saved" by "*breaking through to the objective*" (italics mine). "He deserves not the name [of poet] while he only speaks out his few subjective feelings; but as soon as he can appropriate to himself, and express, the world, he is a poet. Then he is inexhaustible, and can be always new." Earlier in the book Goethe had given similar advice to Eckermann himself. Assigning to Eckermann the task of "sparing no toil" in "studying" and "representing" the particular look of the city of Erfurt, Goethe says: "You must do violence to yourself to get out of the Idea. . . . I know well that it is difficult; but apprehension and representation of the individual is the very life of art."[26]

Goethe's words here bring us back full circle to the beginning of our discussion and provide a summarizing thread to trace through the chapter as a whole. In urging his protégé to break through to the objective and "get out of the Idea," Goethe articulates what Naipaul must have wished to say in his vexed exchanges with the Indonesian villagers. In

Goethe's terms we can now see that Naipaul was frustrated precisely by the man's unwillingness to get out of the idea of the ruined building's mythical antiquity—his refusal to break through to the objective evidence of its real age. By contrast, every one of Emerson's heroes in *Representative Men* can be said to have achieved his special stature by virtue of having courageously carried out precisely such representational breaking through. Plato is credited with having taught the West to use critical reason to break unto truth through the manifold illusions spun out by tradition and convention: "He secures a position not to be commanded, by his passion for reality" (*E&L* 646). Swedenborg is celebrated first for having broken through Christianity's symbolic framing to an encyclopedic apprehension of positive scientific facts and then for attempting to construct a more suitable symbolic ligature with which to link the million facts back together. Montaigne is specially honored for breaking through the medieval symbolic framings of the self. Napoleon's greatness comes from having shattered the medieval sociopolitical symbolic frame. Shakespeare moves beyond symbolism to "perfect representation, at last" (*E&L* 723), and Goethe "pierces" through "the coats of convention" to the objective facts of nature, "putting ever a thing for a word" (*E&L* 753). In each case and in sum, Emerson's representative men confirm Gellner's conception of liberal culture as founded on a world-historical cognitive breaking through from symbolic to empirical modes of representation and consciousness. *Representative Men* is a paradoxical attempt to provide an open, flexible, even critical symbolic frame for a liberal culture defined by its empiricist resistance to symbolic framing.

9

Liberty, Commerce

Biography (1835); English Literature (1835–1836);
English Traits (1856)

I started the first chapter of this book by pointing out Emerson's debt
to the Whig sense of history. It is a mark of the persisting importance of this metanarrative to Emerson's work that it is now necessary
to return to it as we move to the final phase of his career. In chapter 1 I
drew on the writings of Lord Acton to trace the "history of liberty"
from the Hebrew prophets and the Athenians to the Italian Renaissance
and Luther's Reformation in Germany. To understand the liberalism of
Emerson's interesting but largely neglected late work, *English Traits*, it
helps to pick up a parallel thread of Acton's Whig story, which begins in
Anglo-Saxon England.

According to this account, the early Saxon tribes who took England from the Celts were possessed of the same sort of primordial
libertarian-democratic instincts that Tacitus reported of all the ancient
Germans. England's eleventh-century Norman conquerors thus faced a
special challenge in imposing a hierarchical feudal order on a gruffly independent people whose innate egalitarianism had since been fortified
and exalted by a pure form of primitive Christianity. Over hundreds of
years of give-and-take, a complex but salutary balance evolved in which
foreign Norman kings obtained support against their own ever-restive

foreign Norman nobility by granting unusual privileges to the Anglo-Saxon clergy and to the increasingly numerous free-holding and free-spirited Anglo-Saxon commoners. In time, as historian William Stubbs (*Constitutional History of England*, 1873–78) would put it, "the commixture of race and institutions was so completed as to produce an organization which grew into conscious life."[1] And thus a new sort of liberty-loving culture was born. The new hybrid language of this new hybrid culture was English, and its political vernacular was liberal. Its strongest, ever-spreading political roots were one great protoliberal idea and two great protoliberal institutions—the proudly held "rights" of Englishmen, on the one hand, and the "ancient" English Parliament and centuries-old English common-law "constitution," on the other. So it was not surprising that the early-modern liberalizing forces of trade, science, print technology, humanism, and Protestantism first found full political protection in England among all the nations of Europe. Nor was it surprising that Enlightenment liberals from the Continent such as Montesquieu and Voltaire subsequently looked to England as a political model. English "parliaments" had met regularly and exercised real economic and legal power for hundreds of years before their Continental counterparts played any meaningful role. Ordinary Englishmen came to be the proud possessors of a set of traditional "common-law rights" well before early-modern Continental legal and political theorists began to speculate about "natural rights." And thus the Lockean principles of the Glorious Revolution of 1688 set the example and provided the theory almost one hundred years in advance for the yet "more glorious" American Revolution and its French sequel.[2] The political, religious, and cultural turmoil of seventeenth-century England and its almost miraculously bloodless liberal resolution in 1688 was, as Acton put it, "the point where the history of nations turned into its modern bed. It is the point also where the Englishman became the leader of the world."[3]

Emerson had been raised on this Anglo-centric Whig outlook, and it stuck. We saw its prominence in the conception of progress outlined in his early journals. We noted the heroic presence of Lord Russell and Harry Vane in *Nature*. England set the standard for antislavery reform in Emerson's emancipation speech. And, in two lecture series given in 1835–1836, which we have yet to examine, Emerson directly anticipates several of the major themes of *English Traits*. It is worth looking briefly at these lectures as a lead-in to *English Traits* because they help to indicate this book's protracted gestation. Far from an anomalous late-life lapsing into cultural conservatism, *English Traits* emerges in the context of these lecture series as the long-deferred public expression of Emerson's life-long sense of grateful cultural indebtedness to England and the English.

Although the respective titles—Biography and English Literature—do not make this plain, both series are chronologically structured and distinctively Whiggish in their overall pattern as well as in their more local emphases. The first starts with the decidedly Catholic figure of Michelangelo but manages to represent him as a kind of prodigy of the Protestant work ethic: "From his childhood to his death almost at the end of a century he was dedicated to toil. Few men have ever lived as industrious as this worshipper of beauty, none who proceeded more strictly step by step to the height of Art through the appointed means of study of nature" (*EL* 1:102). The next is Martin Luther, the towering founding hero of all Protestant historical epic: "Revolutions never go backward, and this monk and his ethical propositions [were] the revolution" (*EL* 1:123). "He loved, he hated, he feared God, he dared the world and the devils, he prayed, he sang, he desponded, he married, he served his prince, he abhorred dependence and became free" (*EL* 1:142). Thereafter Emerson traces an exclusively Anglo-Protestant liberal succession. John Milton is honored as "an apostle of freedom; of freedom in the house, in the state, in the church; freedom of speech, freedom of the press" (*EL* 1:159). In George Fox, we are told, "Religious Sentiment" found expression as "the most republican principle," the "enormous assertion of spiritual right" before which "topple . . . all the tyrannies, all the hierarchies, all the artificial ranks of the earth" (*EL* 1:167). And Edmund Burke, "believing that in the British Constitution rightly administered would be found . . . a remedy for every mischief, was . . . a steadfast friend of liberty, of humanity, the redresser of wrong" (*EL* 1:194).

The subsequent series, English Literature, adds to the Anglo-liberal historical narrative of Biography but now with more explicit interest in England as a source of American identity and within a classically Anglo-Scottish narrative framework. The English "traits" selected and carried over to the United States are tellingly libertarian and pragmatic: "Are they lovers of freedom? We more. Are they lovers of commerce? We more. Are they lovers of utility? We more" (*EL* 1:233). Emerson asserts that England has reached "the highest point of civilization" on the decidedly secular and materialistic grounds that "it contains at this hour how vast an amount of human comfort and splendor" (*EL* 1:235). In providing a genealogy for this success he nods to the ancient Anglo-Saxon "passion for freedom," noting that they "elected their chiefs by an equal suffrage" and relating an anecdote about the twenty-nine Saxons who "strangled themselves to avoid being brought into the theatre as gladiators" (*EL* 1:237). But Emerson attributes modern English success principally to the energy and acumen with which they made the all-important transition from martial to commercial-technological values.[4]

> If you look in the most general way at the history of the world from the fourth to the ninth centuries, you find it a period of universal war. It is singular that we can draw so firm lines of distinction between modern and ancient history. But it is easy to indicate a period during which the ancient systems of party, of philosophy, of social order were dissolved. If you consult the table of chronology before the 10th century, you shall find no events but wars and their works. Come down a few centuries and you shall find the same table filled up with a quite different record: Invention of paper, of printing, of glass, of linen, the compass; discovery of the solar system; of America; manufacture of watches; the Post Office; the Bank; potato; coffee; tea; and silk. (*EL* 1:254–55)

The feature that most clearly distinguishes modern liberalism from its ancient Greek or classical republican precursors, Leo Strauss and Thomas Pangle emphasize, is its turning away from the austere civic-martial virtues of sacrifice for the patria in favor of the "softer" self-regarding and acquisitive virtues of the bourgeois individual. The pivotal figure was Locke: "The great and chief end of man's uniting into commonwealths and putting themselves under government is the preservation of their property," Locke wrote, and in doing so implicitly overturned much of classical and Christian political thought.[5] "Locke's teaching on property," as Strauss puts it, "and therewith his whole political philosophy, are revolutionary not only with regard to the biblical tradition but with regard to the philosophic tradition as well. Through the shift of emphasis from natural duties or obligations to natural rights, the individual, the ego, had become the center and origin of the moral world, since man—as distinguished from man's end—had become that center or origin."[6] Montesquieu, the Scots, and the American founders then followed Locke's revolutionary lead, giving his revaluation a historical dimension by projecting it diachronically across a new narrative of historical progress. In this account the incrementally global emancipation of human acquisitive energies brings with it not only exponential increases in economic productivity, remarkable leaps in scientific knowledge and technology, and a new spirit of international cooperation, but also a new kind of urbane, tolerant, prudent, and, above all, peaceable human being. "Commerce cures destructive prejudices," Montesquieu wrote, "and it is almost a general rule that wherever there are soft ways of life there is commerce; and that wherever there is commerce, there are soft ways of life."[7] Property, protected by abstract law, replaces honor, protected by the code of vengeance, as the basis of social prestige.

In drawing so firm a distinction between an ancient history dominated by warfare and a commercial modernity improved by the "soft" arts of accumulation and trade, Emerson in the passages above takes over this foundational binary of modern liberal thought—the historical-diachronic counterpart, one might say, to the synchronic opposition between tradition and reason. Indeed, Emerson's rhetorical verve causes him to push this opposition to an extreme. The best qualities associated with ancient history are "hardihood" and "strength of will" (*EL* 1:255). Beyond this, it offers nothing but "universal war," moral "childhood," "boisterousness," domineering selfishness, despotism, narrow interests, pervasive danger, intellectual servility, and a "degraded" social life of mindless solidarity (*EL* 1:255). In characterizing modernity, by contrast, Emerson starts with a striking list of inventions, artfully selected to evoke the multiple adjacent and intersecting spheres of a complex and dynamic form of life, shaped and reshaped by technology and trade. Paper and printing come first, and we are meant to think specifically of the importance of print technology to the Protestant Reformation as well as of the immeasurable general explosion of literacy, communication, and access to knowledge that print had brought about. Emerson could have stopped right here and still have had a strong case for the superiority of modernity. But he moves on to glass, which forms an apt juxtaposition because, like printing, it may be said to be a medium of light to the more strictly material end of admitting the sun's radiance without releasing heat, the possibility of which completely transformed architecture and the quality of human habitation. Then Emerson turns, charmingly, to linen, intending presumably to evoke the cool, light-weight feel of this fabric on the skin of his listeners, who were very likely to have been wearing it as undergarments. The compass then stands in for the whole sphere of modern navigation and travel, which made possible the European discovery of the land on which Emerson's listeners would have been sitting as well as the global trade by which they obtained such commodities as paper, glass, and linen. The "discovery of the solar system; of America" then brings the list to a climax, linking the new world on earth with the new world in the heavens disclosed by the Copernican revolution in astronomy, which in discrediting Christian cosmology was for Emerson, as we have seen, the most decisive turning point in the Western transition to modernity. The denouement of the list then seems designed to confirm that what followed that turning point was not a secularized replaying of feudal-Christian precedents but a startling new multidimensional assemblage built out of oddly juxtaposed pieces: "the manufacture of watches" (clock time); "the Post Office" (politics as the provision of service); "the Bank" (abstract property); "the potato" (cheap, nutritious, easily transported foodstuffs); and "coffee, tea, and silk" (formerly exotic imports made commonplace by trade).[8]

For Emerson, the distinctive character of English literature (and the source of its special importance) is its receptivity to this material and moral transformation. He essentially divides English literary history into two large phases that correspond roughly to the martial versus commercial, or honor versus property, binary schema sketched above. The first phase, which he calls "the age of fable," was typified by what he regards as "extravagant," "childish," and "superstitious" fantasies of chivalric romance. "The Poets sang as we do to children of war and witchcraft. The metrical and prose romances left all nature and common sense far behind them; they set geography, chronology and chemistry at defiance: and piled wonder on wonder for the delight of credulous nations" (*EL* 1: 255–56). But in the aftermath of the Crusades' opening of trade routes to the East, a more realistic literature begins to emerge that does not shy away from facts. In Chaucer, Shakespeare, Jonson, Herrick, and Herbert, Emerson argues, we find "the peculiar genius of English poetry — its homeliness, love of plain truth and strong tendency to explain things as they are and without rhetorical decoration. It imports into songs and ballads the smell of the earth and the breath of cattle and like a Dutch painter seeks a household charm of low and ordinary objects" (*EL* 1: 262–63). In the writings of Francis Bacon we then find this empirical openness radicalized into a complete recasting of the method and structure of human knowledge (*EL* 1:320–36). Emerson's account here is impressionistic and sketchy and clearly biased against all non-English or medieval sources, but it is worth noting that its principal thesis about the evolution of English literature in the direction of ever-greater realism is strongly supported by Erich Auerbach's far more scholarly, multilingual, and widely admired modern study in *Mimesis* of the development of realism in European literature as a whole.[9] Emerson would have relished Auerbach's definition of Western literary realism as "the serious treatment of the ordinary," not least because it would seem to allow for such a large overlap between the radically empirical approaches of modern literature, modern science, and modern commerce.[10] All three "delight," as Emerson says of Shakespeare in these lectures, "in the earth and earthly things" (*EL* 1:300). For Emerson, this new form of mimetic pleasure is an important part of the intimate history of liberty as a history of feeling.

Emerson traveled to Great Britain in October 1847 and stayed until July 1848. He was received as a celebrity and mingled with the country's intellectual, political, and industrialist elite. Lecturing widely to substantial audiences, he saw much of London and booming industrial midland cities such as Manchester and Birmingham. He took careful notes every step of the way. Upon returning to the United States, Emerson began giving lecture series on the topic of England at the same time as he continued to speak out against slavery. In 1856 he published *English Traits,* a full, book-length description of English institutions, economy, and national character. The book was popularly successful at the time (it was by far Emerson's biggest seller), but its twentieth-century scholarly reputation has been negligible. Lacking the transcendental lift and lyrical sparkle of his early prose, deemed to be politically "conservative," and regrettably shadowed at moments by nineteenth-century racialist theories of historical evolution, the book was not even discussed by Stephen Whicher in his otherwise comprehensive and influential study of Emerson's writing. It is still routinely left out of anthologies, seldom written about, and rarely taught.[11] But the concurrence of the composition and publication of *English Traits* with what is newly understood as Emerson's most intense period of antislavery activity has led some recent scholars to take it more seriously. David Robinson, for example, remarks that "the interrelation between [Emerson's] analysis of England and his sense of an American crisis is the subtext of his discussion of 'race' as a causative factor in England's material and imperial success."[12] And Phyllis Cole notes that, "like so many of his American contemporaries—Hawthorne and Melville most notably, Emerson approached travel in England as an exercise in self-definition." Throughout his trip to England, Cole observes, "America was only one thought away at all times."[13] My own reading of *English Traits* in the larger context of Emerson's liberalism as a whole confirms Cole's and Robinson's suggestions about its relationship to the growing crisis over slavery in the United States but also provides some corrective to their conclusions as to the work's ultimate pessimism.

As did Montesquieu in *L'Esprit des lois* (The Spirit of the Laws) and Voltaire in *Lettres anglaises ou philosophiques* (Letters on England), Emerson looked to England in *English Traits* as a model of liberal freedom, especially as the country whose "air . . . is too pure for any slave to breathe" (*AW* 11), and he was by no means entirely disappointed by what he saw. Extending the Whig conception of progress that emerged in Emerson's earliest notebooks and remained prominent throughout his work, *English Traits*, notwithstanding some serious strictures against the excesses of utilitarian materialism, is a robustly optimistic update on the history of liberty from the point of view of a (still) aspiring inheritor and extender of its legacy.

Emerson announces the book's concern with liberal inheritance from the very beginning. In a move that some readers have found structurally extraneous, he devotes the entire first chapter to a recollection of his meetings with eminent artists and intellectuals during his previous trip to England some fifteen years earlier. Emerson generally found these encounters anticlimactic and unsatisfying: Landor was polite but capriciously contrary; Coleridge was snuff addled, abstracted, and offensive; and Wordsworth was awkward and rigid. But by showing Emerson in the posture of a youthful initiate paying respects to great figures from a previous generation, these sketches serve nonetheless to establish the book's larger theme of cultural transmission. And Emerson acts his part in the agon of influence with characteristic rhetorical strength: he creates a perceived need for his own cultural intervention by portraying his predecessors as faded, wearisome, and somewhat forlorn.

The theme of cultural inheritance is then abruptly deepened in Emerson's account of his meeting and conversations with Carlyle, a peer and, as we have seen, a formidable fellow aspirant to intellectual leadership of the next generation. At first Carlyle keeps to what he sees as the most morally urgent topic of the day: "English pauperism, the crowded country, the selfish abdication by public men of all that public persons should perform" (*E&L* 774). But in time the talk turns to the immortality of the soul, a topic Carlyle approaches reluctantly but with characteristically lively historical imagination:

> But he was honest and true, and cognizant of the subtile links that bind ages together, and saw how every event affects all the future. "Christ dies on the tree: that built Dunscore kirk yonder: that brought you and me together. Time has only a relative existence."
>
> He was already turning his eyes towards London with a scholar's appreciation. London is the heart of the world, he said, wonderful only

from the mass of human beings. He liked the huge machine. Each
keeps its own round. The baker's boy brings muffins to the window at a
fixed hour every day, and that is all the Londoner knows or wishes to
know on the subject. (*E&L* 775)

Carlyle thus affirms the astonishing historical efficacy of culture over
vast expanses of time. One symbol—Christ on the tree—has had the
power to influence events in the West at every level of experience for almost two thousand years. But Emerson's inclusion of Carlyle here also
implicitly raises the question as to the continuing relevance of this symbol at a historical moment the newness of which the imposing Scot saw
as clearly as anyone alive. Just before Marx and long before Durkheim,
Carlyle recognized that the new urban-industrial division of labor
exemplified in London was bringing about a complete reordering of
human communities—a new order paradoxically characterized both by
more extensive interdependence and by greater social isolation. Would
the same Christian communal-sacrificial symbols and values—Christ
on the tree—that had shaped England for so long maintain their authority in this new kind of society? Or would some other set of values
and their symbols provide the "subtle links that bind ages together"?
Carlyle would soon begin his lifelong thundering in favor of an authoritarian restoration of the former. But since this meeting Emerson had already begun to forge a new set of post-Christian liberal-symbolic links,
and he here signals that *English Traits* will further extend that effort.

The second chapter, "Voyage to England," mainly provides details of
Emerson's crossing of the Atlantic on his second trip in 1848, which
forms the basis of the book as a whole. But it also quietly conveys serious
concerns about cultural continuity. We are told, for example, without additional comment, that Emerson's ship is named the *Washington Irving*—a
major author of the previous generation whose most influential work,
The Sketch Book of Geoffrey Crayon, emphasized the English roots of American folkways and customs. And then in an aside a few paragraphs later
Emerson tells of how contemplation of the sea during the passage
evoked in him a sudden awareness of the possibility of wholesale cultural erasure:

Is this sad-colored circle an eternal cemetery? To the geologist, the sea
is the only firmament; the land is in perpetual flux and change, now
blown up like a tumor, now sunk in a chasm. . . . The sea keeps its old
level; and 'tis no wonder that the history of our race is so recent, if the
roar of the ocean is silencing our traditions. A rising of the sea, such as

had been observed, say an inch a century, from east to west on the land, will bury all the towns, monuments, bones, and knowledge of mankind, steadily and insensibly. (*E&L* 781)

This is the dark side of Emerson's readiness to contemplate deep time. He is here struck by the obliterating potential of the same immense geological ages that lent "vast flowing vigor" to his ecstatic early essays. Throughout the preceding pages I have argued against the influential reading of Emerson's later work as a lapse into "conservatism," but there is no question that something has changed between his early embrace of historical forgetting and this later anxiety about slow submersion. Advancing age is part of the explanation. Emerson's anxiety here about "silencing our traditions" reflects in part a familiar and all-too-human response to the growing consciousness of mortality as he entered his fifties. But increasing awareness of the fragility of civilization does not necessarily equal political conservatism, and it is revealing in this connection to ask, To whom exactly does Emerson refer above when he speaks of "*our* traditions"? Knowing as we now do that, by this point, Emerson's objections to slavery had pushed him to the point of advocating Northern secession and tearing up the Constitution, we can be assured that his "our" does not principally invoke a *national* collective. Given the immediate ocean setting, it is more likely that he has in mind a shared *transatlantic* culture. And that culture, he will soon make clear, is by no means a conservative one.

"Why England is England?" Emerson asks at the beginning of chapter 3 upon landing at Liverpool (*E&L* 784). Why has this particular nation among all the nations of the globe become so astoundingly prosperous and powerful? The answers he provides over the next twelve chapters may be grouped into two general categories. On the one hand, he identifies an extensive set of popular characteristics that have been conducive to English success and that he elaborates in chapters 4 through 10 under the headings "Race," "Ability," "Manners," "Truth," "Character," "Cockayne," and "Wealth." And on the other, he singles out a set of institutions that he labels roughly in chapters 11 through 15 as "Aristocracy," "Universities," "Religion," "Literature," and "The 'Times.'"

Emerson's use of racial categories throughout the first section has been controversial and will remain troubling to new readers and so needs clarification. To put it starkly, on cursory reading Emerson can often sound like a racist in these chapters to the extent that he seems to attribute England's long-term historical success to the dominant characteristics, or "traits," of the "Saxon" race. This concern would seem to be strengthened by a glance at his journals, where it becomes clear that Emerson read and gave initial credence to some of the important theorists of nineteenth-century racist ethnography.[14] Not least among these was his good friend Harvard professor Louis Agassiz, who lent his weighty support to the spurious "polygenist" theory of racial origins preferred by Southern apologists who defended slavery on the grounds of the racial inferiority of black people. Fortunately, this issue has already received scrupulous scholarly attention from Philip Nicoloff and Len Gougeon, who both find that Emerson seriously considered the possibility of racial determinism in the 1840s and early 1850s but ultimately dismissed it.[15] Nicoloff concludes that "in the opening arguments of his chapter 'Race,' Emerson presented one of the more liberal and perceptive statements on the question of race to be written by a layman in the middle of the nineteenth century. Without at any point denying the unique importance of the 'kind' of men which formed a nation, he had reduced to confusion the glib doctrine of permanent racial distinctions."[16]

Two points in particular from chapter 4 of *English Traits* confirm Nicoloff's contention that Emerson possessed an unusually sophisticated sense of race and history for a mid-nineteenth-century writer. For one, Emerson casts serious doubt on the possibility of isolating race from the large multitude of factors that combine to shape the character and long-term destiny of any group of people. An almost immeasurable array of geographical, social, cultural, economic, and institutional influences, he points out, play a decisive role: "Civilization is a re-agent, and eats away the old traits" (*E&L* 792). "Each religious sect has its physiognomy," he elaborates, "trades and professions carve their own lines on face and form," and "certain circumstances of English life are not less effective; as, personal liberty; plenty of food; good ale and mutton; open market, or good wages for every kind of labor." "It is easy to add to the counteracting forces to race," he continues, including such crucial immaterial determinants as religious beliefs and scientific understanding of nature (*E&L* 792). He argues further that even one such variable can take on great significance when multiplied by the enormous lengths of time over which the peoples of the earth have evolved. Such vast temporal expanses also make it implausible to believe that different races never intermingled. "Though we flatter the self-love of men and

nations by the legend of pure races, all our experience is of the grada-
tion and resolution of races, and strange resemblances meet us everywhere. It need not puzzle us that Malay and Papuan, Celt and Roman,
Saxon and Tartar should mix, when we see the rudiments of tiger and
baboon in our human form, and know that the barriers of races are not
so firm, but that some spray sprinkles us from the ante-diluvian seas"
(*E&L* 793).

And this leads to the second striking aspect of these remarks on race:
Emerson credits English success not to racial purity but to promiscuous
hybridity. "The English composite character betrays a mixed origin.
Every thing English is a fusion of distant and antagonistic elements.
The language is mixed; the names of men are of different nations,—
three languages, three or four nations" (*E&L* 793). "On the whole, it
is not so much a history of one or of certain tribes of Saxons, Jutes, or
Frisians, coming from one place, and genetically identical, as it is an
anthology of temperaments out of them all" (*E&L* 794). Understood as
the biological correlative of commercial exchange, such hybridity, for
Emerson, is implicitly liberal. "The best nations are those most widely
related; and navigation, as effecting a world-wide mixture, is the most
potent advancer of nations" (*E&L* 793).

This decisive rejection of racial purism raises the question, Why
does Emerson use racial or even national categories at all? If he believed
that the English were really an amalgam of different peoples, and if he
denied the plausibility of race as a historical cause, why raise the specter
of biological racial determinism by using the term "traits" in the title
and speaking throughout the book of "Saxon" characteristics? He hints
at part of the answer himself in the canny first paragraph of chapter 5
when he acknowledges the probable inaccuracy of the commonplace
Whig notion that the English aristocracy and the commoners were
descended, respectively, from Normans and Saxons. "Though, I doubt
not, the nobles are of both tribes, and the workers of both, yet we are
forced to use the names a little mythically, one to represent the worker,
and the other the enjoyer" (*E&L* 806). The word "mythically" is revealing here because it both demonstrates Emerson's urbanity with respect
to his own categories and names the kind of symbolic cultural work that
will be performed by the putatively empirical-historical sketch provided
in *English Traits*.[17] Myths, whatever other purposes they may also serve,
tend to provide the societies to which they belong with an orientation to
the long past—to distant, often sacred, origins. Burrow has argued that

nineteenth-century Whig history in general did the work of cultural myth in providing a rapidly changing English society with the symbolic ballast of a long, organic, Burkean narrative of origin and descent.[18] Emerson in *English Traits* tries to perform a similar cultural service for an even more rapidly changing mid-nineteenth-century American society. Emerson writes about English "traits" and "Saxon" virtues in *English Traits* because he wants to secure the deep roots, however mythical, of an Anglo-American commitment to freedom that he worries may be wavering under the increasing pressure of the Southern "slave power" in the United States of the 1850s.

Emerson also finds these admittedly mythical racial categories useful because they help him to write about history on the intimate psycho-social level that, as we saw in chapter 1, he had long advocated. Like the French Annales historians of the twentieth century, Emerson is less interested in major historical events or important leaders and movements than he is in *mentalités*—deep-rooted attitudes and structures of feeling held and transmitted over the *longue durée*. This is why he spends no time on politics in *English Traits* and much on geography, religious belief, social structure, universities, a widely read newspaper, and the values and habits of ordinary people. But I do not want to overstate Emerson's empirical rigor in *English Traits* by associating it with painstaking Annales scholarship characterized by the careful differentiation of microcultures existing within the larger umbrella category of modern nationality. Ultimately, Emerson is only impressionistically interested in one rather general set of attitudes that he finds diffused over English society as a whole—what he sees as a distinctively Anglo-Saxon *mentalité* of liberty. He links this mentality to race not out of any conviction of the importance of genetic determinants but rather, like the Whig historians, in the hopes of thus extending the roots of liberal freedom down toward the nourishing primordial wellsprings of deep time. And in doing so Emerson knowingly but imperceptibly crosses the line between empirically sketching the world's most successful liberal society and adding another dimension to his already multidimensional liberal myth.

The heroes of this myth are not hard to find. They are the members of the English middle class, upper and lower, who are characterized, above all, as paragons of Emerson's favorite liberal virtue—work. The English, we are told, are "the hands of mankind. They have the taste for toil, a distaste for pleasure or repose, and a telescopic appreciation of future gains" (*E&L* 807). "They have tilled, builded, forged, spun, and woven" (*E&L* 816). "They love the lever, the screw, and pulley, the Flanders draught-horse, the waterfall, wind-mills, tide-mills; the sea and wind to bear their freight ships" (*E&L* 811). "They apply themselves to agriculture, to draining, to resisting encroachments of sea, wind, traveling sands, cold and wet sub-soil" (*E&L* 811). For the English, according to Emerson, political position is no sinecure: "The high civil and legal offices are not beds of ease, but posts which exact frightful amounts of mental labor. Many of the great leaders, like Pitt, Canning, Castlereagh, Romilly, are soon worked to death" (*E&L* 814). English stargazing, similarly, is no idle aristocratic pastime but a model of the painstaking cross-generational discipline of empirical-scientific rationality: "Sir John Herschel, in completion of the work of his father, who had made the catalogue of the stars of the northern hemisphere, expatriated himself for years at the Cape of Good Hope, finished his inventory of the southern heaven, came home, and redacted it in eight years more;—a work whose value does not begin until thirty years have elapsed" (*E&L* 815). And the English have embraced technology as an extension of their dedication to efficacious work: "They have reinforced their own productivity by that marvelous machinery which differences this age from every other age" (*E&L* 852). "Steam is almost an Englishman. . . . He weaves, forges, saws, pounds, fans, and now he must pump, grind, dig, and plough for the farmer" (*E&L* 817). "The power of machinery in Great Britain, in mills, has been computed to be equal to 600,000,000 men, one man being able by the aid of steam to do the work which required 250 men to accomplish 50 years ago" (*E&L* 853).

Emerson in the 1850s is no less Lockean with regard to the benefits of work than he was in the 1830s. The mixture of such prodigious labor with the rich raw materials of the British islands has yielded spectacular amounts of property. "When, to this labor and trade, and these native resources, was added this goblin of steam, with his myriad arms, never tired, working night and day everlastingly, the amassing of property has run out of all figures" (*E&L* 853). And Emerson remains committed to the Scottish Enlightenment connection of property with progress. One of the newly dominant institutions of English life—"the Bank"—has provided for the necessary alienability and abstractness of all this new wealth, and "by these new agents our social system is moulded": "It votes an issue of bills, population is stimulated, and cities rise; it refuses loans, and emigration empties the country; trade sinks, revolutions break out, kings are dethroned" (*E&L* 854). Inevitably, such abundance and fluidity of property has an effect on the condition and character of the people. For some, Emerson admits, the effect has been disastrous. The chapter entitled "Wealth" in *English Traits* is one of the few places where Emerson acknowledges the large-scale urban pauperization in England that moved Carlyle and many other writers of the 1840s to howls of protest. But on the whole, Emerson sees the proliferation of what Dickens called "portable property" as not only materially beneficial but also morally productive of historically unprecedented opportunities for self-sufficiency, self-respect, and self-realization. "All that can feed the senses and passions, all that can succor the talent, or arm the hands of the intelligent middle class, who never spare in what they buy for their own consumption; all that can aid science, gratify taste, or soothe comfort, is in open market" (*E&L* 855). The legal barriers of negative liberty ensure the safety of whatever is acquired in the open market, and the feudal social hierarchy is thus subverted: "The house is a castle which the King cannot enter. The Bank is a strong box to which the King has no key. Whatever surly sweetness possession can give is tested in England to the dregs. Vested rights are awful things, and absolute possession gives the smallest freeholder identity of interest with the duke" (*E&L* 856).

Finally, for Emerson in *English Traits* as for Montesquieu in *L'Esprit des lois* the distinctive character of the English is illuminated by a quasi-historical contrast with the French, wherein the Brits are associated with liberal-rational modernity, while the Gauls continue to be defined by premodern aristocratic values. The English, Emerson allows, started their extraordinary modern history under the Norman yoke. But "a century later, it came out that the Saxon had the most bottom and longevity, had managed to make the victor speak the language and accept the law and usage of the victim; forced the baron to dictate Saxon terms to Norman kings; and, step by step, got all the essential securities of civil liberty invented and confirmed" (*E&L* 806). Protobourgeois pragmatism, persistence, and "calm, patient" rationality in time overcame chivalrous martial hauteur. "Sense and economy must rule in a world which is made of sense and economy, and the banker, with his seven *per cent*, drives the earl out of his castle. A nobility of soldiers cannot keep down a commonalty of shrewd scientific persons. What signifies a pedigree of a hundred links, against a cotton-spinner with steam in his mill; or, against a company of broad-shouldered Liverpool merchants, for whom Stephenson and Brunel are contriving locomotives and a tubular bridge?" (*E&L* 807). Thus, France is associated with honor, elegance, and aesthetic refinement, while England is associated with discipline, practicality, sincerity, and work. "The Frenchman invented the ruffle," Emerson writes, "the Englishman added the shirt" (*E&L* 811). "An Englishman," he adds later, "understates, avoids the superlative, checks himself in compliments, alleging that in the French language, one cannot speak without lying" (*E&L* 831). And on the highest level of generality, grandiose aristocratic notions of public honor remain far more important in France than in modest middle-class England. "Glory, a career, and ambition, words familiar to the longitude of Paris, are seldom heard in English speech. Nelson wrote from their hearts his homely telegraph, 'England expects every man to do his duty'" (*E&L* 844).

Emerson's sketch as a whole portrays the English as industrious, acquisitive, commercially minded, practical, technologically competent, and quietly but tenaciously devoted to the free pursuit of private domestic happiness. None of this sounds very heroic or inspiring. Indeed, a gruff impatience with pretensions to heroism is presented as one of the defining characteristics of this bourgeois mentality. And therein lies the deeper liberal-historical argument of *English Traits*. Montesquieu hovers everywhere in the background of this book, and Emerson quotes him explicitly twice: "No people have true common sense but those who are born in England" (*E&L* 810), and "England is the freest country in the world" (*E&L* 810). And Emerson agrees with the great French liberal, favorite sage of the American founders, that these two truths are indissolubly linked. The exercise of "common sense" does not bring about freedom in a direct causal relationship, as if common sense were in itself a great political virtue. On the contrary, the bourgeois regime of common sense works by suppressing or sidelining other more unruly parts of the soul—martial courage, ambition for honor, patriotism, love of fame, eros in general—that are inherently more ennobling but also potentially dangerous to stable liberty. As Pangle has shown, *L'Esprit des lois* makes its case for modern, commercial, bourgeois liberalism by drawing a complex, somewhat ambivalent contrast with ancient, martial, virtue-based republicanism: "The experience of acquisition reveals to men their natural desire for security and property. . . . Men cease to seek satisfaction in devotion to the fatherland or king; they think of themselves. And they lose their taste for personal glory, or salvation after death; they look to their material affairs. They become hard-working, tolerant, and peace-loving."[19] This is an eloquent formulation of what might be called the foundational existential trade-off of bourgeois liberalism. The most ennobling but dangerous aspirations of the soul are suppressed to make room for a safer, more secure, and more tolerant mediocrity of spirit. No one understood the necessity of such existential trade-offs better than the author of "Compensation," and in *English Traits* Emerson praises the English as the principal architects and beneficiaries of this emancipating modern bargain. In chapter 8, entitled "Character," toward the end of the substantial central portion of the book whose description of the English mentality I have been summarizing, Emerson cleverly compresses its multiple dimensions into two words. "If the English race were as mutable as the French, what reliance?" he writes. "But the English *stand for* liberty" (*E&L* 843, italics mine). "Stand for" connotes a degree of boring bourgeois stolidity but also compensatory qualities of strength, steadiness, discipline, and resolution. To "stand for" something is also what symbols do, and Emerson here reveals the larger liberal-symbolic meaning of the image of the English he has constructed.

In the second major part of *English Traits*, chapters 10 to 15, Emerson shifts his focus from the English people to a selection of English economic and cultural institutions under the headings "Aristocracy," "Universities," "Religion," "Literature," and "The 'Times,'" referring in this last case to a nationally distributed newspaper. Recent readers such as Cole, Julie Ellison, and Robinson have drawn principally from these chapters to emphasize what they see as Emerson's ultimately pessimistic attitude in this book. It is certainly true that Emerson occasionally takes a darker, more critical tone toward his subject in these chapters. But this is entirely in keeping with Emerson's dialectical approach to almost any topic he discussed, and nothing that he says here comes close to fully countering in either quantity or intensity the lavish foregoing celebration of the English liberal spirit. Indeed, much of this second section of the book extends the praise of the first, and the two penultimate chapters, "Stonehenge" and "Result," return to the opening theme and stage a rhetorically and symbolically stirring pageant of liberal-cultural transmission.

It is fair, for example, to expect at least some hostility in a chapter on the English aristocracy from so American a writer as Emerson, but these pages are remarkable chiefly for their efforts to paint even this most medieval institution in a favorable liberal-progressive light. "There was this advantage of western over oriental nobility," he writes, "that this was recruited from below. English history is aristocracy with the doors open. . . . All nobility in its beginnings was somebody's natural superiority" (*E&L* 861). Emerson projects backward in time the idea of "natural aristocracy" by which eighteenth-century liberals such as Jefferson and other American founders sought to retain a special leadership role for a talented elite. He then interprets nineteenth-century economic changes and accompanying liberal reforms as further progress in the same direction, not so much putting an end to the institution of aristocracy but rather opening its already open doors wider still: "The revolution in society has reached this class. . . . The tools of our time, namely, steam, ships, printing, money, and popular education, belong to those who can handle them: and their effect has been, that advantages once confined to men of family, are now open to the whole middle class" (*E&L* 872). Emerson asserts that one of the chief aims of liberal reformers everywhere in the nineteenth century—to have "careers open to talent"—has been fully achieved in England. But he insists that this is only an acceleration and intensification of a process at work "throughout English history": "The analysis of the peerage and the gentry shows the rapid decay and extinction of old families, the continual recruiting of these from new blood" (*E&L* 873). It is a mark of the aristocratic affinities of Emerson's own liberalism that he is thus pleased to find the class structure of nineteenth-century England, even after the passing of two great reform bills, as organically continuous with the old regime. The dubious historical accuracy of this claim is not at issue here. It is sufficient to see how it suits Emerson's Whiggish purposes in *English Traits* to suggest that liberalism and aristocracy properly understood are not intrinsically incompatible. "English history, wisely read, is the vindication of the brain of that people. . . . Who now will work and dare, shall rule. This is the charter, or the Chartism, which fogs, and seas, and rains proclaimed—that intellect and personal force should make the law; that industry and administrative talent should administer; that work should wear the crown" (*E&L* 873).

The subsequent chapter on universities is evenhanded and moderately complimentary. It is finally only in chapter 13, "Religion," that we find Emerson allowing himself any very sharp words for the English. But even here, his pointed but relatively brief criticisms are preceded by long passages of sincere historical admiration. English religious architecture, for example, fills Emerson with admiration and praise. "Plainly there has been great power of sentiment at work on this island, of which these buildings are the proofs" (*E&L* 883):

> England felt the full heat of Christianity which fermented Europe, and drew, like the chemistry of fire, a firm line between barbarism and culture. The power of the religious sentiment put an end to human sacrifices, checked appetite, inspired the crusades, inspired resistance to tyrants, inspired self-respect, set bounds to serfdom and slavery, founded liberty. . . . Bishop Wilfrid manumitted two hundred and fifty serfs, whom he found attached to the soil. The clergy obtained respite from labor for the poor on the Sabbath, and on church festivals. . . . The priest came out of the people, and sympathized with his class. The church was the mediator, check, and democratic principle. . . . The Catholic church, thrown on this toiling, serious people, has made in fourteen centuries a massive system, close fitted to the manners and genius of the country, at once domestical and stately. In the long time, it has blended with everything in heaven above and the earth beneath. It moves through a zodiac of feasts and fasts, names every day of the year, every town and market and headland and monument, and has coupled itself with the almanac, that no court can be held, no field ploughed, no horse shod, without some leave from the church. . . .
>
> The English church has many certificates to show, of humble effective service in humanizing the people, in cheering and refining men, feeding, healing, and educating. It has the seal of martyrs and confessors; the noblest books, as sublime architecture; a ritual marked by the same secular merits, nothing cheap or purchasable. (*E&L* 883–84)

The sight of England's lovely old churches brings Emerson to these thoughts, but it is not their time-washed stones, as it might have been with Ruskin, that move him. Rather, in keeping with the role of symbolic expositor that he inherited from his Calvinist past and continues to try to adapt to his liberal present, Emerson is interested in these structures chiefly as the stony nodes of an elaborately interwoven mesh—a "massive system"—of cultural symbolism. Emerson offers here not merely a generous appreciation of the shaping force of Christianity in English cultural history but, indirectly, the fullest account perhaps anywhere in his writing of the work of culture (in the anthropological sense of the word) per se. His ideas themselves are not surprising, but his language is characteristically vivid and evocative. He tells us, to start with, that Christianity "fermented" England along with the rest of Europe. The word suggests chemical transformation in a sealed-off space and is thus carefully chosen to evoke both the protective, preservative function of culture as well as its catalytic agency. Emerson then extends the chemical metaphor in saying that the church also "drew, like the chemistry of fire, a firm line between barbarism and culture," thus evoking with appropriately ominous imagery another of culture's most basic and, often, most dangerous functions—the establishment and reinforcement of group boundaries. Culture is also understood in these sentences to evoke and channel moral feeling, to "check appetite" and "inspire self-respect." Culture orders time, "mov[ing] through a zodiac of feasts and fasts," as well as space, "nam[ing] . . . every town and market and headland and monument." Both "stately and domestic," public and intimate, culture suffuses every aspect of human life, "blend[s] with everything in heaven above and earth beneath," raising the random raw materials of immediate animal experience into the symbolically mediated order of human history. And the direction of this particular national history, we should by now no longer be surprised to find, is toward freedom. Christian culture in England, Emerson suggests, not only "put an end to human sacrifice," "inspired self respect," and "set bounds to serfdom and slavery," but also continues to mitigate the injustices— exploitation of workers, soulless instrumentalism—of the commercial culture that has emerged and continues to grow in the wake of these archaic institutions.

In thus detailing the depth and extent of traditional Christian culture in England Emerson also indicates the formidable challenge that faces him or anyone else (Ruskin, Carlyle, Mill, Marx, Arnold, etc.) who hopes to fashion an adequate substitute. The new network of symbols and its expositors must also manage, at the least, to "humanize," "cheer," "refine," "feed," "heal," and "educate." For a brief moment, two paragraphs later, Emerson allows himself to think that perhaps no such replacement is necessary. He is present at the great cathedral of York for the "enthronization of the new archbishop" and is moved by hearing "the service of evening prayer read and chanted in the choir": "It was strange to hear the pretty pastoral of the betrothal of Rebecca and Isaac, in the morning of the world, read with circumstantiality in York minster, on the 13th of January 1848, to the decorous English audience, just fresh from the Times newspaper and their wine; and listening with all the devotion of national pride. That was binding old and new to some purpose. . . . Here in England every day a chapter of Genesis, and a leader in the Times" (*E&L* 885). This might be described as Emerson's Unitarian moment in *English Traits*. Just as he did for a time in his twenties, Emerson here entertains the hope that traditional Christianity may be happily reconciled with rational modernity, that "old and new," Genesis and the *Times*, the "morning of the world" and 1848, may be, like Rebecca and Isaac, joyfully wed. But now as then the fragile synthesis fails to hold. Emerson sustains it for four paragraphs, as the sublimity on the same occasion of the playing of Handel's *God Save the King* moves him again to remark approvingly upon "the unbroken order and tradition of [the] church; the liturgy, ceremony, architecture; the sober grace, the good company, the connection with the throne, and with history, which adorn it" (*E&L* 885–86). He recalls especially the "learning," "industry," "devotion," and sincere Christian kindness of men such as Wycliffe, Becket, Latimer, More, Cranmer, Herbert, and Butler. But his tone then turns suddenly harsh as he declares abruptly that the age of these men "is gone": "The spirit that dwelt in this church has glided away to animate other activities; and they who are come to the old shrines find apes and players rustling old garments" (*E&L* 886). And in the subsequent paragraphs Emerson again replicates the pattern of his youthful break with Unitarianism by leveling two familiar criticisms at contemporary Anglicanism. For one, he charges that the English church, its architectural and ceremonial grace notwithstanding, is merely an outworn external shell—a lovely but cold form devoid of real religious feeling. "The torpidity on the side of religion of the vigorous English understanding, shows how much wit and folly can agree in one brain. Their religion is a quotation; their church is a doll; and any examination is interdicted with screams of terror" (*E&L* 887). "The gospel it preaches, is, 'By taste are ye saved'" (*E&L* 888). And second, Emerson charges that the Anglican Church, for all its superficial solicitude toward learning, is ultimately hostile to science and concomitant democratic progress: "The church has not been the founder of the London University, of the Mechanics' Institutes, of the Free School, of whatever aims at diffusion of knowledge" (*E&L* 888).

It is then not surprising that Emerson draws upon a scientific-technological metaphor to characterize the vital energy gone missing from Anglicanism. "Where dwells the religion? Tell me first where dwells electricity, or motion, or thought, or gesture. . . . Electricity cannot be made fast, mortared up and ended, like London Monument, or the Tower" (*E&L* 891). Nor is it surprising that in expanding this metaphor Emerson sounds very much as he did in "Nature" and "Self-Reliance": "[Religion] is passing, glancing, gesticular; it is a traveler, a newness, a surprise" (*E&L* 889). "The new age has new desires, new enemies, new trades, new charities, and reads the Scriptures with new eyes" (*E&L* 891–92). As Emerson approaches the concluding chapters of *English Traits*, the paradoxical "twofold office" of his original self-imposed task of cultural transformation still weighs upon him. His time in England has helped Emerson to gain valuable perspective and to push his liberal roots farther down into the soil of time, but he must continue to work on finding a new symbolic arrangement appropriate to the newness of this technological age. Hegel remarked that in the modern age people will read the newspaper on Sunday instead of going to church. Possessed of a similar historical consciousness, to conclude *English Traits* Emerson triangulates between English Christianity, Stonehenge, and the *Times* of London.

If the shadowy nooks of the Gothic churches were to Emerson the spatial embodiment of the regime of monarchic-aristocratic mystery, the glaring inquisitive beam of a free press symbolized the middle-class liberal will to enlightenment. Able to find and disseminate demystifying data to what was for Emerson the astonishing number of fifty thousand readers a day, the *Times* raised the fact-loving empiricist predilection of the English middle class to the status of a formidable social and political force. "No power in England is more felt, more feared, or more obeyed" (*E&L* 909). "No antique privilege, no comfortable monopoly, but sees surely that its days are counted; the people are familiarized with the reason of reform, and, one by one, take away every argument of the obstructives" (*E&L* 908). By way of a remarkable technology, this newspaper thus channeled some potent part of the diffuse energies of a free civil society into a collective but nonetheless critical focus: "When I see them reading its columns, they seem to me becoming every moment more British" (*E&L* 912). "Its existence honors the people who dare to print all they know, *dare to know* all the facts, and do not wish to be flattered by hiding the extent of the public disaster" (*E&L* 913, italics mine). The echo is surely not deliberate here, but it is worth recalling from the beginning of chapter 1 that Kant's Latin motto of Enlightenment—"sapere aude"—translates into these italicized English words.

It is a further measure of Emerson's high estimation of the importance of the mechanisms of civil society as embodied in a free press that he chooses this chapter on "The 'Times'" to bring to the surface a long, lingering countercurrent of *English Traits* as a whole. The theme of America's cultural and political inheritance from England has been prominent in the book from its initial chapter, in which Emerson relates his youthful meetings with Coleridge, Wordsworth, Landor, and others. I noted in my comment on this chapter, however, that some of the ambivalences of influence are implicitly evident in Emerson's less-than-flattering representation of these cultural fathers. Now, as we draw toward the end of *English Traits*, the cultural ephebe begins explicitly to turn the tables. "The tendency in England towards social and political institutions like those of America," he writes, "is inevitable, and the ability of its journals is the driving force" (*E&L* 908). The statement is offered modestly enough, but it amounts to a dramatic reversal of the book's conception of the direction of cultural and political influence. Where hitherto *English Traits* had seemed committed to a linear progression in which English character traits were passed along to form American political-cultural identity, it now suggests a more dialogical conception of the relationship in which each society influences the other, with the balance shifting in America's favor. Just as in "Tradition and the Individual Talent" T. S. Eliot suggests that every new addition to a poetic tradition retroactively realigns the entire preceding order in the light of the present, so Emerson now begins to suggest that the history of Anglo liberty will have to be rewritten in the light of American emergence.

He makes this point more emphatically in chapter 18 when he tells of traveling to Stonehenge with Carlyle just before leaving England, hoping explicitly for a summary symbolic compression of the Anglo-cultural *longue durée:* "It seemed a bringing together of extreme points, to visit the oldest religious monument in Britain, in company with her latest thinker, and one whose influence may be traced in every contemporary book" (*E&L* 915). The combative Carlyle wastes no time in throwing down the glove of cultural precedence, complaining en route of the tendency of American travelers to "run away" to France for "amusement" instead of "confronting Englishmen, and acquiring their culture, who really have much to teach them" (*E&L* 916). Not to be cowed, Emerson responds with sharply double-edged intergenerational diplomacy, bowing to England's preeminence but lovingly advising the father that the son has come most robustly of age: "I surely know, that, as soon as I return to Massachusetts, I shall lapse at once into the feeling, which the geography of America inevitably inspires, that we play the game with immense advantage; that there and not here is the seat and center of the British race; . . . and that England, an old and exhausted island, must one day be contented, like other parents, to be strong only in her children" (*E&L* 916). And, having thus decisively anointed himself as heir to the Anglo-liberal tradition, Emerson then devotes much of the rest of the chapter to staging a striking quasi-ceremonial enactment of this succession.

When Emerson and Carlyle first approach the great megalithic circles, they see larks "soaring and singing" above them. The juxtaposition moves Carlyle to muse upon the at once dense and distanced layerings of deep time, "'the larks which were hatched last year, and the wind which was hatched many thousands of years ago.'" Emerson subsequently clarifies his friend's cast of thought: "The spot, the gray blocks, and their rude order, which refuses to be disposed of, suggested to him the flight of ages, and the succession of religions" (*E&L* 918). The scene is thus set within the largest conceivable cultural-historical frame, and as Emerson and Carlyle clamber about, observe, converse, and move on to other historically significant settings nearby, a long, progressive trajectory is sketched. We pass in thought from the ageless wind, to the era of the Druids, to the English Christian saints, to the late medieval Salisbury Cathedral, to the country seat of an important Renaissance nobleman, and onward, inevitably, to America. When asked by Carlyle and another English friend "whether there were any Americans—any with an American idea," Emerson completes the Anglo-cultural progression by offering a kind of Quaker quintessence of radical-Protestant libertarianism: "I opened the dogma of no-government and non-resistance, and anticipated the objections and the fun, and procured a kind of hearing for it" (*E&L* 922). He reports casually but not insignificantly that, after hearing his high-minded notions, Carlyle playfully refuses to walk out the door ahead of him when dinner was announced—"'he was altogether too wicked'" (*E&L* 923). Emerson "plants his back against the wall," and the situation is only saved when their host walks out first, avowing himself the "wickedest." Carlyle then follows, and Emerson, in what he must have seen as historically appropriate order, "went last."

The whole extended procession unfolds against the backdrop of the awesome, enigmatic colonnades of Stonehenge, and the symbolism therein is pointed. Whatever else these mysterious stone circles may signify, they are clearly associated with ancient Druidical rituals of sacrifice: "The *sacrificial stone*," Emerson tells us, "as it is called, is the only one in all these blocks that can resist the action of fire, and as I read in the books, must have been brought one hundred and fifty miles" (*E&L* 917). From the long view of the history of human culture opened up by

Carlyle at the beginning of the chapter, the foundational liberal idea of natural rights may be seen as a countersacrificial principle at heart, ensuring in theory that no individual may be sacrificed to the larger purposes of collective solidarity. This was symbolized in *"Self-Reliance"* by Emerson's writing "whim" on the lintel of his doorframe. It is symbolized here again in *English Traits* by this image of human progress as an ever-widening spiral, circling out gradually, farther and farther from that dark, archaic, sacrificial core.

In the next chapter of *English Traits* Emerson takes a theoretical step back and lucidly summarizes the importance of England and English history for the United States in terms of the familiar nineteenth-century liberal debate between liberty and equality. He acknowledges that from the point of view of equality England is far from an ideal model. "The feudal system survives in the steep inequality of property and privilege, in the limited franchise, in the social barriers which confine patronage and promotion to a caste, and still more in the submissive ideas pervading these people" (*E&L* 933). But Emerson hews closely to the classical-liberal line of Mill or Tocqueville in giving liberty decisive precedence: "Though we must not play Providence, and balance the chances of producing ten great men against the comfort of ten thousand mean men, yet retrospectively we may strike the balance, and prefer one Alfred, one Shakespeare, one Milton, one Sidney, one Raleigh, one Wellington, to a million foolish democrats" (*E&L* 933). In the end, England and English history are crucial to American identity not because of racial consanguinity but because the English have protected and advanced the liberal conception of freedom against the rising tide of mass democracy. "The English have given importance to individuals":

> Every man is allowed and encouraged to be what he is, and is guarded in the indulgence of his whim. "Magna Charta," said Rushworth, "is such a fellow that he will have no sovereign." By this general activity, and by this sacredness of individuals, they have in seven hundred years evolved the principles of freedom. It is the land of patriots, martyrs, sages, and bards, and if the ocean out of which it emerged should wash it away, it will be remembered as an island famous for immortal laws, for the announcements of original right which make the stone tables of liberty. (*E&L* 933)

As befits the closing paragraph of the book's climactic penultimate chapter, these sentences eloquently reformulate several of the principal themes of *English Traits* and of Emerson's liberalism in general. For "every man [to be] allowed and encouraged to be what he is," to start with, is a disarmingly simple articulation of the broad theoretical outline of Romantic liberalism per se. It sees the purpose of government not as the subordination of individuals to the collective good but as the securing of optimal conditions for the self-realization of each individual. Since human talents and capacities are almost infinitely various and often unpredictable even to their possessors, and since it is impossible to know or plan in advance how any given individual may best fulfill his or her potential, this approach usually entails the placing of substantial limitations on a government's reach. Emerson suggests this defensive orientation by use of the word "guarding" in the first sentence—yet another of many terms we have noted throughout his writing affirming the liberal principle of "negative liberty." Also in keeping with the broader emphases of Emerson's work as a whole, the word "whim" at the end of the first sentence then gives this Romantic negative-libertarian argument a long social-historical provenance and an intimate psychological resonance. It specifically recalls "Self-Reliance," in which Emerson pointedly seeks to spare the self from traditional ethics of sacrifice by symbolic recourse to this term of spontaneous, inward volition. Whim itself is then given a long liberal-historical incarnation by Emerson's striking use of Rushworth's phrase to personify "Magna Charta," the semimythical founding document of English liberalism, as a figure of whimsical defiance—"such a fellow that he will have no sovereign."

The important issue of secularization is then raised again as Emerson shifts into a quasi-religious register in the final two sentences, speaking of "martyrs," "immortal laws," the "sacredness" of individuals, and the "stone tables of liberty." But in reading these climactic lines it is again important to keep in mind Blumenberg's distinction between two conceptions of secularization. On the one hand, secularization may be understood as an unconscious and unknowing *repetition* of religious patterns of experience and frames of interpretation. On the other hand, secularization may be understood as an "occupation" by substantively new secular symbols and values of the *positions* formerly held by traditional religious symbolism. Here as throughout Emerson's work the latter definition is more pertinent. Unlike all Christian accounts of history that hinge upon messianic intervention from on high, the Whig organic narrative employed by Emerson unfolds entirely within secular time—"in seven hundred years evolved the principles of freedom." Indeed, in reiterating the anxiety about cultural erasure that he first experienced during his Atlantic crossing at the very beginning of the book ("if the ocean out of which [England] emerged should wash it away"), Emerson explicitly acknowledges that this "land of patriots, martyrs, sages, and bards" remains subject to time's ravages. Only the "stone tables of liberty" will remain. And herein we have an appropriately conclusive instance of secularization as occupation. The "announcements of original right which make the stone tables of liberty" simultaneously evoke the Ten Commandments and take their place. The doctrine of natural rights occupies the authoritative position in the culture of modern liberalism that the Ten Commandments held in the Hebrew culture of the Old Testament. And while the substantive moralities of the two codes do overlap, they are also fundamentally different in at least one crucial respect. God issues the Ten Commandments as the conditions of a special covenant with a particular tribe whose members must continue to express solidarity with one another and devotion to him through ceremonies of sacrifice: "An altar of earth thou shalt make unto me, and shalt sacrifice thereon thy burnt offerings, and thy peace offerings."[20] Biblical culture thus distinguishes clearly between this tribe and other tribes, conferring special rights through a special rite. But the dissolution in principle of all such tribal rights lies at the heart of the doctrine of natural rights, the foundation of liberal culture and the moral center of Emerson's liberalism.

Conclusion

The Conduct of Life *(1860); "The President's Proclamation" (1862); "The Fortune of the Republic" (1863)*

"We think of poetry (I here use the term to include any work of critical or imaginative cast)," Kenneth Burke writes, "as the adopting of various strategies for the encompassing of situations. These strategies size up the situations, name their structure and outstanding ingredients, and name them in a way that contains an attitude towards them."[1] Burke's formulation, taken together with Emerson's final book of essays (*The Conduct of Life* [1860]) and his two final antislavery statements ("The President's Proclamation" [1862] and "The Fortune of the Republic" [1863]), provides an apt basis from which to reprise our study as a whole and draw it to a conclusion.

Contrary to the many scholars who had judged Emerson to be uninterested in history, I have argued throughout this study that his entire project was based precisely on what Burke calls "a siz[ing] up" of his and his country's world-historical "situation." As far back as 1818 and 1819 and throughout the 1820s the young Emerson read widely in a broad range of historical writing, especially in variants of "Whig" historiography. He became convinced that over the long course of history humankind was slowly advancing toward higher levels of rationality, material

well-being, and respect for human rights, and that a multitude of historical factors placed the United States at the forefront of these advances.
Like Jefferson, Tocqueville, and many other eighteenth- and nineteenth-
century liberals, Emerson came to believe, in other words, that "something new under the sun" was being born in the United States.[2] As I suggested in chapter 1, he embraced "America" then and henceforth in his
work primarily as a symbol of world-historical progress.

But there was a great deal more symbolic work to be done. America
was lucky on the whole to be free of an aristocratic legacy, Emerson believed, but the absence of what he called "the feudal mischief" left a
cultural-symbolic void. The new nation lacked the ordering rituals and
moral guidance of an established church. It had no collective memory
of the high aesthetic standards and cultivation of the European nobility.
Relationships between people had been loosed from the hierarchical
stability enforced by customs of deference. Geographically and socioec-
onomically mobile individuals seemed to feel less and less bonded to any
social class or locale. Private projects and personal ambition took precedence over the collective good. Even Calvinism seemed to be losing its
iron hold. It is indicative of his liberalism that Emerson regarded these
as beneficial developments on the whole: "The energetic action of the
times develops individualism, and the religious appear isolated. I esteem
this a step in the right direction" (*E&L* 1062). But a scion of ministers
who was himself initially trained to be a minister could not help but wonder about the symbolic sustenance of such an untethered society. What
symbolic structures would provide moral inspiration or aesthetic elevation under these new conditions? From what values or concepts would
people derive fundamental existential orientation? What would be the
source of social cohesion? "How is it people manage to live on," Emerson asks in *The Conduct of Life,* "so aimless as they are?" (*E&L* 1058).

Emerson's entire opus, I have been suggesting, was offered as a response to these questions. From his earliest lectures forward he seeks to
distill, clarify, and symbolize what he understood to be the essential concepts and values of the new and freer form of civilization emerging in
the United States, and he seeks to rally his audiences, whether listeners
or readers, to these values. In the late 1820s and early 1830s (chapter 2),
to start with, after a protracted personal struggle, he began publicly to
give precedence to scientific reason over Christian tradition. In 1836
in *Nature* (chapter 3) he presented the entire natural universe as an infinite reservoir of resonant symbols. Approached with holistic-intuitive

rationality, he suggested, nature provided comprehensive guidance more befitting a rational-scientific culture than any traditional Christian symbolic framework. In the lectures, essays, and addresses of the later 1830s (chapter 4) he affirmed and greatly expanded the meaning of the foundational liberal concept of property. In "Experience" in 1844 (chapter 5) he revised and refreshed the value of reason by acknowledging its limits, and he applied this skeptically chastened conception to the political sphere in the contemporaneous libertarian addresses (chapter 6). Natural rights and the self-correcting agencies of civil society became the focus of his antislavery speeches, as exemplified by the 1844 "Address . . . on . . . the Emancipation of the Negroes in the British West Indies" (chapter 7). He celebrated empiricism in the intriguingly self-reflexive portraits of *Representative Men* in 1850 (chapter 8). In 1856 in *English Traits* (chapter 9) he presented England as the historical parent and model of a successful liberal-commercial culture. And finally, in the works we now turn to— *The Conduct of Life*, "The President's Proclamation," and "The Fortune of the Republic"—Emerson revisits many of these themes with a renewed clarity and intensity. It is as if Emerson's lifelong musing on these matters had progressively separated wheat from chaff and finally laid bare what he conclusively presents here as the historical destiny and underlying moral balance of liberal civilization. Perhaps the crisis of American liberal culture occasioned by the Civil War forced Emerson to his sharpest-yet apprehension of its essential character and structure.

The Conduct of Life is a handbook for how individuals may most fully realize the unprecedented opportunities for personal flourishing newly opened to them by the emancipating institutional arrangements of a liberal polity. Even the book's notoriously pessimistic first essay, "Fate," turns out, on close examination, to be an assertion of existential freedom. In keeping with his long-standing commitment to realism, Emerson spends much of the first half of the piece giving due deference to the multifarious facts of human determinism: genetic inheritance, geography, weather, disease, social class, family—the "tyrannous circumstance," "the stealthy power of other laws that 'act on us' daily," "this cropping out in our planted gardens of the core of the world." But, like "Experience," "Fate" turns abruptly at its lowest point, and its second half reappropriates the terms of its rhetorical descent in a countervailing affirmation. Having sketched nature as an array of immeasurably powerful forces in relation to which the lone human organism seems puny, Emerson suddenly shifts ground and grants to individuals a significant share in nature's world-making and world-breaking energies:

> Man is not order of nature, sack and sack, belly and members, link in a chain, nor any ignominious baggage, but a stupendous antagonism, a dragging together of the poles of the Universe. He betrays his relation to what is below him,—thick-skulled, small-brained, fishy, quadrumanous,—quadruped ill-disguised, hardly escaped into biped, and has paid for the new powers by loss of some of the old ones. *But the lightning which explodes and fashions planets, maker of planets and suns, is in him.* On one side, elemental order, sandstone and granite, rock-ledges, peat-bog, forest, sea and shore; and, on the other part, thought, the spirit which composes and decomposes nature,—here they are, side by side, god and devil, mind and matter, king and conspirator, belt and spasm, riding peacefully together in the eye and brain of every man.
>
> Nor can he blink the free will. To hazard the contradiction,—freedom is necessary. If you please to plant yourself on the side of Fate, and say, Fate is all; then we say, a part of Fate is the freedom of man. Forever wells up the impulse of choosing and acting in the soul. Intellect annuls Fate. So far as a man thinks, he is free. (*E&L* 953, italics mine)

Throughout this study I have resisted the recent tendency to associate Emerson with Nietzsche. But it is impossible to deny the proto-Nietzschean resonances in these passages. Among the many Emersonian phrases the brilliant German is said to have absorbed, surely a few of those above sank in deep: "quadruped ill-disguised, hardly escaped into biped"; "has paid for the new powers by loss of some of the old ones"; "the lightning . . . is in him." Indeed, the thrust of the passage as a whole is proto-Nietzschean insofar as it powerfully and poetically asserts human freedom and agency but declines to ground them in the supernatural. And there are a number of similarly proto-Nietzschean moments elsewhere in the essay, such as the soon-to-follow celebration of the power of will, and the stern, concluding reiteration of the tragic classical doctrine of character as fate. I note this Nietzschean connection here, however, only to illustrate that the essays of *The Conduct of Life* are consistent with Emerson's long-standing refusal of the likelihood or need of extrahistorical divine intervention bringing order from on high into human history or human experience. For Emerson as for Nietzsche, it is man, not God, who must hammer the world into habitable form, and the "freedom of man" so forcefully invoked by both writers is imminent in nature itself, not supernaturally superimposed upon it. But to push the Nietzsche connection much further leads to serious distortions. "Fate," like *The Conduct of Life* and, indeed, like Emerson's entire opus, proceeds logically from the assertion of existential freedom to a vigorous endorsement of the rationalist-progressive-humanitarian optimism of nineteenth-century liberalism. For Emerson, it stands to reason that individuals possessed by nature of freedom—and permitted by law to exercise it—will work together to mitigate the harshness of fate and, with due allowance for trial and error, will construct fair, orderly, and maximally prosperous social arrangements. Such moderate, gradualist, and generous-spirited historical optimism runs directly counter to the starkly antirational and explicitly antiliberal bent of much of Nietzsche's writing.

The latter half of "Fate" offers a fresh articulation, and no significant diminishment, of this liberal-historical optimism. Indeed, having arrested the essay's initial descent into determinism by the assertions of freedom quoted above ("so long as man thinks, he is free" [*E&L* 953]), Emerson then explicitly reconstructs his broader liberal outlook in a manner that touches on several of his major themes. I argued in chapters 2, 3, and 5, for example, that Emerson's liberal edifice depends upon a distinctively Romantic and holistic conception of reason that recognizes both the efficacy and the limitations of Cartesian analysis and that incorporates the truth-telling capabilities of intuition, emotion, and imagination. The sustained rhetorical rally that constitutes the latter half of "Fate" is initiated precisely by recourse to human rationality thus broadly conceived—as one of "the noble creative forces": "The revelation of Thought takes man out of servitude into freedom" (*E&L* 955). The moral-historical progression here—from "servitude" to "freedom"—also clearly follows the Whig pattern I have noted everywhere in Emerson's work. And Emerson then redoubles these broad liberal resonances by the terms he uses to graft moral feeling and moral will, also treated at length in the previous chapters, onto this optimistic conception of free, rational, and improving selfhood: "If thought makes free, so does the moral sentiment" (*E&L* 956). The essay then builds from this restored sense of abstract inner freedom toward a conclusive affirmation of its potential for concrete social realization. Emerson points especially to basic but nonetheless epochal scientific and technological advances as evidence of the human power to overcome the forces of fate by a prudent synthesis of reason and moral will. "Right drainage" prevents typhus and cholera. Citrus juices protect against scurvy. Vaccinations break the scourge of smallpox. Previously destructive natural forces such as lightning and flowing water are harnessed to produce electricity and steam power, with immeasurable social benefits: "The mischievous torrent is taught to drudge for man: the wild beasts he makes useful for food, or dress, or labor; the chemic explosions are controlled like his watch. These are now the steeds on which he rides" (*E&L* 959). Thus, "every jet of chaos which threatens to exterminate us, is convertible by intellect into wholesome force" (*E&L* 958). It amounts to a nineteenth-century liberal version of collective Machiavellian *virtù* in which socially shared scientific reason operates as a supple, adaptable, and opportunistic prince, converting the contingencies of natural *fortuna* into opportunities for the general increase of human power. "The Marquis of Worcester, Watt, and Fulton bethought themselves, that, where was power, was not devil, but was God; that it must be availed of, and not by any means let off and wasted" (*E&L* 959).

"Where was power, was not devil, but was God": this statement serves as a succinct summary of the revolutionary and still globally ramifying liberal revaluation of values to which Emerson's opus as a whole gives such distinctive and still vital expression. According to Hans Blumenberg, it was the Renaissance scientists and philosophers of science—men such as Copernicus, Giordano Bruno, Galileo, and Nicholas of Cusa—who launched the modern age by first transgressing the devil-guarded boundary separating putatively ineradicable human ignorance from inaccessible divine omniscience. They and the Enlightenment thinkers who followed them risked excommunication, exile, even death at the stake in pursuit of the intuition that the astounding structures and energies of the cosmos were intelligible to the human mind and thus legitimately available for ameliorative human use. To reiterate Kant's phrase from "What Is Enlightenment" with which I began my discussion of *Nature*, these men "dared to know." They were regarded as dangerous because their inquiries implicitly subverted long-standing Christian binaries by granting reality, value, and even goodness not to a static realm of unknowable spiritual essences but rather to the imminent and dynamic forces of a knowable physical universe. Early modern and Enlightenment political theorists such as Machiavelli, Thomas Hobbes, John Locke, and Montesquieu; Scottish Enlightenment moral philosophers such as Francis Hutcheson and David Hume; and classical liberal political economists such as Adam Smith then applied these empirical methods to the analysis of political, social, and economic life. In doing so they further undermined traditional Christian valuations by implicitly legitimizing the mundane pursuits of material self-interest and the moderate self-regarding sentiments that went with them. I have argued throughout this study that Emerson's work belongs to this revolutionary liberal continuum. His distinctive linking of existential freedom, moral volition, and scientific pragmatism as antidotes to determinism in "Fate" confirms this membership again at what turned out to be a concluding moment in his career.

Four subsequent essays in *The Conduct of Life* not only again assure Emerson's place in this liberal tradition but raise his contribution to an unprecedented and conclusive level of clarity and comprehensiveness. The sequencing in Emerson's collections is often significant, as in the trio of "History," "Self-Reliance," and "Compensation" in his "First Series," but never so pointed as in "Power," "Wealth," "Culture," and "Worship" in *The Conduct of Life*. The first two present the strongest endorsement anywhere in Emerson's writing of the modern liberal emancipation of material self-interest from long-standing Christian stricture. The latter two then present a rhetorically stirring summation of Emerson's long-nourished conception of how a civilization based on such emancipated self-interest can avoid moral and spiritual shallowness. The ideas in play here are not new in Emerson; they appear and reappear throughout his opus, and I have commented on them at length in the foregoing pages. What is new is their almost systematic distillation and integration in these four essays.

"Power," as Emerson presents and celebrates it here, refers not to political domination over other people or to command of resources but rather to a kind of primordial natural energy—an élan vital. It pertains more to individual potential—"vivacity" (*E&L* 974), "buoyancy and resistance" (*E&L* 975), "affirmative force" (*E&L* 973)—than to social relations. He has in mind the sustained elation experienced by a novice who masters a difficult task, the strong exhilaration felt by a student who finally grasps a challenging topic, the deep assurance exuded by an artist, craftsperson, or professional who over time has developed her skills to a high level. "The masters say," he writes, "that they know a master in music, only by seeing the pose of the hands on the keys;—so difficult and so vital an act is the command of the instrument. To have learned the use of tools, by thousands of manipulations; to have learned the arts of reckoning, by endless adding and dividing, is the *power* of the mechanic and the clerk" (*E&L* 984–85, italics mine). It is characteristic of Emerson to thus give priority to the private over the public sphere even when talking about so apparently political a topic as "power." But this preference itself has clear political-cultural connotations, as I have insisted throughout. Indeed, Emerson's happy conviction of the imminent availability of this cosmic quickening to anyone who works for it participates directly in the aforementioned counter-Christian liberal self-assertion initiated by early modern science: "Life is a search after power; and this is an element in which the world is so saturated,—there is not a chink or crevice in which it is not lodged—that no honest seeking goes unrewarded" (*E&L* 971). And the method by which Emerson urges his readers to secure their rightful portion of this ubiquitous elixir—focused labor—also has unmistakable liberal-cultural overtones. For Emerson, lasting self-enhancement and the deep affirmative feelings associated with it are the reward of having learned and heeded what might be called the reality principle of life under the modern liberal division of labor. "Nothing is got for nothing" (*E&L* 971): only by specialized and unstinting labor may the individual tap into the vast energies flowing ever about her. The power-charged world is indeed knowable, delicious, and rightfully available to every human being. But, paradoxically, it may only be possessed by means of a severe kind of self-curtailment:

> You must elect your work; you shall take what your brain can, and drop all the rest. Only so, can that amount of vital force accumulate, which can make the step from knowing to doing. The poet Campbell said, that "a man accustomed to work was equal to any achievement he resolved on, and, that, for himself, necessity not inspiration was the prompter of his muse." (*E&L* 982)

> Concentration is the secret of strength in politics, in war, in trade, in short, in all management of human affairs. One of the high anecdotes of the world is the reply of Newton to the inquiry, "how he had been able to achieve his discoveries?"—"By always intending my mind." Or if you will have a text from politics, take this from Plutarch: "There was, in the whole city, but one street in which Pericles was ever seen, the street which led to the market-place and the council house. He declined all invitations to banquets, and all gay assemblies and company. During the whole period of his administration, he never dined at the table of a friend." (*E&L* 982)

"Diligence passé sens," Henry VIII was wont to say, or, great is drill. . . . Practice is nine tenths. A course of mobs is good practice for orators. All the great speakers were bad speakers at first. Stumping it through England for several years made Cobden a consummate debater. Stumping it through New England for twice seven, trained Wendell Phillips. The way to learn German, is, to read the same dozen pages over and over a hundred times, till you know every word and particle in them, and can pronounce and repeat them by heart. . . . Six hours a day at the piano, only to give facility of touch; six hours a day at painting, only to give command of the odious materials, oil, ochres, and brushes. (*E&L* 984)

The full liberal import of these passages is best grasped by reference to yet another passage from the literature of liberalism. Adam Smith starts *The Wealth of Nations* with a now-classic example of the benefits of the systematic division of industrial labor. He observes that one competent man with no previous knowledge of the tasks involved in pin making and no previous familiarity with special machinery could probably only produce one pin in a day. At most he could produce twenty pins. And yet Smith had himself visited a small factory where the making of a pin had been broken down into eighteen separate specialized tasks, with ten men engaged in performing them. "One man draws out the wire, another straightens it, a third cuts it, a fourth points it, a fifth grinds it at the top for receiving the head," and so on. Although this was a relatively modest factory that made do without the most advanced machinery, these ten men, "when they exerted themselves," "could make among them upwards of forty-eight thousand pins in a day." Even granting the maximum pin-making productivity of each of these ten men working alone, they could not have made even "the two hundred and fortieth part . . . of what they are at present capable of performing."[3] Whatever one's feelings may be about the human cost of such increased efficiency, there can be no doubt that Smith has here identified a fact of immeasurable importance to modern life. The large-scale application of the basic principle illustrated here would soon lead to exponential increases in the human power of production and thus, in remarkably little time, to a complete and pervasive transformation of every aspect of material existence in the West. As Eric Hobsbawm, with whom we began this study, put it, "For the first time in human history, the shackles were taken off the productive power of human societies, which henceforth became capable of the constant, rapid and up to the present limitless multiplication of men, goods and services."[4] In the passages above Emerson recognizes, approves, and adapts this revolutionary principle of enhanced productivity to the individual enterprise of self-realization. Just as the pin-makers gain access to a vast fount of cosmic power by each perfecting and repeating one small task, so the solitary private self may achieve maximum personal efficacy and fulfillment by finding and sticking to the work to which he or she is most suited. Emerson shows no residual Christian compunction here about the moral appropriateness of thus enlisting the colossal mechanisms of the universe for personal empowerment: "If these forces and this husbandry are within reach of our will, and the laws of them can be read, we infer that all success, and all conceivable benefit for man, is also, first or last, within his reach, and has its own sublime economies, by which it may be attained" (*E&L* 985). Nor is Emerson daunted by the specter of human mechanization because he sees the machine itself as a refinement of the human capacity for efficacious labor and thus, startlingly, as an emblem of virtue: "A man hardly knows how much he is a machine, until he begins to make telegraph, loom, press, and locomotive, in his own image. But in these he is forced to leave out his follies and hindrances, so that when we get to the mill, the machine is more moral than we" (*E&L* 986).

It is easy to know if one has heeded the law of power, Emerson contends in the subsequent essay, entitled "Wealth," because such attunement yields tangible rewards. Here again Emerson appropriates a Calvinist symbolic frame but adapts it to his secular liberal context. This essay is striking (and offensive to some) in its candid avowal of a secularized version of the Calvinist formula according to which diligence and success in one's professional calling and the associated material prosperity were interpreted as signs of God's favor. For Emerson, wealth no longer represents the self's accord with God's will and thus its openness to the mysterious visitations of grace; it signifies rather the self's advantageous grasp of a fundamental structure of reality. By disciplined work one activates a quasi-mechanical process of material and moral self-enhancement:

> Success consists in close obedience to the laws of the world, and, since those laws are intellectual and moral, an intellectual and moral obedience. Political economy is as good a book wherein to read the life of man, and the ascendancy of laws over all private and hostile influences, as any Bible that has come down to us. (*E&L* 997)

The interest of petty economy is this symbolization of the great economy; the way in which a house, and a private man's methods, tally with the solar system, and the laws of give and take, throughout nature. (*E&L* 1000)

So there is no maxim of the merchant, e.g. "Best use of money is to pay debts;" "Every business by itself;" "Best time is present time;" "The right investment is in tools of your trade;" or the like, which does not admit of an extended sense. The counting-room maxims liberally expounded are laws of the Universe. The merchant's economy is a coarse symbol of the soul's economy. It is, to spend for power, and not for pleasure. (*E&L* 1010)

I have been arguing throughout this study that Emerson took it upon himself as a lifelong task to find or fashion a new set of symbols for America's new kind of Enlightenment-liberal society. We have seen in chapter 3 how he located in nature a rich network of analogies that linked the autonomous individual to an overarching metaphysical order. We have also seen how, throughout his work, Emerson tied the attainment of individual rights into a grand historical metanarrative of the unfolding of universal human freedom—with the abolition of slavery as the latest astounding chapter. Here in his last major book of essays he identifies money and material wealth as yet another symbolic ligature. But unlike the symbolism of nature and history, which require solitude and the special intuitions of contemplative "reason" to be properly interpreted, the symbolism of money is, at least on the first level, widely socially established and everywhere socially understood. Whether it is the antiliberal Carlyle bemoaning the inescapability of the "cash nexus" or the classical-liberal Hayek "marveling" at the data-transmitting capacity of the free-market price mechanism, few have doubted the vast, intimate, and psychologically potent reach of money as a symbol.[5] So in this essay Emerson seeks not, as in "Nature" or "History," to awaken unwitting readers to a body of radiant symbols that quietly surrounds them but rather, as we saw him do with the language of property, to alert his readers to the larger moral meaning of a utilitarian-symbolic vernacular already spoken at every shop, farm, and kitchen table.

Emerson uses a two-stage strategy. First, at the rhetorical heart of this essay is a piercing and unequivocal assertion of what I have been calling the liberal revaluation of values with regard to the pursuit of material self-interest. Counter to most Christian precedent, Emerson grants moral legitimacy to wealth seeking along the following lines. Human beings have a natural drive, he argues, to see, shape, understand, master, and enjoy their world: "The same correspondence that is between thirst in the stomach, and water in the spring, exists between the whole of man and the whole of nature" (*E&L* 991). In the absence of religious prohibition, which Emerson implicitly rejects by excluding all reference to it, there is no reason to doubt the moral legitimacy of this drive in and of itself. Once this point has been established, a larger moral-cultural reorientation must follow. If wealth is understood primarily as a means to the fulfillment of fundamental human needs and drives, then it not only is morally acceptable but may itself become a standard of moral measurement:

> It is of no use to argue the wants down: the philosophers have laid the greatness of man in making his wants few; but will a man content himself with a hut and a handful of dried pease? He is born to be rich. He is thoroughly related; and is tempted out by his appetites and fancies to the conquest of this and that piece of nature, until he finds his well-being in the use of his planet, and of more planets than his own. Wealth requires, besides the crust of bread and the roof,—the freedom of the city, the freedom of the earth, traveling, machinery, the benefits of science, music, and the fine arts, the best culture and the best company. He is the rich man who can avail himself of all men's faculties. (*E&L* 990–91)

> The rich take up something more of the world into man's life. They include the country as well as the town, the ocean-side, the White Hills, the Far West, and the old European homesteads of man, in their notion of available material. The world is his, who has money to go over it. (*E&L* 994)

> Kings are said to have long arms, but every man should have long arms, and should pluck his living, his instruments, his power, and his knowing, from the sun, moon, and stars. Is not then the demand to be rich legitimate? (*E&L* 994)

It would be hard to overstate the broad liberal-cultural significance of these passages, chosen from among many similar ones in this essay. They represent a thoroughgoing rejection of what Nietzsche would label the morality of resentment. For much of its long history Christianity had consoled the impoverished masses of Europe by denying the ultimate value of their aristocratic overlords' earthly riches. The church,

Nietzsche argued, thus institutionalized economic resentments in the mystified form of world-denying moral strictures against the pursuit and possession of wealth. Emerson here offers a candid, clear, and affirmative substitute for this contorted structure of symbolic denial. If we believe both the world and human beings to be good, and we understand human beings to have a legitimate natural drive to know, understand, and assimilate the world, then wealth, understood as both means and evidence of efficacious human agency in this regard, loses its taint of corruption. Rather than an object of resentment, defensive moral condemnation, and the cause of a turn to world-denying ascetic ideals, wealth in Emerson's essay becomes a compelling symbol of achieved and achievable human fulfillment. "The pulpit and the press," he writes, "have many commonplaces denouncing the thirst for wealth; but if men should take these moralists at their word, and leave off aiming to be rich, the moralists would rush to rekindle at all hazards this love of power in the people, lest civilization should be undone" (*E&L* 994). Without recourse to an otherworldly platform from which to condemn wealth, moreover, one is forced to confront a realistic political question: What legal and institutional arrangements will best give people opportunity to achieve this form of fulfillment without depriving others of the same opportunity? "How," as Emerson puts it later in the essay, "to give all access to the masterpieces of art and nature?" (*E&L* 995). The history of Western liberalism in the nineteenth and twentieth centuries may be told as the story of various ways of answering this question, with U.S. libertarianism at one extreme and Scandinavian social democracy at the other. In this essay Emerson expresses a strong preference for the former—"the basis of political economy is non-interference. . . . Do not legislate. . . . Meddle, and you snap the sinews with your sumptuary laws" (*E&L* 1000). But however this question is answered, the underlying moral reorientation remains in place: where medieval Christian culture had popularly associated wealth with sin, modern liberal culture makes it the measure of a kind of virtue. And thus, not incidentally for Emerson's purposes, the symbolic landscape is transformed and enhanced. It is not just during walks in nature or while reading works of history and literature that Emerson's consciousness is flooded with moral metaphors, analogies, and narratives. On the train from Concord to Boston, in the streets of America's towns and cities as he travels to give his lectures, or in the manufacturing centers of England that he had visited not so many years earlier he finds himself constantly confronting resonant material images of human energies well or badly channeled. In "Wealth" he offers a secular sermon expounding these secular-symbolic images. However lost the traveler, Emerson argues, and wherever he wanders, the social semiotics of wealth ensure that if he pays attention, he will not lack strong moral-symbolic orientation. The moral-mechanical lesson is proclaimed from every building, business, and homestead to every observer: disciplined labor and channeled energy yield power, as symbolized by money and what it buys.

But however pertinent he found this symbolic vocabulary, Emerson was not unaware of the distortions and diminishments to which it was prone. As I noted in my discussion of property in chapter 4, Emerson was especially sensitive to the problem of what we now call "reification." So compelling and inclusive was the language of wealth, he recognized, that it threatened to subsume all of reality within its quantitative grid of exchange value. The result would be a sad reduction not only of the phenomenological reality of nature but of the complexity of human personality and consciousness as well. A person incapable of registering the world in any but abstract instrumental terms might become materially wealthy but would remain impoverished on other levels—a mere thing to himself and to others, dwelling in a universe of mere things. "A man is a beggar," Emerson writes in "Culture," "who only lives to the useful, and, however he may serve as a pin or rivet in the social machine, cannot be said to have arrived at self-possession" (*E&L* 1030). We saw how Emerson tried to address this problem in some of his earlier essays by raising the meaning of "property" into a higher philosophical register, which he played off of more conventional meanings in a fruitful tension. He plays on the term "self-possession" in the same way immediately above, and he employs the same strategy at the end of "Wealth" when he admonishes the reader "always to spend on the higher plane; to invest and invest, with keener avarice, that he may spend in spiritual creation" (*E&L* 1010). But Emerson addresses the problem more systematically in *The Conduct of Life* as a whole by explicitly counterbalancing the instrumental orientation of "Power" and "Wealth" with what we may call the "counterinstrumental" emphases of "Culture" and "Worship."

"Culture," Emerson writes in the first paragraph of the essay of this name, "corrects the theory of success" (*E&L* 1015), and therein lies his hope for the wholeness of liberal civilization. In the immediately following paragraphs he reverses his perspective and tone on many of the principal motifs of "Wealth." Where he had previously celebrated the extraordinary gains in productivity achieved by the division of labor and, accordingly, advocated strict professional self-discipline, he now laments the narrowness, fragmentation, and isolation engendered by these same advances. "Our efficiency depends so much on our concentration, that Nature usually in the instances where a marked man is sent into the world, overloads him with bias, sacrificing his symmetry to his working power" (*E&L* 1015). "So egotism has its root in the cardinal necessity by which each individual person persists to be what he is" (*E&L* 1016). The point is not to retract his foregoing praise of specialization but rather to acknowledge that, like most real benefits, the almost miraculous material progress of liberal society is purchased at a high existential price. It is only by fully acknowledging the immensity of both benefit and loss, Emerson means to suggest, that one is prepared to understand the special role of "culture" in liberal societies. He includes a broad range of pursuits in the category of "culture" in this essay, including a serious engagement with music, painting, sculpture, architecture, gardening, sports, solitude, travel, and, to be sure, literature of every kind—poetry, philosophy, religious writings, history, biography, fiction, and drama. But he nonetheless sees all of these pursuits as united by one common compensatory function. In the context of an economy characterized by an ever more finely differentiated division of labor and a seemingly limitless proliferation of commodities, the activities of culture all serve to restore their participants, however briefly, to a holistic consciousness of nature and of other human beings as radiant ends in themselves rather than as means to any particular practical end. In the following essay Emerson assigns the term "worship" to such grateful, receptive, nonreifying contemplative consciousness of the world—something akin to what Heidegger would call the memory of being. It is consistent with the secularizing strategy we have traced throughout his opus that he presents this worshipful state of mind as the product of high "culture" in general rather than of any particular cult. "There is a principle which is the basis of things, which all speech aims to say, and all action to evolve, a simple, quiet, undescribed, undescribable presence, dwelling very peacefully in us, our rightful lord: we are not to do, but to let do; not to work, but to be worked upon; and to this homage there is a consent of all thoughtful and just men in all ages and conditions" (*E&L* 1061).

Emerson thus traverses two opposite poles in these five major essays in *The Conduct of Life*—"Fate," "Power," and "Wealth," on the one hand, and "Culture" and "Worship," on the other. The first three forcefully embrace the historically unprecedented freedom, dynamism, and sheer material abundance of modern liberal society, while the latter two acknowledge and propose a means for overcoming moral and spiritual deficiencies intrinsic to its productive dynamism. As we follow this self-corrective course we should remember the youthful Emersonian formulation with which we began this study: "The office of a true culture is two-fold: it must rid itself of superstition and deepen the piety." At this late moment in his career Emerson is still attempting to perform this paradoxical twofold office, and he has distilled it down to its essential elements. On the one hand, he attempts to free the liberal self from residual Christian compunctions about material acquisition, thus emancipating human productivity on a scale unprecedented in history. And yet, at the same time, he cautions that same self to slow itself down and, through the mediations of high culture, to allow itself the larger moral-ontological reorientation—the memory of being—that authentic freedom must also include. Well performed, the twofold office of a liberal culture thus yields a twofold bounty: "These wonders," both material and mystical, "are brought to our own door" (*E&L* 48).

In "The President's Proclamation" and "The Fortune of the Republic" Emerson picks up the historical theme where *English Traits* left it off but in a very different tone. Notwithstanding the grievous social inequalities that marked England's cities in the 1840s and that scandalized many European intellectuals, Emerson, as we saw in chapter 9, had effusively praised the English legal system in *English Traits* for securing the rights to property in such a way as to provide seemingly unlimited stimulus to industrial production, trade, and the acquisition of wealth. He had celebrated a robust middle-class work ethic and a vigorous practicality that seemed rooted in a distinctive Anglo-Saxon mentality. And he had marveled at the vibrancy of the English press as an instrument and emblem of a free civil society. Indeed, *English Traits*, published in 1855 on the basis of a trip taken in 1848, could be described as an effort on Emerson's part to lay claim for American inheritance of what he regarded as the world-historical success of English liberalism. He wrote of the English: "The modern world is theirs. . . . [T]hey have made and make it day by day" (*E&L* 915). "The American is only the continuation of the English genius into new conditions, more or less propitious" (*E&L* 785). But by 1863 the homage of the favored heir-apparent had turned to surly disillusion. "Stand aside," Emerson barks at England and the English in "The Fortune of the Republic." "We have seen through you. . . . We who saw you in a halo of honor which our affection made, now we must measure your means; your true dimensions: your population; we must compare the future of this country with that, in a time when every prosperity of ours knocks away the stones from your foundation" (*AW* 145).

What so drastically changed Emerson's feelings toward England between 1855 and 1863? The answer, though large and complex, may be simply stated: the outbreak and progress of the American Civil War. For Emerson, the war, especially after Lincoln's issuing of the Emancipation Proclamation and subsequent Northern military successes, promised nothing less than glorious vindication of his long-held Whig sense of history. In "The Fortune of the Republic" Emerson places the American Civil War as the most recent in a sequence of decisive moments in the world-historical progress of liberty, following "the planting of Christianity," "the rise of towns," "the reformation of Luther," "the decay of the temporal power of the Pope," "the breaking of the power of the Inquisition," "the establishment of free institutions in England, France, and America," and "the revolutions effected in all the arts of life by science" (*AW* 142). Yet in 1862 England, whose liberal example on slavery we saw Emerson use to shame his own nation in the 1844 speech on emancipation in the West Indies, struck a deal to build ships for the Confederacy. And in 1863 the same English nation, whose air was said to be too pure for the breath of a slave, sat poised to offer its military support to the American slave power. English intellectual leadership, moreover, as represented for Emerson especially by his longtime friend and correspondent Carlyle, had also thrown its rhetorical weight behind the South, voicing hateful racist spleen in the process. As with his condemnation of Daniel Webster, the depth of Emerson's foregoing idealization of England is indicated by the bitterness of his subsequent disappointment. "You have failed," he says in "The Fortune of the Republic," "in one of the great hours that put nations to the test. When the occasion of magnanimity arrived, you had none: you forgot your loud professions, you rubbed your hands with indecent joy, and saw only in our extreme danger the chance of humbling a rival and getting away his commerce. . . . Justice is above your aim. . . . [W]e cannot count you great" (*AW* 144–45).

Such disillusion was painful, but it also had a liberating aspect. With the imago of the political-cultural father thus diminished, Emerson was now free to assert the heir's preeminence. While I concurred at the beginning of this study with those scholars who have recently sought to qualify the extent of Emerson's nationalism, there can be no doubt about its prominence in these two late speeches. Emerson greeted the war and Lincoln's proclamation with gratitude for many reasons, but not least among them was that they allowed him, after long and distressing doubt throughout the 1850s, to once again embrace his country as a symbol of freedom's advance:

> These measures provoke no noisy joy, but are received into a sympathy so deep as to apprise us that mankind are greater and better than we know. At such times, it appears as if a new public were created to greet the new event. It is as when an orator, having ended the compliments and pleasantries with which he conciliated attention, and having run over the superficial fitness and commodities of the measure he urges, suddenly lending himself to some happy inspiration, announces with vibrating voice the grand human principles involved,—the bravoes and wits who greeted him loudly thus far, are surprised and overawed. A new audience is found in the heart of the assembly, an audience hitherto passive and unconcerned, now at last so searched and kindled, that they come forward, every one a representative of mankind, standing for all nationalities. (*AW* 129–30)

> Liberty is a slow fruit. It comes, like religion, for short periods and in rare conditions, as if awaiting a culture of the race which shall make it organic and permanent. (*AW* 129)

> Our hurts are healed; the health of the nation is repaired. . . . We have recovered ourselves from our false position and planted ourselves on a law of nature. (*AW* 131–32)

> What a change! We are all of the English race. But climate and country have told on us so that John Bull does not know us. It is the Jonathanizing of John. (*AW* 151)

> For such a gain,—to end once for all that pest of all free institutions,—one generation might well be sacrificed,—perhaps it will be,—that this continent be purged, and a new era of equal rights dawn on the universe. Who would not, if it could be made certain, that the new morning of universal liberty should rise on our race, by the perishing of one generation,—who would not consent to die? (*AW* 153)

> We are coming, thanks to the war, to a nationality. (*AW* 144)

We saw in chapter 1 how Emerson's liberal sense of history was expressed on two levels. On the first and most prominent level he consistently assumed and applied a grand, overarching metanarrative in which the major events of Western history, including the founding of the United States, were understood as steps in the predestined unfolding of universal human freedom. At the same time he showed frequent interest in the history of liberty as manifested in the evolution of more local and intimate moral feeling—such as in the decline of religious persecution. The Civil War speeches excerpted above may serve to conclude our commentary on Emerson's work as a whole because they so explicitly and climactically bring these two levels together. Here as throughout his life Emerson at once announces, enacts, and thus attempts to advance the concrete realization in American society at large of a culture of freedom—what he calls above "a culture of the race" that will make freedom "organic and permanent." He is aided here as throughout his work by what he knows to be his society's deep-rooted cross-denominational Protestant assurance that the human personality itself is radically free—that it may be, at any moment, graciously shattered, shed, and rebuilt anew. Just as Lincoln would do two years later in the Gettysburg Address when he spoke of "a new birth of freedom," Emerson here pointedly links the great national crisis to the familiar, psychologically intimate, and culturally pervasive Protestant narrative of personal spiritual conversion—being born again. "What a change!" he exclaims and casts the war as an opportunity for cathartic transatlantic liberal-cultural regeneration: the "Jonathanizing of John," the birth of "a new era of equal rights," the dawning of "a new morning of universal liberty." And he further appeals to a broad-based cultural Protestantism when he likens the regenerated nation to an audience "searched and kindled," "surprised and overawed" by an inspiring sermon or lecture. Indeed, Emerson names the secularized Protestantism of his own lifetime's cultural work when he imagines "a new public created to greet the new event." He thus expresses his belief that the Emancipation Proclamation and the Civil War not only have legally ended the moral blight of slavery but in doing so began to initiate the entire American public into precisely the new kind of liberal culture he had spent his life promoting. For Emerson, this is the special greatness of Lincoln: he seems not only to be successfully pursuing the war but also to have correctly interpreted its largest cultural meaning. He has managed not only to protect and preserve the legally constituted liberal nation but also to lead its people into a culturally constituted liberal "nationality."

But to thus tap into the resonances of Protestant-Christian symbolism and to take over some of its inspirational functions is not, as I have maintained throughout this study, to subscribe to its extrahistorical apocalypticism, millennialism, or even utopianism. The American society that Emerson hopes will emerge from the Civil War will be decidedly freer and more just than the one that preceded it, and freer and more just than most other societies on earth, but it will not be otherworldly or transcendent. On the contrary, Emerson chooses to speak of the "fortune" of the republic in part to emphasize the inescapable element of geographical, historical, and economic contingency in America's comparatively promising situation. The "ample domain" of a prodigal continent provides vast territory and natural resources. Socially, America continues to benefit immeasurably from being founded after "the feudal mischief": "No inquisition, no kings, no nobles, no dominant church—so no terrorizing of the mind by charges of heresy." Along with this relative social and intellectual freedom came the cultural freedom bred of religious pluralism and tolerance. And these freedoms in turn helped to create an environment hospitable to science, scientific education, and technological innovation. Emerson looks ahead, then, not to the eternal beatitude of a shining kingdom of the righteous but to further incremental amelioration of the human condition by such prosaic means as developments in technology, an educated civil service, opportunities for landownership under the provisions of the Homestead Act, and, most important, the securing of civil rights for all citizens— "freedom of thought, of religion, of speech, of the press, of trade, of suffrage." By these imperfect human means, not by divine intervention, Emerson expects America to achieve an accessible but nonetheless historically unprecedented condition of general rationality, justice, decency, and opportunity, to "pass out of old remainders of barbarism into pure Christianity and humanity . . . a state of things in which crime will not pay . . . a state of things which allows every man the largest liberty compatible with the liberty of every other man" (*AW* 153).

Notes

Introduction

1. Perry Miller, "From Edwards to Emerson," in *Ralph Waldo Emerson: A Collection of Critical Essays*, ed. Lawrence Buell (Englewood, NJ: Prentice Hall, 1993), 13–31.

2. William L. Hedges, "From Franklin to Emerson," in Buell, *Ralph Waldo Emerson*, 42.

3. Sacvan Bercovitch, "Emerson, Individualism, and the Ambiguities of Dissent," in Buell, *Ralph Waldo Emerson*, 101–31.

4. Robert Richardson, *Emerson: The Mind on Fire* (Berkeley: University of California Press, 1995), 251.

5. Lionel Trilling, "The Situation of the American Intellectual at the Present Time," in *The Moral Obligation to Be Intelligent: Selected Essays*, ed. Leon Wieseltier (New York: Farrar, Straus and Giroux, 2000), 275–91.

6. Len Gougeon, *Virtue's Hero: Emerson, Antislavery, and Reform* (Athens: University of Georgia Press, 1990).

7. George Willis Cooke, *Ralph Waldo Emerson: His Life, Writings, and Philosophy* (Boston: James R. Osgood, 1881); Moncure Daniel Conway, *Emerson at Home and Abroad* (Boston: James R. Osgood, 1882); Alexander Ireland, *In Memoriam: Ralph Waldo Emerson* (London: Simpkin, Marshall, 1882), new ed. as *Ralph Waldo Emerson: His Life, Genius, and Writings* (London: Simpkin, Marshall, 1882); Oliver Wendell Holmes, *Ralph Waldo Emerson* (Boston: Houghton Mifflin, 1884); James Eliot Cabot, *A Memoir of Ralph Waldo Emerson*, 2 vols. (Boston: Houghton Mifflin, 1887); Gay Wilson Allen, *Waldo Emerson: A Biography* (New York: Viking, 1981); and John McAleer, *Ralph Waldo Emerson: Days of Encounter* (Boston: Little, Brown, 1984).

8. Stephen E. Whicher, *Freedom and Fate: An Inner Life of Ralph Waldo Emerson* (Philadelphia: University of Pennsylvania Press, 1953); Ralph Rusk, *The Life of Ralph Waldo Emerson* (New York: Charles Scribner's Sons, 1949).

9. As Gougeon puts it, "The image of Emerson that emerges from this study is that of a concerned, sometimes frustrated, but always committed social

activist who was very much involved with, and interested in, the abolition of slavery as well as other important social reforms of his day." But, "as was the case with most major developments in his life, there was a lengthy and thoughtful prologue to the commencement of his public commitment to abolition and a substantial evolution thereafter" (*Virtue's Hero*, 17).

10. Morris Dickstein, ed., *The Revival of Pragmatism: New Essays on Social Thought, Law, and Culture* (Durham, NC: Duke University Press, 1998).

11. Cornel West, *The American Evasion of Philosophy: A Genealogy of Pragmatism* (Madison: University of Wisconsin Press, 1989), 36.

12. Ibid., 38. See also Harold Bloom, "Mr. America," *New York Review of Books*, 22 November 1984.

13. Richard Poirier, *The Renewal of Literature: Emersonian Reflections* (New York: Random House, 1987), 17, 49, 92, 10–11, 14.

14. Ibid., 3, 4, 9.

15. David Robinson, *Emerson and "The Conduct of Life": Pragmatism and Ethical Purpose in the Late Work* (Philadelphia: University of Pennsylvania Press, 1993), 1.

16. Bloom, "Mr. America," 19, 23.

17. Stanley Cavell, "What's the Use of Calling Emerson a Pragmatist?" in Dickstein, *The Revival of Pragmatism*, 72–80.

18. John J. McDermott, *The Writings of William James* (Chicago: University of Chicago Press, 1977), 629.

19. "What does it mean to say that we 'know' something in a world in which things happen higgledy-piggledy? Virtually all of Charles Peirce's work—an enormous body of writing on logic, semiotics, mathematics, astronomy, meteorology, physics, psychology, and philosophy, large portions of it unpublished or unfinished—was devoted to this question. His answer had many parts, and fitting them all together—in a form consistent with his belief in the existence of a personal God—became the burden of his life. But one part of his answer was that in a universe in which events are uncertain and perception is fallible, knowing cannot be a matter of an individual mind 'mirroring' reality. Each mind reflects differently—even the same mind reflects differently at different moments—and in any case reality doesn't stand still long enough to be accurately mirrored. Peirce's conclusion was that knowledge must therefore be social. It was his most important contribution to American thought, and when he recalled, late in life, how he came to formulate it, he described it—fittingly—as the product of a group. This was the conversation society he formed with William James, Oliver Wendell Holmes, Jr., and a few others in Cambridge in 1872, the group known as the Metaphysical Club" (Louis Menand, *The Metaphysical Club: A Story of Ideas in America* [New York: Farrar, Straus and Giroux, 2001], 199–200).

20. For Emerson's Platonism see especially John S. Harrison, *The Teachers of Emerson* (New York: Sturgis & Walton, 1910); and Edmund G. Berry, *Emerson's*

Plutarch (Cambridge, MA: Harvard University Press, 1961). For his love of science see especially Whicher, *Freedom and Fate*; Richardson, *Emerson: The Mind on Fire*; Eric Wilson, *Emerson's Sublime Science* (New York: Macmillan, 1999); and, recently, Laura Dassow Walls's excellent *Emerson's Life in Science: The Culture of Truth* (Ithaca, NY: Cornell University Press, 2003).

21. See Harold C. Goddard, "Unitarianism and Transcendentalism," in *Studies in New England Transcendentalism* (New York: Columbia University Press, 1908); Lawrence Buell, *Literary Transcendentalism* (Ithaca, NY: Cornell University Press, 1973); David Robinson, *Apostle of Culture: Emerson as Preacher and Lecturer* (Philadelphia: University of Pennsylvania Press, 1982).

22. Christopher Newfield, *The Emerson Effect: Individualism and Submission in America* (Chicago: University of Chicago Press, 1996).

23. Ibid., 22–23.

24. Lou Ann Lange, *The Riddle of Liberty: Emerson on Alienation, Freedom, and Obedience* (Athens: University of Georgia Press, 1986).

25. Christopher Lasch, *The True and Only Heaven: Progress and Its Critics* (New York: Norton, 1991), 243–78. In general Lasch performs a valuable corrective to postmodernist criticism by directing our attention to the profound sense of limits that characterizes Emerson's work throughout. He also provides a much-needed reminder of the Puritan roots of Emerson's moral vision, suggesting a compelling connection between Emerson's ecstatic affirmations and Jonathan Edwards's definition of virtue as "consent to Being as a whole." But although I personally find attractive the populist political tradition that Lasch describes here and elsewhere in his work, I believe he is wrong in trying to assimilate Emerson to it. As I hope to make clear, I believe that a profound streak of anti-popular aristocratic sentiment runs through the heart of Emerson's writing.

26. See Goddard, "Unitarianism and Transcendentalism"; Buell, *Literary Transcendentalism*; and Robinson, *Apostle of Culture*. See also Merrell R. Davis, "Emerson's 'Reason' and the Scottish Philosophers," *New England Quarterly* 17, no. 2 (1944): 209–28.

27. "The worst symptom I have noticed in our politics lately is the attempt to make a gibe out of Seward's appeal to a higher law than the Constitution, & Webster has taken part in it. I have seen him snubbed as '*Higher-law*-Seward'" (*JMN* 2:248).

28. Emerson's bitter disappointment in Webster pervades his journals of the early 1850s. It is expressed in distilled form in his speech "The Fugitive Slave Law." "He [Webster] did as immoral men usually do, made very low bows to the Christian Church, and went through all the Sunday decorums; but when allusion was made to the question of duty and the sanctions of morality, he very frankly said, as at Albany, 'Some higher law, something existing somewhere between here and the third heaven,—I do not know where.' And if the reporters say true, this wretched atheism found some laughter in the company" (*AW* 79).

29. Alexander Hamilton, James Madison, and John Jay, *The Federalist*, ed. Max Beloff (1948; New York: Blackwell, 1987), 265, 287.

30. George Santayana, "The Genteel Tradition in American Philosophy," in *Winds of Doctrine and Platonism and the Spiritual Life* (1913; Gloucester, MA: Peter Smith, 1971), 186–215.

31. Van Wyck Brooks, *America's Coming of Age* (New York: R. W. Huebsch, 1915), 77. Later in his career Brooks reversed himself completely on Emerson. His 1935 biography, *Ralph Waldo Emerson*, bathes its subject in a soft haze of impressionistic admiration.

32. F. O. Matthiessen, *The American Renaissance: Art and Expression in the Age of Emerson and Whitman* (London: Oxford University Press, 1941).

33. Quentin Anderson, *The Imperial Self: An Essay in American Literary and Cultural History* (New York: Knopf, 1971), 36.

34. Ibid., 39, 57.

35. Thomas Pangle, *The Spirit of Modern Republicanism: The Moral Vision of the American Founders and the Philosophy of John Locke* (Chicago: University of Chicago Press, 1988).

36. Joyce Oldham Appleby, *Economic Thought and Ideology in 17th Century England* (Princeton, NJ: Princeton University Press, 1978); Appleby, *Capitalism and a New Social Order: The Republican Vision of the 1790s* (New York: New York University Press, 1984); Appleby, *Liberalism and Republicanism in the Historical Imagination* (Cambridge, MA: Harvard University Press, 1992); Isaac Kramnick, *Republicanism and Bourgeois Radicalism: Political Ideology in Late 18th Century England and America* (Ithaca, NY: Cornell University Press, 1990).

37. Three of the major political historians of the period—Arthur Schlesinger, Jr., Daniel Walker Howe, and Charles Sellers—agree on this. Politically minded literary historians Arthur Ladu and William Charvat come to similar conclusions. See Arthur Ladu, "Emerson: Whig or Democrat?" *New England Quarterly* 13, no. 3 (1940): 419–41; Arthur Schlesinger, Jr., *The Age of Jackson* (Boston: Little, Brown, 1945); William Charvat, "American Romanticism and the Depression of 1837," in *The Profession of Authorship in America, 1800–70: The Papers of William Charvat*, ed. Matthew J. Bruccoli (Ohio: Ohio State University Press, 1968); Daniel Walker Howe, *The Political Culture of the American Whigs* (Chicago: University of Chicago Press, 1979); Charles Sellers, *The Market Revolution* (London: Oxford University Press, 1991). Charvat's summary of the issue is the most stark: "Emerson's entries in his journal through the depression years contain the essence of the rebellion of his class against the Jacksonian democracy. . . . [I]n his attitude toward the lowest social strata . . . Emerson reveals the class basis of his thinking and the essential similarity between his social point of view and that of such complacent patricians as Longfellow and Prescott" ("American Romanticism," 61, 64). Sellers's assessment is slightly more nuanced but similar in its conclusions: "This exemplary American scholar was bred in the bosom of Boston Federalism, and breeding told. Preaching a transcendental

Reason evoked by the beauty and metaphor of nature, he could not but see the hard-times market as a 'system of selfishness.' Yet imperatives of class perspective and wealth made Jacksonian insurgency abhorrent and confined his hopes to individual regeneration within the class structure he validated as natural" (*The Market Revolution*, 376). Arthur Schlesinger, Jr., is more gentle. In a book that is generally very tough on Whigs he grants that Emerson was "the wisest man of the day." "Yet," he adds, "politics represent his greatest failure. He would not succumb to verbal panaceas, neither would he make the ultimate moral effort of Thoreau and cast off all obligation to society. Instead he lingered indecisively, accepting without enthusiasm certain relations to government but never confronting directly the implications of acceptance" (*The Age of Jackson*, 384). Arthur Ladu offers perhaps the most balanced account: "To sum up, we see that during the 1830s Emerson believed that the Democrats might have some superior ideas, although he seems never to have felt an enthusiastic conviction that this was true. But following renewed Democratic successes after 1840, and the agitation over Texas, Slavery, and the Mexican War, Emerson became skeptical of the entire party and its ideas. During the decade of the fifties, and thereafter, his skepticism increased and engendered a decided discouragement with American democracy, not only as represented by a party, but also as an idea. In particular, he denounced at this time, as never before, the prescribed tenets of American Democratic faith, belief in the virtue of the masses and in majority rule" ("Emerson," 432–33). Howe shows the extent to which Emerson's thought shared the general emphases of American Whig political culture at a variety of important levels.

38. John Dewey, "Emerson: The Philosopher of Democracy," *International Journal of Ethics*, 13 July 1903, 411–12.

39. One cannot help but wonder if Vernon Parrington read later works such as "Wealth" or *English Traits* when he writes, "[Emerson] was at one with Jefferson in preferring an agrarian to an industrial order. Manchester economics — the doctrine of the economic man, of the iron law of wages, and other obscenities of the school, he frankly loathed" (*Main Currents in American Thought: An Interpretation of American Literature from the Beginnings to 1920* [New York: Harcourt Brace, 1927], 396).

40. Matthiessen, *The American Renaissance*, ix, 4.

41. Daniel Aaron, *Men of Good Hope* (New York: Oxford University Press, 1951), 14.

42. Allen, *Waldo Emerson*, 566.

43. George Kateb, "Democratic Individuality and the Meaning of Rights," in *Liberalism and the Moral Life*, ed. Nancy Rosenblum (Cambridge, MA: Harvard University Press, 1984); Kateb, *The Inner Ocean: Individualism and Democratic Culture* (Ithaca, NY: Cornell University Press, 1992); Kateb, *Emerson and Self-Reliance* (Thousand Oaks, CA: Sage Publications, 1994).

44. Kateb, *Emerson and Self-Reliance*, 178–79.

45. In *The Shaping of American Liberalism: The Debates over Ratification, Nullification, and Slavery* (Chicago: University of Chicago Press, 1993) David F. Ericson suggests that American liberalism has been decisively shaped by a persistent tension between a classical republican-communitarian conception of liberalism and a classical liberal-libertarian conception. In my view, Emerson throws his considerable rhetorical weight behind the latter.

46. Guido de Ruggiero gives a clear and comprehensive account of this central tension in European liberal thought and legislation. "Democracy and liberalism are two inseparable but opposed terms, whose conflicts and treaties of peace will occupy the political thought of the 19th century and our own" (*The History of European Liberalism*, trans. R. G. Collingwood [1927; Boston: Beacon Press, 1959], 82).

47. In his epochal work *The Road to Serfdom* (Chicago: University of Chicago Press, 1994) Friedrich August von Hayek urged socialist-leaning twentieth-century liberals to turn back toward their more libertarian nineteenth-century inheritance.

48. Kateb, *Emerson and Self-Reliance*, 50.

49. Ibid., xxviii, 18.

50. Ibid., 18.

51. "Just as steady as Emerson's praise of vocation is his dismay at most occupations" (ibid., 24).

52. Ibid., 178.

53. Ibid., 170, 18.

54. Walt Whitman, "Song of Myself," in *The Complete Poems*, ed. Francis Murphy (New York: Penguin, 1975), 63; Whitman, "Crossing Brooklyn Ferry," in Murphy, *The Complete Poems*, 189.

Chapter 1. Progress

1. For examples of a few of those readers see A. Robert Caponigri, "Brownson and Emerson: Nature and History," *New England Quarterly* 17 (September 1945): 368–90. See also George Santayana, "The Genteel Tradition in American Philosophy," in *Winds of Doctrine and Platonism and the Spiritual Life* (1913; Gloucester, MA: Peter Smith, 1971); Van Wyck Brooks, *America's Coming of Age* (New York: R. W. Huebsch, 1915); and Quentin Anderson, *The Imperial Self: An Essay in American Literary and Cultural History* (New York: Knopf, 1971).

2. For the now-classic formulation of the issue of Emerson's vocation see Henry Nash Smith, "Emerson's Problem of Vocation," *New England Quarterly* 12 (March 1939): 52–57.

3. Richardson quotes the same phrase in noting the significance of Emerson's reading of Hegel's "Introduction to the Philosophy of History" in Hedge's *Prose Writers of Germany*, published in 1847 (see Robert Richardson,

Emerson: The Mind on Fire [Berkeley: University of California Press, 1995], 473). I use the phrase here to characterize the liberal sense of history that the young Emerson derived from many sources and later found confirmed in Hegel, among others.

4. He was not alone in this intuition. "We can no longer say there is nothing new under the sun," Thomas Jefferson wrote to Joseph Priestley in 1801, "for this whole chapter in the history of man is new" (*Writings* [New York: Library of America, 1984], 1086). "Spirit has broken with the world it hitherto inhabited," Hegel wrote in 1807, "and stands poised to submerge it in the past and in the labor of its own transformation" (Hegel's preface to *Phenomenology of Spirit*, trans. A. V. Miller [Oxford: Oxford University Press, 1977], 6).

5. Rene Wellek, "Emerson and German Philosophy," *New England Quarterly* 16, no. 1 (1943): 41–62.

6. Philip L. Nicoloff, *Emerson on Race and History: An Examination of English Traits* (New York: Columbia University Press, 1961).

7. Gustaaf Van Cromphout, "Emerson and the Dialectics of History," *PMLA* 91, no. 1 (1976): 55.

8. Robert D. Richardson, "Emerson and History," in *Emerson: Prospect and Retrospect*, ed. Joel Porte (Cambridge, MA: Harvard University Press, 1982).

9. Len Gougeon, *Virtue's Hero: Emerson, Antislavery, and Reform* (Athens: University of Georgia Press, 1990).

10. Sacvan Bercovitch, "Emerson, Individualism, and the Ambiguities of Dissent," in *Ralph Waldo Emerson: A Collection of Critical Essays*, ed. Lawrence Buell (Englewood, NJ: Prentice Hall, 1993), 122.

11. Eduardo Cadava, *Emerson and the Climates of History* (Stanford, CA: Stanford University Press, 1997).

12. Lawrence Buell, *Emerson* (Cambridge, MA: Harvard University Press, 2003).

13. Ibid., 262.

14. Nicoloff's assessment of the influence of this pervasive racialism on Emerson is carefully balanced. He sums up as follows: "His intellectual environment considered, Emerson never became more than a relatively mild 'racist' if only because of his impatience with the extreme claims which the radical racialists were making" (*Emerson on Race and History*, 124).

15. Richardson, "Emerson and History," 60.

16. Bercovitch also sees Emerson as turning back to his liberal roots during these years, but for different reasons.

17. Daniel Walker Howe, *The Unitarian Conscience: Harvard Moral Philosophy 1805–61* (1970; Middletown, CT: Wesleyan University Press, 1988).

18. The most significant sources for Emerson were Adam Smith, David Hume (whose *History of England* and *Essays* are unmistakably "Whig" in their overall conception of history's pattern, despite his Tory political sympathies),

William Robertson, and, though he was not a historian in the same sense as these others, Dugald Stewart. There is clear evidence that Emerson himself read all of these, and, as Garry Wills, Daniel Walker Howe, Henry May, and George Callcott, among others, have emphasized, these Scottish writers along with Adam Ferguson fundamentally shaped the moderate historical progressivism of American academic culture generally, especially at Harvard, in the first half of the nineteenth century. The many other historians that Emerson read in the 1820s and 1830s tended to strongly reinforce the Whig orientation of the Scots. Here are just a few exemplary passages. "No unbiased observer, who derives pleasure from the welfare of his species," Henry Hallam writes in *View of the State of Europe during the Middle Ages* (London: John Murray, 1856), 266, an earlier edition of which Emerson checked out in October 1821 and renewed for five weeks on 15 December, "can fail to consider the long and uninterruptedly increasing prosperity of England as the most beautiful phenomenon in the history of Mankind. . . . [I]n no other region have the benefits that political institutions can confer been diffused over so extended a population, nor have any people so well reconciled the discordant elements of wealth, order, and liberty." "Liberty was the spring and principle of their political associations," Sharon Turner writes in the first volume of *The History of the Anglo-Saxons* (London: Longman, Brown, Green and Longmans, 1852), 15, an earlier edition of which Emerson quotes in December 1822 as well as in July 1833 and June and October 1835, "and pervaded the few civil institutions which their habits required, and their humors permitted." Even the non-English historians tended to take a distinctly Whiggish line, as the subtitle of Sismondi's redaction of his great *History of Italy* makes clear: *Italian Republics or, The Origin, Progress, and Fall of Italian Freedom* (Paris: A. & W. Galignani, 1941), which Emerson quotes from in the fall of 1822 and May 1833. In reference to the Peace of Constance Sismondi writes: "Thus terminated, with the establishment of a legal liberty, the first and most noble struggle which the nations of modern Europe have ever maintained against despotism" (ibid., 39). And Guizot follows suit in *The History of Civilization in Europe*, which Emerson probably read in 1838: "There can be no doubt . . . but that this simultaneous development of the different social elements greatly contributed to carry England, more rapidly than any other of the continental states, to the final aim of all society—namely, the establishment of a government at once regular and free" (*Historical Essays and Lectures*, ed. Stanley Mellon [Chicago: University of Chicago Press, 1972], 247). Edward Everett and Daniel Webster, American scholar-statesmen whom the young Emerson revered, also regularly presented more and less-condensed versions of the Whig history of liberty in celebrated speeches, some of which from the early 1820s Emerson collected in his library under the title "American Pamphlets." One of Everett's best speeches, not included in this collection, is entitled "The History of Liberty." In "The President's Protest," also not included in that collection, Webster scolds

Andrew Jackson and his aides as follows: "And now, Sir, who is he, so ignorant of the history of liberty, at home and abroad; who is he, yet dwelling in his contemplations among the principles and dogmas of the Middle Ages; who is he, from whose bosom all original infusion of American spirit has become so entirely evaporated and exhaled, that he shall put into the mouth of the President of the United States the doctrine that the defence of liberty *naturally results to* executive power, and is its particular duty" (*The Papers of Daniel Webster: Speeches and Formal Writings,* ed. Charles M. Wiltse [Hanover, NH: University Press of New England, 1988], 2:61).

19. Herbert Butterfield, *The Whig Interpretation of History* (1931; New York: Norton, 1965).

20. Lord Acton, *Essays in the History of Liberty,* ed. J. Rufus Fears (Indianapolis: Liberty Fund, 1985), 8. The essays, reviews, and lectures containing Acton's classic account of the history of liberty were written and published in England in various venues from 1866 to 1902, too late to have had any direct influence upon Emerson. I draw upon them here rather as the most lucid, elegant, and comprehensive synthesis of a broadly held nineteenth-century Anglo-Whig outlook.

21. Ibid., 10, 62, 11, 25, 24.

22. Acton, "The History of Freedom in Christianity," in ibid., 29–53.

23. See C. B. Macpherson, *The Political Theory of Possessive Individualism* (New York: Oxford University Press, 1962) for a sharply critical exposition of the importance of self-ownership to early modern Anglo liberalism.

24. Butterfield, *Whig Interpretation,* 6.

25. Clifford Geertz, *The Interpretation of Cultures* (New York: Basic Books, 1973).

26. Sacvan Bercovitch, *The American Jeremiad* (Madison: University of Wisconsin Press, 1978), 28, 181.

27. Sacvan Bercovitch, *The Rites of Assent: Transformations in the Symbolic Construction of America* (New York: Routledge, 1993), 63.

28. Bercovitch, *American Jeremiad,* 14.

29. Bercovitch, *Rites of Assent,* 312, 329, 332, 335.

30. Hans Blumenberg, *The Legitimacy of the Modern Age,* trans. Robert M. Wallace (Cambridge, MA: MIT Press, 1983), 33.

31. Ibid., 137.

32. In his classic study *The Idea of Progress: An Inquiry into Its Origin and Growth* (London: Macmillan, 1928), J. B. Bury also argues that the idea of progress is inherently ecumenical. He links it to Stoic universalism as follows: "In the later period of Greek history, which began with the conquests of Alexander the Great, there had emerged a conception of the whole inhabited world as a unity and totality, the idea of the whole human race as one. We may conveniently call it the ecumenical idea—the principle of the ecumene or inhabited world,

as opposed to the principle of polis or city. Promoted by the vast extension of the geographical limits of the Greek world resulting from Alexander the Great's conquests and by his policy of breaking down barriers between Greek and barbarian, the idea was reflected in the Stoic doctrine that all men are brothers, and that a man's true country is not his own particular city, but the *ecumene*" (ibid., 23). Bury links progress to Enlightenment universalism as follows: "Turgot had already conceived 'the total mass of the human race moving always slowly forward': he had declared that the human mind everywhere contains the genius of progress and that the inequality of peoples is due to the infinite variety of their circumstances. This enlarging conception was calculated to give strength to the idea of Progress by raising it to a synthesis comprehending not merely the western nations but the whole human world" (ibid., 168).

33. "Even when it came to commenting explicitly on American mission or identity, Emerson was an intermittent nationalist at best" (Buell, *Ralph Waldo Emerson*, 272).

34. Eric Hobsbawm, *The Age of Revolution: Europe 1789–1848* (1962; London: Abacus, 2002), 44.

35. Reinhart Koselleck, *Futures Past: On the Semantics of Historical Time* (Cambridge, MA: MIT Press, 1985), 256.

36. Richardson, *Emerson: The Mind on Fire*, 126–27.

37. Buell, *Ralph Waldo Emerson*, 16.

Chapter 2. Reason I, Science

1. Immanuel Kant, "What Is Enlightenment?" in *The Portable Enlightenment Reader*, ed. Isaac Kramnick (New York: Penguin, 1995), 1.

2. See Daniel Walker Howe, *The Unitarian Conscience: Harvard Moral Philosophy 1805–61* (1970; Middletown, CT: Wesleyan University Press, 1988); Howe, *The Political Culture of the American Whigs* (Chicago: University of Chicago Press, 1979); also Henry May, *The Enlightenment in America* (New York: Oxford University Press, 1976); Garry Wills, *Inventing America: Jefferson's Declaration of Independence* (New York: Doubleday, 1978); Charles Taylor, *Sources of the Self* (Cambridge, MA: Harvard University Press, 1989); and Robert Richardson, *Emerson: The Mind on Fire* (Berkeley: University of California Press, 1995), 29–33.

3. Howe, *Political Culture*, 31.

4. Peter Gay characterizes these writers in similar terms in *The Enlightenment: An Interpretation*, 2 vols. (1966; New York: Norton, 1969).

5. May, *Enlightenment in America*, 337, 342, 343.

6. Howe, *Unitarian Conscience*.

7. "The first true advance which is made must go on in the school in which Reid and Stewart have labored. Philosophers must agree in terms and discover their own ideas with regard to the moral sense, or, as others term it, the decisions of the understanding" (Ralph Waldo Emerson, *Two Unpublished Essays:*

The Character of Socrates & The Present State of Ethical Philosophy [New York: Lamson, Wolffe, 1895], 76).

8. Merrell R. Davis, "Emerson's 'Reason' and the Scottish Philosophers," *New England Quarterly* 17, no. 2 (1944): 214.

9. For a concise recent review and restatement of this position see Richardson, *Emerson: The Mind on Fire*, 29–33.

10. Taylor, *Sources of the Self*, 251.

11. Ibid., 255.

12. Ibid., 260.

13. For this and the following characterizations of Reid's thought see Wills, *Inventing America*, 184–89.

14. Taylor, *Sources of the Self*, 357.

15. Ibid., 369.

16. Quoted in Richardson, *Emerson: The Mind on Fire*, 222.

17. Taylor, *Sources of the Self*, 364.

18. See Ralph L. Rusk, *The Life of Ralph Waldo Emerson* (New York: Charles Scribner's Sons, 1949), 1–13.

19. See Ralph L. Rusk, ed., *The Letters of Ralph Waldo Emerson*, vol. 1, 1813–1835 (New York: Columbia University Press, 1939).

20. Lewis Simpson, ed., introduction to *The Federalist Literary Mind: Selections from the "Monthly Anthology" and "Boston Review," 1803–1811* (Baton Rouge: Louisiana State University Press, 1962), 32–33.

21. Lawrence Buell, "Neoclassical Continuities: The Early National Era and the New England Literary Tradition," in *New England Literary Culture: From Revolution through Renaissance* (Cambridge: Cambridge University Press, 1988), 84–105, 94.

22. It is no small part of Emerson's literary achievement to have passed on this distinctive imaginative receptivity to the scientific universe to an extraordinary line of poetic heirs—from Whitman and Dickinson to Frost, Stevens, and Ammons. In "Star-Splitter" Robert Frost tells of a man who burnt down his house to get the insurance money so he could buy a telescope. "'The best thing that we're put here for's to see,'" the man is heard to say. "'The strongest thing that's given us to see with / A telescope. Someone in every town / Seems to me owes it to the town to keep one'" (*Collected Poems, Prose and Plays* [New York: Library of America, 1995], 166).

23. Laura Dassow Walls depicts Emerson as drawing on natural science to foster "a culture of truth" throughout his work (*Emerson's Life in Science: The Culture of Truth* [Ithaca, NY: Cornell University Press, 2003]).

24. *JMN* 4:86. Emerson will reiterate this statement three years later when he writes: "The Teacher that I look for & await shall enunciate with more precision and universality, with piercing poetic insight those beautiful yet severe compensations that give to moral nature an aspect of mathematical science" (*JMN* 5:6).

25. Walter Benjamin, *Illuminations,* ed. and intro. Hannah Arendt, trans. Harry Zohn (1968; New York: Schocken, 1969), 263–64.

26. Hans Blumenberg, *The Legitimacy of the Modern Age,* trans. Robert M. Wallace (Cambridge, MA: MIT Press, 1983), 232, 391.

27. Eric Hobsbawm, *The Age of Revolution: Europe 1789–1848* (1962; London: Abacus, 2002), 61.

Chapter 3. Reason II, Virtue

1. Stanley Cavell has been making the case for Emerson's philosophical seriousness for some years. See "Emerson's Aversive Thinking," in *Romantic Revolutions: Criticism and Theory,* ed. Kenneth Johnston et al. (Bloomington: Indiana University Press, 1990), 219–49; *In Quest of the Ordinary: Lines of Skepticism and Romanticism* (Chicago: University of Chicago Press, 1988); *The Senses of Walden* (1972; San Francisco: North Point Press, 1981); *This New yet Unapproachable America: Lectures after Emerson after Wittgenstein* (Albuquerque, NM: Living Batch Press, 1989); *Conditions Handsome and Unhandsome: The Constitution of Emersonian Perfectionism* (La Salle, IL: Open Court, 1990); *Philosophical Passages: Wittgenstein, Emerson, Austin, Derrida* (Oxford: Blackwell, 1995).

2. This includes friendly critics such as Cornel West who enlist him in the pragmatist "evasion of philosophy" as well as hostile critics such as George Santayana who see Emerson as a hopelessly fuzzy subjectivist. See Cornel West, *The American Evasion of Philosophy: A Genealogy of Pragmatism* (Madison: University of Wisconsin Press, 1989); George Santayana, "The Genteel Tradition in American Philosophy," in *Winds of Doctrine and Platonism and the Spiritual Life* (1913; Gloucester, MA: Peter Smith, 1971), 186–215.

3. "Originally, the authority par excellence or the root of all authority was the ancestral. Through the discovery of nature, the claim of the ancestral is uprooted; philosophy appeals from the ancestral to the good, to that which is good intrinsically, to that which is good by nature" (Leo Strauss, *Natural Right and History* [1950; Chicago: University of Chicago Press, 1953], 91).

4. 　　　The poem refreshes life so that we share,
　　　For a moment, the first idea . . . It satisfies
　　　Belief in an immaculate beginning
　　　And sends us, winged by an unconscious will,
　　　To an immaculate end. We move between these points:
　　　From that ever-early candor to its late plural
　　　And the candor of them is the strong exhilaration
　　　Of what we feel from what we think, of thought
　　　Beating in the heart, as if blood newly came,
　　　An elixir, an excitation, a pure power.
　　　The poem, through candor, brings back a candor again
　　　That gives a candid kind to everything.

Wallace Stevens, "Notes Toward a Supreme Fiction," in *The Collected Poems of Wallace Stevens* [New York: Knopf, 1968], 382.

5. In *The Republic* Socrates argues that virtue in general and "justice" in particular are the "health" of the soul. Virtuous action conforms to and nourishes the soul's optimum natural condition of balance and well-being: "And is not the creation of justice the institution of a natural order and government of one by another of the parts of the soul, and the creation of injustice the product of a state of things at variance with the natural order? . . . Then virtue is the health and beauty and well-being of the soul, and vice the disease and weakness and deformity of the same?" (*The Dialogues of Plato,* trans. Benjamin Jowett, ed. William Chace Green [1927; New York: Liveright Publishing, 1954], bk. 4, 328).

6. "Tired of the old descriptions of the world, / The latest freed man rose at six and sat / On the edge of his bed" (Wallace Stevens, "The Latest Freed Man," in *Collected Poems,* 204).

7. Again, Stevens is relevant. Stevens's long poem "An Ordinary Evening in New Haven" is precisely a celebration of the enhanced apprehension of the ordinary in the wake of abandoned religious orthodoxy: "The instinct for heaven had its counterpart: / The instinct for earth, for New Haven, for his room, / The gay tournamonde as of a single world / In which he is and as and is are one" (ibid., 476).

8. See especially the second half of the fifth stanza:

> Shades of the prison-house begin to close
> Upon the growing Boy,
> But he beholds the light, and whence it flows,
> He sees it in his joy;
> The Youth, who daily farther from the East
> Must travel, still is Nature's Priest,
> And by the vision splendid
> Is on his way attended;
> At length the Man perceives it die away,
> And fade into the light of common day.

"Intimations Ode," in *William Wordsworth,* ed. Stephen Gill (New York: Oxford University Press, 1984), 299.

9. I derive this idea of the cultural function of tragedy and comedy directly from Northrop Frye and indirectly from Clifford Geertz. See Northrop Frye, *Anatomy of Criticism* (Princeton, NJ: Princeton University Press, 1957); Clifford Geertz, *The Interpretation of Cultures* (New York: Basic Books, 1981).

10. Guido de Ruggiero suggests that at its heart liberalism is a philosophy of work (*The History of European Liberalism,* trans. R. G. Collingwood [1927; Boston: Beacon Press, 1959]).

11. "A leaf, a drop, a crystal, a moment of time is related to the whole, and partakes of the perfection of the whole. Each particle is a microcosm, and faithfully renders the likeness of the world" (*E&L* 29–30).

12. "I loafe and invite my soul, / I lean and loafe at my ease . . . observing a spear of / summer grass" (Walt Whitman, *Leaves of Grass* [New York: Library of America, 1982], 27).

13. Bernard Bailyn, *The Ideological Origins of the American Revolution* (Cambridge, MA: Harvard University Press, 1967).

14. As Gordon Wood plainly states, "The sacrifice of individual interests to the greater good of the whole formed the essence of republicanism and comprehended for Americans the idealistic goal of their Revolution" (*The Creation of the American Republic* [Chapel Hill: University of North Carolina Press, 1969], 53).

15. Wood again makes this point clear. "Frugality, industry, temperance, and simplicity—the rustic traits of the sturdy yeoman—were the stuff that made a society strong. The virile martial qualities—the scorn of ease, the contempt of danger, the love of valor—were what made a nation great. The obsessive term was luxury, both a cause and a symptom of social sickness. This luxury, not mere wealth, but that 'dull . . . animal enjoyment' which left 'minds stupefied and bodies enervated, by wallowing for ever in one continual puddle of voluptuousness,' was what corrupted a society: the love of refinement, the desire for distinction and elegance eventually weakened a people and left them soft and effeminate, dissipated cowards unfit and undesiring to serve the state" (ibid., 52).

16. Michael Sandel, *Democracy's Discontent: America in Search of a Public Philosophy* (Cambridge, MA: Harvard University Press, 1996).

17. See Thomas Pangle, *The Spirit of Modern Republicanism: The Moral Vision of the American Founders and the Philosophy of John Locke* (Chicago: University of Chicago Press, 1988); Isaac Kramnick, *Republicanism and Bourgeois Radicalism: Political Ideology in Late 18th Century England and America* (Ithaca, NY: Cornell University Press, 1990); and John Patrick Diggins, *The Lost Soul of American Politics: Virtue, Self-Interest, and the Foundations of Liberalism* (New York: Basic Books, 1994).

18. See Joyce Oldham Appleby, *Liberalism and Republicanism in the Historical Imagination* (Cambridge, MA: Harvard University Press, 1992); and David F. Ericson, *The Shaping of American Liberalism: The Debates over Ratification, Nullification, and Slavery* (Chicago: University of Chicago Press, 1993).

19. Thomas Pangle, *The Ennobling of Democracy: The Challenge of the Postmodern Era* (Baltimore, MD: Johns Hopkins University Press, 1992).

20. In *Emerson's Plutarch* Berry provides a thorough and convincing account of the pervasive influence of classical Stoicism on Emerson's work throughout his career.

21. Stephen Whicher, Newton Arvin, and, more recently, Christopher Lasch, who do give Emerson credit for a tragic sensibility, are exceptions in this regard. Whicher's account of Emerson's "tragic sense" is the most searching: "There is an Emersonian tragedy and an Emersonian sense of tragedy, and we

begin to know him when we feel their presence underlying his impressive confidence." Emersonian tragedy, Whicher argues, is "a tragedy of incapacity. Man's reach must exceed his grasp, of course, that is not tragic. Emerson's chasm cuts deeper: between a vision that claims all power now, and an experience that finds none. Emerson's thought of the self was a total Yes and a total No, which could not co-exist, could not be reconciled, and yet were both true. . . . His serenity was a not unconscious answer to his experience of life, rather than an inference from it (even when presented as such). It was an act of faith, forced on him by what he once called 'the ghastly reality of things'" ("Emerson's Tragic Sense," in *Emerson: A Collection of Critical Essays*, ed. Milton R. Konvitz and Stephen E. Whicher [Englewood Cliffs, NJ: Prentice Hall, 1962], 43). See also Arvin, "The House of Pain: Emerson and the Tragic Sense," in *American Pantheon*, ed. Daniel Aaron and Sylvan Schendler (1966; New York: Dell, 1967), 16–38; and Lasch's discussion of the concept of "fate" in Emerson's work in *The True and Only Heaven: Progress and Its Critics* (New York: Norton, 1991). Northrop Frye states this Greek tragic principle in terms of human finitude: "Tragedy revolves around the primary contract of man and nature, the contract fulfilled by man's death, death being, as we say, the debt he owes to nature" (*Fools of Time: Studies in Shakespearean Tragedy* [Toronto: University of Toronto Press, 1967], 4).

22. In *Waldo Emerson: A Biography* (New York: Viking Press, 1981) Gay Wilson Allen describes Emerson's brothers as "career-haunted" (114). Edward Emerson, Ralph Waldo's brilliant, energetic, and ambitious younger brother, went temporarily insane in 1828. His doctor attributed his collapse to his "too-intense application to study" (ibid., 116). Ralph Waldo's older brother, William, also suffered periodic depressions throughout his life.

23. Ibid., 92–102.

24. Up until the most recent generation of postmodernist commentators, major critics of Emerson generally agreed on the centrality of the moral law to his outlook as a whole. See, for example, John Jay Chapman, "Emerson," in *The Selected Writings of John Jay Chapman*, ed. and intro. by Jacques Barzun (1898; New York: Doubleday, 1958); F. O. Matthiessen, *The American Renaissance: Art and Expression in the Age of Emerson and Whitman* (London: Oxford University Press, 1941); Stephen Whicher, *Freedom and Fate: An Inner Life of Ralph Waldo Emerson* (Philadelphia: University of Pennsylvania Press, 1953). See also Ralph L. Rusk, *The Life of Ralph Waldo Emerson* (New York: Charles Scribner's Sons, 1949); Allen, *Waldo Emerson*; and Robert Richardson, *Emerson: The Mind on Fire* (Berkeley: University of California Press, 1995).

25. For fundamental continuities between Puritanism and Emerson see Perry Miller, "From Edwards to Emerson," in *Ralph Waldo Emerson: A Collection of Critical Essays*, ed. Lawrence Buell (Englewood, NJ: Prentice Hall, 1993), 13–31; Lasch, *The True and Only Heaven*.

26. Michael Gilmore, *American Romanticism and the Marketplace* (Chicago: University of Chicago Press, 1985).

27. Emerson read Smith's *Wealth of Nations* sometime between December 1823 and January 1824 (Richardson, *Emerson: The Mind on Fire*, 54).

28. Emerson's first wife, Ellen Tucker, impressed his family early on by declaring her dislike of Jackson. In 1831 Emerson described Jackson's as "the bad party in the country," and he wrote to his brother Edward in the following rather smug and snobbish tone: "Sad political disclosures every day brings. Wo' is me my dishonored country that such poor wretches should sit in the chairs of Washington, Franklin, and Adams." It seemed to him, he said, that "we should all feel dirty if Jackson is re-elected" (Rusk, *The Life of Ralph Waldo Emerson*, 153).

29. See Arthur Schlesinger, Jr., *The Age of Jackson* (Boston: Little, Brown, 1945); Daniel Walker Howe, *The Political Culture of the American Whigs* (Chicago: University of Chicago Press, 1979); Charles Sellers, *The Market Revolution* (London: Oxford University Press, 1991).

30. Harold Bloom worries at length about the affinities between Emersonianism and Reaganism in his review of John McAleer's biography of Emerson in "Mr. America," *New York Review of Books*, 22 November 1984.

31. Irving Kristol, "Adam Smith and the Spirit of Capitalism," in *Neoconservatism: The History of an Idea* (New York: Free Press, 1995), 258–300.

32. See György Lukács, *Soul and Form*, trans. Anna Bostock (Cambridge, MA: MIT Press, 1974).

Chapter 4. Property, Culture

1. G. W. F. Hegel, *Political Writings*, ed. Laurence Dickey and H. B. Nisbet (Cambridge: Cambridge University Press, 1999), 198.

2. "Ideas of progress and the Burkean conception of tradition . . . are the warp and woof of all those 19th Century interpretations of English history which . . . may safely if loosely be described as Whig interpretations" (J. W. Burrow, *A Liberal Descent: Victorian Historians and the English Past* [Cambridge: Cambridge University Press, 1981], 22).

3. See Arthur Herman, *How the Scots Invented the Modern World* (New York: Random House, 2001); Christopher Berry, *Social Theory of the Scottish Enlightenment* (Edinburgh: Edinburgh University Press, 1997); A. S. Skinner, "Adam Smith: An Economic Interpretation of History," in *Essays on Adam Smith*, ed. Andrew Skinner and Thomas Wilson (Oxford: Clarendon Press, 1975), 154–79.

4. For references to Hume see *JMN* 1:187, 2:8, 194, 267, 306–7, 335, 365, 369, 414, 3:65, 4:15, 5:242. For Robertson see *JMN* 1:55–56, 2:108, 194; for Smith see *JMN* 2:213 and Robert Richardson, *Emerson: The Mind on Fire* (Berkeley: University of California Press, 1995), 54; for Gibbon see *JMN* 1:201–2, 253, 322, 393, 2:102, 194, 266, 306, 360–64, 366, 380, 4:232, 5:108.

5. See Bernard Aspinwall, "William Robertson in America," in *Eighteenth Century Scotland: New Perspectives,* ed. T. M. Devine and J. R. Young (East Linton: Tuckwell Press, 1999), 152–76; George H. Callcutt, *History in the United States, 1800–1860* (Baltimore, MD: Johns Hopkins University Press, 1970), 20.

6. Daniel Walker Howe, *The Unitarian Conscience: Harvard Moral Philosophy 1805–61* (1970; Middletown, CT: Wesleyan University Press, 1988), 123.

7. Berry, *Social Theory,* 98.

8. Adam Smith, *The Wealth of Nations* (New York: Modern Library, 1937), 384.

9. John Locke, "The Second Treatise of Government," in *The Selected Political Writings of John Locke,* ed. Paul Sigmund (New York: Norton, 2005), 30, 7.

10. Locke, *A Letter Concerning Toleration,* in Sigmund, *Selected Political Writings,* 129.

11. Isaiah Berlin, "Two Concepts of Liberty," in *Four Essays on Liberty* (London: Oxford University Press, 1969).

12. Guido de Ruggiero, *The History of European Liberalism,* trans. R. G. Collingwood (1927; Boston: Beacon Press, 1959), 26–27.

13. Richard Pipes, *Property and Freedom* (New York: Vintage, 1999), 117.

14. For Cobden see Nicholas Edsall, *Richard Cobden: Independent Radical* (Cambridge, MA: Harvard University Press, 1986).

15. Aurelian Craiutu, *Liberalism under Siege: The Political Thought of the French Doctrinaires* (New York: Lexington Books, 2003).

16. Sacvan Bercovitch, "Emerson, Individualism, and Liberal Descent," in *The Rites of Assent: Transformations in the Symbolic Construction of America* (New York: Routledge, 1993), 324.

17. Michael Gilmore, *American Romanticism and the Marketplace* (Chicago: University of Chicago Press, 1985), 21–22, 30.

18. Howe, *Unitarian Conscience,* 208.

19. Ralph Waldo Emerson, "Ode, Inscribed to W. H. Channing," in *Essays and Poems,* ed. Joel Porte, Harold Bloom, and Paul Kane (New York: Library of America, 1996), 1111–14.

20. Carolyn Porter, *Seeing and Being: The Plight of the Participant Observer in Emerson, James, Adams, and Faulkner* (Middletown, CT: Wesleyan University Press, 1981), 93.

21. Alexander Hamilton, James Madison, and John Jay, *The Federalist,* ed. Max Beloff (1948; New York: Blackwell, 1987), 47–48.

22. Richard Tuck, *Natural Rights Theories* (Cambridge: Cambridge University Press, 1979), 16, 22. Pipes quotes James Madison to the same effect: "In a word, as a man is said to have right to his property, he may be equally said to have a property in his rights" (*Property and Freedom,* xii).

23. Gordon Wood, *The Radicalism of the American Revolution* (New York: Knopf, 1992), 6–8.

24. Stanley Cavell, "An Emerson Mood," in *Emerson's Transcendental Etudes*, ed. David Justin Hodge (Stanford, CA: Stanford University Press, 2003), 22, 23.

25. It hardly needs saying that a genuinely universal right to property was still far from being realized in the United States. African Americans, Native Americans, and women could not, for the most part, own property.

26. Here, without page citations but in the order in which they appear in the essay, is a sampling of some of the many similar series of nouns: "Babylon, Troy, Tyre, Palestine, and even early Rome"; "London and Paris and New York"; "Egypt, Greece, Gaul, England, War, Colonization, Church, Court, Commerce"; "Greece, Asia, Italy, Spain, and the Islands"; "oration of Burke, a victory of Napoleon, a martyrdom of St. Thomas More, of Sidney, of Marmaduke Robinson, a French Reign of Terror, a Salem hanging of witches, a fanatic Revival, the Animal Magnetism in Paris"; "the Pyramids, the excavated cities, Stonehenge, the Ohio Circles, Mexico, Memphis"; "the fly, the caterpillar, the grub, the egg"; "the Foreworld, the Age of Gold, the Apples of knowledge, the Argonaut's expedition, the calling of Abraham, the building of the Temple; the Advent of Christ; Dark Ages: the Revival of Letters; the Reformation; the discovery of new lands; the opening of new sciences, and new regions in man."

Chapter 5. Reason III, Skepticism

1. Stephen Whicher established this narrative schematization of Emerson's development in his influential work *Freedom and Fate: An Inner Life of Ralph Waldo Emerson* (Philadelphia: University of Pennsylvania Press, 1953). In a note on the "Chronology" of Emerson's "outer life" at the beginning of his book, Whicher divides Emerson's career into the following five phases: (1) 1803–1830, Unitarian Period; (2) 1830–1832, First Crisis; (3) 1832–1841, Period of Challenge; (4) 1838–1844, Second Crisis; (5) 1841–1882, Period of Acquiescence (ibid., xxviii). The first half of Whicher's study, entitled "Freedom," deals with the first four of these phases; the second half, entitled "Fate," deals with the long fifth phase. Whicher's commentary on "Experience" initiates the second half and concludes as follows: "His [Emerson's] position is such that a lasting release is no longer to be found in egoistic rebellion, but only in acquiescence" (ibid., 122). While I disagree with this conception of Emerson's development, I nonetheless acknowledge a debt to Whicher's sensitive study.

2. The term "acquiescence" is Whicher's. References to "later" Emerson can be found throughout Emerson scholarship since Whicher's book was published in 1953.

3. Samuel Taylor Coleridge, *Aids to Reflection*, reprinted in *The Collected Works of Samuel Taylor Coleridge*, vol. 9, ed. Kathleen Coburn (Princeton, NJ: Princeton University Press, 1993). This edition also reprints James Marsh's

"Preliminary Essay" to the first American edition of *Aids to Reflection*, an essay that Emerson read and admired.

4. "Taking his lead from Stewart, Emerson was to struggle against Hume for years" (Robert Richardson, *Emerson: The Mind on Fire* [Berkeley: University of California Press, 1995], 30–32). See also Evelyn Barish, *Emerson: The Roots of Prophecy* (Princeton, NJ: Princeton University Press, 1989), 99–116; and John Michael, *Emerson and Skepticism: The Cipher of the World* (Baltimore, MD: Johns Hopkins University Press, 1988).

5. Quoted in Richardson, *Emerson: The Mind on Fire*, 63.

6. As Emerson writes in "Montaigne; Or, the Skeptic," "the interrogation of custom at all points is an inevitable stage in the growth of every superior mind, and is the evidence of its perception of the flowing power which remains itself in all changes" (*E&L* 702).

7. For an account of the basic tenets of academic skepticism in relation to the other major schools of skeptical thought see Charlotte L. Stough, *Greek Skepticism: A Study in Epistemology* (Berkeley: University of California Press, 1969), 35–66. "Pyrrhonists advocate following existing conventions without assent, whereas Academics abandon the requirement of absolute certainty as the sole warrant and justification of assent. That is, they are less rigorous in applying the Skeptic principle of suspense of judgment" (ibid., 65–66). See also R. J. Hankinson, *The Skeptics* (New York: Routledge, 1995). It is unclear whether Emerson ever read Sextus Empiricus directly, but it is certain that Hume did.

8. Hankinson, *Skeptics*, 156–57.

9. Ibid., 155–81.

10. T. S. Eliot, "The Metaphysical Poets," in *Selected Essays of T. S. Eliot*, new ed. (1932; New York: Harcourt, Brace, Jovanovich, 1950), 248.

11. David Hume, *Enquiries Concerning Human Understanding and Concerning the Principles of Morals* (1777; Oxford: Clarendon Press, 1975), 31.

12. David Fate Norton summarizes the received view in *David Hume, Common Sense Moralist, Skeptical Metaphysician* (Princeton, NJ: Princeton University Press, 1982). Thomas Reid, Fate Norton tells us, viewed Hume "as a dangerous skeptic who represented mankind as mere Yahoos and undermined both natural and moral philosophy. James Beattie spread this representation across the learned world, where it became entrenched orthodoxy. Throughout the nineteenth century and much of the twentieth, Hume as philosopher was Hume the universal skeptic who dogmatically denied the existence of knowledge, causes, substances, freedom, values, and God" (ibid., 4).

13. See Norman Kemp Smith, "The Naturalism of Hume," in *Mind* 14 (1905): 149–73, 335–47. See also Norman Kemp Smith, *The Philosophy of David Hume: A Critical Study of Its Origins and Central Doctrines* (1941; New York: Macmillan, 1964); Richard Popkin, "David Hume: His Pyrrhonism and His Critique of Pyrrhonism," *Philosophical Quarterly* 1 (October 1951): 385–407, reprinted in

Richard H. Popkin, *The High Road to Pyrrhonism*, ed. Richard A. Watson and James E. Force (San Diego: Austin Hill Press, 1980), 103–33; Fate Norton, *David Hume*; and Donald W. Livingston, *Hume's Philosophy of Common Life* (Chicago: University of Chicago Press, 1984).

14. Livingston, *Hume's Philosophy*, 28–29.

15. The most eloquent and influential of recent "pragmatist" readings of Emerson is Richard Poirier, *The Renewal of Literature: Emersonian Reflections* (New York: Random House, 1987). See also Cornel West, *The American Evasion of Philosophy: A Genealogy of Pragmatism* (Madison: University of Wisconsin Press, 1989); and David Robinson, *Emerson and "The Conduct of Life": Pragmatism and Ethical Purpose in the Late Work* (Philadelphia: University of Pennsylvania Press, 1993).

16. Richard Rorty, *Consequences of Pragmatism* (Minneapolis: University of Minnesota Press, 1982), xvi.

17. Ibid., xxx.

18. Ibid., xxxi, xxxvii.

19. "The word aretê, which later comes to be translated as 'virtue,' is in the Homeric poems used for excellence of any kind; a fast runner displays the aretê of his feet (*Iliad*, 20.411) and a son excels his father in every kind of aretê—as athlete, as soldier and in mind (*Iliad*, 15.642). This concept of virtue or excellence is more alien to us than we are apt at first to recognize. It is not difficult for us to recognize the central place that strength will have in such a conception of human excellence" (Alasdair MacIntyre, *After Virtue* [Notre Dame, IN: Notre Dame University Press, 1984], 122).

20. Miller originally established the connection between Emersonian metaphysics and Calvinist theology in his important essay "From Edwards to Emerson," in *Ralph Waldo Emerson: A Collection of Critical Essays*, ed. Lawrence Buell (Englewood, NJ: Prentice Hall, 1993), 13–31.

Chapter 6. Limited Government

1. See Carl Guarneri, *The Utopian Alternative: Fourierism in 19th Century America* (Ithaca, NY: Cornell University Press, 1991). Guarneri points out that Matthiessen "labelled the two decades before the War 'the Age of Fourier' in American social thought" (ibid., 9). For an alternative account of Emerson's complex response to utopian-socialist thinking see Sacvan Bercovitch, "Emerson, Individualism, and the Ambiguities of Dissent," in *Ralph Waldo Emerson: A Collection of Critical Essays*, ed. Lawrence Buell (Englewood, NJ: Prentice Hall, 1993), 101–31.

2. This phrase comes from the beginning of the last paragraph of "Experience": "I know that the world I converse with in the city and in the farms, is not the world I *think*. I observe that difference, and shall observe it" (*E&L* 491–92).

3. I take the term "piecemeal" from Karl Popper. In *The Open Society and Its Enemies* (Princeton, NJ: Princeton University Press, 1961) he favors what he calls "piecemeal" social engineering over more radical types of political reform.

4. See Len Gougeon and Joel Myerson, eds., *Emerson's Antislavery Writings* (New Haven, CT: Yale University Press, 1995).

5. See especially Thomas Pangle, *The Spirit of Modern Republicanism: The Moral Vision of the American Founders and the Philosophy of John Locke* (Chicago: University of Chicago Press, 1988).

6. Benjamin Constant, a favorite of Emerson, originally made the distinction between "negative" and "positive" liberty in his essay "On Ancient and Modern Liberty," in *Political Writings*, trans. and ed. Biancamaria Fontana (New York: Cambridge University Press, 1988). Isaiah Berlin eloquently reasserted this distinction in a cold war context in "Two Concepts of Liberty," an inaugural lecture delivered before the University of Oxford in 1958 and published in *Four Essays on Liberty* (New York: Oxford University Press, 1969). For Constant see also Stephen Holmes, *Benjamin Constant and the Making of Modern Liberalism* (New Haven, CT: Yale University Press, 1984).

7. John Gray, *Liberalism*, 2nd ed. (Minneapolis: University of Minnesota Press, 1995), 18.

8. Gray includes "meliorism" in a list of the four defining characteristics of the modern liberal tradition. I include all four terms here because they are illuminating in themselves and because they all apply to Emerson. "Common to all variants of the liberal tradition is a definite conception, distinctively modern in character, of man and society. . . . It is *individualist* in that it asserts the moral primacy of the person against the claims of any social collectivity; *egalitarian* inasmuch as it confers on all men the same moral status and denies the relevance to legal or political order of differences in moral worth among human beings; *universalist*, affirming the moral unity of the human species and according a secondary importance to specific historic associations and cultural forms; and *meliorist* in its affirmation of the corrigibility and improvability of all social institutions and political arrangements" (ibid., xii).

9. Judith Shklar offers a compelling reminder of the central importance of this distrust in her essay "The Liberalism of Fear," in Nancy Rosenblum, ed., *Liberalism and the Moral Life* (Cambridge, MA: Harvard University Press, 1989), 21–39. Shklar explains: "Liberalism must restrict itself to politics and to proposals to restrain potential abusers of power in order to lift the burden of fear and favor from the shoulders of adult women and men, who can then conduct their lives in accordance with their own beliefs and preferences, as long as they do not prevent others from doing so as well" (ibid., 31).

10. Among the founders Hamilton was perhaps second only to John Adams in late Calvinist pessimism about human nature. In *The Creation of the American Republic* (Chapel Hill: University of North Carolina Press, 1969) Gordon Wood

quotes a letter from John Adams to Mercy Warren in 1776 in which he complains that there is "'so much Rascality, so much Venality and Corruption, so much Avarice and Ambition such a Rage for Profit and Commerce among all Ranks and Degrees of Men' that republicanism seemed indeed a precarious experiment" (570).

11. Gray concisely states the case for considering Hume a liberal in *Liberalism:* "[The] Scottish aspiration to a science of society in which liberal ideals are given a foundation in a theory of human nature and social order is present even in the writings on political and economic questions of the great sceptic, David Hume. In Hume, by contrast with the thinkers of the French Enlightenment, the defence of a liberal order invokes the facts of man's imperfection. In the *Treatise in Human Nature,* Hume cites men's restricted benevolence and intellectual limitations and the unalterable scarcity of the means of satisfying human needs as causes of the emergence of the basic principles of justice. In his essay on 'The Idea of the Perfect Commonwealth,' Hume goes further and sketches in utopian spirit the main outlines of a form of political order in which these laws of nature are fully embodied and individual liberty guaranteed under the rule of law. It is in Hume, indeed, despite his reputation as a conservative theorist, that we find the most powerful defence of the liberal system of limited government" (24). I refer to Montaigne as a liberal only in the very broad and limited sense in which skepticism and liberalism may be said to have an affinity. Shklar makes the connection most clearly in "The Liberalism of Fear": "The liberalism of fear is thus not necessarily tied to either skepticism or to the pursuit of natural sciences. There is, however, a real psychological connection between them. Skepticism is inclined toward toleration, since in its doubts it cannot choose among the competing beliefs that swirl around it, so often in murderous rage. Whether the skeptic seeks personal tranquility in retreat or tries to calm the warring factions around her, she must prefer a government that does nothing to increase the prevailing levels of fanaticism and dogmatism. To that extent there is a natural affinity between the liberal and the skeptic. Madison's discussion in the *Federalist* of how to end sectarian and similar factional conflicts through freedom is the perfect example of the fit between skepticism and liberal politics" (23).

12. John Gray, *Hayek on Liberty,* 3rd ed. (New York: Routledge, 1998), 39.

13. Ibid., 30. The ensuing summary of Hayek's position is partially derived from Gray as well as from Hayek's works themselves.

14. Guarneri, *Utopian Alternative,* 52.

15. Ibid., 94.

16. Ibid., 2.

17. "That we cannot have everything is a necessary, not a contingent, truth. Burke's plea for the constant need to compensate, to reconcile, to balance; Mill's plea for novel 'experiments in living' with their permanent possibility of

error, the knowledge that it is not merely in practice but in principle impossible to reach clear-cut and certain answers, even in an ideal world of wholly good and rational men and wholly clear ideas—may madden those who seek for final solutions and single, all-embracing systems, guaranteed to be eternal. Nevertheless, it is a conclusion that cannot be escaped by those who, with Kant, have learnt the truth that out of the crooked timber of humanity no straight thing was ever made" (Berlin, "Two Concepts of Liberty," 170).

18. Václav Havel, *Summer Meditations* (New York: Knopf, 1992), 62.

19. Tocqueville worried about this quality of American civilization:

> As social conditions become more equal, the number of persons increases who, although they are neither rich nor powerful enough to exercise any great influence over their fellows, have nevertheless acquired or retained sufficient education and fortune to satisfy their own wants. They owe nothing to any man, they expect nothing from any man; they acquire the habit of always considering themselves as standing alone, and they are apt to imagine that their whole destiny is in their own hands.
>
> Thus not only does democracy make every man forget his ancestors, but it hides his descendants and separates his contemporaries from him; it throws him back forever upon himself alone and threatens in the end to confine him entirely within the solitude of his own heart. ("Of Individualism in Democratic Countries," in *Democracy in America*, trans. Henry Reeve and intro. by Daniel Boorstin [New York: Knopf, 1972], 2:99)

20. A willingness to learn from conservatives in this respect was shared by many of the most thoughtful progressive voices of the 1990s. See Shelby Steele, *The Content of Our Character: A New Vision of Race in America* (New York: St. Martin's Press, 1990); William Galston, *Liberal Purposes: Goods, Virtues, and Diversity in the Liberal State* (Cambridge: Cambridge University Press, 1991); E. J. Dionne, *They Only Look Dead: Why Progressives Will Dominate the Next Political Era* (New York: Simon and Schuster, 1996); and Jacob Weisburg, *In Defence of Government: The Fall and Rise of Public Trust* (New York: Scribner, 1996). Michael Sandel states the point most broadly: "But we are beginning to find that a politics that brackets morality and religion too completely soon generates its own disenchantment. A procedural republic cannot contain the moral energies of a vital democratic life. It creates a moral void that opens the way for narrow, intolerant moralisms. And it fails to cultivate the qualities of character that equip citizens to share in self-rule" (*Democracy's Discontent: America in Search of a Public Philosophy* [Cambridge, MA: Harvard University Press, 1996], 24). For a broader theoretical discussion of the important, if somewhat uneasy, position of virtue in the liberal thought of Hobbes, Locke, Kant, and Mill see Peter Berkowitz, *Virtue and the Making of Modern Liberalism* (Princeton, NJ: Princeton University Press, 1999).

21. Quoted in Berkowitz, *Virtue*, 3.

22. Václav Havel, "What I Believe," in Havel, *Summer Meditations*, 61.

23. Václav Havel, "Politics, Morality, and Civility," in Havel, *Summer Meditations*, 1.

24. Ibid., 8.

25. Alexandre Kojeve, *Introduction to the Reading of Hegel* (Ithaca, NY: Cornell University Press, 1969), 29–30.

26. James Melvin Washington, ed., *A Testament of Hope: The Essential Writings and Speeches of Martin Luther King, Jr.* (San Francisco: HarperCollins, 1991), 13, 19, 20.

27. For connections between Emerson and Martin Luther King, Jr., see Anita Haya Patterson, *From Emerson to King: Democracy, Race, and the Politics of Protest* (New York: Oxford University Press, 1997).

Chapter 7. Natural Rights, Civil Society

1. David Brion Davis, *The Problem of Slavery in Western Culture* (Ithaca, NY: Cornell University Press, 1966), 31.

2. David Brion Davis, *Slavery and Human Progress* (New York: Oxford University Press, 1984), 107; Davis, *The Problem of Slavery in the Age of Revolution, 1770–1823* (1975; New York: Oxford University Press, 1999), 42.

3. The term "hypostasize" is from Davis, *The Problem of Slavery in Western Culture*, 297.

4. The Mennonites also survived and maintained a principled antislavery position.

5. Davis, *The Problem of Slavery in Western Culture*, 350.

6. See Garry Wills, *Inventing America: Jefferson's Declaration of Independence* (New York: Doubleday, 1978).

7. Edward Shils, "The Virtue of Civil Society," in *The Civil Society Reader*, ed. Virginia A. Hodgkinson and Michael W. Foley (Hanover, NH: University Press of New England for Tufts University, 2003), 300–301.

8. Adam B. Seligman, *The Idea of Civil Society* (New York: Macmillan, 1992), 3.

9. The term "uncoerced" is taken from Michael Walzer, "A Better Vision: The Idea of Civil Society," in Hodgkinson and Foley, *The Civil Society Reader*, 306.

10. Alexis de Tocqueville, *Democracy in America*, trans. Henry Reeve and intro. by Daniel Boorstin (New York: Knopf, 1972), 1:193.

11. Seligman, *The Idea of Civil Society*, 3.

12. Ibid., 28, 30.

13. Emerson employs this strategy in later antislavery speeches as well. In "Address to the Citizens of Concord on the Fugitive Slave Law" he declares, "As long as men have *bowels,* they will disobey" (*AW* 60–61). And in "The Fugitive

Slave Law" he says, "There is no help but in the *head* and *heart* and *hamstrings* of a man" (*AW* 83, italics mine).

14. Norbert Elias, *The Civilizing Process*, trans. Edmund Jephcott, 2 vols. (1978; New York: Pantheon Books, 1982).

15. "At the still point of the turning world. Neither flesh nor fleshless; / Neither from nor towards; at the still point, there the dance is. / But neither arrest nor movement. / And do not call it fixity, / Where past and future are gathered" (T. S. Eliot, "Burnt Norton," in *The Complete Poems and Plays 1909–1950* [New York: Harcourt, Brace, 1980], 119).

16. George M. Frederickson, ed., *William Lloyd Garrison* (Englewood Cliffs, NJ: Prentice Hall, 1968), 30.

17. John Stuart Mill, *On Liberty*, ed. and intro. by Currin V. Shields (1859; Indianapolis: Bobbs-Merrill, 1956), 24–25.

18. John Rawls, *Political Liberalism* (New York: Columbia University Press, 1993), 217, 218.

19. Thomas Clarkson, *The History of the Rise, Progress, and Accomplishment of the Abolition of the African Slave-trade by the British Parliament* (London: J. S. Taylor, 1836).

20. Emerson was joined in this hope by many antebellum reformers. For further explorations of the larger culture of antebellum reform in relation to liberal conceptions of civil society and the public sphere see Robert Fanuzzi, *Abolition's Public Sphere* (Minneapolis: University of Minnesota Press, 2003); and T. Gregory Garvey, *Creating the Culture of Reform in Antebellum America* (Athens: University of Georgia Press, 2006).

Chapter 8. Empiricism

1. Ernest Gellner, *Plough, Sword, and Book: The Structure of Human History* (London: Collins Harvill, 1988), 51.

2. Ibid., 61.

3. Ibid.

4. Joseph Slater, ed., *The Correspondence of Emerson and Carlyle* (New York: Columbia University Press, 1964), 98.

5. Ibid., 103–4.

6. Ibid., 171.

7. Thomas Carlyle, *Sartor Resartus* (1838; Oxford: Oxford University Press, 1987), 160, 169.

8. Thomas Carlyle, *On Heroes, Hero-Worship, and the Heroic in History* (1841; Berkeley: University of California Press, 1993), 20, 23, 39, 66.

9. Ibid., 140–41.

10. Ibid., 134.

11. Ibid., 148, 147, 149.

12. Erich Auerbach, *Mimesis* (1968; Princeton, NJ: Princeton University Press, 1974), 310.

13. Ernest Benz, *Emanuel Swedenborg: Visionary Savant in the Age of Reason*, trans. Nicholas Goodrick-Clarke (West Chester, PA: Swedenborg Foundation, 1969), 21–22, 84–85, 42–43.

14. Ibid., 60–65, 84–85, 87, 85.

15. Ibid., 358–59.

16. Judith Shklar, *Ordinary Vices* (Cambridge, MA: Harvard University Press, 1984).

17. Michel de Montaigne, *The Complete Essays of Montaigne*, trans. Donald M. Frame (Stanford, CA: Stanford University Press, 1958), 5, 3, 4, 5, 16, 18.

18. G. Douglas Atkins, *Tracing the Essay: Through Experience to Truth* (Athens: University of Georgia Press, 2005), 31.

19. Auerbach, *Mimesis*, 310.

20. Quoted in ibid., 286.

21. Montaigne, *Complete Essays*, 816.

22. Auerbach, *Mimesis*, 310–11.

23. For a reading of Lacan that preserves the agency of the subject see Mari Ruti, *Reinventing the Soul: Posthumanist Theory and Psychic Life* (New York: Other Press, 2006).

24. Friedrich Nietzsche, *Twilight of the Idols*, secs. 12, 13, quoted in Kenneth Marc Harris, *Carlyle and Emerson: Their Long Debate* (Cambridge, MA: Harvard University Press, 1978), 164.

25. Stanley Cavell has most sensitively explored issues of skepticism in Emerson's work. For a list of Cavell's work see chap. 3, n.1.

26. Johann Wolfgang von Goethe, *Conversations of Goethe with Eckermann* (London: J. M. Dent, 1930), 8, 19, 14, 46, 125–26, 16.

Chapter 9. Liberty, Commerce

1. J. W. Burrow, *A Liberal Descent: Victorian Historians and the English Past* (Cambridge: Cambridge University Press, 1981), 147.

2. Lord Acton, *Essays in the History of Liberty*, ed. J. Rufus Fears (Indianapolis: Liberty Fund, 1985), 119.

3. Ibid., 97.

4. Here as later in *English Traits* Emerson seems oblivious or indifferent to the contribution of imperialist exploitation to English wealth.

5. Quoted in Leo Strauss, *Natural Right and History* (1950; Chicago: University of Chicago Press, 1953), 245.

6. Ibid., 248.

7. Quoted in Thomas Pangle, *Montesquieu's Philosophy of Liberalism: A Commentary on "The Spirit of the Laws"* (Chicago: University of Chicago Press, 1973),

206. Adam Smith similarly dispensed with both classical and Christian norms in linking ethical *propriety* with the prudent and moderate behavior of middle-class *proprietors*. Hume also, in "Of Refinement in the Arts," among other essays, delivered a sharp, historically based rejoinder to classical republican strictures against luxury: "*Industry, knowledge,* and *humanity,* are linked together by an indissoluble chain, and are found, from experience as well as reason, to be peculiar to the more polished, and what are commonly denominated, the more luxurious ages." "Industry, knowledge, and humanity," Hume went on, "are not advantageous in private life alone: They diffuse their beneficial influence on the *public,* and render the government as great and flourishing as they make individuals happy and prosperous. The increase and consumption of all the commodities, which serve to the ornament and pleasure of life, are advantageous to society; because, at the same time that they multiply those innocent gratifications to individuals, they are a kind of *storehouse* of labour, which, in the exigencies of the state, may be turned to the public service" (*Essays,* ed. Eugene F. Miller [Indianapolis: Liberty Fund, 1987], 271–72). And Hamilton, Madison, and Jay, the American authors of *The Federalist,* as Douglas Adair has long since demonstrated, had carefully read their Locke, their Montesquieu, and their Hume: "The prosperity of commerce is now perceived and acknowledged by all enlightened statesmen to be the most useful as well as the most productive source of national wealth, and has accordingly become a primary object of their political cares. By multiplying the means of gratification, by promoting the introduction and circulation of the precious metals, those darling objects of human avarice and enterprise, it serves to vivify and invigorate all the channels of industry and to make them flow with greater activity and copiousness" (*The Federalist* 12: 91). Even the farm-loving Jefferson concurred: "All the world is becoming commercial," he wrote to George Washington in 1784. "Our citizens have had too full a taste of the comforts furnished by the arts and manufactures to be debarred the use of them" (*Writings* [New York: Library of America, 1984], 784).

8. On politics as the provision of service see Hannah Arendt, *The Human Condition* (Chicago: University of Chicago Press, 1958).

9. Erich Auerbach, *Mimesis* (1968; Princeton, NJ: Princeton University Press, 1974).

10. Both are further supported by Gellner's suggestion that the transition from agrarian to industrial forms of economic organization brings with it a fundamental cognitive shift from purely symbolic to empirically oriented conventions of representation and thought. See *Plough, Sword, and Book.*

11. The Library of America's recent paperback edition of *Essays and Poems* (1996), edited by Joel Porte, Harold Bloom, and Paul Kane, for example, contains every book Emerson published between 1836 and 1860 except for *English Traits.* I note this not to dispute the editorial decision but only as an example of the relatively low critical regard for the book.

12. David Robinson, *Emerson and "The Conduct of Life": Pragmatism and Ethical Purpose in the Late Work* (Philadelphia: University of Pennsylvania Press, 1993), 115.

13. Phyllis Cole, "Emerson, England and Fate," in *Emerson: Prophecy, Metamorphosis, and Influence,* ed. David Levin (New York: Columbia University Press, 1975), 84, 85.

14. See, for a few examples, *JMN* 6:494–95, 7:53, 8:421, 226.

15. See Philip L. Nicoloff, *Emerson on Race and History: An Examination of "English Traits"* (New York: Columbia University Press, 1961), 97–187; Len Gougeon, *Virtue's Hero: Emerson, Antislavery, and Reform* (Athens: University of Georgia Press, 1990), 179–86.

16. Nicoloff, *Emerson on Race and History,* 151.

17. See Julie Ellison, "The Edge of Urbanity: Emerson's *English Traits,*" *Journal of the American Renaissance* 32, no. 2 (1986): 96–109.

18. See Burrow, *A Liberal Descent.*

19. Pangle, *Montesquieu's Philosophy of Liberalism,* 204.

20. Exodus 20:24 (AV).

Conclusion

1. Kenneth Burke, *The Philosophy of Literary Form: Studies in Symbolic Action,* 3rd ed. (1941; Berkeley: University of California Press, 1973), 1.

2. Thomas Jefferson, *Writings* (New York: Library of America, 1984), 1086.

3. Robert L. Heilbroner, ed., *The Essential Adam Smith* (New York: Norton, 1986), 162.

4. Eric Hobsbawm, *The Age of Revolution: Europe 1789–1848* (1962; London: Abacus, 2002), 43.

5. Friedrich August von Hayek, "The Use of Knowledge in Society," in *The Essence of Hayek,* ed. Chiaki Nishiyama and Kurt R. Leube (Stanford, CA: Hoover Institution, 1984), 220.

Index

Aaron, Daniel, 22

abolition. *See* antislavery movement

Acton, John, 32–33, 108–9, 255, 311n20, 328n2. *See also* liberalism: and Victorian "history of liberty"; Whig history

Adair, Douglas, 328–29n7

Adam, 90, 123

Adams, Henry, 166

Adams, John, 21, 46, 54, 56, 323n10

Adams, John Quincy, 104

Addison, Joseph, 55

African Americans, 14. *See also* Emerson: antislavery writings of; slavery

Agassiz, Louis, 265

Alger, Horatio, 191

Allen, Gay Wilson, 6, 23

American Constitution, 41, 55, 116

American Enlightenment, 54, 55. *See also* May, Henry

American jeremiad, 38–39, 42. *See also* Bercovitch, Sacvan

American Renaissance (Matthiessen), 22

American Revolution, 46, 47, 48, 56, 119, 256

America's Coming of Age (Brooks), 18

Anabaptists, 197

anatomy: early practitioners, 241–42

Anderson, Quentin, 19–20, 21, 308n1; *The Imperial Self*, 19–20

Annales school of historiography, 45, 267

antifoundationalism. *See* Emerson: antifoundationalist readings of; postmodernism; pragmatism

antislavery movement, 29, 31, 214–15, 256; religious and intellectual antecedents of, 195–200

antiutopianism, 170–74

Appleby, Joyce, 21, 94, 97

Arendt, Hannah, 329n8

Aristotle, 153, 156

Arnold, Matthew, 8, 24, 26, 69; *Culture and Anarchy*, 24

Atkins, G. Douglas, 246

Auerbach, Erich, 237–38, 246, 248–49; *Mimesis*, 260–61

Augustine, St., 34, 60, 61, 62, 81, 153, 196; *The City of God*, 34, 81

Aurelius, Marcus, 60, 153

Austin, J. L., 120

Bacon, Francis, 9, 21, 68, 260

Bailyn, Bernard, 93, 94

Barlow, Joel, 56

beauty, 88, 90, 93, 97, 121, 122; moral beauty, 92

Benjamin, Walter, 74

Bennett, William, 186

Bentham, Jeremy, 71, 72, 172

Benz, Ernest, 240, 328n13

Bercovitch, Sacvan, 5, 29, 30, 38–40, 116, 117, 309n16, 322n1

Berkeley, George, 62

Berkowitz, Peter, 325n20

Berlin, Isaiah, 113, 172, 177, 323n6, 324–25n17

Bernstein, Richard, 7

Bible, 213, 227–28, 274–75, 276, 281, 291